D1126164

Medieval Southampton

Medieval Southampton

The port and trading community, A.D. 1000-1600

Colin Platt

Department of History
University of Southampton

Routledge & Kegan Paul

London and Boston

First published in 1973
by Routledge & Kegan Paul Ltd
Broadway House, 68–74 Carter Lane,
London EC4V 5EL and
9 Park Street,
Boston, Mass. 02108, U.S.A.
Printed in Great Britain by
The Camelot Press Ltd, London and Southampton

ISBN 0 7100 7653 3

Library of Congress Catalog Card Number: 73–80377

To Mr E. A. Chalk and his associates, the officers and members of the Southampton Commons and Parks Protection Society, the Friends of Old Southampton and the Southampton Civic Trust, whose determined defence of burgess rights of common, taken to a successful conclusion in the High Court action of October 1969, reassuringly recalls the spirit of their long-time predecessors and fellow burgesses of Southampton, the salt-marsh enclosure objectors of 1500 and 1517.

Contents

Part IV 1400–1500

Part V 1500–1600

Appendices

Plates

Figures

Preface and acknowledgments

From small beginnings as an historical introduction to the archaeology of medieval Southampton, this book has taken on a life of its own. But it still bears many of the marks of its original purpose, remaining primarily a social history of the port, with a firm topographical bias. More than has been usual in equivalent urban histories in the past, it returns to the physical setting of the burgesses and to the changes imposed on that setting by the altering circumstances of the men who lived there. The book is not an economic history. It says little of the relative wealth of the borough, and attempts no tabulation of its trade. These are omissions I regret, but which were dictated by the material at my disposal when I came to write the book. It is my hope that this book itself may encourage others to make them good.

Happily, I do not expect to be the last student of Southampton's history, as I have not been the first. I have benefited myself from discussions and correspondence with Dr E. O. Blake, of my own university, and Mr J. M. Kaye, of the Queen's College, Oxford. It is to them that we may look in the future for authoritative editions of the cartularies of St Denys and God's House. Dr Alwyn Ruddock, of Birkbeck College, London, continues her work on the Italian mercantile community in the late-medieval port, with particular reference to Christopher Ambrose, one-time native of Florence, later burgess and twice mayor of Southampton. The most recent product of Mr L. A. Burgess's long concern with the problems of Southampton's history and topography has been an edition, for the Southampton Record Series, of that very useful fifteenth-century survey of properties in the town, the so-called 'terrier' of 1454. There is work in progress on the valuable late-medieval internal accounts of the hospital at God's House. And Miss Margaret Vowles, for two years my research assistant on this project, is now herself at work on the final stages of a doctoral thesis on Southampton during the Hundred Years War, in which she treats aspects of the shipping, trade and defence of the late-medieval borough mentioned only in passing by myself. Throughout my own work, I have had the benefit of Mr Patrick Faulkner's expert advice on the dating of the standing medieval buildings of Southampton. His paper on these buildings is to be included in the projected volumes of archaeological reports and catalogues, covering the last two decades of excavations in the town, shortly to be published by the Leicester University Press.

Over the years, my debts have mounted. Above all, I am obliged to Margaret Vowles, without whose selfless and always efficient labour this book could never have been written. I have been helped, too, by Miss Sheila Thomson, the Southampton city archivist, by Mr P. S. Peberdy, curator of the city museums, and by Mr G. Hampson, keeper of special collections at the university library, Southampton. Mr A. S. Burn and his staff, of the university cartographic unit, have done far more than merely tidy up my sketches. In my archaeological work in the town, I can look back with particular satisfaction on six years of harmonious co-operation with my fellow director of excavations, Mr Richard Coleman-Smith. Of the many who assisted me, whether in committee or on the sites, it is only just to single out Professor Frank Hodson, deputy-chairman of the Southampton Excavation Committee, as the source of particularly valued support and encouragement throughout. Mr J. A. Sugden and Mr D. W. Stirling, some of whose photographs I am using in this book, have been both expert colleagues and good friends. In the preparation and the writing of this book, it is a pleasure to acknowledge a grant towards cartographic expenses by my own university, and to record with real appreciation the Leverhulme fellowship which enabled me to share a year of freedom from academic duties between historical writing and the preparation of archaeological reports. I am indebted to my brother, Professor D. C. M. Platt, for a careful reading of the text, and to my wife, Valerie, for finding me the leisure to write it.

All the line drawings published here are the work of the cartographic unit, Southampton University. For permission to publish the following plates, I am grateful to Aerofilms Ltd (Plate 1), Mr J. A. Sugden (Plates 3 and 7), Echo Commercial Photos (Plates 5, 9, 10 and 16), Mr R. G. Lock (Plate 8), and Mr D. W. Stirling (Plates 2, 4, 11, 12 and 15). The copyright of Plates 5, 8, 9, 10 and 16 is held by Southampton Corporation; otherwise, it rests with the photographers.

Abbreviations

Assize of Bread Book	Anderson, R. C. (ed.), *The Assize of Bread Book, 1477–1517*, Southampton Record Society, 1923
B.M.	British Museum, London
Black Book	Chapman, A. B. Wallis (ed.), *The Black Book of Southampton*, 3 vols, Southampton Record Society, 1912–15
Bodleian	Bodleian Library, Oxford
Book of Examinations	Anderson, R. C. (ed.), *The Book of Examinations, 1601–1603*, Southampton Record Society, 1926
Books of Examinations and Depositions	Hamilton, G. H., and Aubrey, E. R. (eds), *Books of Examinations and Depositions, 1570–1594*, Southampton Record Society, 1914
Book of Remembrance	Gidden, H. W. (ed.), *The Book of Remembrance of Southampton*, 3 vols, Southampton Record Society, 1927–30
Brokage Book, 1439–40	Bunyard, Barbara D. M. (ed.), *The Brokage Book of Southampton, from 1439–40*, Southampton Record Society, 1941
Brokage Book, 1443–4	Coleman, Olive (ed.), *The Brokage Book of Southampton, 1443–4*, 2 vols, Southampton Record Series, 1960–1
Bull.Inst.Hist.Res.	*Bulletin of the Institute of Historical Research*, London
Cal.C.R.	*Calendar of the close rolls preserved in the Public Record Office*
Cal. Chancery R., Various	*Calendar of various chancery rolls preserved in the Public Record Office*
Cal.Ch.R.	*Calendar of the charter rolls preserved in the Public Record Office*

Cal. Fine R.	*Calendar of the fine rolls preserved in the Public Record Office*
Cal.Inq.Misc.	*Calendar of inquisitions miscellaneous (chancery) preserved in the Public Record Office*
Cal.Inq.P.M.	*Calendar of inquisitions post mortem and other analogous documents preserved in the Public Record Office*
Cal. Liberate R.	*Calendar of the liberate rolls preserved in the Public Record Office*
Cal. Memoranda R.	*Calendar of memoranda rolls (exchequer) preserved in the Public Record Office*
Cal.P.R.	*Calendar of the patent rolls preserved in the Public Record Office*
Cal.Pap.Reg.	*Calendar of entries in the papal registers relating to Great Britain and Ireland, papal letters*
Cal. State Papers Colonial	*Calendar of state papers, colonial series, preserved in the State Paper Department of Her Majesty's Public Record Office*
Cal. State Papers Domestic	*Calendar of state papers, domestic series, of the reigns of Edward VI, Mary, Elizabeth, preserved in the State Paper Department of Her Majesty's Public Record Office*
Cal. State Papers Foreign	*Calendar of state papers, foreign series, of the reign of Elizabeth, preserved in the State Paper Department of Her Majesty's Public Record Office*
Cal. State Papers Spanish	*Calendar of letters and state papers relating to English affairs, preserved principally in the archives of Simancas*
Cal. State Papers Venetian	*Calendar of state papers and manuscripts relating to English affairs, existing in the archives and collections of Venice, and in other libraries of northern Italy*
Cat. Anc. Deeds	*A descriptive catalogue of ancient deeds in the Public Record Office*
Charters	Gidden, H. W. (ed.), *The Charters of the Borough of Southampton*, 2 vols, Southampton Record Society, 1909–10
Court Leet Records	Hearnshaw, F. J. C., and Hearnshaw, D. M. (eds), *Southampton Court Leet Records*, 1 vol. in 4, Southampton Record Society, 1905–8
Davies	Davies, J. Silvester, *A History of Southampton*, Southampton and London, 1883
E.H.R.	*The English Historical Review*

Ec.H.R.	*The Economic History Review*
God's House Deeds	A typescript calendar: copies at the Southampton Civic Record Office and elsewhere
H.R.O.	Hampshire Record Office, Winchester
History of Parliament	Wedgwood, Josiah C., *History of Parliament (Biographies and Register), 1439–1509*, 2 vols, London, 1936–8
J. Speed, *History of Southampton*	Aubrey, Elinor R. (ed.), *The History and Antiquity of Southampton, with some conjectures concerning the Roman Clausentum, by John Speed, written about the year 1770*, Southampton Record Society, 1909
L. & P. Henry VIII	*Letters and papers, foreign and domestic, of the reign of Henry VIII, preserved in the Public Record Office, the British Museum and elsewhere in England*
Letters	Anderson, R. C. (ed.), *Letters of the Fifteenth and Sixteenth Centuries from the Archives of Southampton*, 1 vol. in 2, Southampton Record Society, 1921
Letters Patent	Gidden, H. W. (ed.), *The Sign Manuals and Letters Patent of Southampton*, vol. 2, Southampton Record Society, 1919
Local Port Book, 1439–40	Cobb, Henry S. (ed.), *The Local Port Book of Southampton for 1439–40*, Southampton Record Series, 1961
Oak Book	Studer, Paul (ed.), *The Oak Book of Southampton of c. A.D. 1300*, 3 vols, Southampton Record Society, 1910–11
P.R.O.	Public Record Office, London
Pipe Roll	*Pipe Roll Society Publications*, London, 1884– (in progress)
Port Books, 1427–30	Studer, Paul (ed.), *The Port Books of Southampton, or Anglo-French accounts of Robert Florys, water-bailiff and receiver of petty customs, A.D. 1427–1430*, Southampton Record Society, 1913
Port Books, 1469–81	Quinn, D. B., and Ruddock, Alwyn A. (eds), *The Port Books or Local Customs Accounts of Southampton for the Reign of Edward IV*, 2 vols, Southampton Record Society, 1937–8
R.C.H.M.	*Royal Commission on Historical Manuscripts*
Register of Edward the Black Prince	*Register of Edward the Black Prince preserved in the Public Record Office*
Rot.Parlm.	*Rotuli parliamentorum; ut et petitiones, et placita in parliamento*, 6 vols, London, 1783 and 1832

Rymer, *Foedera*	Rymer, Thomas (ed.), *Foedera, conventiones, litterae, et cujuscunque generis acta publica,* 20 vols, London, 1727–35
S.C.R.O.	Southampton Civic Record Office
St Denys Cart.	A typescript calendar: copies at Southampton University and elsewhere
Sign Manuals and Letters Patent	Gidden, H. W. (ed.), *The Sign Manuals and Letters Patent of Southampton*, vol. 1, Southampton Record Society, 1916
Southampton Excavations	Platt, Colin, and Coleman-Smith, Richard, *Excavations in Medieval Southampton, 1953–69*, 2 vols, Leicester, in press
Statutes of the Realm	*The statutes of the realm, from original records and authentic manuscripts*, 11 vols in 12, Record Commissioners, London, 1810–28
Stewards' Books	Gidden, H. W. (ed.), *The Stewards' Books of Southampton, from 1428*, 2 vols, Southampton Record Society, 1935–9
Third Book of Remembrance	Merson, A. L. (ed.), *The Third Book of Remembrance of Southampton, 1514–1602,* 3 vols, Southampton Record Series, 1952–65
T.R.H.S.	*Transactions of the Royal Historical Society*
V.C.H.	*The Victoria History of the Counties of England*, London, 1900– (in progress)
Win.Coll.Mun.	A typescript calendar: copies at Southampton University and elsewhere

Part I

1000-1200

Chronological table I

1004 Sweyn invades England for the second time

1007 Ethelred II buys off the Danes for two years

1009 Sweyn winters in Kent

1012 Ethelred II again buys off the Danes

1013 Sweyn attacks England

1014 Death of Sweyn; Cnut chosen to succeed him

1015 Cnut obtains the submission of Wessex

1016 Deaths of Ethelred II and Edmund Ironside; Cnut recognized as king of England

1035 Robert of Normandy succeeded by William; Cnut dies, to be succeeded by Harold Harefoot and Harthacnut, reigning jointly

1040 Harold Harefoot dies; accession of Harthacnut

1042 Harthacnut dies; accession of Edward (the Confessor)

1051 William, on a visit to England, is promised the succession

1053 Harold becomes earl of Wessex

1064 Harold visits Normandy, doing homage to William

1066 Death of Edward; coronation of Harold; defeat of Harold at Hastings; coronation of William

1001 Danes plunder Southampton (*Roger of Hoveden*, i:70)

1006 Danes plunder Southampton (*Roger of Hoveden*, i:72; *Walter of Coventry*, i:29)

1009 Danes plunder Southampton (*Roger of Hoveden*, i:73; *Walter of Coventry*, i:31)

1011 Danes plunder Southampton (*Roger of Hoveden*, i:75; *Walter of Coventry*, i:33)

1014 Cnut proclaimed king at Southampton by an assembly of notables (*Liber monasterii de Hyda*, pp. 216–17)

1042 On Harthacnut's death, Edward arrives at Southampton, to be received there by Godwin (*Annales Monastici*, ii:19)

1066 William ravages the south (*Walter of Coventry*, i:82)

1086 Domesday survey 1087 Death of William I; accession of William II 1088 Odo of Bayeux's rebellion suppressed	
	1098 William II embarks at Southampton for Barfleur (*Lestorie des engles*, ii:184)
1099 William II subdues Maine, crushing the rebellion there 1100 Death of William II; accession of Henry I 1101 Robert of Normandy invades England and is bought off 1105 War between Henry and Duke Robert 1106 Battle of Tinchebrai; defeat and capture of Robert 1109–13 Henry at war with the king of France	
	1116 Henry I at Southampton, 'in transitu regis' (Farrer, 'An outline itinerary', p. 381)
1117–20 Henry at war with William Clito of Normandy and his ally Louis VI of France 1120 Peace with Louis VI; Henry's heir drowned off Harfleur 1126 Matilda accepted as heir	
	1127 Henry I at Southampton (*Regesta regum anglo-normannorum*, ii:207) Henry grants the site at Portswood to the Augustinian canons of St Denys (*Regesta regum anglo-normannorum*, ii:210)
1128 Matilda marries Geoffrey of Anjou 1131 The English barons renew their oath to Matilda 1135 Death of Henry I; accession of Stephen	
	1136 Stephen at Southampton in pursuit of Baldwin de Redvers, earl of Devon (*Gesta Stephani*, p. 29)
1139 Matilda lands in England; outbreak of civil war 1141 Battle of Lincoln; defeat and capture of Stephen; Matilda proclaimed queen at Winchester; Stephen exchanged for Robert of Gloucester	
	1142 Robert of Gloucester dissuaded from attacking Southampton (*Historia Novella*, p. 75)
1144 Geoffrey of Anjou becomes duke of Normandy	
1147 Capture of Lisbon by Alfonso I of Portugal	1147 The men of Southampton take part in the Lisbon crusade (*De Expugnatione Lyxbonensi*, pp. 102–3)
1151 Geoffrey of Anjou dies; Henry succeeds to Anjou and Touraine	

1153 Treaty of Wallingford; Stephen recognizes Henry of Anjou as his successor	
1154 Death of Stephen; accession of Henry II	
1158 Henry obtains Brittany on the death of his brother, Geoffrey of Anjou	1158 Henry II at Southampton on his way to France (Delisle, *Recueil des actes de Henri II*, i:198–9)
1162 Thomas Becket elected archbishop of Canterbury	1162 Henry and Becket meet affectionately at Southampton (*Thómas saga erkibyskups*, i:120)
1163 Henry quarrels with Becket	1163 Henry lands at Southampton (*Ralph de Diceto*, i:308)
1170 Formal reconciliation of Henry and Becket; Becket returns to Canterbury and is murdered there	
1173 Henry's sons rebel against him	*c.* 1173 Leper hospital of St Mary Magdalene founded at Southampton (*Pipe Roll 19 Henry II*, p. 53)
1174 Henry does penance at Canterbury; Treaty of Montlouis between Henry II and Louis VII	1174 Henry lands at Southampton on way to Canterbury (*Ralph de Diceto*, i:383; *Roger of Hoveden*, ii:61; *Benedict of Peterborough*, i:72)
	1176 Geoffrey and Richard land at Southampton to join Henry II at Winchester (*Benedict of Peterborough*, i:114)
	1177 The fleet musters at Southampton (*Benedict of Peterborough*, i:167)
1181–3 Second rebellion of Henry's sons	
1184 Third rebellion of Henry's sons	
1186 Death of Geoffrey of Brittany	1186 Henry lands at Southampton (*Ralph de Diceto*, ii:40; *Benedict of Peterborough*, i:345)
1187–9 Rebellion of Richard and John, allying (1188) with Philip II	
1189 Death of Henry II; accession of Richard I	1189 Duke Richard lands at Southampton on way to coronation (*Gervase of Canterbury*, i:457) Richard I grants the burgesses of Southampton freedom from toll, passage and pontage (*Charters*, i:12–13)
1190 Richard departs for the Holy Land	*c.* 1190 With such major stone houses as West Hall, the rebuilding of Southampton begins
1192 Richard, returning from the Holy Land, is imprisoned by Leopold of Austria	
1194 Richard is released by the emperor Henry VI	
	1196/7 Gervase le Riche founds and endows God's House Hospital at Southampton (God's House Deeds 310, 313, 802)
1199 Death of Richard I; accession of John	1199 John grants the fee farm to Southampton (*Charters*, i:12–13)

Chapter one

The urban setting

The origins of settlement in Southampton are obscure. They fade irrecoverably into the seventh century A.D. But a tradition of town-dwelling, established in the Anglo-Saxon borough, was already antique by the Conquest. There were substantial men in Hampton, on the day that King Edward was alive and dead, who held their land by burgage tenure as tenants-in-chief of the king. And while their property lay partly in the neighbouring fields, to plots in which many would have been able to lay some claim, their setting, essentially, was urban. Their houses clustered within the limits of the borough. They lived by craft or trade. Within twenty years of the landing of the Normans, they were joined by sixty-five co-burgesses of French origin and by another thirty-one English-born, settled there by inducement of the king.[1] Some, in the process, may have lost their lands, and most endured a change in overlordship. But a wholesale expropriation of the existing borough community could scarcely have suited the purpose of a king concerned, above all, to emphasize the elements of continuity in his regime. Nor was it so much the Conquest as the evolution of the entire North European economy which promoted new initiatives in the borough.

Already, perhaps as much as half a century in advance of the Normans, settlement had intensified on the site of what was to become the Anglo-Norman borough, shifting the focal point of the long-established community away from its old centre by the minster at St Mary's, and from the inadequate, perhaps silted-up, harbour beyond it to the east. The archaeology of the Saxon community at St Mary's has established a falling-off of settlement through the length of the tenth century and a virtual abandonment of the site within a few years either way of A.D. 1000.[2] By 1066 the burgesses were well established on the higher land to the west of their former settlement. They had been there for at least a generation, for a hoard of Norman *deniers*, struck *c.* 1030, has recently been recovered from a rubbish pit on the junction of Broad Lane and English Street, now High Street.[3]

It was English Street, 'the great street of Hamton' also known as 'Great English Street', that was the central axis of the new town.[4] It was a broad thoroughfare, running north and south, owing its direction to what has been termed the 'strong natural dominant', the water frontage to the west and to the south. In essence, the plan was a very simple one, conforming to the 'ladder' pattern typical of many coastal towns.[5] In due course it built up, if it had not already done so by the Conquest, in streets parallel to the main thoroughfare, serving the area between it and the gravel cliff to the west. These were named, or renamed, Bull Street and French Street, and they came to constitute the French quarter of the post-Conquest town. It seems that the influential Seal, or Veal, family, supporters of Matilda, chose to live 'in the French street (*vicus*) known as the Bull Street'.[6] And it was here that the new churches of St Michael, patron saint of Normandy, and St John were founded. The other three churches of the town, All Saints, St Lawrence and Holy Rood, each of an antiquity that probably pre-dates the Conquest, were sited along the line of English Street, to the east.

To the north and north-east lay the fields of the town, Houndwell and the Hoglands, with beyond them the commons that came to be known, after the leper hospital sited within them, as the Marlands (or Magdalenes), East and West (Fig. 1). No measure exists of the concern of the burgesses, whether as individuals or as a group, in agriculture. But they lived as near neighbours to purely agricultural communities, and the services that the men of Portswood traditionally owed on Kingsland, next to the Hoglands, were probably such as the husbandmen of Hampton would themselves have acknowledged to their overlords as the price to be paid for their plots. Indeed, the recorded routine of the men of Portswood splendidly evokes an agricultural society scarcely touched by the activity of the harbour and trading community sited so close to the south-west. It is true that an obligation existed to take rushes to the dwelling of the reeve of Hampton for the festival at Easter and for the other great ceremonies of the year. But further than this, the list of obligations slips easily into the routine of the traditional farming calendar. In the early summer the meadows were mown, the hay gathered and stored in the barns, the sheep tended, and the folds and weirs repaired. After Michaelmas (29 September) the apples were gathered and cider made. Church-scot and pannage were due on St Martin's day (11 November), and then there was hedging and ditching.[7]

It may be, after all, that the burgesses of Hampton, like their equivalents at Lincoln, set more store by the pasture than by the tillage of their lands.[8] But their livelihood had depended from the first on dealings in agricultural produce, whether victuals or wool; in some part, it would continue to do so in the future, although the emphasis might shift to wine.[9]

Southampton, as perhaps we may now call it, lies almost central to the gravels and clays of the Hampshire basin, in close touch with the markets at Salisbury and Winchester and with the wool-producing regions that surround them, the chalkland pastures of Wiltshire and the Hampshire downs. Its sheltered roadsteads, its unique double tides, its inevitable association with Winchester, the administrative capital of ancient Wessex: these were the factors that guaranteed the early growth of Southampton as a commercial centre and as a place of resort for the pre-Conquest kings. Canute, it is said, was elected king at Southampton.[10] Ethelred made clandestine visits to the port in 1013, while planning his return to the realm.[11] It was at Southampton that Edward chose to land, to be received by Godwin and to be proclaimed

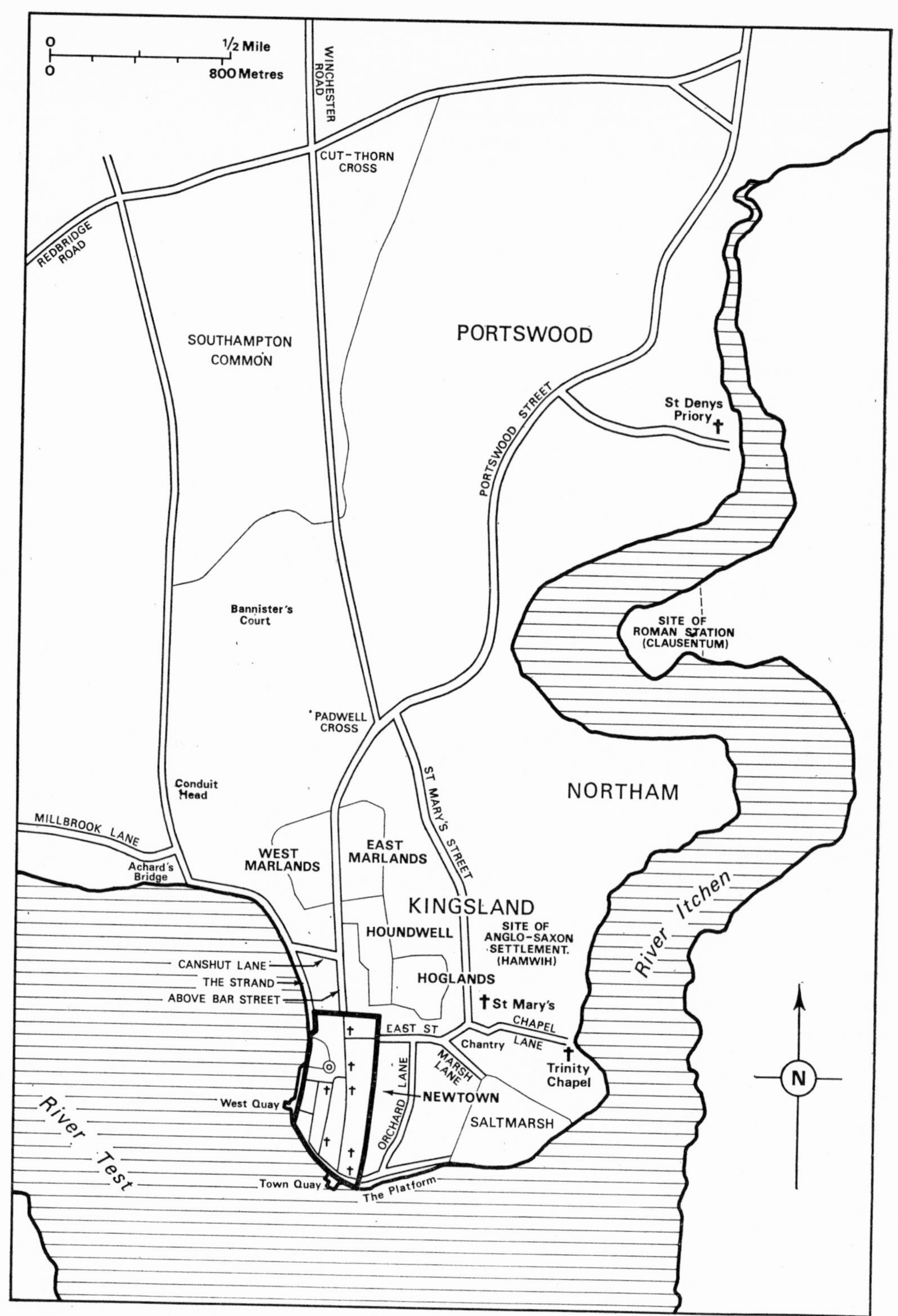

Figure 1 The liberties of the borough of Southampton

king in succession to Harthacnut, the Dane.[12] There are even Arthurian associations at Southampton, for Arthur himself is alleged to have brought a fleet to Southampton in transit to Barfleur,[13] and it was at Southampton that Arthur's nephew reputedly arrived, bringing a relief fleet in aid of his uncle, beset by the Saxon invaders.[14]

Yet the conditions that favoured Southampton's growth were precisely those that attracted its enemies. The Danes were at Southampton at least twice in the ninth century.[15] They were there again in the tenth century during the troubled aftermath of the reign and death of King Edgar.[16] And in one attack after another they plundered Southampton in the last years of the tenth century and the first decade of the eleventh.[17] The roadsteads at Southampton, throughout the Middle Ages, were to show themselves of more value in the protection of shipping against the weather than against piracy. And no doubt it was the exposed siting of the harbour and its adjoining township that explained the evacuation of St Mary's in favour of a more defensible cliff-top setting to the west, just as, in the fourteenth century, it would lead after comparable disasters to an intensive effort, ruinously expensive, to wall the re-sited town in stone. Yet neither before nor immediately after the Conquest is there evidence of more than token defences at the town. There is nothing to suggest that the ramparts at the north end of the settlement were thrown up earlier than the reign of King John.[18] Indeed, in severing the ancient parish of All Saints, they would seem to have been planned deliberately to exclude an important sector of the old town, memories of which might still persist in 'the field called Hampton', known as such from the thirteenth century to the seventeenth at least, and sited north of the town ditch and west of Above Bar Street.[19] Nor is there much reason yet to believe that the castle took shape, in anything approaching its later form, much before the beginning of recorded building expenditure in the middle years of the twelfth century, early in the reign of the first Angevin ruler, Henry II.[20]

A visitor to Southampton in the time of King Stephen would have known a town not substantially different from the borough of Edward the Confessor. Construction throughout would have been of timber, as it had been in the Anglo-Saxon settlement before.[21] Some development must have been noticeable, especially in the south-west quarter of the town, and there were a few major buildings to admire: the Seal family house in Bull Street, the hall of the king's reeve, the meeting-place, perhaps also a hall, of the increasingly powerful gild merchant, and the fortified residence (*munitio*) of the king.[22] But to the sea, then as now, the town presented a ragged and unimposing façade. Naturally low-lying, it lacked even the bulk of the royal castle that would soon come to dominate the Angevin port. It straggled across a wide area, trailing eastwards towards the already waste settlement at St Mary's, and northwards along the king's highway to Winchester. It was largely free of the precise definition of walls or ramparts, and was girdled in their place by a ring of salt-marsh and mud-flat, defending the approaches from the east, the south and the west.

It would seem likely that, in the years since the Conquest, the Norman borough of Southampton had lost at least some of the purpose of its Anglo-Saxon progenitor.

The new dynasty, in making less use of the ancient capital at Winchester, had deprived Southampton of an important part of its functions as an outport. Soon after Hastings, the Conqueror had laid waste the county of Southampton and had probably burnt the town.[23] His successors were to come there only occasionally. William Rufus, in an ill-substantiated legend, is said to have taken ship at Southampton in 1098, characteristically brushing aside the objections of the steersman, who would have held back for a better wind:[24]

> 'Brother', said he, 'hold your peace.
> You never saw a king drowned,
> Nor shall I be now the first.
> Set your ships afloat.'

But Henry I, although he is known frequently to have awaited a fair wind for France nearby, rarely chose to visit Southampton in person. He lingered instead at Westbourne, in Sussex, or nearer at hand at Romsey, Bishops Waltham or Fareham. We know that Henry was at Southampton, *in transitu regis*, probably in 1116. He was there again on the way to Normandy in 1127. But it was from Portsmouth that he usually sailed, and the intense activity that was to characterize Southampton as a royal port of entry, victualling centre and even naval base in the later years of the century, was markedly absent in the earlier.[25] Another change of dynasty would be required before the relative stagnation of the port was healed. For many years already, the Angevin interest on the Continent had been building up at the expense of Normandy and of the enfeebled kingdom of France. The death of Stephen in 1154, as it confirmed the association of the kingdom of England with the dominions of Anjou, drew Southampton ineluctably into a trading partnership with south-central and south-western France, the source, and ultimately the guarantee, of its later extraordinary prosperity.

Notes

1 Henry Moody, *Hampshire in 1086*, pp. 26–7, 58; for J. H. Round's comments on the Southampton Domesday entry and for another transcript of the survey, see *V.C.H., Hampshire*, i:433, 516.

2 P. V. Addyman and D. H. Hill, 'Saxon Southampton: a review of the evidence', *Proc. Hampshire Field Club*, 25 (1968), especially pp. 76–7; also L. A. Burgess, *The Origins of Southampton*, passim.

3 *Southampton Excavations*, forthcoming.

4 God's House Deeds 694; *Cat.Anc. Deeds*, ii:B3377.

5 R. E. Dickinson, 'The town plans of East Anglia', *Geography*, 19 (1934), p. 41.

6 God's House Deeds 506. A messuage 'Domus le Veel' is recorded in Bull Street in a quitclaim dated 1236. In 1127 Robert de Sigillo witnessed a charter of Henry I concerning St Denys lands (H. W. C. Davis *et al.* (eds), *Regesta regum anglo-normannorum*, ii:210). It was the Seals who, because of the very close relations they had in the town, dissuaded Robert of Gloucester from sacking it in 1142 (K. R. Potter (ed.), *The Historia Novella by William of Malmesbury*, p. 75). And the brothers William and Ralph led the men of Southampton on the Lisbon crusade of 1147 (C. W. David (ed.), *De Expugnatione Lyxbonensi*, pp. 101–3). An undated charter records that Nicholas de Sigillo, who features in the Hampton account in the Pipe

Roll of 1161, gave land to St Denys in St Michael's (*Pipe Roll 7 Henry II*, pp. 58–9, and St Denys Cart. 37b).

7 St Denys Cart. 367, 370. The list purports to detail services due to the king in the reign of Henry I, before the foundation of the priory at St Denys.

8 J. W. F. Hill, *Medieval Lincoln*, p. 332.

9 For a view of the importance of the pre-Conquest wool trade, see P. H. Sawyer, 'The wealth of England in the eleventh century', *T.R.H.S.*, 5th series, 15 (1965), pp. 145–64. Professor Sawyer is currently working on an elaboration of his argument. It received striking confirmation recently in an analysis of the bone content of Middle Saxon levels at North Elmham, Norfolk. The analysis demonstrated a ratio of cattle : pig : sheep of 1 : 3 : 5. Most of the sheep were found to be over six years old, the implication being that they were kept for wool production (Peter Wade-Martins, 'Excavations at North Elmham 1970. An interim note', *Norfolk Archaeology*, 35 (1971), p. 266).

10 H. R. Luard (ed.), *Flores historiarum*, i:541, and E. Edwards (ed.), *Liber monasterii de Hyda*, pp. 216–17.

11 William Stubbs (ed.), *Willelmi Malmesbiriensis monachi de gestis regum anglorum libri quinque*, i:208.

12 H. R. Luard (ed.), *Annales monastici*, ii:19.

13 William Hardy and Edward L. C. P. Hardy (eds), *A collection of the chronicles and ancient histories of Great Britain*, i:325.

14 J. E. B. Mayor (ed.), *Ricardi de Cirencestria speculum historiale de gestis regum Angliae*, i:30.

15 Thomas Arnold (ed.), *Henrici archidiaconi Huntendunensis historia Anglorum*, p. 139, and William Stubbs (ed.), *Willelmi Malmesbiriensis monachi de gestis regum anglorum libri quinque*, i:122.

16 Thomas Arnold (ed.), op. cit., pp. 168–9; also William Stubbs (ed.), op. cit., i:186, and Thomas Arnold (ed.), *Symeonis monachi opera omnia*, ii:135.

17 William Stubbs (ed.), *Memoriale fratris Walteri de Coventria*, i:29, 31, 33, and William Stubbs (ed.), *Chronica Rogeri de Houedene*, i: 70, 72, 73, 75.

18 J. S. Wacher, taking a section through the rampart west of Bargate, found twelfth-century pottery in the underlying layers. He is inclined to date the construction of the rampart to the early thirteenth century (*Southampton Excavations*, forthcoming).

19 God's House Deeds 723; S.C.R.O. SC4/2/11 and SC4/3/146. The possible implications of the extra-mural boundaries of All Saints parish are discussed by L. A. Burgess, *The Origins of Southampton*, pp. 20–1.

20 Excavations, both on the north-east bailey bank and on the castle *motte*, have agreed in placing the building date no earlier than the twelfth century, although it would be hard on this evidence alone to say when in the century the work was undertaken (*Southampton Excavations*, forthcoming).

21 Ibid. There is no archaeological evidence of stone buildings in the town before the last years of the twelfth century.

22 An agreement between Stephen and Henry, dated 1153, makes a clear distinction between the *castrum* at Winchester and the *munitio* at Southampton (H. W. C. Davis *et al.* (eds), *Regesta regum anglo-normannorum*, iii:98). The first notices of considerable works at the 'castle' of Southampton are preserved in the early Pipe Rolls of Henry II (*Pipe Rolls 2, 3 and 4 Henry II*, pp. 53, 107).

23 William Stubbs (ed.), *Memoriale fratris Walteri de Coventria*, i:82, and William Stubbs (ed.), *Chronica Rogeri de Houedene*, i:116.

24 T. D. Hardy and C. T. Martin (eds), *Lestorie des engles solum la translacion Maistre Geffrei Gaimar*, ii:78. The story, sadly, is probably another of Gaimar's many inventions.

25 William Farrer, 'An outline itinerary of King Henry the First', *E.H.R.*, 34 (1919), pp. 381, 544 and passim.

Chapter two

Royal borough

When Payn was reeve of Southampton in the last years of Henry I, his responsibility, as an official of the king, lay not to the burgesses he governed but direct to the king himself. With William de Pont de l'Arche, the sheriff, he collected the taxes of the borough, conducted its court, and published the decrees of the king.[1] Essentially, Southampton, in company with many (although not all) boroughs, was demesne of the king. It was exposed to the king's intervention on all matters of government and justice. It had travelled only a short way on the road to practical self-government, the milestones on which would be the charters of the Angevin, John (1199), and of the Lancastrians, Henry IV (1401) and Henry VI (1445, 1447).[2] Already a measure of recognition had been accorded to the members of the gild merchant, protected by Henry I together with 'all their liberties and customs by land and by sea'.[3] But there is no suggestion as yet of the generous freedoms which the citizens of London had secured from the ageing king.[4] And if the burgesses of Southampton enjoyed judicial and mercantile privileges of any substantial kind, as very probably they did, they would have known that these could last only as long as the good will of the king persisted. Within a few years, London lost the substance of its independence from the sheriff, nor was it quick to regain the full range of the freedoms conceded by Henry I. Southampton waited still longer. Henry II, although prepared to tolerate the communal movement on his continental domains, showed no wish to encourage the independence of his English boroughs. Richard's finances compelled him to take a less authoritarian view, and it was during his reign that the citizens of London once more regained control of their farm. But it was not until the end of the century that an Angevin king was prepared generally to concede the exclusion of his sheriffs from the boroughs. John did it because he needed the money. And he found a ready purchaser, among others, in the free burgesses of the prospering port of Southampton.[5]

In the meantime, the activity of the new dynasty in Southampton took the form of regular visits in transit to, or from, the Continent, together with a parallel concern to improve the amenities of the royal castle at the port, to perfect its facilities for storage of the king's wines, and to supply it with a quay of its own. Henry II was at Southampton in 1158 on the way to France.[6] He met Becket there in 1162, and the next year landed at the port on one of his periodical visits to the realm.[7] His celebrated pilgrimage to Canterbury, in expiation of the murder of Archbishop Becket, began at Southampton, after a night's rest in the town, on 9 July 1174.[8] His sons, Richard and Geoffrey, disembarked at Southampton on 2 April 1176, on their way to celebrate Easter with their father at Winchester.[9] The next year, while the king's army mustered at Winchester, his fleet assembled at Portsmouth and Southampton.[10] The old king disembarked at Southampton on 27 April 1186, accompanied by Eleanor, his queen.[11] And it was at Southampton that Duke Richard elected to land on 12 August 1189 on his way to Winchester, to continue from there to London for his coronation.[12]

A useful index to the degree of direct royal interest in, and experience of, the borough is preserved in the record of expenditure on the castle. Nothing of Henry's doing could compare in scale with the great campaigns of work that were undertaken by his sons, Richard, in 1191–5, and John, in 1204–9. Nevertheless, throughout his reign lesser works were recorded regularly at the castle, making it year by year more appropriate for use as an occasional residence of the king. The mound (or *motte*) and moats of the castle were probably already finished some years before 1156–7, for expenditure on the castle bridge is an important item in the earliest surviving group of building accounts. They may, of course, have originated very much earlier than this. There was a chapel at the castle in the first years of the reign, and there are regular entries in the Pipe Rolls recording the payment of a stipend and wages to the chaplain, doorkeepers and watchmen. In 1160–1 the sum of £12 was spent on the chambers of the king and the queen. They were re-roofed a quarter of a century later in Devon slate, perhaps as a precaution against fire. And this may have been the reason for the provision, in 1187 also, of a new treasury in stone.[13]

As one year succeeded another through the reigns of Henry II, Richard I and John, the entries in the Pipe Rolls diversify, demonstrating the wide range of royal concern in what was by now again a flourishing port. The king's treasure was shipped out of Southampton in 1162.[14] His wines were unloaded there in 1163, and his cows were transported overseas.[15] In 1167, alms for the Eastern Church were put aboard a ship in the harbour, especially hired for the purpose.[16] The king's venison and other victuals were shipped overseas regularly, for his own enjoyment or for that of allies and friends.[17] Slate and other stones were brought to Southampton for the king's works at Winchester.[18] And the enlargement of the castle at Southampton itself absorbed considerable shipments of materials.[19] The king bought hemp seeds, walnuts and lead.[20] He sent 250 salted pigs to Exeter.[21] He arranged that wine should be taken from Southampton to stock his cellar at Clarendon.[22] Glimpses of a wider world outside the port are afforded from time to time in the accounts. For the duration of the baronial uprisings of 1173–4, the king maintained a garrison of five knights at the castle.[23] Hostages were brought there in 1190–1. Their keep featured as a heavy charge on the account, but they were not released until the spring of 1195, spanning years during two of which Richard himself had been a captive, first of Leopold of Austria, then of the emperor Henry VI.[24] John's galleys were lying-up at the port in

1211–12; they were there again in 1214–15, for the king bought hemp that year to renew their cables.[25]

The activity of the king and his agents in the port undoubtedly advanced the fortunes of the burgesses. The association throughout was close. The founders of the great mercantile dynasties of the thirteenth century begin to appear regularly in the royal accounts of the twelfth. Here, for the first time, are featured the Fortins, the Isembards, the Gloucesters, the St Laurences and the Barbfletes. All were prominent in the thirteenth century, and the lines of the Isembards and the Barbfletes would continue far into the fourteenth century as well. They were brought together in the service of the king, but other alliances and inter-relationships were still more permanently binding than this. A St Laurence (Joan) married an Isembard (Ralph). Their daughter, Petronilla, married John le Fleming, son of the great Walter. With Claramunda, of the Gloucester clan, she was one of the great ladies of the thirteenth-century town, the recipient of the favours of the queen.[26] Alice of St Laurence, sister of Joan, married John de la Bulehuse, a founding member of another family prominent in Southampton politics from the early thirteenth century.[27] A Fortin (Lucya) married a Barbflete (Robert), and their son (Nicholas) sold the family tenement in English Street to a notable burgess of fourteenth-century Southampton, Nicholas de Moundenard, merchant and servant of the king.[28] For these and their forebears, it was the king's favour that determined their fortunes. For though it would be said, with good reason, that 'when every man has his part, the king has the least', the king himself thrived on the activity of his burgesses, whom he could make and break as he willed.[29]

It was in the royal service, for example, that Fortin and Walter of Gloucester joined John, the 'counter-tallyer', in supervision of works at the castle in 1173.[30] In 1190–1 Walter of Gloucester, this time in association with Gervase of Hampton, called 'le Riche', again acted as clerk-of-works for the king.[31] Robert Isembard and Robert de Barbflete (*Barbefluvio*) were among those burgesses of Southampton who made a large purchase of wines for the king in 1195–6.[32] And Walter Fortin, probably the son of the Fortin of 1173, assumed in 1202–3 the role once held by his father as supervisor of the castle works.[33] But it was less the direct service of the king than the early association of the same men in the collection of the town farm that had its impact on the constitutional development of the borough. Henry II had steadfastly refused to relinquish his control of the borough farms, at least by grant in perpetuity to the burgesses. Nevertheless, his policy of temporary, or short-term, leases of the farm is reflected, at Southampton as elsewhere, in the assumption by prominent burgesses of the role of tax farmer to the town. In the early uncertainties of taxation, the farm of Southampton had been set at an exorbitant £300. Emma, viscountess of Rouen, who had held the farm between 1158 and 1163, retired owing a considerable debt to the crown. And this precedent no doubt persuaded three burgesses (Roger, son of Milo, Fortin and Robert of St Laurence), when they came to assume the responsibility of accounting for the farm, to do so, on their own insistence, not as farmers but as keepers (*custodes*) for the crown.[34] By 1167 a more realistic target of £200 had been agreed. Robert of St Laurence, now alone, was again accounting for the borough farm from 1173. Like Gervase of Hampton, his successor, he seems to have served as farmer in his own right, rather than as servant of the king. And if both he and Gervase incurred debts to the Exchequer while in office, both found it possible to wipe them out by a compromise settlement with the king.[35]

These, then, were the conditions – the resolution of an attainable figure for the farm at £200, and the willingness of responsible burgesses to collect it – that enabled John, within barely one month of his accession, to grant away in perpetuity the farm of his borough of Southampton. 'Know ye', he said, addressing his church, his aristocracy and his faithful subjects, 'that we have granted and by this present charter have confirmed to our burgesses of Southampton, the town of Southampton to farm for ever, with the port of Portsmouth with all their appurtenances, liberties, and free customs, and all others which pertained to the farm of the said town of Southampton, in the time of Henry our father, to be held from us and our heirs for ever to farm, on rendering thence yearly on Michaelmas Day to our treasury £200 sterling.'[36] Some years elapsed before the association with the new borough of Portsmouth was firmly resolved in an amicable partition of rights and profits, agreed in 1239, by which the harbour alone of Portsmouth was recognized as the sphere of the burgesses of Southampton and local customs were shared equally between the two communities.[37] But the value of this early link between Portsmouth and Southampton, not formally severed for many years, lay in its recognition of the status and authority of Southampton as the head-port of its locality. The case for the preservation of this authority was to be argued still in 1572, in a draft of 'Alegacyons why porstmoth sholde have no Cust hows', preserved among the records of Southampton. The erection of a customs house at Portsmouth, it was held, would ensure that Sussex and a great part of Surrey and Hampshire, which hitherto had usually been served with wines, woad, canvas and other commodities from Southampton, would then be served for the same commodities by Portsmouth, 'to the great decay & utter undoing of the said towne of Suthampton which of auncient time hath bene & yet is worthelie maynteynid by thonlie trade of merchaundize'.[38]

Notes

1 H. W. C. Davis *et al.* (eds), *Regesta regum anglo-normannorum*, ii:269. Precepts of Henry I concerning land of Reading Abbey in Southampton were addressed to Payn, the reeve of Hampton, probably in 1133. His predecessor in office seems to have been Warin of Southampton, mentioned in notifications of August 1127.

2 *Charters*, i:2–5, 40–50, 54–81. The charters are helpfully discussed, and many of them are re-dated, by Edwin Welch, *Southampton City Charters*, passim.

3 *Charters*, i:10–11.

4 D. C. Douglas and C. W. Greenaway (eds), *English Historical Documents, 1042–1189*, pp. 945–6.

5 No original of the charter survives, though its concession is recorded in the *Pipe Roll*

2 John, p. 206, and a copy is preserved in Edward III's general confirmation of 1340 (*Charters*, i:12–13).

6 M. Leopold Delisle (ed.), *Recueil des actes de Henri II*, i:198–9.

7 Eiríkr Magnusson (ed.), *Thómas saga erkibyskups*, i:120, and William Stubbs (ed.), *Radulfi de Diceto decani Londoniensis opera historica*, i:383.

8 Almost all the chroniclers make much of this incident, but see, for example, William Stubbs (ed.), *Memoriale fratris Walteri de Coventria*, i:230, and *Chronica Rogeri de Houedene*, ii:61.

9 William Stubbs (ed.), *Memoriale fratris Walteri de Coventria*, i:262.

10 Ibid., i:292

11 William Stubbs (ed.), *Gesta regis Henrici secundi Benedicti abbatis*, i:345.

12 William Stubbs (ed.), *The historical works of Gervase of Canterbury*, i:457, ii:86.

13 For a convenient summary of the royal works at the castle from the twelfth century to the sixteenth, see H. M. Colvin (ed.), *The History of the King's Works*, ii:840–4.

14 *Pipe Roll 8 Henry II*, pp. 35, 39.

15 *Pipe Roll 9 Henry II*, p. 56.

16 *Pipe Roll 13 Henry II*, p. 194.

17 *Pipe Roll 14 Henry II*, p. 190; *15 Henry II*, p. 158; *17 Henry II*, pp. 42–3; *21 Henry II*, p. 16.

18 *Pipe Roll 18 Henry II*, p. 98; *21 Henry II*, p. 207; *22 Henry II*, p. 200; *23 Henry II*, p. 177; *26 Henry II*, p. 149.

19 *Pipe Roll 33 Henry II*, pp. 143, 195; *3 John*, p. 284; *4 John*, p. 78; *6 John*, p. 120.

20 *Pipe Roll 32 Henry II*, p. 179.

21 *Pipe Roll 2 Richard I*, p. 6.

22 *Pipe Roll 9 Richard I*, p. 17.

23 *Pipe Roll 19 Henry II*, p. 53; *20 Henry II*, p. 134.

24 *Pipe Roll 2 Richard I*, p. 137; *4 Richard I*, p. 293; *5 Richard I*, p. 140; *6 Richard I*, p. 220.

25 *Pipe Roll 13 John*, p. 187; *16 John*, p. 127.

26 For the Isembard, St Laurence and Fleming connection, see God's House Deeds 695; P.R.O. E326/9331; and *Cal.P.R. 1266–72*, pp. 242, 325. For Claramunda and the Gloucesters, see P.R.O. E210/5324; and *Cal.C.R. 1279–88*, p. 87. For tables demonstrating family alliances, see Appendix 1b and Fig. 10.

27 St Denys Cart. 63.

28 S.C.R.O. SC4/2/41, 42, 44.

29 B. J. Whiting, *Proverbs, Sentences and Proverbial Phrases*, p. 388 (other proverbs quoted below are taken from this same source). The St Laurence family, in crossing King John, risked much and lost more. Ralph of St Laurence, in 1208, was fined 60 marks for 'having the benevolence of the king' (*Memoranda Roll 10 John*, p. 68). Bovo, probably the son of Simon of St Laurence, spent much of his life paying off the debt incurred by Simon as bailiff in 1213–14 (P.R.O. E372/62–100).

30 *Pipe Roll 19 Henry II*, p. 53.

31 *Pipe Roll 2 Richard I*, pp. 131–2.

32 *Pipe Roll 7 Richard I*, p. 226.

33 *Pipe Roll 4 John*, p. 78.

34 James Tait, *The Medieval English Borough*, p. 170, and *Pipe Rolls 10, 11, 12 and 13 Henry II*.

35 *Pipe Roll 26 Henry II*, p. 133, and *2 Richard I*, p. 136.

36 *Charters*, i:12–13.

37 *Oak Book*, ii:132.

38 *Letters*, pp. 88–9.

Plate 1 Oblique aerial view of the medieval quarter from the south, showing the original street plan broken by the insertion of a new inner ring road, now known as Castle Way

Plate 2 A late-twelfth-century Norman wine jug

Plate 3 The twelfth-century Tournai marble font at St Michael's church

Chapter three

The gild merchant

John's charter of 1199 had protected only in the most general terms the liberties and free customs of the borough on which the king was conferring new privileges. Yet these were already ancient in John's day, and to contemporaries they needed little defining. An early list of the customs of Newcastle upon Tyne has survived from the reign of Henry I. Here the protection and regulation of trade ranked equally with juridical rights as a matter of concern to the legislators. A burgess of Newcastle was shielded against outsiders not of his franchise, in the purchase of goods as in the collection of debts He was answerable, in matters not touching the crown, to the courts of his own borough. He was free to dispose of his property as he willed, and he could pass on his privileges to his son.[1] Very probably the liberties and customs of the gildsmen of Southampton, contemporaneously granted the protection of Henry I, would have found parallels in these.[2] Certainly, a Southampton burgess of the twelfth century, while still subject in matters of taxation to the sheriff, might unite with his fellows in the regulation of local trade. He might found, together with them, a protective association, or gild, to exclude the competition of outsiders, even of fellow franchisers, and to nurture the economy of his borough. He might reasonably expect the benevolence of the king, and he might build, with the king's implicit consent, an administrative structure within the borough capable, in due course, of assuming its government.

Already, from its early Frankish beginnings, the gild had combined religious and social functions, some of which touched on government. Its preoccupations might be military or mercantile. But whatever its original purpose, it shared the principal characteristics of other such social alliances: the religious ceremonies centring on saints' days and burial of the dead, the almost ritual alms-giving, the mutual insurance against natural or political disaster, symbolically secured by convivial sessions in the hall. Nothing in the surviving record can place the origins of the Southampton gild merchant before the reign of Henry I, but very probably it owed its form to a similar association of traders in the Anglo-Saxon borough.[3] It would have met, as did the *probi homines* of Winchester, in a convenient hall.[4] It provided its members with an excuse for the customary drinking-bout (*potacio*). It saw to their entertainment with suitably heroic tales: the romance of *Sir Beves of Hamtoun* may well have been first shaped in the vicinity, and would certainly have been known in one form or another in the twelfth-century port.[5] It flattered both their individual and their corporate pride. It was before just such an 'honourable gathering' at Huntingdon, to attend the wants of a 'great throng of nobles', that the blessed Christina of Markyate was to be summoned as cup-bearer. For the saint, the day-long assembly of the gild merchant of Huntingdon, 'one of the merchants' greatest and best-known festivals', was an ordeal only to be endured by constant recourse to the thought of the Mother of God. For the merchants of Huntingdon, their gild in session was an entirely necessary demonstration, both to themselves and to others outside their community, of the strength and solidarity of their fellowship.[6]

At Southampton, the gild was held twice yearly, on the Sunday next after St Hilary (13 January) and on the Sunday following the feast of John the Baptist (24 June). The gildsmen assembled at the hour of prime, and were fined for a late appearance. No member of the gild might leave the town while the gild was in session, unless he had the permission of the steward. Non-attendance, if not the result of sickness, was heavily fined, at the same rate as unauthorized absence from the town. The gild might be expected to last through to the evening, and could continue for several days. It was conducted by elected officials: an alderman, a steward (*seneschal*), four discreets (*echevins*), an usher and a chaplain. A clerk was in attendance on the chaplain, and sergeants were apportioned to the officials. Strangers, not of the gild, were excluded from its deliberations. They might attend the gild only by express sanction of the alderman or of the steward.[7]

After the manner of similar associations elsewhere, the Southampton gild, from its earliest years, protected both the person and the property of its members. It forbade quarrels between its gildsmen, punished swearing, and set a tariff on fisticuffs and cases of more serious assault. It required attendance on the sick, and provided for those in its ranks who had come upon bad days and had fallen at the last into poverty. As an association of practising Christians, it was particularly concerned that a proper respect should be shown to the dead. 'When a gildsman dies, all those who are of the gild and in the town shall be at the service of the dead, and gildsmen shall carry the body, and bring it to the place of sepulture. And he who will not do this shall pay, on his oath, twopence to be given to the poor. And those of the ward where the dead man shall be, shall find a man to watch with the body the night that the dead person shall lie in his house. And as long as the service of the dead shall last, that is to say, the vigil and the mass, there shall burn four wax tapers of the gild, each taper of two pounds or more, until the body be buried. And these four tapers shall remain in the keeping of the seneschal of the gild.'[8]

Every gildsman was of the franchise of the town, but not every franchiser was a member of the gild. There is no way of telling either when the distinction originated, or how long it persisted. Nevertheless, in the formative years of the borough, it remained very real. 'If anyone', in the words of the thirteenth gild ordinance, 'who is not of the gild, but is of the franchise, offend [or] strike a gildsman and be reasonably attainted, he shall lose his franchise and go to prison for a day and a night.' A stranger, neither of the gild nor of the franchise, if convicted of the same offence, served twice the sentence.[9] Membership of the gild, although it might be purchased by agreement, was usually hereditary. On the death of a gildsman, his seat at the gild descended to his eldest son or to his nearest heir by birth. Membership could not be obtained by marriage, nor did it descend automatically to sons of a gildsman other than the eldest, although these might expect to be admitted to membership on the taking of an oath and the payment of a fine. Important financial incentives maintained recruitment to the gild. Gildsmen were obliged to share with their fellows such merchandise as was available for purchase, and might be refused the right to trade if they failed to observe the obligation. But their co-operation, once secured, was usually richly rewarded. Exemption from local tolls and customs was shared with every franchiser, as was some part at least of the retail trade of the borough. But a gildsman was privileged before all others to bargain for goods brought for sale to the town. Furthermore, 'no one shall buy honey, seim [fat], salt herring, or any kind of oil, or millstones, or fresh hides, or any kind of fresh skins, except a gildsman; nor keep a tavern for wine, or sell cloth by retail, except on a market day or fair day; nor keep above five quarters of corn in his granary to sell by retail, if he is not a gildsman; and whoever shall do this, and be attainted [thereof], shall forfeit all to the king'.[10]

The sense of community in the gild, kept alive by regular meetings and by the daily co-operation of its members in concerns of social welfare and trade, could, and most probably did, develop the corporate spirit of the borough. There is no evidence of a genuine communal movement in twelfth-century Southampton, a deliberate attempt by the burgesses to organize themselves as a self-governing community on an elective basis. But in the conduct of the gild merchant throughout the century there existed already what has been called an 'active communal principle'.[11] The gild elected its alderman, its steward, its *echevins*, and its usher. In the collection of entry fees and fines, it built up a common treasury of its own. It conducted its business at assemblies at which every gildsman was present and at which, presumably, each had a voice. No comparable organization existed in the regulation of affairs of the borough. There was no machinery to build up a town fund distinct from the annual payment of the farm. The portmoot, or borough court, was headed by the reeve, still an official of the crown. The liberties and free customs of the borough were such as to protect its trade and to confer rights of judgment in the existing courts of the king. They were not in any real sense the starting-point of municipal independence on the model so frequently demonstrated during that same century on the Continent.

The details of the evolution of the Southampton gild merchant into a genuine municipal governing body are obscure. But there is little reason to doubt that it had happened, in almost every sphere, before the middle of the thirteenth century. The surviving gild ordinances of the thirteenth century are ordinances that concern directly the government of the town. An assembly of the whole community of the town (*toute la commune de la vile*), meeting annually on 30 September and charged with the election of a council of twelve to keep the king's peace in the borough, perhaps perpetuated some of the spirit of the former borough organization, and existed side by side with the gild.[12] But at Southampton, as equally at Leicester, Andover or Lincoln, the same men who held office in the gild might hold, either then or at some other time, positions of comparable responsibility in the borough. And it was in their persons, rather than in any deliberate reallocation of borough offices, that the two organizations, borough and gild, merged.[13] Such an evolution, if it appears at this distance virtually inevitable, need not at the time have been smooth. In a progress otherwise sparsely recorded, one event cannot fail to stand out. On 25 October 1249 the burgesses of Southampton, headed by Walter le Fleming, obtained from the king the unusual right of exemption from the obligation to elect a mayor.[14] It may be that the move owed something to a personal rivalry between Walter le Fleming, the wealthiest merchant of his generation, and Benedict Ace, the outgoing mayor. But they had been partners in many joint enterprises in the past, and for several years had shared municipal office.[15] Perhaps more to the point, Benedict for some considerable time had held jointly the offices of mayor and keeper of the king's wines; like Walter le Fleming himself, he had worked on frequent commissions for the king.[16] The association of municipal office with royal service, while never entirely absent at any time in the later Middle Ages, was less tolerable in the thirteenth century than it had been in the twelfth. In natural sequence from the development of the municipal responsibilities of the gild merchant, it followed that the chief officer of the gild, the alderman, should seek to assume the role formerly held by a royal official, once reeve and now seemingly mayor also, in the direction of the affairs of the borough.[17] 'The alderman', in the definition of a contemporary gild ordinance, 'is chief of the town and of the gild, and should principally be at pains and careful to maintain the franchise and the statutes of the gild and of the town; he shall have the first voice in all elections and in all matters that concern the town and the gild.'[18] In the course of time, the mayoralty re-emerged, to bring Southampton into line once again with what had become the usual practice elsewhere. But for at least half a century after 1249, the chief officer of the town commonly described himself as 'alderman'. And when his title reverted to the earlier style, as it began to do, on occasion, several years before 1300, it carried with it no necessary connotation of some special relationship with the king. The old battles were over. There was no need to fight over identical ground again.

The very strength of the gild organization of Southampton, a classic example of its kind, flowed naturally from an economic setting that daily increased the dependence of the town on trade. With the exception of some ship-building and of the inevitable small-scale local crafts, the borough enjoyed no industrial role comparable with that of the great cloth-producing centres close at hand to the north, at Winchester, and to the west, at Wilton. There were thus few natural oppositions at work within the trading community, and nothing existed to prevent the growth of a single powerful association for the protection and encouragement of trade. Very much more is known of the circumstances of such trade in the thirteenth century and later. But already in the twelfth century there are indications enough both of its extent and of its variety, and it is surely not without significance that the first steps in the direction of municipal independence took the form of guarantees of trade. Four days before John published his concession of the farm in perpetuity to Southampton, he had already confirmed his brother's earlier grant of a sweeping exemption from tolls. A copy of Richard's charter, dated within a month of his accession, survives in the general confirmation of Edward III. It probably repeated earlier concessions, perhaps less explicit or far-reaching. The burgesses of Southampton, from the start of the new reign, were to be quit of 'toll and passage and pontage both on land and sea, both in fairs and markets, and from all secular customary services and throughout all our dominions on this side of the sea and beyond and throughout our whole realm. And we forbid any hereafter to disturb them or cause them injury, trouble, or hardship in respect to that which pertains to our authority, under pain of our displeasure.'[19]

Richard protected an existing trade, already long-established by his day. Imports by sea included wine and the more exotic victuals, building materials (limestone, slate and tile) and lead; by road came supplies of corn. Ale, livestock and salted venison were exported to provision the king's fortresses; raw wool and cloth, the staples of the Southampton export trade of the thirteenth century, were probably as important in the twelfth (Fig. 2).[20] Trading contact with south-west France was clearly on the increase in the later years of the twelfth century. But the archaeological evidence, imperfect though it is, suggests that the main emphasis of trade remained throughout the century in the north. Between 1203 and 1205, in a series of disastrous campaigns, John was to lose his paternal fiefs in Normandy, Maine and Anjou. Brittany fell to Philip Augustus in 1206. But until this happened, the natural flow of Southampton trade continued to be towards the south-east and the north. Archaeologically, the links with these regions are obvious. A probable by-product of the wine trade, the crudely incised jugs of Normandy, decorated with a characteristic wavy, or zig-zag pattern (Plate 2), were being imported into Southampton in increasing numbers through the length of the twelfth century. Of a cream-buff ware, frequently carrying decorative applied strips, broad and thumb-pressed along their length, these jugs are easily recognizable alongside the heavy, round-bottomed cooking-pots of the native pottery industry.[21] Yet there is no comparable evidence in a twelfth-century archaeological context of trade on this scale to the south. Shipping, calling at Southampton in the twelfth century, evidently still came almost exclusively from Normandy, Flanders or the far north. The bulk of the heavy trade remained with Normandy, on the short haul due south across the Channel. Caen stone was an habitual ingredient of late-twelfth-century construction work at Southampton as elsewhere, and it is likely that the wine came through Normandy down the river route via Paris, Rouen and Honfleur. But the quickest profits were already to be found not so much in Normandy as in the wool and cloth markets of Flanders, and it was from there, predictably, that the finest products of contemporary craftsmanship derived.

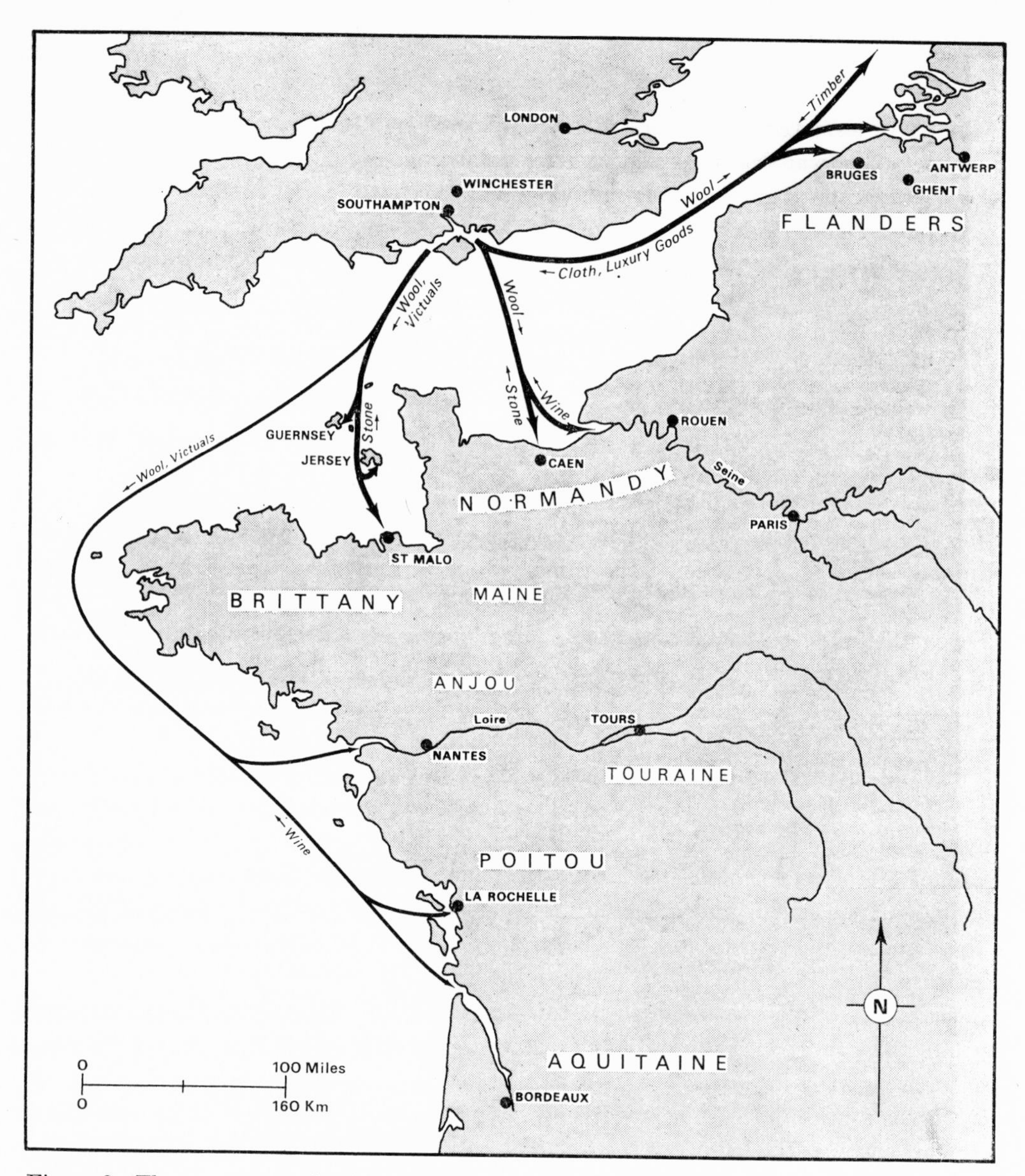

Figure 2 The overseas trade of Southampton in the twelfth century

The remarkable Tournai marble font (Plate 3) preserved in the parish church of St Michael is of Flemish workmanship. A close parallel has been recognized at Dendermonde, near Ghent, and there are many similar survivals in northern France, Belgium and Germany.[22] Equally, the finest pottery vessel to have been found in the early Angevin town is most probably a product of the kilns of Andenne. A remarkable tripod pitcher in a rich amber glaze, it is painted with great 'Maltese' crosses (Plate 4) evocative of a wider world of adventure and crusade, the proper sphere of the Knights of St John.[23]

Notes

1 D. C. Douglas and C. W. Greenaway (eds), *English Historical Documents, 1042–1189*, pp. 970–1.
2 *Charters*, i:10–11. The debate, however, continues as to how exactly one set of borough privileges may be held comparable with another.
3 Emile Coornaert, 'Les ghildes médiévales (Ve–XIVe siècles)', *Revue Historique*, 199 (1948), pp. 22–55, 208–43, argues convincingly the case for continuity.
4 J. S. Furley, *City Government of Winchester*, pp. 70–1.
5 Eugen Kölbing (ed.), *The Romance of Sir Beves of Hamtoun*. Early English Text Society, extra series, 3 vols in 1, 1885–94.
6 C. H. Talbot (ed.), *The life of Christina of Markyate, a twelfth-century recluse*, p. 49.
7 *Oak Book*, i:24–7, 32–3, 78–9 (gild ordinances).
8 Ibid., i:26–33, 36–7.
9 Ibid., i:32–3.
10 Ibid., i:30–1, 34–9.
11 James Tait, *The Medieval English Borough*, p. 230.
12 *Oak Book*, i:44–5.
13 James Tait, *The Medieval English Borough*, p. 233; also G. H. Martin, 'The English borough in the thirteenth century', *T.R.H.S.*, 5th series, 13 (1963), p. 134; and J. W. F. Hill, *Medieval Lincoln*, pp. 186–7.
14 *Cal.Ch.R. 1226–57*, p. 345; *Cal.C.R. 1247–51*, p. 257; and P.R.O. E372/94, m.1.
15 P.R.O. E372/86, m. 13; *Cal.C.R. 1227–31*, p. 285, *1234–7*, p. 94, and *1237–42*, p. 286; *Cal. Liberate R. 1245–51*, p. 209. For their association in municipal office, see Davies, p. 170; to this might be added at least one other year (1244–5) in which, while Benedict Ace served yet again as mayor, Walter le Fleming and Sampson de Puteo were bailiffs (P.R.O. E326/4492).
16 Regular entries, in which Benedict Ace is represented as keeper of the king's wines at Southampton, begin at least as early as the Pipe Roll of 1232–3 (P.R.O. E372/77 and thereafter passim).
17 A. Ballard and J. Tait (eds), *British Borough Charters, 1216–1307*, pp. lvii, 386. The identity of mayor and reeve was perhaps never very firmly established. When Walter Fortin was mayor, early in the century, Ralph Isembard held jointly the offices of reeve of Hampton and steward of God's House (God's House Deeds 348).
18 *Oak Book*, i:60–1.
19 *Charters*, i:2–3, 10–13.
20 Some idea of the commodities of twelfth-century trade in the port may be obtained from the published Pipe Rolls of Henry II (e.g. for wine, see *9 Henry II*, p. 56, *12 Henry II*, p. 109, *22 Henry II*, p. 188; for ale, see *14 Henry II*, p. 190; for livestock, see *9 Henry II*, p. 56, *14 Henry II*, p. 190, etc.). For a useful discussion of a comparable trading situation, including a survey of activity in this early period, see Eleanora Carus-Wilson, 'The medieval trade of the ports of the Wash', *Medieval Archaeology*, 6–7 (1962–3), pp. 182–201.
21 For a general discussion of these wares and of their dating, see *Southampton Excavations*, forthcoming.
22 Cecil H. Eden, *Black Tournai Fonts in England. The Group of Seven Late Norman Fonts from Belgium*, pp. 17–18, 29–30.
23 *Southampton Excavations*, forthcoming.

Chapter four

The Church

Where the commercial expansion of twelfth-century Southampton brought to life its stagnating economy, the Church paid regard to its soul. 'I do not think', boasted William Fitz Stephen in praise of London, 'there is a city with a better record for church-going, doing honour to God's ordinances, keeping feast-days, giving alms and hospitality to strangers, confirming betrothals, contracting marriages, celebrating weddings, providing feasts, entertaining guests, and also, it may be added, in care for funerals and for the burial of the dead.'[1] And Fitz Stephen's 'genial vision' of the metropolis in the final decades of the twelfth century has certainly its relevance elsewhere. At Southampton, the merest flavour of the robust and colourful religious life of Fitz Stephen's London survives in the text of an agreement not many years later in date. In 1225 a settlement was reached between the then rector of St Mary's, Philip de Lucy, and the prior and convent of the neighbouring Augustinian house of St Denys, holders of the advowsons of the churches, or chapels, of St Michael, Holy Rood, St Lawrence and All Saints. It had been claimed, in a petition to Pope Honorius III the previous year, that the rights and dues of the mother church had been prejudiced by the unwarranted activity of its juniors. From now, 'the common procession of the town of Southampton shall come to St Mary's church on the day of the Ascension, with chaplains, crosses and banners, but on the days of the Assumption of the Blessed Mary and of St Leodegar without crosses and banners'. The agreement concerning tithes and offerings, stated only in general terms in the settlement of 1225, was elaborated within a few years as follows.[2]

> The parochial chapels are to receive tithes from the sale of fish by their parishioners, living within the bounds of the parish, wherever the fish have been caught; and from the two wind-mills which are situated between the town of Southampton and the house of the lepers; and the tithes of piglets within the walls of the town. All other tithes shall go to the church of St Mary. The Prior and Convent of St Denys shall have the tithes of one water-mill by their court on the north, and of gardens existing within the enclosure of their house at the time of this agreement. If anyone dies on board ship or in a house *inhonesta* unsuitable for the performance of the

> service of the dead in the town of Southampton, his body may be carried to the parochial chapel, but no mass may be celebrated while it lies there, nor any other service that could not be held in the house of some parishioner if he had been taken there.

Little enough may be recognizable of the constructive piety of Fitz Stephen's Londoners in the dry record of a parochial squabble in Southampton. But the care for the dead that Fitz Stephen admired is echoed, albeit for a different reason, in the text of the settlement, and there are suggestions here too of that contemporary surge of popular piety which had brought before a wide, sometimes fanatical, twelfth-century audience the concepts of the humanity of Christ and the accessibility to prayer of the Blessed Virgin Mary. Certainly there can be no question of the enthusiasm of the wealthy Southampton burgesses in the later years of the century for works that would demonstrate in some permanent manner the practical Christianity of their generation. At the parish church of St Michael, the Tournai marble font still serves us today as a reminder of that spirit. In their own day the burgesses, although comparatively slow to come to the assistance of the existing royal foundation at St Denys, competed to endow what they must have considered in a special sense the charge and responsibility of their borough, the leper hospital of St Mary Magdalene and, still more, the hospital for the aged and infirm at St Julian, commonly known as God's House.[3]

Indeed, an inventory of the charters of God's House, taken in 1290 within a century of the foundation of the hospital, reads like a roll-call of the merchant plutocracy of the town. Ralph, Roger and John, the sons of Azo of Hampton, had all granted property to the hospital; there were the gifts of James Isembard, of Turstin the Clerk, of Richard of Leicester and Benedict Ace; individual transactions of Gervase of Hampton, founder of the hospital and the leading burgess of his generation, are listed with the extensive confirmation charters of Master Roger, his brother.[4] In themselves, the lists of witnesses testifying to these charters are ample demonstration of the interest taken by the leading burgesses, at the turn of the twelfth and thirteenth centuries, in the fortunes of the new foundation. The witnesses of Turstin's charter included Simon and William of St Laurence, Richard of Leicester, Roger Bonhait and Benedict Ace.[5] A contemporary document, the charter of Golditha, daughter of Vitalis and one of the last of that important twelfth-century family of 'Seals', was attested by Benedict Ace and Richard of Leicester, Walter Fortin, Walter le Fleming, John de la Bulehuse and Robert the Monk.[6] Master Roger's important confirmation of the hospital lands attracted a particularly impressive gathering of the *probi homines* of the borough. Among those ready to add the force of their names to the document were the Fortins (Walter, Denys and Amys), the Flemings (Walter and James), the St Laurences (Bovo and Robert), Richard of Leicester, Ralph Isembard, John de la Bulehuse, Walter of Colchester, Robert the Monk, 'and many others'.[7]

Inevitably, other deserving religious bodies, in particular the house of Franciscan friars which was established next to the hospital within half a century of its foundation, would first threaten, then replace God's House in the primacy of the affections of the burgesses. Walter le Fleming, for example, while he was to be a generous friend to the friars, did not appear in the 1290 inventory as a benefactor of the hospital. On his death in 1257 he left only ten shillings to the hospital 'to maintain the beds of the poor', the legacy comparing ill with the outright gift of £5 to his protégés, the Franciscans, together with the residue of his property.[8] Indeed, by the end of the century, and probably for many years before, the flood of donations had subsided. God's House had become institutionalized, so much an accepted part of the social machinery of the town that the burgesses would claim in 1286, against all the evidence the bishop of Winchester could produce, the right of presenting to the wardenship.[9]

The claim was unsuccessful, but it may serve to illustrate, nevertheless, the particular sense in which the hospital belonged to the economy of the borough. No such special relationship seems to have held in the case of the royal foundation at St Denys. Although senior to the hospital by almost three-quarters of a century, and a near-neighbour to the borough from the start of its mounting prosperity, the Augustinian priory at St Denys remained significantly ill-endowed.[10] Inescapably, it played its part in borough affairs, for it held, by grant of Henry II, the advowsons of all the major churches in the town, with the exception of St John's, in French Street, and of the mother church at St Mary.[11] Edward III reinforced the connection by the gift, in 1347, of the lands and other assets of the leper hospital at St Mary Magdalene, in partial compensation for the losses sustained by the priory in the raid of 1338.[12] And Henry IV attempted to lift the poverty of the house by licensing, in 1405, its appropriation of the four parish churches to which his ancestor had first given it a claim.[13] But it was the king, throughout, who remained the chief benefactor of the priory. Remembering St Denys in their wills, the burgesses contributed in some part to its endowment. The wealthy Claramunda was a benefactress of the priory, and her contemporary John Horn (d. 1279) left it the reversion of his considerable English Street and suburban properties to sustain a canon 'who shall celebrate three times a week in St Denys church for the souls of the testator, of Rose his wife and of all the faithful departed'.[14] Nevertheless, the product of their piety, at least in this particular, was to remain a thing of shreds and patches. The burgesses may, on occasion, have been generous. They were rarely exceedingly so.[15]

By the turn of the twelfth and thirteenth centuries, the character of the religious and socio-religious life of the town had, in the main, been set. It is true that the Franciscan friary, an important addition to this life, had yet to be founded, but in other respects there would be little fundamental change before the great upheaval of the Dissolution in the fourth decade of the sixteenth century. In 1173, or perhaps before, the leper hospital of St Mary Magdalene had been established at a convenient distance to the north of the town, beyond the common field of Houndwell and surrounded by lands of its own.[16] It drew its support partly from the revenue of its own endowment, partly from legacies, and partly also from a charge on the local customs, a duty of a penny on each tun of wine imported, whether by 'natives or aliens, men of the town excepted'.[17] Before the end of the century, the hospital at God's House had begun to care for another category of the old: the poor and the infirm. Both institutions were to be remembered, in one of the earliest of its ordinances, as deserving of the charity of the gild merchant. While the gild sat, two sesters of ale were sent to the lepers of *la Maudeleyne*, another two to the sick of God's House.[18]

Less than two miles to the north-east of the town, the canons of the Augustinian house of St Denys had long combined the service of religion as a community of regulars with the cure of souls in the borough. As clerks in holy orders, the canons, at least in these early years, most probably found members of their own community to serve the churches that they held. Later, as their expenses mounted and as satisfactory recruitment fell, they appointed vicars to the cure in their place. But in the interval their participation in person in the day-by-day religious routine of the community of the borough was as acceptable as it must have been familiar. With the precentor, or chanter, of St Mary's, as in due course with the brethren at the Franciscan friary, they kept in motion a continual round of intercession with the Almighty. It was the pleasure of pious benefactors to see that the work should never be interrupted. Most specifically, Claramunda of Southampton made this the condition of a grant of rents deriving from properties on the western shore. To God and the church and canons of St Denys, she gave eight shillings of rents in free alms for her soul and for the souls of Brunus and Stephen, her late husbands, of her father, her mother and all the faithful departed. She directed that the revenue should be used to provide 'wine for the church of St Denys in the sacrament of the altar, by which every day the body and blood of our Lord Jesus Christ crucified, is consecrated through the ministry of a priest in the form of bread and wine, for all the faithful living and departed'.[19]

Something of the enveloping spiritual life of the twelfth-century borough may be recognized in this daily celebration at St Denys of the mystery of the Eucharist. The display of the sacred host had become for the first time in the twelfth century an accepted part of the routine of the mass. In a new way, it united priest and congregation, taking its part alongside a genuinely popular devotion centring, usually, on the more readily understandable concepts of the new-found humanity of Christ and the demonstrable benevolence of the Virgin. Marian art, Marian legend and Marian prayer provided the outlets for a great out-pouring of the spirit, at least as common in the lower ranks of society as in the higher. The events of the Passion, the lives and works of fashionable saints, the mystery of the Godhead, these were the materials of a genuinely popular faith which, while it continued to pay regard to the older surviving traditions, dwelt increasingly on the tenderness and the suffering of Christ, and on the sweet devotion of his womenfolk. There were major processions, we have seen, on the feasts of the Ascension and the Assumption of the Blessed Mary. The hospital for lepers, in the spirit of a widespread tradition, was dedicated to St Mary Magdalene. The chapel of Holy Trinity, on the shore due east of St Mary's, must date back at least to the twelfth century.[20] And the dedications of the new churches in the French quarter, to St Michael and St John Baptist, followed a twelfth-century fashion current throughout the West.[21] In yet another direction, the increasing practice of pilgrimage, whether overseas to Jerusalem and Santiago, or closer at hand to Canterbury, opened new avenues to devotion in the town. We know of Agnes Sweyn's proposed pilgrimage to the Holy Land in 1269, for she was persuaded to appoint the prior of St Denys as her executor, 'in view of the danger attending the pilgrimages'.[22] There is evidence also of a visit by Richard of Southwick to Canterbury later in the same century, where he purchased two *ampullae*, or badges, as souvenirs to commemorate his excursion.[23] But the habit of pilgrimage, in Southampton as elsewhere, was far older than this. In 1174 Henry II had landed at Southampton at the start of his expiatory journey to Canterbury. Pilgrims from Spain and western France followed in the king's tracks, making their way, as he had, from Southampton to Winchester, and thence by the long land route to Canterbury. 'Pylgrymesgate', opening on West Hithe on the seaward side and on Simnel Street to the east, was their point of entry to the town. For centuries thereafter, the name 'Pilgrims' Pit' attached to the west end of Simnel Street, or more commonly to a garden plot adjoining it on the south.[24]

Nevertheless, for all the apparatus of religion in the town, and for all the public piety of its burgesses, there still persisted a division, as old as St Augustine, between what the Church could demand of itself and what it might expect of its penitents. A Christian congregation in the twelfth century, as readily as its equivalent in the fifth, recognized its own manifest limitations. It sought not to attain the perfection of the saints, but rather to work off its inevitable sins by penance. Unwilling though the Church might be to tolerate such a double standard of morality, it found itself powerless to stop it. In Southampton, the canons of St Denys, arming themselves for the struggle, equipped their library with a copy of the popular *Penitential* of Bartholomew Iscanus (d. 1184), sometime archdeacon, then bishop of Exeter. They would have used it as a guide in their ministry in the town, employing the tariff of penance it presented. But their task could scarcely have been more formidable. Just below the surface of the emotional piety of their generation lay a network, barely concealed, of antique pagan practice and deep-rooted superstition. The canons met it on every side.[25]

> If anyone pays respect to soothsayers, augurs, enchanters, or makes use of philters, let him be anathema. Whoever by any magic turns aside a judgment of God, shall do penance for two years. He who is a magician for the sake of love and does not bring it to success shall do penance for two years. If he does, five years. If adultery results, ten years. . . . He who strives to take away another's supply of milk or honey or of other things by any incantation, or [tries] by magic to gain it for himself, shall do penance for three years. . . . They who by any incantation disturb the calm of the atmosphere or who by invocation of demons confuse the minds

> of men shall do penance for five years. They who, deceived by the illusion of a demon, believe and profess that they go or ride in the services of her whom the stupid crowd call Herodias or Diana with a countless multitude and and obey her commands shall do penance for one year. She who lays a table with three knives for the service of the Fates, that they may predestinate good things to those who are born there, shall do penance for two years. A woman who by a magical trick [prevents the consummation of a legal marriage] shall do penance for five years.

To the bishop, and to those of his persuasion, it was clear enough that if faith in his day came easily, it was as much in necromancy as in God. Against all odds, the canons of St Denys must play the Pelagian, insisting that perfectionism was both desirable and attainable within the entire body of the Christian church. But the task was such that even the best might falter.[26]

> O Jesus, good Shepherd, O Jesus, kind and loving Shepherd, a wretched and miserable shepherd cries out to you. Although he is weak, ignorant and useless, still he is the shepherd of your sheep. O good Shepherd, a shepherd who is not good cries out to you, anxious for himself, anxious for your sheep.

Notes

1 D. C. Douglas and C. W. Greenaway (eds), *English Historical Documents, 1042–1189*, p. 959. Fitz Stephen's *Description of the most noble city of London* is made use of extensively by Sir Frank Stenton, 'Norman London', in *Social Life in Early England*, ed. Geoffrey Barraclough, pp. 179–207.

2 St Denys Cart. 283, 284.

3 For useful summaries of the endowments of of these houses, see Davies, pp. 433–42, 448–63. The internal organization of God's House was discussed by H. T. Riley in his report on the hospital accounts preserved with the Queen's College muniments (*R.C.H.M.*, 6th report, pp. 551–69); see also Richard Harris, 'God's House, Southampton, in the reign of Edward III', Southampton M.A. dissertation, 1970.

4 Cecil Deedes (ed.), *Registrum Johannis de Pontissara*, Canterbury and York Society, 30 (1924), pp. 698–705.

5 God's House Deeds 472.

6 Ibid., 522.

7 Ibid., 313.

8 Bodleian, Queen's College MS. 1071.

9 Cecil Deedes (ed.), *Registrum Johannis de Pontissara*, Canterbury and York Society, 19 and 30 (1915–24), i:xxxvi–vii, 319–20, ii:695–711; also Davies, p. 457. For an exactly contemporary claim, successfully upheld, to the patronage of the leper hospital of St Mary Magdalene, see Davies, p. 448.

10 The gift by Henry I of 'the part of his land lying between Portswood and the river Itchen' presumably constitutes, as this was to be the site of the priory buildings, a foundation grant to the canons. It was dated 1127 (H. W. C. Davis *et al.* (eds), *Regesta regum anglo-normannorum*, ii:210).

11 *Cal.Ch.R. 1300–1326*, p. 337. A record of Henry's grant of the advowsons of the chapels of St Michael, Holy Rood, St Lawrence and All Saints is preserved in an *inspeximus* of 1317. The advowson of the church of St John Baptist belonged from an early date to the Norman abbey of Lyre, becoming a part of the assets of its dependent priory at Carisbrooke (*Cal.P.R. 1391–6*, p. 5).

12 For the circumstances of the gift, see *Cal.P.R. 1345–8*, pp. 298–9, *1399–1401*, p. 505.

13 *Cal.P.R. 1405–8*, p. 26.

14 St Denys Cart. 79, 80, 87 and 208. Also, for Claramunda's legacy, see P.R.O. E210/5324.

15 The slight income of St Denys in 1291 (T. Astle *et al.* (eds), *Taxatio ecclesiastica Angliae et Walliae, circa A.D. 1291*, p. 213) and again in 1535 (J. Caley and J. Hunter (eds), *Valor ecclesiasticus, temp. Henrici VIII*, ii:19) contrasts strangely with its siting next to one of the wealthiest boroughs of the realm (see David Knowles and R. Nevill Hadcock (eds), *Medieval Religious Houses, England and Wales*, pp. 125–60, for a list of the English Augustinian houses, giving their incomes in these years).

16 *Pipe Roll 19 Henry II*, p. 53. For comparable siting of leper hospitals beyond the margin of settlement, see M. D. Lobel (ed.), *Historic Towns*, Gloucester (p. 6), Hereford (p. 6), Nottingham (pp. 3–4). A list of the Magdalene lands is preserved with a schedule of St Denys rents dated 1349, after the appropriation of the hospital; another was compiled in 1396 (P.R.O. SC12/14/62, SC6/981/28).

17 *Cal.C.R. 1389–92*, p. 110.

18 *Oak Book*, i:26–7.

19 St Denys Cart. 87.

20 O. G. S. Crawford, 'Trinity chapel and fair', *Proc. Hampshire Field Club*, 17 (1949–52), p. 49.

21 Jean Leclercq *et al.*, *La Spiritualité du Moyen Age*, p. 312.

22 St Denys Cart. 31.

23 *Southampton Excavations*, forthcoming.

24 Both Pilgrim's Gate and Pilgrims' Pit appear regularly in the town records. See, for example, S.C.R.O. SC13/1 (Terrier of 1454) and, for the siting of Pilgrims' Pit, God's House Deeds 642.

25 John T. McNeill and Helena M. Gamer, *Medieval Handbooks of Penance*, p. 349. The Southampton Penitential is preserved at the British Museum (Royal MS. 5E. vii), and is listed, with the other surviving copies of this work, by Adrian Morey, *Bartholomew of Exeter, Bishop and Canonist*, p. 164.

26 Anselm Hoste and Rose de Lima (ed. and trans.), *For Crist Luve. Prayers of Saint Aelred, Abbot of Rievaulx*, pp. 39–40.

Part II

1200-1300

Chronological table II

1202 Anglo-French war
1203 Murder of Arthur of Brittany
1204 John loses Normandy, Maine, Anjou, Touraine and Poitou, holding Gascony
1208 England and Wales laid under interdict
1209 John is excommunicated

1214 Battle of Bouvines; Philip II defeats Otto IV and his English allies
1215 John cedes Poitou, Anjou and Brittany to France, retaining Guienne and Gascony; he consents to the Great Charter, but has it annulled by Innocent III; civil war begins
1216 Prince Louis of France lands in England; death of John; accession of Henry III
1217 Prince Louis defeated at Lincoln; French fleet defeated off Sandwich; the French withdraw from England
1220 Henry III is crowned
1224 Anglo-French war; first Franciscans reach England
1225 Fall of La Rochelle to the French

1227 Henry III declares himself of age
1230 Henry campaigns unsuccessfully in France

1202–4 John makes a two-year grant to the men of Southampton of £100 out of their farm, 'to close their town' (*Pipe Roll 4 John*, p. 78)

1211–15 The king's galleys lie at Southampton (*Pipe Roll 13 John*, p. 187, *16 John*, p. 127)

1216/17 The mayor and men of Southampton concerned in the arrest of Sir Richard Scarcaville's horses and armour (*Royal and historical letters, Henry III*, i:8–10)

1225 Agreement between the church of St Mary and the priory of St Denys concerning tithes and other payments (St Denys Cart. 283–4

1233/4 Franciscan friars settle at Southampton (God's House Deeds 760; *Cal.C.R. 1234–7*, p. 96)
1239 Agreement with the burgesses of Marlborough concerning tolls (*Sign Manuals and Letters Patent*, pp. 44–5)
Concord with Portsmouth (*Oak Book*, ii:132–7)

1242 Henry campaigns, again unsuccessfully, in France

1243 Five-year Anglo-French truce; Henry abandons his claim to Poitou

1249 Anglo-French truce renewed

1250–1 Rebellion in Gascony

1253 Anglo-French truce renewed

1255 Henry III accepts the crown of Sicily for Edmund, his son

1258 Alexander IV revokes the grant of Sicily to Prince Edmund; the barons force Henry to agree to the Provisions of Oxford

1259 Treaty of Paris, defining English rights and possessions in France; Provisions of Westminster

1263 Mise of Amiens: Louis IX supports Henry against his critics

1264 Battle of Lewes; Henry defeated

1265 Battle of Evesham; defeat and death of Simon de Montfort

1272 Death of Henry III; accession of Edward I

1274 Edward returns from the Seventh Crusade, and is crowned at Westminster; commercial treaty with Flanders

1275 Reorganization of the customs; imposition of the Ancient Custom on wool, woolfells and hides

1249 Grant to the burgesses of Southampton that they may never have a mayor (*Cal.P.R. 1247–58*, p. 51)

1251–4 Dispute and settlement concerning St Giles Fair, Winchester (Goodman, *Chartulary of Winchester Cathedral*, pp. 193–4; *Cal.P.R. 1247–58*, p. 109)

1252 Henry III orders the men of the Cinque Ports to stop interfering with the trade of Southampton and Portsmouth (*Charters*, i:6–7)

1256 Charter of Henry III granting protection in actions of debt, the return of writs and the power to elect coroners (*Charters*, i:8–9, 14–17)

1260 Reports and inquisition concerning the decay of the castle buildings at Southampton (*Cal.Inq.Misc. 1219–1307*, p. 162; *Cal.P.R. 1258–66*, p. 104) Beginning of a long series of murage grants (*Cal.P.R. 1258–66*, p. 126)

1263 Henry grants protection to Spanish merchants visiting the town (*Cal.P.R. 1258–66*, p. 258)

1264 Similar protection granted to the men of Bordeaux (*Cal.P.R. 1258–66*, p. 335)

1265 Agreement with the burgesses of Winchester concerning tolls (Bird, *Black Book of Winchester*, p. 50)

1274 Anti-Jewish riot at Southampton; Adam de Wynton is appointed keeper of the town (Rigg, *Calendar of Plea Rolls of Exchequer of Jews*, ii:130–1, 137–8, 216–17, 219–20, 249; P.R.O. E372/119)

1276–7 First Welsh war	1276 The government of the town is restored to its elected officers, at the price of a permanent increase on the farm (P.R.O. E372/120)
1279 Statute of Mortmain; gifts of property to corporations forbidden	
	1280 The friars begin building their new stone church, completing it seven years later (J. Speed, *History of Southampton*, p. 133)
1282–3 Second Welsh war	1282 Beginning of a new series of murage grants, to be applied also to repair of the castle (*Cal.P.R. 1281–92*, p. 13)
	1286–90 Dispute between the burgesses of Southampton and the bishop of Winchester concerning the patronage of God's House; also between the king and the bishop concerning St Mary Magdalene Hospital (*Rot.Parlm.*, i:18–20, 30, 39–41, 45; Deedes, *Registrum Johannis de Pontissara*, i:319–20, ii:695–8, 705–11)
1290 The Jews are expelled from England	1290 Nicholas de Barbflete grants the spring in Hill to the friary, to feed its conduit (*Cal.P.R. 1281–92*, p. 365) A royal officer is assaulted at Southampton; the town is seized by the king, and a fine is imposed (*Rot.Parlm.*, i:58; P.R.O. E372/138)
1294 Philip IV declares Gascony confiscated; Anglo-French war; rebellion in Wales	1294–5 Royal galley built at Southampton (P.R.O. E101/5/2,12)
1297 Anglo-French truce, confirmed in 1298 (Tournai) and 1299 (Montreuil); the greater part of Gascony is now French	
	1299 For services in Gascony and elsewhere, the king grants John of London a free burgess-ship at Southampton (*Cal.P.R. 1292–1301*, pp. 398–9)

Chapter five

Topography of a prospering borough

When, in 1202–3, a beginning was made on the construction of a system of rampart defences in Southampton, an artificial limit was set on the borough to the north and to the east, defining for the first time the area of intensive settlement. Throughout the twelfth century, substantial buildings might still, on occasion, have been erected north of the limit. One such, a multi-phase structure possibly of two storeys in its later years, was recently excavated immediately beyond the line of the northern ditch. Significantly, it appears to have gone out of use within a few years of the construction of the rampart and ditch it adjoined.[1] But in the next century the great stone houses of subsequent generations were to be sited within the borough enclosure, rarely outside it. They were erected in the shadow of the recently enlarged royal castle, and were shielded by the rampart and ditch on the two landward quarters, by mud-flats and the water towards the sea. There is no evidence, of course, that King John's grant to the burgesses of £100 out of their farm 'to close their town' initiated the process of fortification.[2] At the core of the present Bargate, a surviving round-headed archway of three orders, now partially cut away, may be as much as twenty years earlier in date. But it is likely, nevertheless, that it was the contemporary débâcle in Normandy, coupled with the threat to the king's entire continental empire, that hastened the work of enclosure in the town. John, we have seen, spent heavily on the castle in 1204–9. He kept a fleet of galleys in the port to meet an invader, if necessary, at sea. What a Norman and an Angevin had already done, a Capetian might yet do. The king did everything in his power to prevent it.

But the tradition of urban fortification in England was not strong, nor would it ever become so. In sharp contrast to the continental practice, which might lead, in the larger centres, to a repeated extension and elaboration of the fortified enclosure, an English borough, even a major one, might remain throughout the Middle Ages with none but the most primitive defences. Reading, Derby, Salisbury and Bedford were never enclosed, and Banbury may serve as an example of the many smaller market towns at which the gates served rather as toll-points than as defensive barriers.[3] At Southampton, despite the more obvious dangers of its seaboard situation, there was never more than one major ring of fortifications; it changed little, if at all, in outline from the thirteenth century to the sixteenth. Civil disorder, held in check by a strong monarchy, was rarely a continuous threat in England after the Conquest. If an attack were made on Southampton, it would come not from the land but from the sea. And it was precisely the king's loss of the command of the sea, a product of his failure in Normandy, that compelled the burgesses, against all their instincts of economy, to look seriously to the problems of defence.

For all that, it is not hard to see the reasons for their reluctance to make a sound beginning. There is only one recorded instance in the twelfth century of a threat of assault on the borough, and that had been averted. In 1142, in the thick of the Matildine wars, Robert of Gloucester had briefly considered sacking the town. He had been diverted by his allies, the Seals, who had family interests in the port, and landed at Poole instead.[4] By 1200, as the king's fortunes deteriorated in western France, the danger of piracy mounted, but the resources to meet it were not easily found. The king's grant, chargeable on the town farm, was less generous than it might seem. Much of the cost of any major programme of public works in the town would fall directly on the burgesses themselves, and they were still comparatively few in number. In 1228, despite the increasingly satisfactory trading record of their port, the men of Southampton were to plead their poverty before the king.[5] Needless to say, municipal poverty and private wealth are frequent companions at any time, but at Southampton in these years the burgesses may indeed have had cause for their complaint, for the work that was currently proceeding on the fortifications must have strained their resources to the limit. Mentions of a town ditch become relatively frequent in the charters after about 1220.[6] And although it is true that successive murage grants begin again in 1260, the major work of clearance and excavation must have been completed by the earlier date. Certainly, by the mid-century a bank and ditch, the former crowned with a timber palisade or even a light wall, enclosed the town on its northern and eastern flanks. Supplied with strong stone gateways, of which the Bargate, since drastically transformed, is the only surviving example, the fortifications resembled the early defences of York, finding parallels also at contemporary Shrewsbury, Nottingham, London and elsewhere.[7] But they were not to be completed within the century, and it would be many years before the circuit of the defences was joined.

Towards the sea, the problem of devising an effective defence, acceptable to all parties within the town, remained intractable. The castle guarded the north-west quarter, and may have been considered adequate to shelter much of the exposed western shore. But on the south and south-west, the water-frontages most open to commercial exploitation, any proposal that could have been thought to threaten continued easy access to the sea would have met the objections of some of the most powerful burgesses and property-owners of the time. Dame Claramunda was one of these, Walter le Fleming another. For Claramunda held a major property at Ronceval (*Roncevaux*), which she leased from the priory of that name. It was sited on the western shore, at the foot of the cliff and to the north of the street now 'Westgate Street'.[8] Adjoining it was Martin's Hall, late of John Martin and purchased from him by Walter le Fleming.[9] No doubt gates were early supplied to the streets leading down to the sea, and other defensive precautions may well have been taken to bar access to the centre of the town.[10] Eventually, too, the disaster of the French raid of 1338 would lead to the completion of the defences in this quarter. But in the mid-thirteenth century, as just before the raid itself, every combination of self-interest in the town operated towards maintaining ease of access to the sea. When that access was closed, the houses for which it had been preserved were allowed to fall into disrepair, and their wealthy occupants moved elsewhere. But it took a disaster to stir the burgesses into taking action of this kind, and it was disaster, or the threat of disaster, that accounted for every such move they made.

Indeed, the resumption of expenditure on fortification in the 1260s was determined by just such conditions. In January 1260 Earl Simon returned to England, to defy almost immediately the authority of the king. In November that same year the murage grants began.[11] Already, a full decade before, the Hampshire region had acquired a reputation for lawlessness.[12] But it required, nevertheless, the peculiarly disturbing conditions of the baronial revolt to stir the burgesses into fresh activity in their own defence. Open war began on the Welsh border early in 1264, and the king, while waiting for his army to muster at Oxford, took the opportunity, on 28 March, to order the gift of ten oaks to his burgesses of Southampton 'to make barriers in the said town'.[13] Henry's defeat at Lewes on 14 May, while it solved few problems in the long term, must have restored temporarily a degree of stability to the countryside. But peace could scarcely be maintained for long, and the commission of Simon de Montfort the younger, issued to him on 2 March 1265, required him specifically to 'keep the peace in the parts of Southampton and Portsmouth and repress those persons who coming by sea and land to those parts incessantly commit plundering and other grievous trespasses there'. He was to do this as constable of Portchester.[14] Shortly afterwards, on 10 May 1265, the south-coast ports were warned to be on their guard against possible invasion.[15] Southampton, avoiding the fate of Portsmouth which was sacked and burnt by the barons of the Cinque Ports, seems to have come through the events of these years unscathed.[16] Its burgesses, where they suffered at all, did so as individuals, not as a group. Nevertheless, it would have been surprising if some at least of their number had not been implicated in the rebellion. One such was John Fortin, a former bailiff and member of a family prominent in borough affairs in the first half of that century. It was reported in September 1265 that he had been an associate for a time of Simon de Montfort the younger, taking his livery. His land, though he refused to yield it up, was declared forfeit to the crown.[17]

For thirty years the murage grants continued, but there is little to show how they were applied. Misappropriation of such moneys by leading burgesses responsible for their collection was to occur early in the next century.[18] It may have happened in the thirteenth century as well. Yet there is little need to postulate dishonesty where it is clear that the heavy charge of maintenance alone, on the earthwork and timber defences of the time, must have absorbed much, if not all, of the money that was raised. When it came to the point of trial, the town's system of fortification was to prove entirely inadequate. It was based on a strategy that exalted the private above the public interest. It failed just where that private interest was strongest: on the valuable water-frontage to the south and south-west of the town.

However, looked at another way, it was precisely the value of this property, at its highest in the thirteenth century, that explains the reluctance of the wealthier burgesses to embark on fresh programmes of costly public works in their town. An unprecedented building boom had already begun at Southampton some years before the end of the twelfth century. It gathered momentum early in the thirteenth century and seems still to have been alive as the century drew to its close. Where so much personal wealth was committed to the rebuilding of the town in stone, little could have been left for defensive precautions of debatable merit and great immediate cost. The treaty of Paris of 1259, for all its manifest imperfections as a settlement of permanent value, brought peace between England and France for the term of thirty-five years. These were conditions to favour a vast expansion of the Bordeaux trade to which Southampton was heavily committed. They were scarcely conducive to the evolution of a logical policy of defence.

In the twelfth-century town, as in its Saxon and Saxo-Norman predecessors, domestic building, whatever its scale, was exclusively of timber, commonly in-filled with wattle and daub. Recent excavations, conducted at the south end of the town where, in the later Middle Ages, the stone houses were to be at their finest, have confirmed the presence of an underlying spread of earlier timber structures, datable, from their associated artefacts, to the eleventh and twelfth centuries. Beam-slots (in which the timber ground-sills were laid), post-holes and rubbish pits are all that have survived of these early buildings. But it has become evident, nevertheless, that timber construction after this fashion persisted in Southampton throughout the twelfth century; further, that its replacement by stone can have begun no earlier than the last years of the century, more generally the beginning of the next.[19] Fragments of burnt daub, identifiable in most twelfth-century contexts and occasionally found crammed closely into pits dug designedly for the purpose, suggest everywhere the frequency of fires. And it is of particular interest, in view of Southampton's own late-twelfth-century conversion to building in stone, that the earliest known English building legislation, Fitz-Alwyne's London assize of 1189, concerned itself with precisely this problem, ordering, exactly as was actually happening in contemporary Southampton, the substitution of stone for wood, and tiles for thatch, as a timely precaution against fire.[20]

As to the fact of this substitution, the archaeological evidence is unequivocal. Further, it is strongly supported by the wording of the earliest charters of the late-twelfth-century foundation at God's House, in particular the confirmation charters, datable within the first three decades of the thirteenth century, of the founder's brother. Master Roger, The founder, Gervase, had built his own mansion at West Hall, probably in stone, some years before the end of the twelfth century. And Master

Roger's charters depict a scene of considerable building activity, in which many of the leading burgesses of his time were taking a lively part. Roger himself built two stone houses, equipped with cellars, and bought another two. Of those who witnessed the charters, Richard of Leicester, Walter le Fleming and John de la Bulehuse each built houses, and James le Fleming, brother of Walter, held, and may well have lived in, the stone houses formerly of Roger de Tankerville.[21]

Building activity, certainly present at this date in the parishes of St Lawrence, Holy Rood and St Michael, rapidly extended over the entire area of the enclosed town. It is recorded in charters that span the length of the century. By 1221 Richard of Leicester had built, and no longer held, his 'great stone houses' on French Street. These were to be cited as landmarks in the placing of another lesser tenement on the opposite side of the street, on which a quit-rent was owing to St Denys.[22] They are mentioned again, still 'late of Richard of Leicester', in the endowment of Robert Bonhait's chantry, founded in 1273 in the name of his late wife Alice, daughter of Walter le Fleming. Robert and Alice had lived opposite the great stone houses in French Street, presumably on much the same site as the tenement described in the charter of 1221. It was Robert's intention that his former house, with the quit-rent from a vault at the south-east end of English Street, and a cash payment of £14, should endow in perpetuity a chaplaincy at the church of St Michael, charged with a daily mass at the altar of St Theobald in that church.[23]

Late in the century, the work of building continued, the chosen material still being stone. Thomas of Andover, a wealthy merchant active in the wine and wool trades in the sixties and seventies of the century, built himself a stone house (*petrinum*) and stone cellar (*celarium lapideum*) on the west side of English Street, in the parish of Holy Rood. He was also the owner of the property next door, and was concerned to pay off in a single lump sum the quit-rent owed on his new house to St Denys.[24] A few years later, on the same side of the street and not many doors away, John de Byndon built a house adjoining property of the priory. In so doing, and probably unwittingly, he had encroached on priory land, demolishing a stone wall which belonged by rights to St Denys. Both sides sought a settlement of the resulting 'grave dispute', submitting in 1292 to the judgment of a panel of 'trustworthy burgesses', among them the then alderman and bailiffs. John, adjudged in the wrong, conceded his claims to the disputed property. In return, the prior and convent, while requiring of him a formal instrument to this effect, graciously remitted his offence, 'together with the rancour which they had conceived towards him for his building of the house'.[25]

Yet stone, for all its regular use in the re-shaping of the thirteenth-century town, could never have been an inexpensive building material in Southampton. No suitable native stone was readily available, and the limestone commonly used in building had to be shipped from the Isle of Wight, from Dorset, or from Normandy, the source of the fine Caen stone so much in demand for the more intricate work on mouldings. Purbeck marble, enjoying a vogue at the turn of the twelfth and thirteenth centuries, was employed occasionally at Southampton. Granite, brought in from time to time from the Channel Islands, was shipped, perhaps, as ballast. Whatever its source, suitable stone was both difficult to come by and expensive. And it is the frequency of its use, despite this, together with the comparatively narrow restriction of the main building period to little more than a century, that lends particular significance to this apparently massive reconstruction of the thirteenth-century town. It is not, of course, that building could be said to have come to a halt in 1300. Obviously it continued, but it made increasing use of timber. Nor is it the case that Southampton stood alone in the adoption of so costly a building practice. London, we have seen, was legislating for a fire-proof, stone-built city from the beginning of the thirteenth century. Simultaneously, at Canterbury, Terric the goldsmith and his fellows were building their own stone houses, as were the burgesses, some of them perhaps Jewish financiers, at Lincoln, Norwich and Bury St Edmunds.[26] While, at the far end of the great trade route to the south, the citizens of Bordeaux, already perhaps as influential as any of the regular visitors to Southampton, had begun to use stone in their buildings.[27] But at Southampton, as at few other places, the scope and extent of the thirteenth-century rebuilding of the town remains recorded in its numerous surviving stone structures, together signifying a degree of material prosperity in the borough so much the more striking for being so magnificently preserved.

Recently, a survey of the surviving medieval stonework in Southampton, conducted and recorded in 1944 while much still remained exposed after the bombing, has demonstrated the spread of major stone buildings through the length of the medieval walled town.[28] It would be impossible, on the evidence presented, to date the majority of those buildings. But many, either at that time or since, have been individually recorded in detailed plans and sections. Others, datable by archaeological associations, have since been exposed by excavation. In addition, there survive, more or less intact, those remarkable copy-book examples of 'Norman' domestic architecture known, quaintly, as 'King John's House' and 'Canute's Palace' (Plate 5), the one next to Blue Anchor Postern, on the western shore, the other on Porters Lane, at the southernmost limit of the medieval town. Neither has been, or perhaps can be, closely dated, whether on architectural or documentary grounds. But both seem likely to date from the final decades of the twelfth century, and both conform to a recognizable 'house over warehouse' type.[29] In each, the domestic quarters of the owner were sited on the upper, not the lower floor. Each was equipped with a hall, and each would have had at least one other, more private chamber. A small side-wall fireplace, probably serving to heat the chamber, has survived in the north wall of 'King John's House'. Fenestration was by pairs of round-headed lights, set in round-arched frames. On the ground floor at 'King John's House', arches gave directly on to the neighbouring quay, or strand, and both houses originally faced the shore. The lower storeys served as warehousing, possibly also as shops, in the fashion of the vaulted undercrofts more characteristic of the thirteenth- and fourteenth-century buildings in the upper town. They were roofed plainly with a simple structure of pillars and beams, supporting the floor of the upper chambers. It was a technique which permitted greater width in the building, and which must also have contributed considerably to the flexibility on both floors of the interior design.[30]

Adjoining 'King John's House', on the south, was the property known as Ronceval, held for a time by Claramunda. To the south again, at a remove of a tenement or two, was another great property, now underlying the line of Cuckoo Lane, and then sited, like its neighbours, on the flat clay strand at the base of the gravel cliff which bounded the town on its west. A recent reconstruction of the town wall at this point has revealed fragments of the house preserved within it. Excavations have further determined its plan (see Fig. 5), and have helped to establish details of ownership and date. In keeping with the width of the shore, the Cuckoo Lane house was long where 'King John's House' was square, but in many other respects it was strikingly similar in design. Like its near-neighbour to the north, it had been conceived on a considerable scale. At an estimated length of over thirty metres, it was a building of royal or baronial dimensions, nearly twice as long and more than twice as wide as the contemporary country manor-house at Boothby Pagnell, Lincolnshire. The recent excavations, revealing a line of three carefully-shaped limestone pillar bases sunk deep into the clay of the floor, have established that the roof of the ground-floor warehouse was set on a pillar-and-beam structure such as that employed in the contemporary buildings at 'King John's House' and 'Canute's Palace'.[31] The warehouse, which was probably approached through arches from the shore, was lit by small square-headed windows, one of which has been preserved in the fragment of north wall incorporated in the fourteenth-century town defences. Immediately over it were found the remains of a two-light window, still fitted with the base of a Purbeck marble central shaft. It would have served an upper chamber, or hall, and was sited nearly opposite the external door on the south wall, the east jamb of which had likewise been preserved in a fragment of the house built into the later town wall. An external stair from a courtyard to the south gave access through this door to the private apartments of the owner. They would have consisted of the conventional hall and chambers, but might also have included domestic offices at the rear, for a large rubbish pit had been constructed in stone against the south-east corner of the building, close up beneath the cliff and external to the building it served. In the courtyard to the south, a lime-kiln, dug in the clay of the shore, had clearly been designed to provide slaked lime for mortar during the building. On the completion of the work, which may have extended over a period of years, the sweepings of the yard were used to help fill the northern end of the sunken kiln. They included shattered fragments of the original brown-glazed roofing-tiles, the earliest to survive in a datable context in the town. With them was a short section of a Purbeck marble shaft, of the same material and workmanship as the column base surviving at the centre of the upper-storey window preserved in the fragmentary north wall of the mansion.[32]

These remarkable buildings – 'King John's House', 'Canute's Palace' and the unnamed tenement on Cuckoo Lane – cluster in date around the final years of the twelfth century. They were the direct contemporaries of Gervase le Riche's great mansion at West Hall, and were the immediate forerunners of a number of capital messuages conceived on a similar scale, the centres, or head-houses, of important family groups in the town. One such building was 'Martin's Hall', of which we know only that John Martin sold it before 1258 to Walter le Fleming, who left it in that year to Henry, his eldest son, describing it as his 'manor'.[33] Another was the 'great house called la Bulehuse', sited within a few paces of West Hall, on the junction of Bull (now Bugle) Street and Westgate Street, not far, presumably, from the family house of the 'Seals'.[34] Bull Hall, as it came to be known to later generations, was probably built originally for Thomas de la Bulehuse, bailiff with William of St Laurence in 1205 and listed with other leading burgesses of the town in the Pipe Roll of 1211–12.[35] His son, or grandson, Roger de la Bulehuse, quitclaimed the mansion in 1270 to James Isembard, who seems to have sold it shortly afterwards to Thomas le Halveknight.[36] But it had remained a family centre for the Bulehuse clan for two generations at least, and ever after bore its name.[37]

Indeed, continuity in ownership, while the family itself persisted, might rather have been the rule than the exception. The Barbflete family house, a considerable mansion sited on the east of English Street immediately north of the friary, was sold in 1329 to Nicholas de Moundenard. The seller, Nicholas de Barbflete, son of the Robert whose residence it had been, was not the last of his line. Yet the mansion may already have been in the family hands for somewhat over a century, for there were Barbfletes, Robert and Matilda, prominent in Southampton at the turn of the twelfth and thirteenth centuries, and it is known that Matilda held a tenement on English Street.[38] At least as long is the story of the continued use by the Fleming family of Walter le Fleming's great capital messuage on the south junction of Broad Lane and English Street. It was probably at this tenement that Petronilla la Fleming, wife of John le Fleming the elder, housed alien merchants in the 1260s, among them visitors from Flanders and from Spain. Another John le Fleming, great-grandson of Walter, made the mansion his residence after an interval during which William le Horder had held it, probably on lease. John lived there until his death in 1336, leaving it to his eldest son, Walter, who sold it almost immediately to a leading burgess of the time, Henry de Lym.[39] It was such great stone structures as these, material demonstration of the wealth and authority of a new class of merchant capitalists, that dominated the thirteenth-century port. Further, they were set off to advantage by the parallel series of fine streets, connected by a mesh of linking alleys, which had first taken shape within a century of the Conquest, and which had been added to, and improved upon, ever since.

By the middle years of the thirteenth century, the town, taken as a whole, had achieved both the plan and the setting it would retain, scarcely changed, for a full four centuries or more. The broad thoroughfare known as English Street, although it was to remain interrupted for another half-century by the intrusive bulk of the original church of Holy Rood, was the main artery of the town (Figs. 3 and 4). Many of the principal merchants of the era either lived on it or sought to hold property

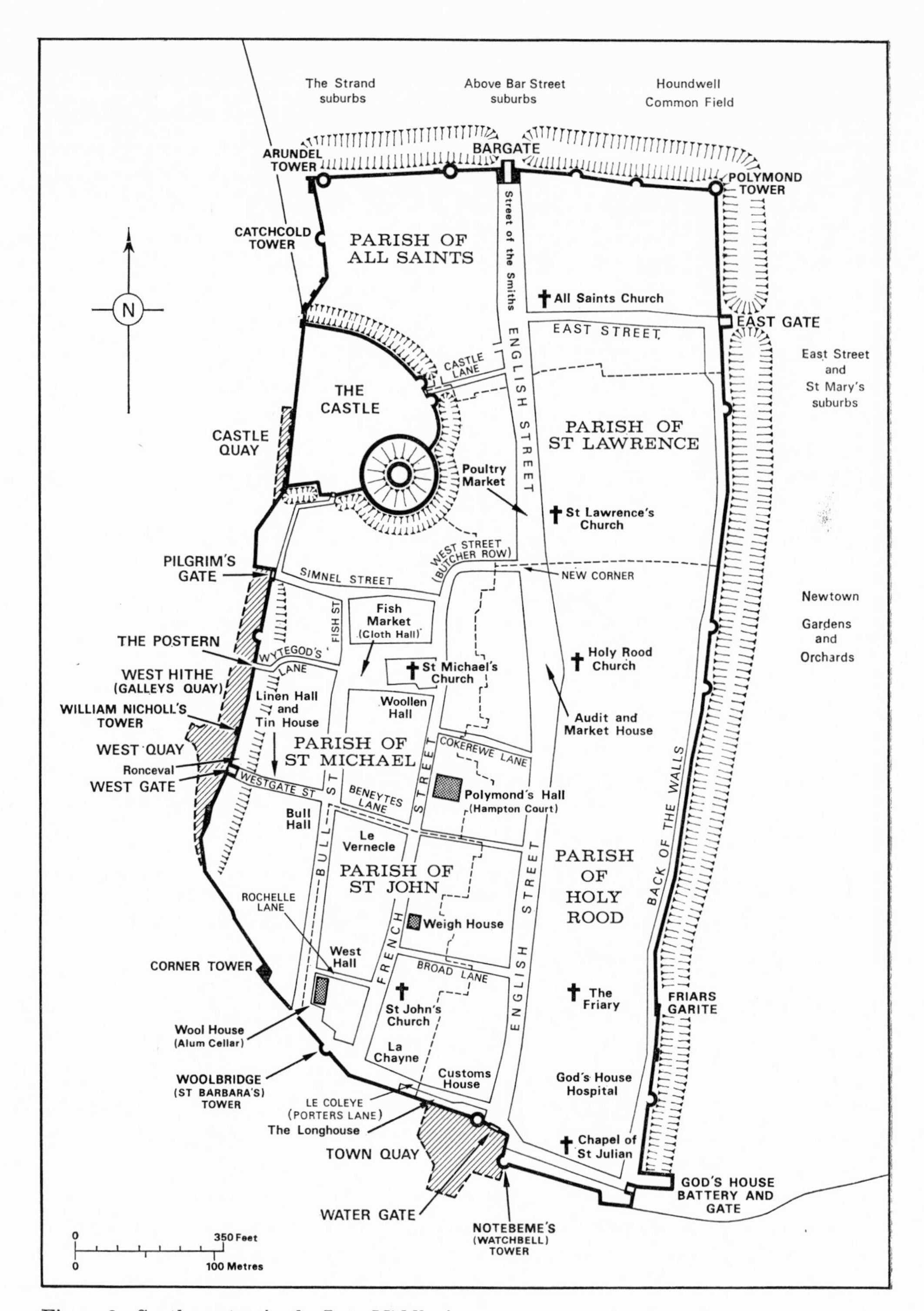

Figure 3 Southampton in the Late Middle Ages

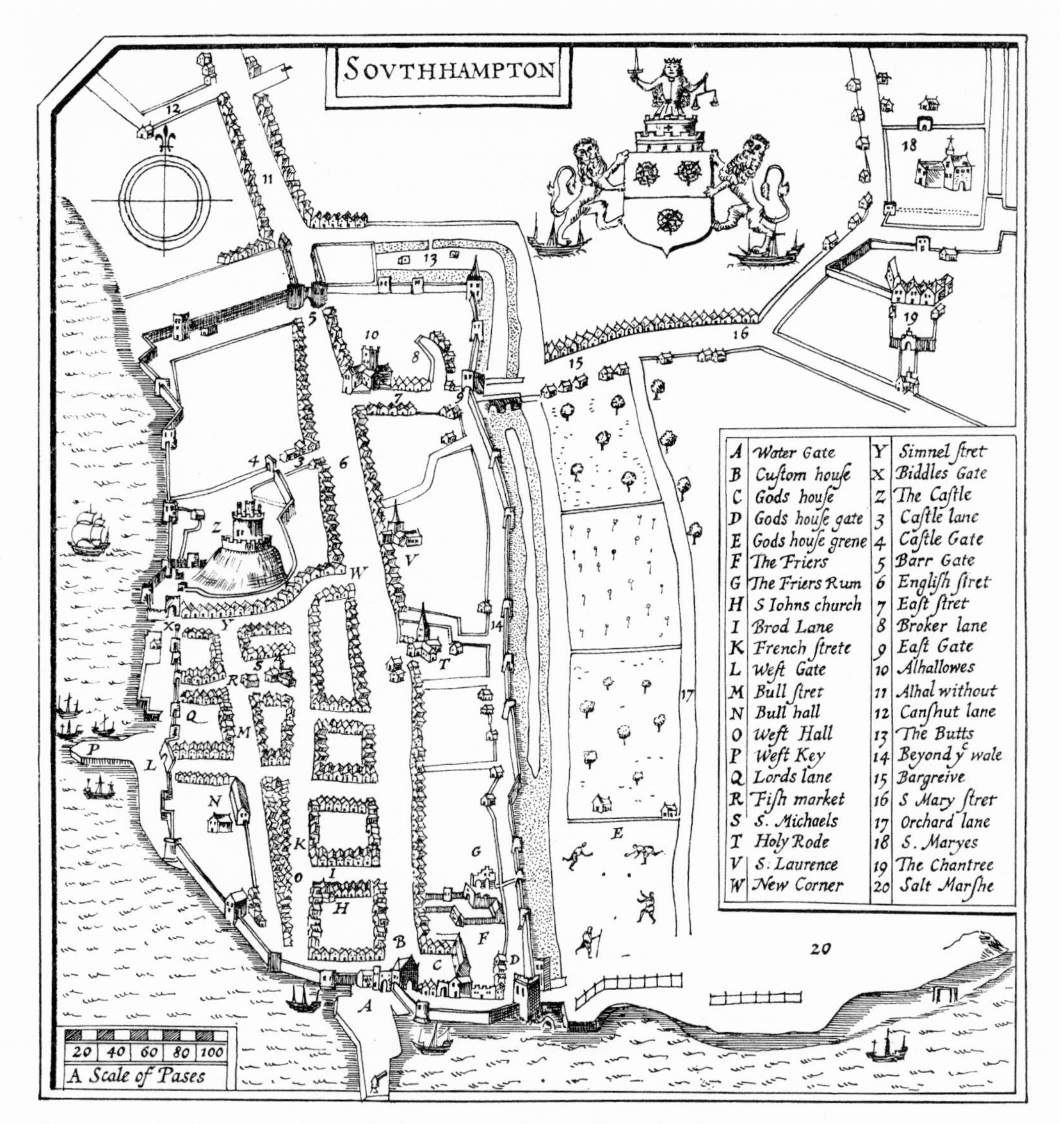

Figure 4 Southampton in 1611, from a map by by John Speed

there. Shops, or open stalls, spread along most of its length: the smiths congregating at the north end, in the parish of All Saints, the butchers more dispersed, in St Lawrence, by the junction with West Street, or in Holy Rood, south of the friary gate.[40] More shops lined East Street, the only major thoroughfare to cut the segment of the town between English Street, on the west, and the town defences, on the east. Then, as now, it was a shopping street of great importance, the means of access, through the East Gate (Plate 6), to the populous suburb of St Mary's. Prominent landholders in the medieval town did their best to acquire an interest there: Petronilla la Fleming in the thirteenth century, Nicholas le Barber in the fourteenth, with the prior of St Denys heading the list with a grand total of fourteen shops, recorded in his fifteenth-century rentals.[41] There were shops, too, in French Street and in Simnel Street, and the fishmarket, with a market house of its own, was held in the square outside the west door of the parish church of St Michael.[42] Too much, assuredly, should not be made of the distinction between the retailing and the residential quarters of the town. A merchant's dwelling was usually his manufactory also, and his shop. But, in general, the markets and major shopping centres of the town concentrated on the line of its principal thoroughfares, penetrating very little behind them. Typically, a shop and its chamber would be sited in front of a major tenement. It might continue throughout its history to be leased as a separate unit, and need have had no access to the property at the rear.[43] Behind it, the tenement, equipped with independent access to the street, stretched back, sometimes to a considerable length. Frequently, its presence there explains the situation of one of those many diminutive service lanes which fed off the principal thoroughfares of the town. But these, of course, were to multiply still further in later generations, as a progressive subdivision of many of the original tenement plots increased the demand for access.

In the thirteenth century, the relations of tenement plots to service lanes and of both to the main dispositions of the town, were still comparatively straightforward. The great tenements on English Street, in the absence of any continuous system of secondary roads to the rear, generally ran back to meet the nearest considerable obstacle. In the centre of the town, in the parish of St Lawrence, this might have been the castle ditch to the west of the street, or the ramparts to its east.[44] In Holy Rood, to the south, the considerable area absorbed by the sites of the Franciscan friary and the hospital of St Julian, or God's House, limited the size of the plots in that quarter, and prevented them from being drawn out eastwards to the ramparts. On the west of English Street, in Holy Rood, St Michael's and St John's, similar limitations on the length of individual plots were imposed first by French Street, then by Bull Street beyond it to the west, partitioning the space available for building. Individual houses might still be found to stretch from a frontage on English Street through to the line of French Street.[45] And it was not unusual for a tenement on the west side of French Street to have another door on Bull Street, to the rear.[46] A more common practice seems to have been to site houses on both sides of each of these streets, wasting as little street frontage as possible. To the west of Bull Street again, a natural limit was set by the line of the gravel cliff. Here the gardens of the Bull Street tenements overlooked the great stone houses set on the sea shore at West Hithe – 'King John's House', perhaps, or Ronceval, or the mansion on Cuckoo Lane to the south.[47]

There was to be no standard size, it is evident, for the tenement plots of the borough. In 1339, a vacant plot on the west side of English Street, between two standing tenements, measured 112 feet by 11 feet, the latter undoubtedly the frontage.[48] A few years before, another vacant plot, this time on French Street, had a frontage of 16 feet, but was no more than 26 feet in depth.[49] A Corporation terrier of 1617 lists the borough's properties and gives the dimensions of their plots. Some must have been affected by subdivision or amalgamation in the later Middle Ages, others distorted by family arrangements, disputes and compromises of one kind and another. But there were many plots listed, nevertheless, which very probably retained the dimensions held since the thirteenth century. A great tenement, for example, at the north-east end of English Street, parish of All Saints, is given a frontage of 29 feet 9 inches. With its brewhouse and its garden together, the length of its plot is calculated at 220 feet. Further to the south, one of the great tenements of the medieval town had extended from English Street, on the west, to the ramparts, or wall, on the east. The tenement, with its garden, stable and coal-house, contained 'in Length from the said Street to a Lane leading by the Towne Wall 300 ffoot and in Breadth at the East End next the said Lane 13 ffoot and at the West End next the said English Street 19 ffoot'. Smaller tenements, more typical, perhaps, of the general run of properties in the town, usually averaged somewhat less than 100 feet in length, with a street frontage rarely exceeding 20 feet. One of these, on the west side of English Street, in Holy Rood, measured 70 feet back from the street and 20 feet along it. Another, in St Michael's to the west of Bull Street, extended, with its garden plot, 'in Length from the Bull Street to westward 92 ffoot & in Breadth at the West End 22 ffoot and at the East End next to Street Side 20 ffoot and an half'. The great house 'called Romsevall' was by now sadly decayed. In 1617 its length, once constituting sea frontage but now, because of the blocking town wall, taken back from a front on Westgate Street to the south, is recorded as 84 feet. The site, from the wall eastwards (or, as here, from the Linen Hall westwards), was 44 feet deep, 'in which is contained a Cellar with a Loft over it, one skeeling [shed] or Tenemt all along under the Towne Wall and one Shop with two Roofs next to the Lane there'.[50]

Dividing these properties, and serving them, were the lanes and alleys that honeycombed the medieval town. Few of these have survived in any recognizable form to the present day, for they were as transient as the properties they adjoined. Many, perhaps, were never given names at all, and even among the more important there were some the names of which changed regularly from one generation to another. The confusion, surely disheartening to the contemporary lawyer, is reflected frequently in the records. A garden between English Street and French Street is said to be bounded on the south by 'Halfknyghteslane, *alias* Cokerewelane, *alias* Braggeryslane'.[51] A contemporary document, dated 1420, describes the identical alley as 'la Smalelane', perhaps in contrast to 'Broad Lane' further to the south.[52] 'Beneyteslane' was otherwise known as 'Forstislane'.[53] In the suburb of St Mary's, the street formerly called 'Bradeweye' had become known by 1439 as 'Baggerewe'.[54]

Commonly, it was a strong family interest in the neighbourhood which determined the choice of a name. The Halveknights of 'Halfknyghteslane', a name sometimes applied to Rochelle Lane as well, were wealthy landholders in the late-thirteenth-century borough. In the early 1270s Thomas le Halveknight had bought Bull Hall from James Isembard, and had acquired other neighbouring properties on Bull Street; before the end of the century, he was the owner of Gervase's great tenement at West Hall.[55] In much the same way, 'Beneyteslane', which would become 'Forstislane' and is now 'Vyse Lane', most probably recalled the Beneyts, heirs of Benedict Ace and the holders in the thirteenth century of property on French Street as well as on the western shore.[56] But from early in the following century, the Forsts were to become dominant in their place. 'Forstislane' commemorated the new interest, although the older 'Beneyteslane', first appearing late in the thirteenth century, persisted at least into the fifteenth.[57]

In such company Broad Lane, still known today by the name familiarly applied to it as early as the fourteenth century, stands out as an example of an impressive, certainly an unusual, continuity. It was, of course, as its name implies, exceptionally wide; for at 17 feet its width compared favourably indeed with that of another, London, 'Brodelane' which at its widest touched eight feet, at its narrowest barely six.[58] But it was also one of the few available throughways linking French Street, on the west, with English Street, on the east. And this may have lent it a public quality rarely attaching to those service lanes which, usually on private initiative, had been provided to give access to individual tenements in the borough. Something of this, too, may explain its origins, for it would appear, on the archaeological evidence, to have been laid down as a part of a post-Conquest re-shaping of the town, overlying late-Saxon and Saxo-Norman occupational debris and differing appreciably in alignment from the structures it replaced.[59] Naturally, much will remain hypothetical until the make-up of the other parallel lanes can be investigated. But it may be suggested, on the Broad Lane example, that the lines of at least the major east-west throughways of the town were already decided by the twelfth century or by early in the thirteenth century at latest, and that such a decision, however arrived at, constituted a part of a considered scheme to re-apportion, once and for all, the tenement plots in the south-west quarter of the borough. From this, then, stemmed the chessboard pattern of the predominantly Norman quarter of the town. To use the names current in the nineteenth century, Broad Lane, Brewhouse Lane and Market Lane joined English Street to French Street on the west. Rochelle Lane, Vyse Lane and St Michael's Square (via Church Lane) effected the link with Bull Street. Westgate Street extended the line of Brewhouse Lane and Vyse Lane to meet the western shore. And Simnel Street, continued by West Street, closed off the northern end of the quarter under the shadow of the castle wall, providing access, more or less direct, from the shore at West Hithe to the markets along the length of English Street. There is no planning as systematic as this anywhere else in the town. Nor was there, perhaps, ever so deliberate a settlement.

Indeed, the closest adducible parallel to such planning may be found not in the town itself, but rather in its suburbs and immediately adjoining fields. From an early date, in the twelfth century or before, the most familiar unit in the suburban settlements was the acre, or more usually half-acre, plot. Such plots were the standard measures of thirteenth-century transactions, and it is obvious that they could from the beginning command a high price, attracting the investment of the dominant landholding families of the borough. Before the mid-century, Richard of Leicester sold

Plate 4 A tripod pitcher, missing rim and handle, probably from Andenne, *c.* 1200

Plate 5 'Canute's Palace', a late-twelfth-century merchant's house on Porters Lane

Plate 6 The East Gate in the eighteenth century, shortly before its demolition

land and buildings 'in the suburb of Southampton outside the north gate'; the purchasers were Stephen Jociaume and Claramunda, his wife. Richard himself had earlier acquired the property from John de la Bulehuse, to whom an annual quit-rent of eighteen pence was still due. The purchase price was sixty shillings sterling.[60] Claramunda, a few years later, bought a quit-rent of two shillings, payable on a half-acre plot in the same northern suburb. It lay between the half-acre of Mistress Alice de la Bulehuse on the one side, and the half-acre of Peter Dikeman on the other.[61] Claramunda died the owner of considerable properties in the suburb north of the Bar and in the street called 'the Strand', also beyond the ramparts to the north-west.[62] Likewise, her contemporary, the wealthy John Horn, with whom she sometimes did business, built up an important suburban interest of his own, including two acres of land in Kingsland and a tenement, with appurtenances, above the Bar, which had once been the property of Claramunda. But neither, it should be said, chose to live on a suburban holding, and it seems clear that Southampton burgesses of their generation, whatever the practice elsewhere, had not yet contracted the habit of residing outside their community, usually preferring to maintain their capital messuages in the more crowded conditions of the town. Claramunda herself lived down by the shore at West Hithe, and John Horn went to great lengths to assemble a formidable group of properties about his capital messuage in St Lawrence, on the west side of English Street. On his death in 1279, it is there that he is recorded to have dwelt.[63] In the next century, men of comparable stature in the town, Thomas of Abingdon, Nicholas de Moundenard, William le Horder, and the Flemings, John and Henry, all had considerable holdings in the suburbs, divided still into lots of half an acre, or multiples of the same. But they treated these primarily as investments, choosing to live themselves within the ramparts of the town: Thomas of Abingdon probably on French Street, Nicholas de Moundenard, William le Horder and the Flemings, on English Street.[64]

It is some measure of the value placed on a suburban interest that the collection and exploitation of suburban plots brought together some of the leading families of the town. One such association is detectable, by inference if nothing more, between the Stouts, the Englishes and the Nostschillings, each with relations in common. Early in the fourteenth century, the Stouts were a wealthy landholding family, with property centred on Bull Street and on French Street, at the extreme south end of the town.[65] Like the Englishes, they were ship-owners, and both families held plots in the suburbs, as well as in the town itself. Further, the two were related by marriage, for Rosya Stout, daughter and co-heir of Thomas, head of the family, married Bartholomew le English, by whom she had a son, William. Florence Stout, widow of Thomas and the holder for life of a substantial portion of his estate, subsequently married Thomas Nostschilling, three times bailiff of Southampton.[66] The first record of the suburban transactions which brought the families together is dated 1301. It concerned the purchase by Luke Stout, perhaps the brother of Thomas, and, like him, a prospering burgess, of a thirty-two-year lease on four acres in Westgarston field, next to the Magdalene hospital. The seller was John Bonhait, son of the Robert

Bonhait who had married Walter le Fleming's daughter, Alice, and who would have been a neighbour of the Stouts in French Street.[67] In due course, these acres reverted to the original freeholder, the priory of St Denys. But the long lease taken on them by Luke Stout illustrates a family interest in the suburbs that undoubtedly complemented tenements already possessed in the town. Following his marriage to Florence Stout, Thomas Nostschilling entered the market in 1325–6, with a purchase of one and a half acres in Hoglands, to the east. He acquired these plots from Richard le English to enlarge his holding to the north, which he had received as a gift from John le English, Richard's brother. Bounding his new possession on the south was another English holding, the property now of William le English, cousin of Richard and John, and son and co-heir of Bartholomew.[68] Thomas Nostschilling, it can be assumed, further consolidated his suburban holdings, and already Florence Stout, on her re-marriage, had probably brought him at least a life interest in some of the Stout suburban inheritance. Certainly, when their son, John, died in 1361, his estate included a considerable suburban holding. By 1374 these lands had come, by neglect of the terms of the mortmain legislation, into the hands of the crown. They totalled six acres, divided between Hoglands and the Magdalene fields.[69]

A family might choose to concentrate its holdings in one area. It could well attempt to relate them to some tenement already held on one of the three built-up suburban streets: perhaps on the street called 'Bovebarrestreete', north of the Bargate, as Claramunda and John Horn seem to have done, or on St Mary Street beyond East Gate, or again on that more elusive 'king's highway called the Strand', in the parish of All Saints Without, over by the western shore.[70] But it need have done neither, and undoubtedly there continued to be available, throughout the later Middle Ages, a wide choice of cultivable plots in the common fields of the town, free grazing for the cattle of the commonalty once the crop had been harvested, very much private property before. In 1549, an 'ancient old' man, called upon to give evidence in the long-lasting salt-marsh dispute, remembered 'Mr bakers closse, Mr ryges closse, and Mr James closse, and the chauntery closse, hondewell, Kingslonde, hoggeland, madelin twoo fyldes, Lobery mede, the closses in Saynt Maris Lane and where the pryour of St Denis made his garden' as common land of the town on which cattle might be run after cropping.[71] And there is little reason to question that the lands the old man listed were in fact the ancient cultivable fields of the town, property of the burgesses from time out of mind. He was not the only witness so to describe them.

Almost as important to the burgesses were the commons to which they could lay a claim beyond the limits of these fields. Southampton Common, preserved to this day, lies to the north of the town. It became indisputably the property of the borough in 1228. Pasturage on the salt-marsh to the east, between Newtown suburb and the Itchen, was claimed at least as early. But it encountered a parallel claim of the master of God's House, who, in the first years of the sixteenth century, asserted a prescriptive right to the salt-marsh to justify its enclosure. On 28 December 1500, the burgesses, led by their mayor, broke down the hedges and filled the ditches of the hospital on the marsh.[72] And it was this same strong instinct towards the preservation of an ancient right that prompted the borough officers to preserve carefully in an iron-bound coffer under one of the windows of their Audit House, in amongst the most precious of their charters and instruments, a 'fyniall concord and agreement made betwene the burgeases of Suthampton of thonpartie and nicolas of sirlie of thotherpartie for the comon of the same towne in the xii[th] yeare of the reigne of king henry the sonne of k. John'.[73] The charter, supported by two fifteenth-century inspections, related that on 13 May 1228 Nicholas, lord of the manor of Shirley, had met the burgesses of Southampton at the castle in their borough before the justices of the king. Nicholas disputed the grazing rights claimed by the burgesses, and their representatives, one of them Richard of Leicester, had moved a plea against him in the courts. By the terms of the settlement reached on that occasion, Nicholas gave up all claim to control of the common pasture of the borough, this to remain to the 'burgesses and their heirs for ever'. In return, he received the small payment of ten marks in silver, with the promise that the action pending against him would be dropped, and that his men, living within the liberty of the borough, would be entitled, as were the burgesses themselves, to rights of common.[74] In 1253 the limits of the Common, as Nicholas and the burgesses had agreed them, were included within that liberty, forming a part of the borough boundaries on the north and west sides. These, as found at an inquisition held on 28 October 1253, extended from 'Achard's bridge [at the south end of Hill Lane] as the road runs by the Crosses to the north as far as Cutthorn [by Bassett cross roads], and from Cutthorn as far as Burleston [on Burgess Road] as far as the aqueduct at Fursewell [in South Stoneham] where it flows into the Itchen'.[75]

Notes

1 *Southampton Excavations*, forthcoming.
2 *Pipe Roll 4 John*, p. 78.
3 H. M. Colvin, 'Domestic architecture and town-planning', in *Medieval England*, ed. A. L. Poole, i:65–7; also M. D. Lobel (ed.), *Historic Towns*, Banbury (p. 4). For an instructive summary of the continental evidence, see F. L. Ganshof, *Étude sur le développement des villes entre Loire et Rhin au Moyen Age*, pp. 35–63.
4 K. R. Potter (ed.), *The Historia Novella by William of Malmesbury*, p. 75.
5 *Cal.C.R. 1227–31*, p. 32.
6 The first mention of the ditch occurs in Master Roger's second, and more extensive, confirmatory charter of the lands of God's House (God's House Deeds 313). For another early reference, in a charter of 1248, see *Cat.Anc. Deeds*, ii:B3383.
7 Angelo Raine, *Medieval York*, p. 1; also for notes on recent relevant excavations at Shrewsbury, Nottingham and London, see *Medieval Archaeology*, 3 (1959), pp. 312–14; 9 (1965), pp. 164–7; and 11 (1967), p. 294. For a discussion at length of J. S. Wacher's excavations on the Southampton wall, see *Southampton Excavations*, forthcoming. Mr Wacher is critical of some of the conclusions of B. H. St J. O'Neil, 'Southampton town wall', in *Aspects of Archaeology in Britain and Beyond*, ed. W. F. Grimes, pp. 242–57.
8 *Cal.C.R. 1279–88*, p. 87.
9 Bodleian, Queen's College MS. 1071.
10 Gating of the streets is discussed by Anthony M. Carr, 'A documentary survey of property in medieval Southampton', typescript deposited at Southampton University Library, pp. 10–12.
11 Murage grants begin in earnest on 11 November 1260; for this and other grants

within the century, in 1270, 1282 and 1286, each for a period of years, see *Cal.P.R. 1258–66*, p. 126; *1266–72*, p. 492; *1281–92*, pp. 13, 229.

12 H.R. Luard (ed.), *Matthaei Parisiensis, monachi sancti Albani, chronica majora*, v:59–60.

13 *Cal.C.R. 1261–4*, p. 338.

14 *Cal.P.R. 1258–66*, p. 481.

15 *Cal.C.R. 1264–8*, pp. 121–2.

16 P.R.O. E372/110.

17 *Cal.Inq.Misc. 1219–1307*, p. 216. For John Fortin as bailiff, see Davies, p. 170, and God's House Deeds 761.

18 *Cal.P.R. 1340–3*, p. 326. The enquiry, ordered in 1341, was to concern itself equally with malpractices in the previous reign.

19 *Southampton Excavations*, forthcoming.

20 H. T. Riley (ed.), *Munimenta Gildhallae Londoniensis*, i:328–9.

21 God's House Deeds 313.

22 St Denys Cart. 251–3.

23 God's House Deeds 356, 369, 517.

24 St Denys Cart. 229. Thomas of Andover, with his partner William Thomas, was a principal in an abortive purchase of 60 tuns of wine in 1267 (*Cal.P.R. 1266–72*, p. 282). In 1273 he was granted a licence to export twenty sacks of wool (Ibid., 1272–81, p. 22).

25 St Denys Cart. 233; P.R.O. E327/695.

26 William Urry, *Canterbury under the Angevin Kings*, pp. 174–5, 192–4; also Margaret Wood, *The English Medieval House*, pp. 1–7, 14; and V. D. Lipman, *The Jews of Medieval Norwich*, pp. 22–32.

27 Charles Higounet, *Bordeaux pendant le haut moyen âge*, p. 272.

28 A MS. plan, the product of the survey, is preserved at the Department of the Environment (Inspectorate of Ancient Monuments). A collection of plans and sections of individual buildings is also held by the Department. Copies of these may be inspected at the office of the Southampton City Architect, where they are usefully supplemented by the Architect's own plans of buildings affected by post-war development of the sites.

29 Mr P. A. Faulkner discusses the Southampton architectural survivals in *Southampton Excavations*, forthcoming.

30 Norman town houses as a class are discussed by Margaret Wood, *The English Medieval House*, pp. 1–15.

31 Another example of a use of the same technique has been noticed in the basement cellar of the present Duke of Wellington public house. It is discussed by P. A. Faulkner in *Southampton Excavations*, forthcoming.

32 A full account of the building is given in *Southampton Excavations*, forthcoming.

33 Bodleian, Queen's College MS. 1071.

34 *Cat.Anc. Deeds*, ii:B3447. Mr L. A. Burgess has argued, somewhat unconvincingly, that La Bulehuse, whether this or another, was sited in Holy Rood ('A topographical index of Southampton', typescript deposited at Southampton City Reference Library).

35 Davies, p. 170, and *Pipe Roll 13 John*, p. 186.

36 God's House Deeds 600, 601.

37 The mansion was still known as Bull Hall up to the date of its eighteenth-century demolition.

38 S.C.R.O. SC4/2/44. For Robert de Barbflete, see *Pipe Roll 7 Richard I*, p. 226; for Matilda, see God's House Deeds 749.

39 For the use of the tenement as lodgings for alien merchants, see *Cal.P.R. 1258–66*, p. 258, and *1266–72*, pp. 242, 325. John le Fleming's will is preserved in the Bodleian (Queen's College MS. 1076); Henry de Lym is recorded in possession in a God's House rental of 1340 (Queen's College MS. 339).

40 A 'street of the smiths', seemingly the north end of English Street, is mentioned in the will of Matilda Wrangy, dated 1328 (Bodleian, Queen's College MS. 1073). The name recurs the following year in a St Denys charter concerning a dispute with God's House (St Denys Cart. 106). For the 'Fleshambles' and 'Flesmangarestrete' in St Lawrence, see Win.Coll.Mun. 17842, 17843, 17898. Certainly, a butcher held property here on the west side of English Street, and the area was known as the meat market (*macecraria*), as early as the second half of the thirteenth century (St Denys Cart. 189–90). For 'Butcher Rowe' in the same place, see P.R.O. SC11/597; and for 'the streat caulid the butcher Rewe within the newe corner', see *Black Book*, iii:114. It may be that the butchers did not set up in business south of the friary gate as early as the thirteenth century, but there were certainly shops there before 1250 (P.R.O. E327/328). The 'Modern Laws' of the fifteenth-century town include regulations for the conduct of butchers keeping their market there (*Oak Book*, i:142). There are constant references to repairs on the stalls in the contemporary Stewards' Books, including at least one major rebuilding of the 'butcher's rew' in 1497–8 (S.C.R.O. SC5/1/24B).

41 P.R.O. E326/9317, 9318, 9314, SC11/596 and 597.

42 A quit-claim of 1296 records four shops, with their cellars, on the west side of French Street (God's House Deeds 525); for other, fourteenth-century references to shops in the street, see P.R.O. E210/8123, and S.C.R.O. SC2/6/2. For shops in Simnel Street, see God's House Deeds 643, 658. The siting of the fishmarket in St Michael's Square is well

attested in the fifteenth-century Stewards' Books.

43 For an example of this practice in Southampton, see a quit-claim of 1321 relating to a shop and chamber on the east side of English Street, sited in front of a tenement of which they were not a part (Win.Coll.Mun. 17846). See also H. E. Salter, *Medieval Oxford*, pp. 81–3.

44 S.C.R.O. SC4/2/67, and God's House Deeds 450.

45 S.C.R.O. SC4/2/209.

46 West Hall was the most important of these, but see also the shops in God's House Deeds 525.

47 Recent excavations in the garden at 49 Bugle (Bull) Street revealed two small windows, eastward facing, in the stone retaining wall against the cliff on the west. They would originally have been upper-storey windows in the north wall of Ronceval (*Southampton Excavations*, forthcoming).

48 God's House Deeds 717, 718.

49 S.C.R.O. SC4/2/33.

50 S.C.R.O. SC4/1/2.

51 *Black Book*, ii: 42.

52 Ibid., ii: 22. In the eighteenth and nineteenth centuries, the lane was known as Market Lane.

53 Ibid., ii: 17.

54 Ibid., ii: 64.

55 God's House Deeds 476, 601,605; St Denys Cart. 242.

56 J. M. Rigg (ed.), *Calendar of the Plea Rolls of the Exchequer of the Jews*, ii: 119–20; God's House Deeds 353, 524. John Beneyt, later rector of Gussage All Saints, was Benedict Ace's first-born son.

57 P.R.O. E210/5745.

58 Philip E. Jones (ed.), *Calendar of Plea and Memoranda Rolls, 1437–57*, pp. 68–9. In this context, the road widths determined for Edward I's fresh Gascon foundation at Montpazier are instructive. Here the principal streets were to be 24 feet wide, the secondary streets 16 feet, and the lanes only 6 feet (Caroline Shillaber, 'Edward I, builder of towns', *Speculum*, 22 (1947), pp. 297–309).

59 *Southampton Excavations*, forthcoming.

60 St Denys Cart. 67.

61 The price, at twenty shillings, was a ten-year purchase (St Denys Cart. 36). At a similar date James Isembard adopted the same principle in offering to sell, at a rate of ten marks down for every one mark of rent due, the quit-rent owed to him by Thomas le Halveknight on Bull Hall (God's House Deeds 601).

62 See, for example, St Denys Cart. 78–80, 87.

63 Ibid., 201–6, 208. It is known, however, that Sampson de Puteo and Isabella, his wife, lived in the northern suburb, on the east side of Above Bar Street (Ibid. 143), and certainly the burgesses of Warwick, if wealthy enough to do so, frequently settled in their suburbs (*V.C.H.*, *Warwick*, viii: 487).

64 Bodleian, Queen's College MS. 340.

65 S.C.R.O. SC2/6/2; the group of charters collected under this accession number contains much of the material used here and not subsequently annotated.

66 Davies, p. 171.

67 P.R.O. E210/6997.

68 P.R.O. E329/193.

69 P.R.O. C143/376/19, E326/9381; Win.Coll. Mun. 17779; *Cal.Inq.P.M.*, xiii: 272.

70 *Black Book*, ii: 68–9.

71 Ibid.

72 The record of the dispute survives in unusual detail (S.C.R.O. SC4/2/314–32). It was followed shortly by another wrangle, quite as bitter, between the mayor himself and the commonalty. It concerned once again the enclosure of the salt-marsh, this time on the initiative of the borough officers, designed to help support the cost of the sea defences (*Third Book of Remembrance*, i: 20–6, 33, 37, and *Sign Manuals and Letters Patent*, i: 35–7).

73 *Black Book*, iii: 149. A list of these charters was drawn up in 1570.

74 *Black Book*, iii: 134–9.

75 Ibid., iii: 140–5; also *Oak Book*, ii: 138–41. For an identification of the boundary marks, unchallenged since, see Davies, pp. 41–8.

Chapter six

Municipal government and the great families

In circumstances everywhere of growth, a workable system of self-government in Southampton evolved simultaneously with the physical development of the borough. Much of this was already anticipated in the operation of the twelfth-century gild merchant, and substantial portions of the gild regulations were incorporated in the ordinances copied into the 'Oak Book', or 'Paxbread', of the town. But in the thirteenth century, as the organization and personnel of gild and borough progressively merged, the ordinances of the one became those of the other, together comprising an acceptable constitution, or working code, for the town. William Overy, the late-fifteenth-century translator of the ordinances, while he recognized the distinction between gild and borough, clearly considered it of small importance to his readers. The clauses of the Paxbread, in his view, were of a general application. They constituted the 'olde rules and ordinaunces of the good towne of Suthampton, made by greate deliberacon by the awncyent fathers in time passed, for the utilitie and comon welthe, as well for the burgeasses and bretheren of the gilde, as for all the Dwellers and inhabitantes within the franchis and liberties of the saide towne'. The book, he said, had been made of old time in the French tongue as the 'firste sadd [steadfast] and good rule to be had and setted amounge them [the fathers]'. It was to persist in the same 'unto the worldes ende'.[1]

The fathers, in their wisdom, had assembled a code that took something from the practice of each of the competing authorities in the town. The *alderman*, a gild official, was 'chief of the town and of the gild'; his voice was first (and, the Modern Laws add, last) in all matters touching the town, in elections and in the protection of the statutes; he headed the courts, supervised, and where necessary corrected, the activities of the borough officers, kept the peace, summoned town meetings, and took charge of the municipal funds. He was assisted by another leading gild official, the *seneschal* or *steward*, second only to the alderman himself in the direction of the borough courts, and concerned chiefly with the care and administration of property, whether of the gild or of the town. Below the alderman and the steward, gild officials both, extended an administrative structure essentially the creation of the borough, controlled electorally by the franchisers meeting in common council:[2]

> Every year, on the morrow after St Michael's day [30 September], shall be elected by the whole community of the town, assembled in a place provided to consider their estate and treat of the common business of the the town . . . twelve discreets [*prudhommes*], to furnish the king's commands, together with the bailiffs, and to maintain the peace and protect the franchise, and to do and keep justice to all persons, as well poor as rich, denizens and strangers, all that year; and to this they shall be sworn in the form provided. And these twelve discreets shall choose the same day two discreets from among themselves and the other profitable and knowing men to be bailiffs for the ensuing year, of whom the community hold themselves well pleased: and they shall receive their bailiwicks on the morrow after St Michael's day, as has been customary. And this shall be done from year to year; so that the bailiffs shall be removed every year, and the twelve aforesaid, if occasion be. The same shall be done with regard to the clerk and of the town sergeants as to making and removing them.

In effect, the *bailiffs*, appointees of the entire body of franchisers and chosen without reference to gild membership, were to remain the principal executive officers of the borough. Under the alderman, they were charged with the maintenance of the law, with control of markets and the supervision of agreed standards in the victualling trades, with registering debts, and with keeping the accounts of customs levied in the town. They enjoyed the advice and support of the elected *prudhommes*, and they were further assisted in their duties by other officials of the town. The four *jurats* of the markets enforced the statutes maintaining quality controls on the sale of fish, meat, poultry and bread; the twelve *guardians*, or *aldermans de la garde*, answered for the keeping of the peace in the five wards of the borough; and the *brokers* watched the interests of the burgesses in 'all manner of purchases and sales, and in all kinds of merchandise, before all other merchants', preserving the advantage of townsman over alien in every way that they could. With the *clerk*, the *sergeants* and the *echevins*, the first a shadowy figure before the phenomenal expansion of the office in the sixteenth century, the second exercising a police role in the borough, and the third a group of four elder statesmen, the essentials of the borough administration were complete.[3] There would be, and perhaps were already, the *constables*, *water-bailiffs*, *Bargate brokers* and a host of lesser office-holders to carry municipal officialdom into every sphere of the social and economic life of the later medieval borough. But in the thirteenth century these offices, for the most part, were as yet ill-formed. Certainly they found no place in the Paxbread, or seemed, as in the case of the *porters*, to relate rather to a working condition than to an office sought after for its customary profits and frequently performed by delegation.[4]

Within this structure, the role of the ordinary burgess, compounded of privilege and obligation, was well-defined from the first. Whatever the realities of power in medieval Southampton, they were clothed in a form that made much of the duty of consultation. The community met frequently: 'as often as necessary', in the formula of the Paxbread; more specifically, as the fifteenth-century Modern Laws defined it, on the Friday before St Matthew's day, on Michaelmas day, on the Friday after Michaelmas day and the Saturday following, on Christmas day, Easter day, Trinity eve, at the Quarter Sessions and Gaol Delivery, and at the coming and departure of the king.[5] In common council, the franchisers would receive the king's commands, attending to the business, common and extraordinary, of the town. Attendance at these regular assemblies was an understood obligation of citizenship, written into the oath that every burgess swore:[6]

> You shall be faithful and loyal to our lord the king and his heirs; you shall maintain the franchise of the town and the points of the gild; you shall keep secret their counsel; you shall, upon reasonable summons, come to the courts and assemblies; you shall enter into no partnership with any stranger by which the customs of the said town would be lessened; you shall not hold, or suffer to be held, except by common consent of the said town, any meetings or assemblies by which any man of the said town may be damaged or defrauded; and if any such confederacies or evil combinations shall come to your knowledge, by your oath you shall cause to be warned the mayor and the good people [of the town] to hinder such iniquitous practice; with your best skill, and with your body, goods and chattels, you shall maintain the above points. So help you God and the Saints.

But the oath, phrased in the most general terms, was intended to acquaint the burgess as much with what he should not do, as with what he should. And it could give little idea of the manifold burdens that he might, during his lifetime, have to shoulder. For a guide to these, with obvious later extensions, we can do no better than look ahead a century or so to the terms of the letters patent granted by Henry IV to Thomas Armorer, burgess of Southampton. Thomas subsequently presented his letters to an assembly of burgesses, held on Saturday 10 November 1414. In consideration of his past services and the heavy labours he had undertaken for the town, the assembly conceded the exemptions he claimed and caused them to be enrolled in the Black Book. They read:[7]

> Henry, by the Grace of God, King of England and France and Lord of Ireland, to all his bailiffs and faithful subjects to whom the present letters may come, greeting. Know that of our special grace we have granted to our dear liege Thomas Armorer, of our town of Southampton, that for the term of his life he may have this liberty, that is to say, that he shall not be placed on any assizes, juries, attaints, inquisitions or recognitions whatsoever, although they may concern us or our heirs, and that he shall not be made mayor, coroner, reeve, bailiff, constable, nor any other servant of us or of our heirs whatsoever, and that he shall not be made a tryer of panels, juries, inquisitions, attaints, or of any person placed on assizes,

> juries, inquisitions or attaints, and that he shall not be made commissioner of array, or tryer or leader of men-at-arms, hobblers or archers, nor any other official or servant of ours or of our heirs, and that he shall not be made collector, assessor or valuer of any tallages whatsoever, nor collector, assessor, valuer, supervisor, or controller of tenths, fifteenths or other subsidies or aids granted to us or to our heirs or about to be granted, and that he shall not be made customer, controller, searcher, alnager, weigher, troner, supervisor, nor any official or servant whatsoever of ours or of our heirs. And therefore we command you that you shall not injure or in any way annoy the said Thomas against this our grant. In witness whereof we have caused these our letters patent to be made. Witness myself at Westminster the fifteenth day of December, in the fourteenth year of our reign, [etc.]

Thomas had delayed presentation of his patent for almost two years, and when he finally submitted it to the assembly, had already been elected for the ninth time as bailiff of the borough.[8] A generation before, John Polymond, who was as many times mayor, had secured for himself on 28 October 1383 a closely equivalent exemption.[9] It is a measure of his public spirit, at least as much as of his self-interest, that he does not appear to have acted upon it.

In the close-knit community of their borough, to which they gave, and from which they received, so much, it is little wonder that, over the years, the burgesses of Southampton should have built up an intense local patriotism, founded on civic pride. This 'notabill and worshipfull Towne of Suthampton', in the artless fifteenth-century phrase, devoted much attention to the cultivation of the dignity of its officers. It rewarded their industry with perquisites and banquets, and bolstered their self-regard by decree. 'Those', the Paxbread provided, 'who are summoned to come to the court or assembly to hear and furnish the king's command, or for the common business of the community of the town, and come not at the summons . . . shall be amerced as often as they shall offend in this sort, whoever they be, poor or rich, by the award of the aldermen of their ward, and the fine shall be immediately levied to the use of the town'.[10]

Further, the power of such rivals as may have threatened their authority was steadily whittled away. One of the most notable victories over that perennial enemy, the sheriff, was won on 14 July 1256. Henceforth, by grant of Henry III, the burgesses themselves replied in their own name to the writs sent down to them by the king's courts or to the summonses from the Exchequer, 'so that no sheriff or bailiff or other servant of ours hereafter shall intermeddle concerning the making of summons of this kind or attachments or distraints in the aforesaid town except by default of the said burgesses or bailiffs of the same town'. To free them equally from the intervention of the county coroner, they were granted the right to elect coroners of their own. Pleas touching their property within the liberty of the town might be heard in their own courts. And they were protected from the serving of writs in their borough, except writs of right, of novel disseisin and of dower.[11] The king, of course, might still intervene in the affairs of the town, and might do so, if he wished, through his sheriff. But now, for the most part, the borough officials held in their own hands those powers once claimed for the county. They might deal, should it suit them to do so, direct with the central government in London. Fresh recognition had been granted their courts by the king, and they might expect to by-pass the sheriff, in matters of law as of taxation, with impunity.

The confidence and self-esteem of the burgesses, promoted by triumphs such as this, fed on aggression. An inevitable opponent was the bishop of Winchester, an economic as well as a spiritual force sited uncomfortably close to the north. In 1251, in the first year of the uncertain tenure of Aymer de Valence, elected bishop on 4 November 1250 but not consecrated for a further decade, the burgesses of Southampton chose their moment to dispute the conditions of attendance at the bishop's great fair at St Giles. The fair, held on St Giles's Hill for a fortnight each September, was an event on the scale of Boston Fair, drawing custom from every quarter. Locally its effect was to bring to a halt every sort of commercial transaction, directing to the bishop's exchequer such dues as might have been derived therefrom by the towns. In 1251, the bishop-elect complained, the burgesses of Southampton had not come, as was their usual practice, to display their goods for sale on St Giles's Hill during the weeks of the fair. Instead, they had continued to trade at home in their own town, levying on their own account the tronage and pesage that would otherwise have come to Aymer himself as an essential perquisite of the fair. Nor would they make amends for their neglect.[12] The dispute lasted a full three years, and although the terms of the settlement, agreed in good time for the fair of 1254, supported in essence the claims of the bishop-elect, there is little doubt that the burgesses also had negotiated some concessions for themselves. Victuals alone were to be sold in Southampton while the fair lasted; no tronage or pesage might be levied during that period in the town; and all burgesses with goods to offer were constrained to display them at St Giles. However, a merchant arriving at the town during the fair, if he swore that he had not come specifically to visit it, might be allowed to pass unhindered, return or abide, provided always that he sold nothing in Southampton save victuals.[13] Later in the century, the burgesses would test their power again in disputes with John of Pontoise, then bishop, concerning the patronage of their hospitals at St Mary Magdalene and God's House. Yet here their opponent, in both causes, would be less the bishop than the king, and they seem to have surrendered to superior right with at least a reasonable grace.[14]

In general, as was only to be expected, the burgesses were on stronger ground where matters of commercial interest were at stake. It was in 1252, for example, that they won the first round of that long-lasting dispute with the Cinque Ports which flared up expensively in 1321 and which remained unresolved as late as the first years of the sixteenth century. The men of the Cinque Ports had been tampering with cargoes at the port of Portsmouth, held at farm from the king by the burgesses of

Southampton. On the complaint of the latter, Henry III required of his 'barons' of the Cinque Ports that 'for the future ye take no cargo in their aforesaid port nor execute any attachment, nor do them injury contrary to their liberties and customs granted by us under penalty of our displeasure'.[15] On a more personal issue, the dispute which centred on the custody of the Weigh House, long a perquisite of the earls of Warwick, was at least as typical of the aggressive self-confidence of the burgesses. An enquiry, ordered on 16 February 1275, was established to discover the circumstances of the arbitrary arrest and detention of the balance and weights at the Weigh House, removed by a group of Southampton burgesses led by Nicholas de Barbflete, Robert Benet (Bonhait) and Thomas of Andover. With three such notable burgesses in the van, it is not surprising that the alderman and bailiffs had themselves done nothing to remedy the injustice, if injustice it was. And though both the nature of the dispute and its resolution are unknown, the mere fact that it should have arisen at all, particularly in the form that it did, is indication enough in itself of the extreme unwillingness of the thirteenth-century burgess to allow himself to be imposed upon in any way or by anybody, no matter what power in the land such stubbornness might provoke.[16]

There was a limit, even so, to aggression. In their dealings with the king, the burgesses of Southampton took liberties they would, in due course, repent. The reasons for the king's action are obscure, but it may have been as a consequence of the dispute over the fair at St Giles that he took the town into his own hands on 29 September 1251, releasing it nearly a month later on the payment of a fine of twenty marks.[17] There was to be, in the spring of 1274, a still more serious confrontation, the consequences of which would remain with the burgesses and their successors for almost three centuries. A Jewish money-lender, Deudoné of Winchester, was assaulted in the town, to which he had ridden in the company of the king's sheriff to collect outstanding debts. But whereas the assault was popular locally, implicating such great figures as Bernard le Moigne and Robert le Mercer in its support, it was not such as the king could ignore. Edward I seized the town, delivering it to Adam de Wynton as keeper in his name. Though called to account by the king, Southampton's bailiffs were dilatory, dragging their feet over a settlement. It was a full two years on this occasion before the burgesses were permitted to resume their liberties, to do so then only at the cost of an immediate fine of £20 and the recognition for the future of a permanent increase of forty marks on their farm.[18] Although there was to be trouble again in 1292–3,[19] it must already have been plain to at any rate the more substantial of the burgesses that their best interests lay rather in co-operation with, than in opposition to, the king. Edward I had taught them a bitter lesson. The experience continued to cost the town more than it could properly afford for many generations to come. While this happened, as before, it was in the traditional association of royal and municipal office that the greater merchants shaped their fortunes. It is not difficult to see how this was done.

The determining factor in the domestic politics of thirteenth-century Southampton was the small size and great cohesion of the dominant ruling caste. The names that mattered in the first half of the century were the Flemings (Walter, James and John), the St Laurences (Simon and Bovo), the Bulehuses (Thomas and John), and the Fortins (Denys, Amys, William, Walter and John). The list becomes virtually complete with the addition of Benedict Ace, Ralph Isembard, Richard of Leicester, Robert le Moigne, William Bonhait, John Blancbuilly, and Sampson and Thomas de Puteo. By the second half of the century, the Flemings were still in evidence, with Petronilla, Roger, Henry and John the younger, as were the Bonhaits, Robert, Roger and John. There was a James Isembard, a John de Puteo (also known as John atte Barre), a Bernard le Moigne, and a Bartholomew de la Bulehuse. And there were new names: the Prises (Walter, Henry, Richard and Philip), the Passelewes (Hugh, Robert and William), the Horders (Adam, Walter and Thomas), and, towards the end of the century, the Englishes (Robert, Richard, William and Bartholomew). Of the outstanding individuals who first made an appearance in these decades, some were to found lines of their own. There had been Barbfletes in Southampton since the last years of the twelfth century, but it was probably the wealthy Nicholas de Barbflete (d. 1295) who set the family firmly on its feet. Thomas le Halveknight, by the end of the century, had acquired full ownership of the great mansion at West Hall, which he was to divide among his children, John, Thomas the younger, Roger, Walter and Petronilla, the wife of William Bassingrom. John de Byndon and Robert le Barber each had notable successors. Between these men, or, not infrequently, their widows, there developed an intricate web of cross-allegiances, fostered by office, expanded by trade, and confirmed by intermarriage. If the king's commissions demanded exceptional resources or particular skills, two or more burgesses would be found ready to come together to complete them. If a trading venture were launched, it would be conducted, usually, in partnership. If an estate required rounding-off, or a fortune a beginning, there were the daughters or the widows of associates to be courted. Within the warm circles of gild and borough, parish, ward and family, the way ahead was clear. 'Each man', it was said, 'must have a beginning, for the fair lasts but a while.'

Undoubtedly, there were opportunities enough for individual profit in the works and purchases of the king. The two major figures of the first half of the thirteenth century, Benedict Ace, keeper of the king's wines and repeatedly mayor, and Walter le Fleming, the 'faithful and trusty' of Henry III's formula, built their fortunes in large part in the service of the king. And there were many others, both contemporaries and successors, who with varying degrees of effectiveness executed crown commissions. Thomas de Puteo, member of an important local family, was overseeing repairs at the castle in 1245–6.[20] Until his death in 1253, William Fortin, just as well connected in the town, was keeper of the king's buildings, an office his son would inherit. But lineal succession, as is too often the case, brought a bad man in place of the good. John Fortin seriously neglected his charge. During the seven years of his tenure, he allowed the king's houses and the walls of his court to fall down, turning a blind eye to the removal, by persons unknown, of timber and roofing materials, doors, windows, bolts and hinges. In the thick of the building boom, there were many among his relatives and friends who would gladly have profited at the king's expense. And when, in 1260, the king commissioned an enquiry to assess the extent of the damage, it is at least suggestive that he should have employed outsiders to do it. Peter de Nevill was one; the sheriff, William de Wintershill, the other.[21] Yet the king's dependence on the services of local men was quite as great as their own reliance on his patronage. When the recommended repairs were undertaken in 1260–1, John Horn, the associate of Claramunda, was one of the two overseers appointed for the work.[22] And when once again, in 1286, the castle was reported to be ruinous, it was the turn of Nicholas de Barbflete, one of the wealthier burgesses of his generation, to be instructed to attend to its rebuilding.[23]

Above all else, the building of the royal galley at Southampton during the winter of 1294–5 illustrates the degree of co-operation that the king might expect, in this case at very short notice, from his burgesses. The galley was to be one of a fleet of twenty, commissioned by the king for his new French wars and intended to be built at the principal ports of the realm. The writ ordering the work was addressed to Southampton on 17 November 1294, and on 28 November, within a few days of receipt of the command, the project was actually begun. With Peter de Lyon, the bailiff, in overall charge, the direct supervision of the work was entrusted to two of the ablest burgesses, Robert le Mercer and John of Holebury. Immediately, boys were sent to Shoreham and to the Isle of Wight to summon four master-builders. Thirty skilled workmen, plankers, clenchers and their mates, were assembled, again from Shoreham and the neighbouring ports. Down by the sea-shore, an empty plot was hired for a boatyard, to be enclosed with a hedge of hurdles and thorn. Neighbouring houses were rented, one as a workshop, another as a store, and two boys were hired to keep watch night and day on the materials and equipment at the yard. Throughout the seventeen weeks it took to build and launch the galley, the supervisors were kept hard at work, overseeing and paying the workmen, ordering and accounting for the stores. In the second week, they obtained the help of a master-builder from Bayonne, whom they fetched from Portsmouth to assist them in matters of design. They bought timber, iron and miscellaneous stores, and sent their own master-builders to Poole and the Isle of Wight to buy sails, the mast and spars. When, finally, the fighting-castles were fitted, the galley was hauled to the sea down a ditch it had taken twenty men six days to dig. It was a creditable performance by any criterion, especially for a winter over which, according to the Worcester annalist, the rains continued right through from the summer of 1294 into the following spring.[24] Only general co-operation within the borough, particularly amongst its leaders, could have secured it. Characteristically, when Peter de Lyon, in the sixth week of building, went to London to discuss finance at the Exchequer, he took with him Robert le Barber, formerly alderman on at least two occasions and a close business associate of Robert le Mercer. At the end of the work, Robert le Barber made a second trip to London to collect wages for the crew, accompanied on this occasion by the supervisor, John of Holebury. John le Fleming, probably the great-grandson of Walter, undertook the provisioning of the galley, armed it, and paid its master, three constables and 120 sailors to take it on the four-day journey to Winchelsea, there to join the royal fleet and become the charge of the crown. He bought hawsers, cables and stays. He furnished the cooks with a hand-mill and an oven for baking, with mortars, pots and other cooking utensils, with barrels for the storage of water and wine, with bags for flour and corn, and with tubs for the salt-meat and remaining victuals. When he sent it to sea, the galley was already heavily armed. He had found for it a full set of helmets, padded tunics and other personal armour, and had supplied sixty cross-bows with 6,000 bolts, 120 lances, 100 halberds and 240 javelins. When it left harbour in the spring of 1295, the galley must have made a brave spectacle. It carried pennons, or streamers, at the mast-head, and bore, by way of identification as a ship of the king, no fewer than twenty-five banners.[25]

In more than one way, the group of able men that had assembled to get the galley into the sea with such despatch displays important characteristics of the ruling class to which each of its members belonged. It was not a particularly stable class, nor could it afford to be exclusive. It was subject to bankruptcies, and exposed to failure of heirs. Like the London aldermanic class, which it resembled in so many ways, it was the prey of high infant mortality even before the plague years.[26] Confident and aggressive in the short term, in the long term its morale as an urban élite was low. A successful burgess, as likely as not, would seek to educate his heir out of that commercial society into which he had been born. Great merchants bred landed proprietors, rarely entrepreneurs; it was the best they could do for their kin. For many years yet, the distinction between usury and the honest pursuit of gain (the *honestus questus* of the canonists) would remain far from clear. If profit were pursued for its own sake, it would be counted illicit. Interest rates, even modest ones, could so easily be held to be usurious, and it was difficult at all times to determine a 'just' price without finding some authority to dispute it.[27] Bending before such moral pressures as these, even the most hard-headed and successful of burgesses might exhibit a marked tenderness of conscience on the approach of death. It was Walter le Fleming's desire, for example, that an appreciable part of his great fortune should go to the support of the many religious institutions in the vicinity. He remembered most particularly the friars, with whom he had been closely associated during the last years of his life. But he also made liberal bequests to all the parish churches in the town, to the hospitals there and in Portsmouth, to the nuns of Romsey, the canons of St Denys and Southwick, the monks of Netley, Beaulieu and Winchester. His grandson, John, was then being educated at the schools. The old man left him twenty marks to maintain himself. By 1296–7 John Fleming was to reappear in the town as a 'clerk', granting property in East Street to St Denys to endow an obit in memory of his Fleming and Isembard relations.[28]

A family like the Flemings, fortunate in its heirs, might last through many generations. Yet even in the second generation there were already signs of those pressures at work that would combine to remove its senior branches from the town. Henry, the eldest son of Walter, inherited from his father in 1258 the means to carry on his business. He acquired Martin's Hall, a suitable property on the western shore, with a great ship, one of the two owned by his father, and the considerable sum of £200 in cash. But with these came also tenements in Chichester, Portsmouth and Winchester, and rents in Southampton itself. Thirty years later, in 1288, his non-residence in the town was regarded as disqualification for the post of keeper of customs, to which he had been lately appointed. Like his nephew John, although in a different cause, Henry Fleming had removed himself from the urban environment which had suited his father so well. He had set himself up as a landed proprietor, and had joined the ranks of the gentry.[29]

Indeed, it was the steady drain of wealth and talent away from the town, at least as much as a failure of heirs, that accounted for the brief life-span of many of the leading burgess families. In two generations, or three at most, the irresistible draw of rural landownership could splinter and disperse a dynasty. The financial difficulties of Adam le Mercer and Juliana, his wife, contracted within a few years of the death of Robert le Mercer, their wealthy relative, could well have derived entirely from their own incompetence. Many families collapsed that way. But it was also true that Robert had begun buying lands outside the town at least as early as 1291. In his long and successful commercial life, he could have been syphoning wealth out into the surrounding countryside for a matter of three decades or more. On his death in 1314, little need have remained in the borough to support the lesser branches of his family.[30] Much the same instinct would have prompted the powerful Barbflete family to acquire an interest in the neighbouring manor of Shirley and Hill, immediately to the north-west of the borough. By 1329 the manor had gone, on the dispersal of their fortunes, to Roger Norman, who came to hold in his own generation perhaps the widest extent of rural properties ever owned by a burgess of Southampton.[31]

Bankruptcies added their toll to the already rapid turnover of the major burgess families. Trading overseas, in which many of them were engaged, had its hazards from the beginning. And John Blancbuilly cannot have been alone in contracting large debts to the merchants of Normandy and Anjou in the 1230s. He was exceptional, and unlucky, only in the fact that the crown showed an interest in their recovery.[32] In a situation at least as typical, a Bulehuse, shortly before the disappearance of his line, was bound in a debt of 100 marks to Benedict, Jew of Winchester.[33] And there is nothing in the records as heartbreakingly prolonged as the collapse of the fortunes of Nicholas and Cecily la Weyte, whose piecemeal sales, 'for their great necessity', of the family tenement on English Street allowed their neighbour, John Horn, to consolidate his own considerable holding in the parish of St Lawrence, between the street and the castle, on the west.[34] John Horn himself, dying without heirs, would illustrate another weakness of his class. And it was this situation precisely, combining every sort of pressure on the resources and the numbers of a dwindling ruling caste, that compelled the burgesses of Southampton to open their doors to outsiders. Of the men who launched the galley in 1295, we know nothing of the origins of either Robert le Mercer or Robert le Barber, each of whom owed his surname to a trade. But the Fleming family name recalled the boom in the

Flanders trade during the reigns of the early Angevins; the alien origins of Peter de Lyon are obvious enough; and John of Holebury had come to the town from the village of that name, on the far side of Southampton Water, rather less than three miles from Hythe. Already, there had been men of Leicester and of Gloucester important in the town, of Bordeaux, Barfleur, Arundel and Andover.

Nothing, given such circumstances, could have been more characteristic of this wealthy but frequently unstable burgess class than its welcome in 1233/4, to the first Franciscan friars to settle in the town. It might have been said, unkindly, that 'the sea shall be dry when the poor man has a friend'. But the burgesses of Southampton, as elsewhere, had long been schooled in the obligations of charity. They believed that 'God loves a glad giver', and understood, perhaps better than we do now, that the poor, deserving their compassion, also had a right to their generosity.[35] Some decades before, they had set up and endowed their hospitals at St Mary Magdalene and God's House. In the new friary to be established in their midst, they were to find a near-perfect vehicle for giving.

A site had been chosen, very probably on the initiative of Walter le Fleming, in the south-east quarter of the town, directly opposite Walter's house. With other landholders in the area, in particular the Fortins and Isabel Chekehull, Walter worked to extend it and to supply the friars with garden plots in the suburb of Newtown, to the east.[36] In clear contravention of the directions of St Francis, the burgesses rallied to furnish the brethren with fine stone buildings, after the fashion already commonplace enough in the town. They were soon to watch them demolished, although not without protest, on the orders of a purist provincial minister, Albert of Pisa.[37] For some years, building proceeded on the prescribed lines. The founder had wished his followers to live as humbly as they might, in houses of mud-plaster and of wood. The timber, in part at least, was supplied by the king, drawing on the resources of his neighbouring forests. But there were many eager to be listed with the benefactors, and Nicholas of Shirley was surely not the only local landowner to add his gift of timber to the king's.[38] There was more than just piety at stake. If the burgesses were not to acquire an unjustified reputation for parsimony, they would have to signify their devotion in stone. Within only a few years of the completion of the first church, for which a grant of roofing timber was made in 1268, the original plan was overtaken by a fresh project for entire reconstruction in stone.[39] It was Robert le Mercer, already a leading figure in the town, who bought a fresh plot for the friary, adjoining the existing site, on which the new church might be built. In seven years, from the laying of foundations in 1280, the work was complete, to be celebrated by a feast and treat for the brethren on the occasion of their first use of the church, on St Francis's day 1287. By 1291 the new dormitory was ready, and in the same year a chapter-house was built.[40] At the suppression of the convent in 1538, its buildings were listed and their contents inventoried. They included, besides the church, a vestry, chapter-house, frater, infirmary, parlour, kitchen and 'tailor's house'.[41]

The location of a friary in their midst opened to the burgesses of Southampton a variety of new facilities. They found the solemn atmosphere and implied spiritual sanctions of a church well suited to the conclusion of business deals, and it was not uncommon, and certainly not held strange, for transactions of this kind to be completed there. In 1276 the parish church of St Lawrence had been used for just this purpose; in 1341 it was agreed that an outstanding debt should be settled at the church of the Friars Minor.[42] As a place of sanctuary, the church again found a predominantly lay purpose. It was in the friary church that Bernard de Perers, merchant of Bayonne, chose to lodge himself for more than forty days in 1301, while he negotiated the terms of his removal with the king.[43] And there again that John Piggesden, self-confessed felon, acknowledged his crimes in 1413 to the coroners of the town, to be granted a royal pardon a little over a year later, on 9 March 1414.[44]

But if these were passive services of the friary, a more positive civic achievement of the brethren themselves was the construction, under their auspices, of a water conduit from a spring beyond the borough boundaries at Colewell in Hill, to where the water-house still remains on Commercial Road, and thence by way of English Street to the friary. Friaries in other parts of the country had been, or more often would be, associated with the organization of water supplies.[45] At Southampton, the first step in this direction was taken in 1290, on the grant of a suitable spring by Nicholas de Barbflete within his manor of Shirley. Work began in 1304, and was completed over the next three decades, to bring a piped supply of fresh water down to the lower reaches of the town. In 1420 it would become a truly municipal service on the borough's purchase and repair of the watercourse.[46]

With no, or very few, possessions outside the borough, the friars remained for the three centuries of their residence inescapably concerned in its affairs. There is little to be said of their pastoral work, for only scanty indications of its nature have survived. But we know, at least, that in 1318 John Sandale, bishop of Winchester, licensed six of their number to preach and hear confessions, and that their names were Brother John Oyle, Brother Baldwin, Brother Nicholas, Brother Jordan, Brother John Gregory and Brother William.[47] No doubt, their work as preachers was important. They took the teaching of Christ to the market-place, and ministered to the poor both in the borough itself and in its neighbouring villages. Nevertheless, for many of the burgesses their worth stood as high in their function as custodians of the dead. It was not, certainly, a role they had sought from the beginning. At Southampton, it would have threatened the established rights of the rector, or precentor, of St Mary's, to whom the charges of death constituted an important source of revenue. And any such conflict with the local secular clergy, present as it might be already on issues of unlicensed preaching and the hearing of confessions, could seriously have jeopardized their ministry. But on this, as on the matter of their buildings, the Friars Minor had to bend to the wishes of the burgesses who supported them. Walter le Fleming, drafting his will in January 1257/8, would still be loyal to the mother church of the town in electing to be buried in its cemetery. He had, as he made clear, long reserved a plot there.[48] Yet of succeeding generations, many chose to lay their remains in the shadow of the friary church, designing to take advantage of the perpetual round of prayer that they knew would continue within it. In the seventies of the next century, the friars' cemetery had to be extended. The new ground, consecrated in 1382, was sited at the west end of the church, between the church and English Street. It measured 120 feet in width by 100 feet in length.[49]

Indeed, so popular did the practice of burial at the friary remain, that the burgesses themselves in the fifteenth century united with the friars to resist any threatened encroachment upon it. A rector of St Mary's, not satisfied with his bare canonical portion of the dues, had begun to insist on the carriage of the bodies of the deceased to his own church, there to receive the final obsequies before being taken to the friary for burial. A judgment, delivered in his favour by the dean of Wells, was contested by the friars and their allies, the townspeople, and appeal was made to Rome. In 1425, accordingly, Martin V instructed the abbot of Abingdon to examine the circumstances of the case. He should respect the 'ancient custom' of the friars to bury whomsoever might request it. If he found in their favour, he was to restore the situation to the status as before, and to license the friary for burials.[50] The victory, evidently, was complete.

A few decades before, the poet William Langland had found it strange that the friars 'would rather bury people than baptize children who want to enter the Church'. And in claiming not to be alone in his confusion, he was certainly voicing criticisms that were gathering force in his day. In Southampton, however, there is little to demonstrate a decline in the popularity of the Franciscans. There had, it is true, been some threat to their position in the last decades of the fourteenth century, for both Edward III (in 1375) and Richard II (in 1382) felt called upon to grant them some protection.[51] But the circumstances of these troubles are unknown, and they seem, in any case, to have had little impact on the permanent position of the friars, high in the affection of the townsfolk. Most burgesses remembered them generously in their wills, and the more notable figures choosing to be buried in their church included Sir Henry Peverel and Nicholas Moundenard in the fourteenth century, John Barbflete, Alice Whitehead and William Soper in the fifteenth century, and Thomas Thomas, 'next to my mother', in the sixteenth.[52] The preference is surely significant. Whatever may have been the experience elsewhere, at Southampton, at least, the friary retained its popularity. In its last days as an Observant house, in the reigns of the early Tudors, it may even be expected to have increased it.

Notes

1 *Oak Book*, i:85.
2 *Oak Book*, i:44–5.
3 Ibid., i:xxiii–vii, 24–81. For the later development of the office of town clerk, see *Third Book of Remembrance*, i:xiii.
4 *Oak Book*, i:70–5.
5 *Oak Book*, i:60–1, 117.
6 Ibid., i:22–3.
7 *Black Book*, ii:2–5.
8 Davies, p. 173.

9 *Cal.P.R. 1381–5*, p. 320.
10 *Oak Book*, i:48–51.
11 *Charters*, i:14–17.
12 *Cal.P.R. 1247–58*, p. 109.
13 *Cal.Ch.R. 1226–57*, p. 445; also A. W. Goodman (ed.), *Chartulary of Winchester Cathedral*, pp. 193–4.
14 Cecil Deedes (ed.), *Registrum Johannis de Pontissara*, Canterbury and York Society, 19 (1915), pp. xxvi–vii, and *Rot.Parlm.*, i:45.
15 *Charters*, i:6–7.
16 *Cal.P.R. 1272–81*, pp. 66, 117.
17 *Cal.C.R. 1247–51*, pp. 563–4, and P.R.O. E372/95.
18 P.R.O. E372/119, 120 and 168; *Cal. Fine R.*, i:24, 69; *Rot. Parlm.*, i:58; J. M. Rigg (ed.), *Calendar of the Plea Rolls of the Exchequer of the Jews*, ii:130–1, 137–8, 200, 216–17, 219–20, 249, 286, 302; the incident is related by Mrs Patricia Allin, to whom I owe the reference to the Jewish records, in 'Medieval Southampton and its Jews', *Trans. Jewish Historical Society*, 23 (1970–1).
19 P.R.O. E372/138.
20 P.R.O. E372/90, m. 12.
21 *Cal.Inq.Misc. 1219–1307*, p. 162; *Cal.P.R. 1258–66*, p. 104.
22 P.R.O. E372/105, m. 10.
23 *Cal.P.R. 1281–92*, p. 229.
24 C. E. Britton, *A Meteorological Chronology to A.D. 1450*, p. 130.
25 P.R.O. E101/5/2, 12. For a transcript of the building account, see R. C. Anderson, 'English galleys in 1295', *The Mariner's Mirror*, 14 (1928), pp. 220–41. Anderson describes the completed Southampton galley as a 'clinker-built vessel with a keel comprising two pieces, with two stems and with frames composed of rungs and futtocks. . . . She had a single mast, yard and sail, and apparently only 60 oars' (Ibid., p. 235). But the same vessel is described in 1312 as a 'good and beautiful galley of six score oars'; money was still owing on her by the crown in 1327 (*Cal.C.R. 1302–13*, p. 477; *Cal. Memoranda R. 1326–7*, p. 357). For a general discussion of the medieval English galley, see R. C. Anderson, *Oared Fighting Ships*, pp. 42–51.
26 Sylvia Thrupp, *The Merchant Class of Medieval London*, pp. 191–206.
27 For a recent discussion of the teaching of the Church on such matters, see J. Gilchrist, *The Church and Economic Activity in the Middle Ages*, pp. 53–70.
28 Bodleian, Queen's College MS. 1071; P.R.O. E326/9331.
29 *Cal.C.R. 1279–88*, p. 504. For the will of Walter le Fleming, see Bodleian, Queen's College MS. 1071.
30 Adam and Juliana le Mercer had acquired their house on English Street, parish of St Lawrence, in 1297. They sold it in 1320, retaining a life interest in the shop on the street frontage (Win.Coll.Mun. 17842, 17843, 17846). Robert le Mercer was active in the wool trade already by 1277. His purchase of land at South Stoneham in 1291 need not have been his first (*Cal. Chancery R., Various, 1277–1326*, p. 2; *Cal.C.R. 1288–96*, p. 245).
31 *Cal.C.R. 1346–9*, p. 258. In 1337, Roger Norman's demesne lands included extensive properties in Hampshire, Wiltshire, Gloucestershire, Essex and Suffolk (*Cal.Ch.R. 1327–41*, p. 389).
32 An order for Blancbuilly's arrest was made on 5 May 1236 (*Cal.C.R. 1234–7*, p. 353). His confiscated lands were granted to Richard, earl of Cornwall, on 6 May 1242 (Ibid., *1237–42*, p. 425). They were in Walter le Fleming's custody in 1254 (Ibid., *1253–4*, p. 122).
33 *Cal.C.R. 1264–8*, p. 462; J. M. Rigg (ed.), *Calendar of the Plea Rolls of the Exchequer of the Jews*, i:167. The original Bulehuse debts may have dated back as far as the reign of King John (Patricia Allin, 'Medieval Southampton and its Jews', *Trans. Jewish Historical Society*, 23 (1970–1).
34 St Denys Cart. 198–206; also P.R.O. E326/6669, 9151 and 9166, and E327/157. For another sale 'through great necessity', dated 1244, see E326/4492.
35 For a useful discussion of charity and the relief of the poor, see Brian Tierney, *Medieval Poor Law. A sketch of canonical theory and its application in England*, passim.
36 For the situation of Walter le Fleming's house in relation to the friary, see P.R.O. E327/328; for details of early benefactions, *Cat.Anc. Deeds*, iii:D121, and God's House Deeds 760. An early register, now lost, is the sole source for many details of the subsequent history of the house. It was seen and transcribed in the eighteenth century by Dr John Speed, *History of Southampton*, pp. 133–6.
37 Demolition must have occurred before 1239 (A. G. Little (ed.), *Fratris Thomae, vulgo dicti de Eccleston, tractatus De adventu fratrum minorum in Angliam*, p. 79; also Rosalind Brooke, *Early Franciscan Government, Elias to Bonaventure*, p. 188).
38 P.R.O. E372/86 (m. 13), 97 (m. 15); also *Cal. Liberate R. 1240–5*, pp. 133, 222; *Cal.C.R. 1247–51*, p. 167, and ibid., *1251–3*, p. 295.
39 *Cal.C.R. 1268–72*, p. 12.
40 J. Speed, *History of Southampton*, pp. 133–4; also C. T. Martin (ed.), *Registrum epistolarum fratris Johannis Peckham, archiepiscopi Cantuariensis*, i:255–6; and Alwyn Ruddock, 'The Greyfriars in

Southampton', *Proc. Hampshire Field Club*, 16 (1944–7), p. 139.

41 P.R.O. E36/115. For a discussion of friary buildings, see A. R. Martin, *Franciscan Architecture in England*, in particular pp. 10–40. Excavations on the site of the friary have recently uncovered a part of what may have been the church (*Southampton Excavations*, forthcoming).

42 P.R.O. E210/4644, and *Cal.C.R. 1339–41*, p. 254.

43 *Cal.C.R. 1296–1302*, p. 455.

44 *Cal.P.R. 1413–16*, p. 173.

45 There are examples of such at Bridgnorth, Bristol, Chichester, Coventry, Lichfield, Lincoln, London, Richmond, Carmarthen, Newcastle, Oxford, Scarborough and Exeter (A. R. Martin, *Franciscan Architecture in England*, p. 39). Sections of the Exeter conduits were seen and recorded by Lady Fox in 1950. The Southampton conduit is known to have been fitted with lead pipes, and at Exeter, a lead pipe, three inches in diameter, was found to be set at the base of the vaulted masonry channel of the cathedral conduit, first constructed in the mid-fourteenth century (Aileen Fox, 'The underground conduits in Exeter, exposed during reconstruction in 1950', *Trans. Devonshire Association*, 83 (1951), pp. 172–8).

46 *Cal.P.R. 1281–92*, p. 365, *1327–30*, p. 12; P.R.O. C143/190/2; J. Speed, *History of Southampton*, p. 134; and S.C.R.O. SC4/2/238.

47 F. J. Baigent (ed.), *The registers of John de Sandale and Rigaud de Asserio, bishops of Winchester* (*A.D. 1316–1323*), p. 85.

48 Bodleian, Queen's College MS. 1071.

49 Davies, pp. 445, 447. Several skeletons were disturbed on the site of the excavation, in 1966, of foundations for the new Telephone Manager's Office.

50 *Cal.Pap.Reg.*, *Papal Letters*, vii:409.

51 *Cal.C.R. 1374–7*, p. 137, and *Cal.P.R. 1381–5*, p. 121.

52 Bodleian, Queen's College MS. 1083 (Peverel), 1091 (Barbflete); P.R.O. E326/8581 (Whitehead), 11798 (Thomas); S.C.R.O. D/LY/23/3 (Moundenard); and *Black Book*, ii:98–9 (Soper).

Chapter seven

The trading staples: wine and wool

When the burgesses claimed in 1306 that the Gascon wine trade was the livelihood of their town, they may not have been presenting the whole of the picture, but it was a large part of it nevertheless.[1] Without appreciable industries of its own, and with competing market centres at Winchester, to the north, and Salisbury, to the west, Southampton existed on its overseas trade, its prosperity depending directly on the activity of its port. Beyond doubt, the burgesses themselves were fully aware of what they owed to the continued good will of foreign merchants. There were disputes, to be sure, between them. There was trouble with the Bordeaux merchants in 1264, with the men of Flanders in 1265 and 1274–6, with the Normans in 1293, and with the Spaniards in 1294.[2] But the cause of these disagreements frequently lay outside Southampton itself, and there is much to show that the burgesses shared the concern of the king to prevent a breach, or to heal it, wherever it might threaten their trade. In 1263 they had been admonished by the king not to burden the merchants of Spain, 'who used to come with ships and merchandise to Southampton, to the profit of that town and those parts', with exactions 'beyond the due and ancient customs' of the borough.[3] But the following year it was they themselves who resisted the arrest of the goods of certain alien merchants dwelling in their midst, and the favour they were prepared to show the Italian trading community in the fifteenth century would become, for its time, notorious.[4]

The mutually profitable exchanges of which such trade was made led naturally to close personal contacts between native and alien merchants. The daughter and heir of Bernard le Moigne married an Italian, a merchant of Lucca, to whom she brought considerable properties on the east side of Bull Street, directly opposite Bull Hall and bounded on the north by 'Beneyteslane' (now Vyse Lane).[5] And it was in the houses of many of the leading contemporary burgesses that the aliens commonly were lodged. Petronilla la Fleming, in her widowhood, maintained lodgings for foreign merchants in the great houses of her father, Ralph Isembard, and her father-in-law, Walter le Fleming. It was here that the Spanish merchants were directed in 1263, and here again that the merchants of Bruges were dwelling in 1268–9, quit of murage by decree, and protected against distraint of their goods for debts not incurred by themselves.[6] In such direct associations as these, an ambitious burgess might expect to make his fortune. Nicholas Barbflete, who died in 1295 a very wealthy man, was host to merchants of Spain in 1267.[7] For his services, he would have expected a fair cut on their trade. We know what the burgesses of Ipswich demanded; it cannot have been much different in Southampton:[8]

> No one in the said town [Ipswich], unless he is a burgess denizen of the town and a peer and commoner, shall be the host of foreign merchants who come to the said town by water with their merchandise to sell there, and such hosts shall be advisers to their merchants how and to whom to sell their merchandise. And the host ought to have the fourth part, and not more, of such merchandise, according to the price at which the merchandise is sold, and the three other parts shall be sold to the other good people of the town. And if the hosts themselves sell the goods of their merchants by their own hand, then they are to be held answerable to their merchants for the amount for which the merchandise was sold. And even if the said merchants sell their goods privately, without the advice of their hosts, nevertheless their hosts shall have their fourth part of the said merchandise, just as much as if they had been the advisers and sellers.

Nevertheless, few Southampton burgesses of the thirteenth century were content to remain only at the receiving end of trade. In conditions approaching a boom, it paid them handsomely to go out and look for trade themselves. Walter le Fleming, we know, died the owner of two valuable seafaring vessels, a new cog called *La Pauline* and a 'great cog', which he neglected to name in his will.[9] Something, too, may be discovered of the movements of his ships. In 1224, for example, Walter obtained a safe-conduct to send his ship *La Heitee* to La Rochelle, laden with merchandise of his own to exchange for the wine, salt and other produce of Poitou.[10] It may never have reached its destination, for La Rochelle was besieged by Louis VIII on 15 July 1224, and fell on 3 August that same year. However, in September 1229 it was *La Heitee* again which was pressed into service for the king, probably for a cargo to Gascony, and six years later the same ship was making a trading voyage for Walter himself, licensed to take his merchandise 'to parts beyond seas throughout the king's power', presumably once more to Gascony.[11] The licence could well have been a reward for a service just completed. A ship of Walter's, perhaps *La Heitee*, had arrived in Southampton in February 1235, laden with a valuable cargo of the fine wines of Anjou. On the command of the king, it was brought with all possible speed to London, to replenish the royal cellars before the end of the following month.[12] In 1242 another ship, *La Jonette*, was granted a safe-conduct for a single trip 'beyond seas' to trade.[13] And the next year, when Walter, as bailiff of Southampton, was at Portsmouth on his way to London to render account of his office at the Exchequer, he was turned back, again at the request of the king, to prepare one of his ships, a cog, to carry the royal treasure to Gascony.[14] It was probably the same vessel that returned to Southampton in January 1244 with a cargo of ninety-eight tuns of the king's wines. Of these, eighteen were to be off-loaded at Southampton, to replenish the king's cellars below the castle; the remainder was shipped on to London.[15] In 1252, one of Walter's ships was carrying a cargo of Anjou wines, and the following year the king requisitioned his best ship to take William of Bitton, bishop of Bath and Wells, on the royal business to Spain.[16] Some four years later, one of his ships, sailing off the coast of Poitou, broke the truce between England and France by attacking a ship of Bernard Papun, merchant of La Rochelle. The king, who was anxious to conclude a formal peace with France, acted quickly to obtain compensation for the outrage. Walter, convicted of receiving some of the stolen wine, was summoned in February 1257 to answer for it before the king. On 16 April he agreed to a composition payment of three hundred marks in silver, together with the expenses of the collector. He was an old man now, and death was fast approaching. He would have been little inclined to argue the merits of the case with the king to whom, in so many other respects, he already owed so much.[17]

When one of Walter le Fleming's ships is given a description, it is usually called a 'cog'. In his day, the cog was a vessel frequently seen in northern waters and well adapted to the long hauls of the Anglo-Gascon trade. It was a sturdily-built craft, high-sided and rounded at stem and stern; it was commonly very broad for its length. In the fourteenth century, the cog would be developed as a ship-of-war, to be enlarged and equipped in keeping with that role. But for Walter and his contemporaries, it remained strictly a carrier, little ornamented and seldom of great size.[18] The cog which returned from Gascony in 1244 with a cargo of ninety-eight tuns of wine was probably of about the average size for its period. But the great cog that Walter bequeathed to his son, Henry, might very well have been somewhat larger, in keeping with the development both of the type of ship and of the trade. Certainly, by 1326, a list of shipping at Southampton, some of it locally owned, suggests an all-round increase in burden. Tonnage was measured in tons burden, calculated on the standard wine-cask of approximately 250 gallons, the *tun* of the Anglo-Gascon trade.[19] This, for example, was the measure used in 1324 to determine the desirable crewing of ships taken in the royal service to Gascony. A ship of 240 tons would have a crew of 60 mariners; of 200 tons, 50; of 180 or 160 tons, 40; of 140 tons, 35; of 120 tons, 28; of 100 tons, 26; of 80 tons, 24; and of 60 tons, 21.[20] Two years later, on Whit Sunday 1326, Hugh Sampson and Henry Forst, acting on the instructions of the king, arrested the wine fleet in the port. Of the ships they listed, *La Gracedieu* was the largest at 180 tons; it was captained by William atte Hurne and had a crew of 48 mariners. Richard Kempe's *La Cogge Johan*, at 160 tons, had a crew of 47; Roger le Smyth's *La Trinite* and Edward le Palmer's *La Nicholas*, each of 150 tons, had crews of 44 and 39 mariners respectively; John Selde's *La Godyere*, at 120 tons, was crewed by 32; William atte Burgh's *La Seintemaricogge*, at 60 tons, by 22 mariners only.[21]

The trade which, early in the fourteenth century, enabled Southampton to put to sea a small fleet of its own, was founded on the balance of two primary products, the wool of England and the wine of western France. It is only for the seventies of the thirteenth century that it becomes possible to obtain some idea of the bulk of wool exports through the borough, and detailed figures do not become available for some years after that. But the merchandise that Walter le Fleming took to La Rochelle in 1224 undoubtedly included some wool, for wool had been the most valuable export of the nation for centuries already, and it was wool as well as wine that was the making of the fortunes of many of Walter's contemporaries and immediate successors.

Even before the imposition of the new Wool Custom in 1275 and the beginning of more systematic accounts, the issue of royal licences to export wool had begun to place on record the names of the principal exporters. For the most part, these exporters were aliens, usually Italians. But they included denizens amongst them, and at Southampton these were just the men we might have expected in that role. In July 1272, Peter de Lyon and Henry le Fleming both obtained licences to ship wool anywhere but Flanders. Later that same year, in November, it was the turn of Geoffrey de la Prise and Robert Bonhait, Henry le Fleming's brother-in-law, exporting between them no fewer than a hundred sacks.[22] The dispute with Flanders had been the reason for the issue of these licences, and they multiplied as the quarrel persisted. Through the length of 1273, the leading Southampton burgesses were obtaining the licences they needed, always excluding Flanders as the destination for their wool. Forty sacks were authorized in the names of Geoffrey de la Prise and Peter de Lyon; twenty in those of Thomas of Andover, Richard le English, Bernard le Moigne and William de Beaubek. Henry le Long and Walter le Horder, Stephen Dyset and Robert le Mercer, joined as partners in exporting twenty the pair. And a licence for the export of the unusually large total of two hundred sacks was obtained jointly by Bernard of Hampton and John le Long, perhaps acting as agents for others.[23] In the general licences of 1277, Southampton features as an important point of departure for considerable quantities of shorn wool and woolfells (sheepskins with the wool attached), handled by local as well as by alien merchants. Of the former, there were representatives from Winchester and Salisbury, Newport (Isle of Wight), Andover, Newbury and Bristol; of the latter, merchants from Lucca and Florence, from Rouen, Amiens and Malines, the Italians still dominating the trade. Robert le Mercer and Adam le Horder, merchants of Southampton, were granted export permits for thirty and fifty sacks of wool respectively.[24] A single sack, it should be remembered, would have held the clip of some 250 sheep. It was a commodity such as only the very rich might handle.

The Wool Custom of 1275, which became known as the *Ancient Custom*, was rated at half a mark (6*s*. 8*d*.) per sack. It was assessed and accounted for locally, the record being entered up in summary form each year in the Enrolled Customs Accounts of the Exchequer. The individual, or *particular*, accounts, compiled at the port of exit, have occasionally survived among the public records. They give, for Southampton as for many other ports, a patchy but useful impression of the nature of the local trade. At first, it is evident, the imposition of the new tax created confusion in the ports. At Southampton, Adam de Wynton, then keeper of the town, showed excessive zeal in distraining the men of the borough for alleged trespasses against the terms of the custom. On 26 January 1276 he had to be ordered to desist.[25] There was at least one other instance, in 1297, of uncertainty in the handling of the tax.[26] But the surviving particular account of 1287–8 is already very explicit. It lists the ships that left the port with cargoes of wool during the Exchequer year Michaelmas 1287 to Michaelmas 1288. One was a ship of William le English, and most carried the wool of several merchants, combining to make up a cargo. Robert le Mercer, with thirty-four sacks in one ship and six in another, was among the more notable of the exporters. In total, custom received over the year amounted to £696. 7*s.* 7¾*d.*[27]

Some complication of the accounts followed the imposition, in 1303, of the *New* (or *Petty*) *Custom*, directed specifically at aliens. It added 3*s.* 4*d.* to the 6*s.* 8*d.* already paid by all exporters on each sack to leave the country. But the distinction between the two levies is often made plain enough in the heading of the account, and it was as collectors of the *Ancient Customs* that Henry de Lym and John of Shirley submitted their account for the months between 14 December 1307 and 27 October 1308. The work, clearly, was no sinecure. Ships were loaded, sometimes two or three in a day, in every month of their office. Many carried a mixed cargo of shorn wool, woolfells and hides. And each commodity had to be listed separately, with the duty charged, in the name of the merchant who handled it. Among those prominent in the export trade, Robert le Mercer was still, quite obviously, a dominant figure, although new names had begun to make an appearance. Henry de Lym, the collector, was himself a major exporter; he would become one of the most notable burgesses of his generation. And he was joined by others: Robert Norman, Robert le Horder, John le English, and the Forsts, Walter and John, members of families that had made, or would yet make, their impression on the story of the borough.[28]

In terms simply of personal fortunes, the importance of the wool trade to Southampton is obvious enough. Within the next century, as wool exports declined, the cloth trade increased in compensation. But more characteristic of the thirteenth-century town, the determinant of its basic commercial allegiance, was the traffic in the wines of Bordeaux. Wine, as an import, was at least as old as its equivalent export, wool. Yet the wines that had been favoured in the eleventh- and twelfth-century kingdom were not those generally in demand a century later. And Southampton profited by the change. Of course, the alteration of tastes was not immediate, nor was it ever complete. But the loss of Normandy and then of Anjou had laid extra charges on the wines of Burgundy, the Seine basin and the Loire. And Bordeaux, at the head of the surviving royal dominions in the south, rapidly became what Rouen once had been, the capital of the English wine interest. In 1224 the fall of La Rochelle, its last considerable rival, accelerated the expansion of Bordeaux. Encouraged by the special trading incentives offered by the English crown, the growth of the city was immediate and phenomenal.[29] Southampton, sharing the Gascon trade with Bristol, Sandwich, Hull and London, participated in the boom. Its own growth accompanied that of its great trading associate, Bordeaux, differing from it only in proportion.

Inevitably, a great part of the activity of the wine trade proceeded from the personal interest of the king himself. In northern Europe generally, French wine might rarely be drunk in quantity outside the ranks of a comparatively restricted class. It remained throughout the Middle Ages, very much as it does today, an occasional luxury item, beyond the budget of even the better-paid artisan.[30] But for the king, for the aristocracy, and for the greater merchants, wine had become something of a necessity. Year after year, the new vintage was eagerly awaited. Year after year, supplies were exhausted by the summer, some weeks before the fresh wines could be expected to arrive. Very often, the king would act as his own importer, but he was accustomed also to take much of his wine in the form of a levy in kind. Before its conversion to a money payment, the so-called 'ancient prise' of wine required the setting aside for the king of two tuns from every cargo of twenty tuns or more, or one from a cargo of more than ten tuns and less than twenty. Consequently, when the king sited his houses on the shore at Southampton, his purpose was only incidentally defensive. It was there that his quay and his cellars must be placed, and there that he would build his castle to defend them. Significantly, when the king's houses in Southampton, with all their appurtenances, were delivered to Robert de le Estre in 1269, he received them not in a military capacity but as 'taker of the king's wines in England'. He was to store the royal wine there, and would be expected to ensure that the king, at least, should never run short of supplies.[31]

It cannot always have been an easy task. A vintage might be poor, or storms might scatter the wine fleet, spring the casks and spoil the wine. When the king heard of the arrival of Walter le Fleming's cargo of fine Anjou wines at Southampton in February 1235, he ordered it in haste to London. Five years before, in January 1230, he had instructed Walter le Fleming and Benedict Ace to set aside some of the best of the recently-arrived Gascon wine for his use. In August 1231, when stocks everywhere might have been expected to be low, he required an immediate pause to all sales of wine, whether at Southampton or elsewhere. Whatever remained was to be sent with all speed after the king's army to Wales, perhaps to restore the sagging spirits of the host lingering at Painscastle in the fiasco of the Elfael campaign.[32]

Regular entries in the Pipe Rolls, recording the transactions of the king's agents in every part of the realm, give some idea of the continuous royal concern in the trade. In 1224–5, for example, the young king's officials were despatching wine from Southampton to Portsmouth, and to the castles at Corfe and at Portchester. The following year they hired three extra cellars in the town, the property of leading burgesses, to store the surplus of the king's wines, or to house it while the king's own quay and cellars were repaired. In 1229–30, wine was sent to Windsor and to Kennington. And there was a constant traffic of wines to Winchester and to Clarendon, near Salisbury, or to the many religious houses enjoying the favour of the king.[33] It is, perhaps, a fair measure of the importance which the king and his advisers set on the trade, that Peter des Rivaux should have been granted, among his many offices, the custody of the royal houses at Southampton and the prise of wine in the port.[34] And it may well have been on Peter des Rivaux's direction that Benedict Ace, for so long the leading figure in the town, assumed principal responsibility for the local handling of the king's wines, an office he continued to hold for many years and which he was still performing in November 1248, not long before the mayoral crisis of the following year.[35] Certainly, the king himself preserved his personal interest in the appointments to this office in Southampton. On 4 February 1264 he wrote to Roger le Fleming, requiring him not to assume the post. John de Swineford, taker of the king's wines, had assigned the local charge to Roger, but 'we do not wish at present that you should enter this office, because we have substituted John le Blund in your place until we decide otherwise'.[36] Mute evidence of the scale of this early royal investment in the town is the massive surviving castle vault, sited below the west curtain wall, where it would have fronted directly on to the king's private quay. Lying parallel to the line of the wall, it is some 55 feet in length, tunnel-vaulted and lit by a single round-headed window to the south of the quayside door (Plate 9). With an equivalent chamber, not yet cleared, immediately to the south of the adjoining castle watergate, it made formidable provision for storage, dating back, on the evidence of preserved vaulting corbels, to *c.* 1180.

The movements of Walter le Fleming's ships establish at least a measure of direct burgess participation in the wine trade. Southampton ships, certainly, took part in the carrying of the wine; Southampton cellars housed it when it arrived. Nevertheless, when good trading figures first became available, early in the fourteenth century, it was alien importers who dominated the trade, leaving comparatively little to the native merchant. Somewhere in between stood men of the calibre of John of London, burgess of Southampton and citizen of Bordeaux. Formerly a servant of the king in Gascony, he was rewarded in 1299 with a free burgess-ship of Southampton, subsequently extended in 1303 to include his wife and his children.[37] He would have used his privileges to secure better terms for himself as an importer. Probably in that capacity, he was hiring a 'great' cellar from God's House Hospital in 1304–6.[38] As a wealthy man with connections in the south and with the ships he needed to maintain it, his position in the wine trade was secure. But, like others of his generation, his interests were by no means confined to it. As deputy to the king's chief butler, he would have handled the royal wines as well as his own. In addition, his holding of the cocket seal before November 1311 suggests an interest in wool and in woolfells, and we know for certain that he traded in wax.[39]

The circumstances of the Southampton wine trade, and in particular its later vicissitudes, have been very fully discussed elsewhere.[40] Whether directly, through the trade itself, or indirectly, as a product of the services it required, wine brought wealth to the town, with an independence and an initiative born of the experience of international trade. The contemporary records of the borough reflect something of this invigorating internationalism. At some time in the fourteenth century, a copy of the antique Rolls of Oleron (*The Charter of Oleron of the Judgements of the Sea*) was transcribed into the 'Oak Book' of the town. It echoes earlier texts, and the fundamentals of the decisions recorded in the rolls would certainly have been known in the borough in the thirteenth century, or possibly even the late twelfth. Essentially a document of the wine trade, although it came to assume the force of a general law of the sea, the Rolls of Oleron have much to tell us of the circumstances of the rich traffic to Bordeaux. They outline the responsibilities of masters and shippers, protect the rights of the crew, and make exacting provision for the apportionment of losses, where sustained. At Southampton, the decisions concerning unloading would have been of particular interest to the borough courts. Few medieval ports were adequately equipped with quays. Bordeaux itself never had deep-water wharves, and at Southampton the improvement of the port facilities, including the provision of cranes, proceeded still in the fifteenth century, never matching the requirements of the shipping. For the most part, unloading remained by block and tackle into lighters lying alongside. A master needed to be alert to the risks, whilst the borough courts themselves must have welcomed an unequivocal definition of responsibility:[41]

> A master of a ship comes in safety to her port of discharge; he ought to show the merchants the ropes with which he will hoist, and if he sees that there is something to repair, the master is bound to repair them, for if a tun is lost by fault of the hoisting tackle or ropes, the master is bound to make compensation, he and his mariners; and the master ought to share as much as he receives for the hoisting, and the hoisting money ought to be set to restore the damage in the first place, and the residue ought to be shared amongst them. But if the ropes break without their having shown them to the merchants, they will be bound to make good all the damage. But if the merchants say that the ropes are fair and good, and they break, each ought to share the loss, that is to say, the merchants to whom the wine belongs alone. And this is the judgement in this case.

Notes

1 *Rot.Parlm.*, 1:193.
2 *Cal.P.R. 1258–66*, p. 335; *Cal.C.R. 1264–8*, p. 126, *1272–9*, pp. 124–5, 307, *1288–96*, pp. 300–1, 370–1, 408–9.
3 *Cal.P.R. 1258–66*, p. 258.
4 Ibid., p. 388, and Alwyn Ruddock, *Italian Merchants and Shipping*, pp. 156–61 and passim.
5 P.R.O. E210/5745.
6 *Cal.P.R. 1258–66*, p. 258, *1266–72*, pp. 242, 325.
7 Ibid., *1266–72*, p. 169.
8 Mary Bateson (ed.), *Borough Customs*, Selden Society, 21 (for 1906), p. 181.
9 Bodleian, Queen's College MS. 1071.
10 *Cal.P.R. 1216–25*, p. 452.
11 *Cal.C.R. 1227–31*, p. 252, and *Cal.P.R. 1232–47*, p. 105.
12 *Cal.C.R. 1234–7*, pp. 53, 64.
13 *Cal.P.R. 1232–47*, p. 301.
14 *Cal.C.R. 1242–7*, p. 102, and *Cal. Liberate R. 1240–5*, p. 178.
15 *Cal.C.R. 1242–7*, pp. 150–1.
16 Ibid., *1251–3*, p. 355.
17 *Cal.C.R. 1256–9*, pp. 123, 138; *Cal.P.R. 1247–58*, pp. 591–2. One of the more recent demonstrations of the king's favour to Walter had been the grant, in 1251, of freedom from distraint throughout the king's dominions, whether in England or in Gascony, for debts of which he was neither chief debtor nor surety (*Cal.P.R. 1247–58*, pp. 86, 103).
18 L. G. Carr Laughton, 'The cog', *The Mariner's Mirror*, 46 (1960), pp. 69–70; also F. W. Brooks, *The English Naval Forces, 1199–1272*, pp. 75–7. A cog features on the fourteenth-century common seal of Southampton.

19 Including the cask, the wine *tun* weighed approximately 2,240 lb. (1,016 kg.). For this, see F. C. Lane, 'Tonnages, medieval and modern', *Ec.H.R.*, 2nd series, 17 (1964–5), p. 218.
20 *Cal.P.R. 1321–4*, p. 417.
21 *Cal.C.R. 1323–7*, p. 611; *Cal. Memoranda R. 1326–7*, p. 130.
22 *Cal.P.R. 1266–72*, pp. 702, 713.
23 Ibid., *1272–81*, pp. 13, 15, 22–4, 35, 38.
24 *Cal. Chancery R., Various, 1277–1326*, pp. 2–10.
25 *Cal.C.R. 1272–9*, p. 266.
26 Ibid., *1296–1302*, p. 104.
27 P.R.O. E122/136/1.
28 P.R.O. E122/136/6.
29 E. M. Carus-Wilson, 'The effects of the acquisition and of the loss of Gascony on the English wine trade', *Bull.Inst.Hist.Res.*, 21 (1946–8), pp. 146–9; Yves Renouard, 'Le grand commerce des vins de Gascogne au moyen âge', *Revue Historique*, 221 (1959), pp. 271–9, and *Bordeaux sous les rois d'Angleterre*, pp. 58–60, 85–9.
30 The point is developed by Jan Craeybeckx, *Un grand commerce d'importation: les vins de France aux anciens Pays-Bas*, pp. 40–3. At Southampton, the fourteenth-century domestic accounts of God's House demonstrate very clearly the luxury quality of the drink, even in a major wine-importing centre. Wine was bought for the hospital when the warden visited the house, but even then never in great quantity. Usually, home-brewed ale was the familiar drink of the inmates, to be supplemented in the summer by stale wine on occasion, or more rarely cheap wine from Spain (Richard Harris, 'God's House, Southampton, in the reign of Edward III', Southampton M.A. dissertation, 1970, pp. 76–7).
31 *Cal.C.R. 1268–72*, p. 16.
32 Ibid. *1227–31*, pp. 285, 596.
33 P.R.O. E372/69, 70, 74 and passim.
34 *Cal.Ch.R. 1226–57*, p. 163.
35 *Cal. Liberate R. 1245–51*, p. 209.
36 *Cal.C.R. 1261–4*, p. 375.
37 *Cal.P.R. 1292–1301*, pp. 398–9, *1301–7*, p. 102.
38 *R.C.H.M.*, 6th report, p. 560.
39 *Cal.P.R. 1307–13*, p. 190; *Cal.C.R. 1307–13*, p. 386; P.R.O. E122/197/5.
40 Margery James, 'The non-sweet wine trade of England during the fourteenth and fifteenth centuries', Oxford D.Phil., 1952, in particular pp. 112–18, and 'The fluctuations of the Anglo-Gascon wine trade during the fourteenth century', *Ec.H.R.*, 2nd series, 4 (1951), pp. 170–96. In an earlier work, Miss James had made a specialized study of the fifteenth-century trade of the port, 'The Gascon wine trade of Southampton during the reigns of Henry VI and Edward IV', Oxford B.Lit., 1948. A selection of her writings, edited by Elspeth M. Veale, has recently been published under the title *Studies in the Medieval Wine Trade*, Oxford, 1971. It includes chapters from her Oxford doctoral thesis, not otherwise readily available. For another discussion of the Gascon trade, making use of Dr James's work, see Yves Renouard's 'Le grand commerce des vins de Gascogne au moyen âge', *Revue Historique*, 221 (1959), pp. 261–304.
41 A good text of the rolls is given in full in the *Oak Book*, ii:54–99.

Chapter eight

The port as entrepôt

The consolidation of the trading position of a medieval borough depended, in great part, on the construction of a network of commercial alliances. Local tariff barriers could be high, and each borough, as a matter of course, exerted itself to secure the maximum exemption from the more onerous of the tolls. In the case of Southampton, a trading centre and entrepôt with little of its own produce to offer, such mutual agreements and exemptions were especially important. They secured the outlets for its wine, smoothed the way for the collection of raw wool and cloth for export, and opened up buying and selling markets all over the country for the many miscellaneous goods which accompanied, whether as imports or exports, the two major trading commodities of the borough. It has been shown already that royal guarantees of exemption from tolls preceded even the grant of effective self-government to the borough. In the thirteenth century, while further privileges were sought, and obtained, from the king, an important series of inter-borough negotiations opened the way to local free trade, to be jealously guarded and fought over as the balance of advantage shifted from one party to another.

General concessions of exemption, although granted freely by the king, were not always recognized without dispute. At Southampton, such details as survive of agreements negotiated between the boroughs have usually resulted from rivalries resolved in a settlement acceptable to both parties. But the town records preserve, in addition, a document of unusual interest. It is a list, incomplete but still very full, of the boroughs that could claim, like Southampton, a degree of exemption from local taxes and tolls. The list, as Professor Studer suggested many years ago, was probably prepared to assist the borough officials to decide whether or not a trader, visiting the town, could rightfully claim exemption from toll by virtue of his status as a burgess elsewhere. It includes no fewer than forty major towns of the realm, extending north as far as Newcastle upon Tyne, west to Shrewsbury and Bristol, and east to Canterbury, Ipswich and Yarmouth. A contemporary memorandum of the towns for which enquiries would still have to be made as to the precise circumstances of exemption, included, among others, Oxford, Andover, Basingstoke and Guildford, Devizes, Weymouth, Dartmouth and Plymouth.[1] Although not completed until the fourteenth century, the list was probably begun a century earlier, during the reign of Henry

III. It demonstrates effectively the wide spread of traffic, much of it by road, over the greater part of the realm, and it includes a record of the Marlborough charter of 20 June 1204, itself the cause of a long-lasting dispute, settled on the intervention of Henry III, 15 June 1239. The terms of the Marlborough settlement are worth repeating, for they would have held good for many less formally negotiated agreements:[2]

> Know ye that whereas a suit had been commenced in our court before us between our good men of Marlborough plaintiffs and our good men of Southampton defendants concerning the toll which the aforesaid men of Southampton took from our men of Marlborough contrary to their liberties which they had by the charter of our lord King John our father and by our own charter, as they alleged, at length by our licence it was thus agreed between them, that all the men of Marlborough who are of the merchant gild, and who are willing to swear to that effect, shall for ever be quit of all custom and all manner of toll in the town of Southampton and all its appurtenances, from which tolls our men of Southampton can acquit the men of Marlborough within their liberty, notwithstanding that the charter of the aforesaid men of Southampton is prior to the charter of the aforesaid men of Marlborough, and likewise the men of Southampton shall be quit of all custom and toll in the town of Marlborough.

A quarter of a century later, on 7 July 1265, a dispute with the burgesses of Winchester was similarly resolved. Murage and other tolls had been the cause of disagreement between the traders of the neighbouring boroughs. All such taxes were to be waived by both parties in the interest of mutually profitable trade.[3]

Needless to say, the conflicting interests and commercial rivalries which had led to the negotiation of each settlement were rarely fully resolved. In 1315 the men of Southampton were to be found complaining to the king that certain magnates of the realm and other lords holding property in the area had been extorting for their own profit 'divers customs and prests, which are due to the burgesses in aid of their farm from men staying within the liberty as well in lands as in waters, and which the burgesses and their ancestors had been accustomed to receive'.[4] No doubt, they would have been alluding, among others, to the bishop of Winchester, an old enemy with whom they were conducting a lawsuit at the time. The argument hinged on the right of the bishop's tenants to claim exemption from toll in the borough. It had begun with the confiscation in 1311/12 of an ox-hide and knife, the property of John le Coupere, of Farnham, a tenant of the bishop. Alleging attempted evasion of toll, the burgesses of Southampton argued that hitherto, time out of mind, they had been 'used to levy toll and stallage of all things bought in the same town for merchandise, as well from the men and tenants of the said bishop as from others'. But in 1316, some four years after the original alleged trespass, the jurors found against them. The bishop and his men, they maintained, had always been quit of toll on all their goods and merchandise in Southampton. Their exemptions, superior to the rights of the burgesses, should be upheld.[5] Already in 1290, the bailiffs of Southampton had been found at fault for wrongfully distraining, on alleged non-payment of tolls, the goods of the abbot of Netley, against the terms of his exemptions.[6] And within twenty years of the Winchester judgment, the burgesses again needed to be reminded of their obligations. They had recently appealed to the king for a relief on their fee farm to meet the heavy charges of maintenance on the roads and bridges in the vicinity, in particular the crossing at Redbridge.[7] Exemptions had deprived them of much of the revenue designed to meet these costs, and it may well have been a general rise in maintenance charges that persuaded the burgesses to enforce the antique gild regulations governing the purchase of goods by merchant strangers in their town. Swiftly, in 1334, the merchants of Winchester, Salisbury and elsewhere joined in a petition to Parliament, in defence of free trade in the borough. They obtained an order to restore it.[8]

The elements of toll exemption were straightforward. Public works in the borough, whether they took the form of wall-building, road and bridge repairs, or the maintenance of quays, were frequently financed, at least in part, by local tolls, the burden of which might be expected to fall principally on outsiders. As most boroughs had to meet the same, or similar, expenses, it was inevitable that the burgesses of each should seek, whether by mutual arrangement or by grant of the king, to be relieved of the multiple payment of dues. Richard I, as early as 1189, had confirmed the burgesses of Southampton in their exemption from 'toll and passage and pontage'. And, as wall-building and other programmes of public works everywhere got under way, they tried to extend their privileges, reasoning, no doubt, that the heavy charges they themselves were meeting at home warranted exemption elsewhere. Edward II, on 4 June 1317, added to a general confirmation of the liberties of the borough the further concession that the burgesses and their heirs 'for ever may be free from murage and pavage on their goods and merchandise throughout our whole realm'. On 4 April 1341, his son, Edward III, enlarged the right, freeing the burgesses from the toll known as 'quayage'.[9] Complementary to these exemptions, an important concession, granted many years before, had protected the goods of Southampton burgesses trading outside the boundaries of their liberty. It was a concession that had been granted already in 1251 as a special mark of favour to the ageing Walter le Fleming. And it was one of the chief inducements held out to the merchants of Bruges in 1269 to persuade them to set up as traders in the town.[10] Dated 14 July 1256, it read:[11]

> Know ye that we have granted and by this our charter have confirmed for us and our heirs to our burgesses of Southampton that they and their heirs for ever shall in all parts of our dominions and authority have this privilege, namely, that they or their goods wheresoever found within our jurisdiction, shall not be arrested for any debt for which they are not either sureties or principal debtors, unless perchance the debtors shall be

Plate 7 The Undercroft, a fourteenth-century basement shop on Simnel Street

Plate 8 The common seal of Southampton, *c.* 1250

Plate 9 Castle Vault, a late-twelfth-century wine store on the former Castle Quay

> of their body, and have wherewithal to satisfy their debts in whole or in part, and that the said burgesses shall fail to do justice to the creditors of the same debtors and that this be reasonably proved.

The trade so worth protecting had become wide-ranging indeed. It stretched from the Baltic in the north to the Mediterranean in the south, taking in Flanders, the western seaboard of France, Spain and Portugal. Not only did Southampton merchants have to accustom themselves to long journeys by sea; they had also to cultivate a variety of highly specialized skills. Some of these skills, of value in the trade to southern France, Portugal and Spain, are recalled in the much later sixteenth-century Bristol handbook, John Browne's *The Marchants Avizo.* Sound advice on the determination of quality, the product of centuries of experience, covers many of the principal commodities of this flourishing traffic to the south. In the case of pepper, mace, nutmeg and ginger, 'the largest and greatest are best'; for cloves, 'the longest and smallest stems are best'; and for cinnamon, 'the largest and thinnest rinde is best, and those which are of fayer and bright orenge colour, and which are quickest and pleasantest on the tong'. Of the dyes, cochineal is best when it is of the brightest grey or silver in colour, 'and that which doth cast the quickest & most orient red in the palme of your hand, after you haue rubbed and mingled it with a little spitle'. But woad is difficult to judge before it is brought to the proof in boiling, and 'men chuse it either by experience or good report of the Soyles where it groweth, or els of the fatnes of the ode [woad]'. Iron is best when 'smallest and thinnest drawen, and which hath least crackes though most flawes'. Oil may be judged by its sweetness, its clarity, and the purity of its colour, yellow or green. Of 'Portingale' soap, 'the whitest, hardest, dryest, and swetest is best, and which hath most of the blew vains & the colour cleer & faire'. Salt may be known by the brightness and whiteness of its grains. But of wines, 'it cannot be set downe by pen or words, the right knowledge of it, for it is perceiuable only by the taste and fauor. But the best sorts of wines generally are, when they doe tast pleasant and strong withall, and when they drinke cleane and quicke in the pallet of the mouth, and when they are cleere & white hued if they be white Wines, or of faire orient red, if they be red wines. But if they drinke weake, rough, foule, flat, inclining to egernesse, or long: they are not good.'[12]

John Browne was a Bristol merchant, and an Elizabethan. But the burgesses of Southampton, trading to those same regions in the thirteenth and fourteenth centuries, would have learnt many such skills long before. A cargo of exotic foodstuffs, arrested at Southampton in January 1255 for the king's personal use, included almonds and ginger, figs, raisins and dates, cinnamon, saffron and pepper, galingale and cumin.[13] The basic materials of victualling, wheat, corn and flour, barley, bacon and fish, were frequently shipped out of the port to provision the king's garrisons overseas. In 1297–8, for example, seven great ships were so loaded for Gascony. They included three vessels from Southampton, *La Cog St. Crucis, La Cog St. Marie* and *La Trinite,* with ships from Guernsey, Beaulieu, Lymington and Christchurch.[14] When Adam de Wynton, keeping the town for the king in 1274–5, accounted at the Exchequer for the customs he collected on goods passing through the town, his brief list included wheat, wine and wool, leather, cheese, alum and spices.[15] But he was intentionally vague, perhaps, on the less routine trading commodities, for a full record of these, had the clerks at the Exchequer required it, would undoubtedly have taxed his skills. Two centuries later, the appointment of garbler for the king in the ports of Sandwich and Southampton was granted to John Stokes, citizen and grocer of London. His brief included the selection of a wide range of products, spices, drugs and dyes: 'anise, cumin, worm seed, wax, alum, grains of paradise, ginger, cloves, mace, cinnamon, galingale, rhubarb, scammony, spikenard, senna, turpentine, dyers' grains, zedoary, almonds, rice, dates, euphorbium, stavesacre, cassia, fistula, nutmeg, long pepper, mastic, frankincense'.[16]

Many of these products, and a great deal more besides, were listed in a table of customs tariffs drawn up for the guidance of the appropriate officials at the turn of the thirteenth and fourteenth centuries. Southampton, now perhaps the major port on the south coast, had become the centre for the redistribution of a great variety of imported goods. They might leave the town either by road or by sea. Wine, for example, might follow either of these routes, as differing rates in the tariff certainly suggest, though there were few goods so unsuitable for transport by road as not to be listed in the preferential tariff negotiated with the citizens of Salisbury in 1329, and entered, immediately after the original list, in the 'Oak Book' of the town. By 1300, it is clear, the traffic through Southampton was active in many directions. Corn and livestock were brought in, usually for export. Imported victuals, a product of the trade to the south, included honey and almonds, walnuts, figs, raisins, rice, garlic and onions. Supplies of fish, fresh and salted, were drawn from both the north and the south: red and white herring, sardine, conger, cod, stockfish, mackerel, mullet, haddock, sturgeon, salmon, lamprey, porpoise and whale. Spices came with the wines: pepper and ginger, zedoary, cinnamon, galingale, mace, cubeb, cloves, saffron and cumin. And there were dyes, again from the south: woad, grain, brazil, alum and litmus. Baltic and other timber, tar and pitch, laths, Devon slate and plaster of Paris were shipped in to serve the needs of the local builders and shipwrights. There was cloth from Ireland and hides; flax, iron, leather, oil, wax and wool from Spain; ropes and canvas from Brittany; furs from the north. Tin and lead came from Cornwall and, to a lesser degree, from Derbyshire; coal from Northumberland and Durham; salt from La Rochelle and the Bay. A rate was recorded for armour, another for bowstaves, yet others for charcoal and quicksilver, copper and brass, silk, linen and coverlets, tallow, millstones, cooking utensils in copper and tin, and earthenware vessels, drinking-cups, bowls, plates and saucers.[17]

Customs accounts, much enriched in detail from just about this date, amply confirm the evidence of the 'Oak Book' tariffs. When Henry de Lym and John of Shirley collected the custom on general merchandise, the property of aliens entering and leaving the port in 1308–9, they listed bacon, mutton and beef, carpets, blankets and cloth among the principal exports, although the very much more valuable trade in wool and woolfells was, of course, accounted for separately. Imports included haddock, conger and herring, liquorice, leather, oil, tin, iron, wheat and barley, in addition to those more important commodities, woad and Spanish wool. Familiar re-exports were iron and fish-oil, salt and, rather surprisingly, coal.[18] A generation later, a summary account of the local customs, prepared by John Forst and Nicholas Sampson for the Exchequer year 1341–2, recorded wine and wool, leather and hides, woad, wax, barley, wheat, alum, madder, cloth, salt, herring, conger, hake and mackerel, tin, lead, iron, coal, plaster, slates and millstones.[19] That same year, wine stood out in another account as by far the most valuable of the imported products subsequently traded out of the town. It was followed in importance by woad and then by herring, with weld, leather, pitch, tar, oil, slates and other assorted commodities bringing up the rear.[20]

Little recalls the nature of this trade so vividly as the few details that have survived of unloading practice in the port. A schedule of lighterage charges, determined at a common assembly of the town on 26 January 1414, informs us that wine, oil, iron and fruit were commonly handled in the great casks known as 'tuns'. Wool was imported by the pack; woolfells and the skins of lamb and calf, by the bundle; soap and sugar, by the chest; tin and pewter vessels, by the barrel; and cloth, wax, woad, alum, anise, pepper, ginger, cumin, cotton, dyestuffs, almonds and dates, by the bale. Tin and lead were handled by the piece.[21] Porters, licensed by the borough authorities, gained a livelihood by transporting the goods from the lighters drawn up on the hards to the cellars and warehouses scattered through the town. Their tariff survives among the ancient gild ordinances of the borough, a splendidly revealing document in the commercial history of late-thirteenth-century Southampton:[22]

> It is provided that the porters of Southampton shall take 1½d for lodging a cask of wine in cellars upon the sea-shore, and this shore extends in English Street to the lane that was Walter le Fleming's [Broad Lane], and in French Street to the house where James le Weyte used to live [possibly at the west end of Broad Lane], and to the West Quay, as far as the cellars which belonged to Sampson de Puteo, the king's castle and the great house which belonged to Dame Claramunda, where she used to live [Ronceval]. Also for carrying a tun of wine on a drag or a hand-barrow beyond the shore aforesaid to the church of St Cross [Holy Rood] or the church of St Michael, 3d; and beyond those churches, wherever they carry a cask of wine to any other place in the town, 4d. Also for loading a cask of wine in a cart to carry to any part of the town, 3½d; and for putting a cask of wine on board ship, 3d, and into a boat, 2d; and for unloading and lodging that cask, 3½d; and for loading a cask of wine to be sent out of town, 3½d. Also to carry a large pack of wool from the warehouses (*sendes*) in St Lawrence parish to the sea, and put it in a boat, or on board ship, 2d. Likewise for a small pack of wool, 1½d, that is, for carriage, ½d, and for putting it on board (he shall) receive 1d. Likewise for carrying a last of

hides from the aforesaid warehouses to the sea and stowing it on board ship, 12d, that is, for carriage, 8d, and for stowage, 4d. Also for carrying four weys of cheese to the boat, 2d. Likewise for carrying salt and corn, and other things which are carried by hundred (weight), except sea coal, two shillings for carrying the hundred (weight) from the sea to the aforesaid warehouses. Likewise for lodging a pair of millstones bought on the sea shore, 2d, and for unloading and lodging a pair (of millstones), 6d, and for loading and putting a pair of millstones into a boat, 8d. The porters aforesaid shall do the business of the burgesses of Southampton before that of any stranger, in all points; and if they do not, and offend against the statutes aforesaid, they shall be imprisoned for a day and a night without bail, and shall not bear the office of porters for a year and a day.

Notes

1 *Oak Book*, i:ix, 6–21.
2 The settlement is quoted by A. Ballard and J. Tait (eds), *British Borough Charters, 1216–1307*, pp. 257–8; see also *Sign Manuals and Letters Patent*, i:44–5.
3 W. H. B. Bird (ed.), *The Black Book of Winchester*, p. 50.
4 *Cal.P.R. 1313–17*, pp. 308–9.
5 *Oak Book*, ii:46–53.
6 *Rot.Parlm.*, i:20.
7 P.R.O. SC8/73/3640.
8 *Rot.Parlm.*, ii:87.
9 *Charters*, i:10–13, 32–5.
10 *Cal.P.R. 1247–58*, p. 103, *1266–72*, p. 325.
11 *Charters*, i:8–9.
12 Patrick McGrath (ed.), *The Marchants Avizo by I(ohn) B(rowne), Marchant, 1589*, pp. 22–5.
13 *Cal.C.R. 1254–6*, p. 30.
14 P.R.O. E372/143, m. 9d.
15 P.R.O. E372/119, m. 6d.
16 Stokes's appointment was dated 17 May 1480 (*Cal.P.R. 1476–85*, p. 205).
17 *Oak Book*, ii:xvi–xxi, 2–17.
18 P.R.O. E122/136/8, published by N. S. B. Gras, *The Early English Customs System*, pp. 360–73.
19 P.R.O. E122/137/11.
20 P.R.O. E122/193/10, and N. S. B. Gras, op. cit., pp. 174–6.
21 *Black Book*, iii:172–7.
22 *Oak Book*, i:70–5. I have substituted the more acceptable forms 'James le Weyte', 'Sampson de Puteo', and the now common 'Dame Claramunda', for Professor Studer's 'Jack le Wyte', 'Sampson del Puytz', and 'Lady Cleremond'. Sampson de Puteo, of whom Professor Studer at the time could find no record, appears as witness to several mid-century charters, in two of which, dated 1241 and 1244, he is described as bailiff (*Cat.Anc. Deeds*, iii:D121, and P.R.O. E326/4492). In 1247 and 1251 he witnessed the sale of the Weyte tenement on English Street to John Horn, Nicholas and Cecily la Weyte being presumably relatives of the James le Weyte above (P.R.O. E326/9151 and 9166). The St Lawrence warehouses, mentioned in the ordinance, would have been sited on English Street.

Part III

1300-1400

Chronological table III

1300 Anglo-Scottish war

1303 Treaty of Paris: Gascony restored to England; imposition of the New Custom on alien traders

1307 Death of Edward I; accession of Edward II

1308–9 Exile and return of the king's favourite, Piers Gaveston

1310 Lords Ordainers appointed

1311 Scots ravage the north; Ordinances published

1312 Baronial rebellion; Gaveston executed

1314 Scottish victory at Bannockburn

1315–17 Years of famine and plague in northern Europe

1302 Southampton required to find ships for the king's war in Scotland (*Cal.C.R. 1296–1302*, p. 612, *1302–7*, p. 78; *Cal.P.R. 1301–7*, pp. 52–3, 75)

1303/4 Partition of West Hall between the heirs of Thomas le Halveknight (P.R.O. E327/163; God's House Deeds 476; St Denys Cart. 242; S.C.R.O. SC4/2/396)

1306 The burgesses of Southampton petition to be allowed to continue trading in wine to Gascony, despite the prohibition: it is the livelihood of their town (*Rot.Parlm.*, i : 193)

1307–8 Royal orders to the keeper of the castle at Southampton to fortify and safely guard it (*Cal.C.R. 1307–13*, pp. 29–30, 50)

1311 Southampton to supply three ships for the war in Scotland (*Cal.P.R. 1307–13*, pp. 352–3)

1312–16 Dispute with the bishop of Winchester concerning the tolls payable by his tenants (*Oak Book*, ii:46–53)

1315 Burgesses of Southampton complain that certain magnates, holding lands locally, have been evading tolls in their town (*Cal.P.R. 1313–17*, pp. 308–9)

1317 Charter of Edward II, granting freedom from murage and pavage throughout the kingdom (*Charters*, i:32–3)

	1319 The Venetian galley brawl (*Cal.C.R. 1318–23*, p. 696; *Cal. State Papers Venetian, 1202–1509*, p. 5; *Cal.P.R. 1321–4*, pp. 276, 368, *1324–7*, p. 195; Rymer, *Foedera*, ii:514)
	1320 The re-siting of Holy Rood Church is agreed (P.R.O. C143/140/19; *Cal.P.R. 1317–21*, p. 535)
	1321 The men of Winchelsea raid Southampton and burn shipping there (*Chronicles of Edward I and II*, i:298; *Rot.Parlm.*, ii:413; Rymer, *Foedera*, ii:456; *Cal.C.R. 1318–23*, pp. 486, 490; P.R.O. SC8/17/833)
1322 Thomas of Lancaster rebels, and is defeated at Boroughbridge	**1322** Southampton supplies two ships and eighty armed men for the war in Scotland (*Cal.C.R. 1318–23*, pp. 524, 530–1, 559)
	1322–6 Dispute concerning an assault on Genoese merchants visiting Southampton (*Cal.P.R. 1321–4*, pp. 250–1, 450, 453, *1324–7*, pp. 225, 315)
1323 Anglo-Scottish truce	
	1325 Troops muster at Southampton and Portsmouth for passage to Gascony (*Cal.P.R. 1324–7*, p. 141)
1326 Queen Isabella and Roger Mortimer invade England; capture of Edward II	**1326** Grant of a new toll of 1*d.* in £1 to complete the town wall and quay (*Cal. P.R. 1324–7*, p. 252)
1327 Edward II resigns the throne; accession of Edward III; murder of Edward II	**1327** The friars secure a licence to lay pipes for their conduit from Hill to the friary itself (P.R.O. C143/190/2; *Cal.P.R. 1327–30*, p. 12) Charter of Edward III: protection granted against actions in courts outside the town concerning property within it, freedom from quayage throughout the realm (*Charters*, i:18–19; *Cal.Ch.R. 1327–41*, p. 9)
1328 England and Scotland conclude the Treaty of Northampton	
1333 Anglo-Scottish war renewed	
	1334 The men of Winchester, Salisbury and elsewhere complain that they are being denied free trade at Southampton (*Rot.Parlm.*, ii:87)
1335 Edward III invades Scotland	**1336** Grant of a toll of 1*d.* in £1 to build a barbican (*Cal.P.R. 1334–8*, pp. 240–1)
1337 Edward III formally claims the throne of France	**1337** Edward orders warning beacons to be prepared on the hill tops near Southampton, in anticipation of a French attack (*Cal.C.R. 1337–9*, p. 179; Rymer, *Foedera*, ii:996)
1338 Edward lands in Flanders	**1338** Men of Southampton required (February) to provide ships and men for the king's intended expedition to

			France (Rymer, *Foedera*, ii:1015) Southampton raided (October) by a French and Genoese fleet; taken into the king's hands (*Les Chroniques de Sire Jean Froissart*, i:72–3; *Cal. Fine R.*, v:97, 102)
		1339	Edward III visits Southampton; he restores the government of the town to its elected officers, and orders the completion of the town wall (*Cal.P.R. 1338–40*, p. 237; *Cal. Fine R.*, v:124)
1340	Battle of Sluys: French defeated at sea; Anglo-French truce agreed at Espléchin		
		1341	The king orders an enquiry into the misappropriation of tolls and evasions of customs by Nicholas de Moundenard and others (*Cal.P.R. 1340–3*, pp. 312, 326, 441)
		1342	A French fleet threatens Southampton (Rymer, *Foedera*, ii:1210)
		1344	Grant of God's House Hospital to the Queen's College, Oxford (*Cal.P.R. 1343–5*, p. 215)
		1345	Troops, bound for Gascony, muster at Southampton (Rymer, *Foedera*, iii:44; *Cal.C.R. 1343–6*, p. 674)
1346	Battle of Crécy: French defeat	1346	French attack expected at Southampton (Rymer, *Foedera*, iii:78, 86)
1347	English capture Calais; Anglo-French truce	1347	St Mary Magdalene Hospital granted to St. Denys Priory (*Cal.P.R. 1345–8*, pp. 298–9)
1348	The Black Death reaches England	1348–9	The Black Death ravages Southampton (*Chronicon Henrici Knighton*, ii:61)
1351	Statute of Labourers: wages regulated	1351	Accumulated debts on the borough farm are cancelled; the farm is reduced, for an eight-year term, to £100 (*Cal.P.R. 1350–4*, p. 56; P.R.O. E372/196)
1355	Anglo-French war renewed, with Scotland as an ally of France; Scots defeated at Nesbit	1355	Invasion scare: French fleet setting sail (*Cal.C.R. 1354–60*, p. 214) Murage grant for ten years, to complete the town wall (*Cal.P.R. 1354–8*, p. 254; *Charters*, i:22–5; *Oak Book*, ii:118–21)
1356	Battle of Poitiers: French defeat	1356	Troops muster at Southampton for Normandy (*Robert of Avesbury*, p. 462)
1357	Anglo-French truce		
1359	Treaty of London rejected by French estates; Edward III invades France		
1360	Preliminary Peace of Brétigny confirmed at Calais	1360	Invasion scare: the king believes the French to be on their way (*Cal.C.R. 1360–4*, pp. 17, 97–8, 102) Inquisition and report on the defences

	(*Cal.Inq.Misc. 1348–77*, pp. 154–5) Winchester, Southampton and Portsmouth excused tax, 'for the poverty which they are undergoing in these days' (*Cal.C.R. 1360–4*, p. 90)
1362 English staple settled at Calais	
1364 John II of France dies in England; accession of Charles V	
1369 Anglo-French war begins, to be followed by successive English reverses	1369 Burgesses leaving the town, forbidden to do so by the king; a captain and keeper appointed; all townspeople are to contribute to the cost of the defences; the king pardons arrears on the farm to further the programme of wall-building (*Cal.C.R. 1369–74*, pp. 18–20; Rymer, *Foedera*, iii:866, 878; *Cal.P.R. 1367–70*, pp. 270, 304, 474; P.R.O. E372/216)
	1370 Order to array all fencible men in Southampton and its suburbs (*Cal.P.R. 1367–70*, p. 474)
1373 John of Gaunt invades France	1373 Invasion thought to be imminent; no one is to leave the town (*Cal.C.R. 1369–74*, pp. 579–80) Bishop of Winchester ordered to array the clergy of his diocese and to send them to Southampton for its defence; Sir John de Montague and others appointed military commanders (Rymer, *Foedera*, iii:988)
1375 Anglo-French truce at Bruges	1375 The king issues an order of protection for the Southampton friars minor (*Cal.C.R. 1374–7*, p. 137)
1376 The Black Prince dies	1376 The burgesses request the king to take the town into his own hands: they cannot support the cost of the defences (*Rot.Parlm.*, ii:346)
1377 Death of Edward III; accession of Richard II; first poll tax; French and Spanish raids on the English coast	1377 The prior of St Denys complains that he is unable to collect the ancient dues on wine imported, which should have come to him with the hospital of St Mary Magdalene (*Cal.P.R. 1374–7*, p. 485) Invasion scare; Sir John Arundel appointed keeper; survey of walls ordered; extensive works carried out on the walls and towers; remission of the town farm is granted on this account (*Cal.P.R. 1377–81*, pp. 4, 7–8, 12, 76, 80; P.R.O. E364/12/E, E372/222, SC8/86/4263–4, SC8/140/3640, SC8/141/7046, SC8/142/7088)
	1378 Work on the new tower-keep at Southampton Castle begins (*Cal.P.R. 1377–81*, pp. 174, 199, 241–2, 264)

1379 Poll tax	1379 A Genoese merchant, proposing a plan to centre all Genoese trading activity at Southampton, is murdered by Londoners (*Chronicon Angliae*, pp. 237–8)
1380 Richard declared of age; a third poll tax is agreed	
1381 Anglo-French truce; Peasants' Revolt	
	1383 Invasion scare: a great enemy fleet is on its way to besiege the town (*Cal.C.R. 1381–5*, p. 314)
	1384 Pavage grants begin at Southampton (*Cal.P.R. 1381–5*, p. 448)
	1384–90 The Venetians debate the advisability of sending their galleys to Southampton (*Cal. State Papers Venetian, 1202–1509*, pp. 30–2)
1385 Anglo-French war renewed	1385 Invasion scare: hostile fleet on its way from France (*Cal.C.R. 1385–9*, p. 6)
	1386 A survey of Southampton's defences is ordered, 'in view of imminent invasion this summer' (*Cal.P.R. 1385–9*, pp. 177, 258)
1387 Richard's powers are limited by the Lords Appellant	1387 Invasion scare: no ships or men are to leave the port (*Cal.C.R. 1385–9*, pp. 327, 329)
1388 Scots defeat English at Otterburn (Chevy Chase)	
1389 Anglo-French truce concluded at Boulogne	1389 Richard II has heard that the burgesses of Southampton have been misapplying their murage moneys; an enquiry is ordered (*Cal.P.R. 1388–92*, pp. 57–8)
1394 Anglo-French truce agreed for another four years	1395–8 Reports of mishandling cause the king to take St Mary Magdalene Hospital into his own hands; he restores it to St Denys Priory (*Cal.Inq.Misc. 1392–9*, pp. 63–4; P.R.O. C47/60/8/303, E364/32, SC6/981/28)
1394–5 Richard II in Ireland	
1396 Richard marries Isabella of France; Anglo-French truce extended	
1399 Henry of Lancaster invades England; Richard II is deposed; accession of Henry IV	

Chapter nine

The merchant capitalists

The successful practice of international trade brought to the fore, in early-fourteenth-century Southampton, a group of exceptionally able men. Roger Norman, Thomas de Byndon, Hugh Sampson, Henry de Lym, John le Fleming and Nicholas de Moundenard lived as near-neighbours; they were associated frequently in municipal office; they held posts in the service of the king; they participated in joint trading ventures overseas. John le Fleming might have owed some part of his fortune to the strength of the family tradition, and Roger Norman must certainly have advanced his by an astute marriage to Joan, widow and joint-heir of a great Anglo-Gascon capitalist, John of London. Nevertheless, oligarchy, maintained by family alliances, is no real explanation of the configurations of wealth and authority in fourteenth-century Southampton. These were men, often emerging from obscurity, who took great risks, made great profits, and sometimes sustained great losses, in an intensely competitive trade. They were men very obviously to be reckoned with; inevitably, they ran the town. John le Fleming and Nicholas de Moundenard were both alderman once; Roger Norman, twice; Henry de Lym, three times; Hugh Sampson on four occasions, and Thomas de Byndon on at least five. In addition, at least three of them had served as bailiff before elevation to the chief municipal office: Nicholas de Moundenard four times.[1]

Such marked concentration of power in the hands of the few clearly provoked tensions in the borough. There will be nothing yet to compare with the open civic rivalries of John Payne and Walter Fetplace 'junior' in the mid-fifteenth-century town.[2] But there are obvious signs, for all that, of intense personal antagonisms at work, occasionally breaking out in violence. While there is little to explain the motivation of individual incidents of this kind, it might yet be significant that the Forst family was implicated in at least two of the better recorded of them. And it may well be that, in the second of these, the Forst brothers, Walter, John and Henry, found themselves momentarily at the head of a genuine popular movement against the ruling faction. Their opposition could have begun as early as 1303, for it was in that year that Walter Forst, bailiff three years before, was to be found complaining to the king that he had been forcibly dispossessed by Peter de Lyon, Richard de Barbflete and others, of a ship and its gear, the whole valued at £100.[3] In 1327, it was the Forsts themselves who took the initiative in violence. Designing to recover what they claimed to be a fraudulent appropriation from the town farm, they attacked, with the support of a number of fellow townsmen, the property and ships of Thomas de Byndon and of John and Henry le Fleming, father and son. They assaulted John le Fleming at Shirley, burnt his property in the borough, carried off his goods, and imprisoned him until he wrote them an acquittance on a debt of £72. Henry le Fleming's ship, returning with merchandise from Flanders, was boarded in Southampton Water, and the goods carried off to the town.[4] But it was Thomas de Byndon, by his own account, who suffered the worst of the three. Henry, Walter and John Forst, he complained, had come with other 'malefactors' to his house at Southampton. They forced the doors and 'took and carried away silver vessels and other goods and chattels to the value of £200, and assaulted, beat and wounded his men and servants, whereby he lost their service for a long time'. They had also gone to 'two of his ships lying at anchor in the port of that town, which were loaded on the king's behalf to go to Gascony to carry salt and wine thence into this realm for the use of the king and of Edmund, earl of Kent, and entered them, and took and carried away the tackle of the ships and other goods and chattels of the king and of his found in the ships to the value of £100, and arrested the ships wilfully, and detained them under arrest so long that the king and he lost the voyage of the ships aforesaid for that season'. But these were difficult times, and it is doubtful whether either the Flemings or Thomas de Byndon could have expected much immediate satisfaction. The Forsts had chosen their ground well. In claiming to protect the property of the queen-mother, to whom the farm belonged by gift of the late king, they had invoked the greatest authority in the land. Neither Isabella nor Mortimer, her paramour, would have lifted a finger in support of claims in any way prejudicial to their interest. On 25 December 1327, on the intervention of the queen-mother herself, the process already initiated in the courts against the Forsts and their companions was dropped, it being held that 'it is not consonant with reason that Henry Forst and the others shall be molested for this reason, and wishing to obviate the malice of the said Thomas [de Byndon]'.[5]

The discomfiture of Thomas de Byndon and his associates would not have lasted long: their value to the crown was too well known and their personal wealth too great. Even while the Forst case proceeded, they were attempting, in the more promising circumstances of the new reign, to reverse an injustice suffered in the old. In 1324–5 a group of the more important Southampton burgesses, among them Thomas de Byndon himself, John le Fleming, Henry de Lym, Nicholas de Moundenard and Richard Forst, had been compelled to buy bad wine, the property of the king, at Portchester, on which they owed still the sum of £90. On 20 February 1328, they were able to secure an order to the justices, cancelling their own acknowledgment, or recognizance, of the debt.[6]

Acting together, their expertise must have been formidable. All, at one time or another, had handled goods or done some service for the king, while Thomas de Byndon and Roger Norman, in particular, were regular purveyors and merchants of the crown. By the time of the 1328 decision, both Henry de Lym and Hugh Sampson had already served in the port as collectors of the royal customs on wool and wine; Nicholas de Moundenard and Thomas de Byndon took their turn in the decade to follow.[7] In 1330, John le Fleming had the satisfaction of attending, as one of the two representatives of the borough, the Winchester parliament of March that year, at which the fall of the Forsts' protector, Roger Mortimer, was engineered.[8] And the following February the king summoned Hugh and Thomas Sampson to his council at Westminster, to inform him 'concerning matters newly arisen upon which he wishes to have [their] advice and counsel'. He would have been referring, probably, to the evasions and frauds known to have been hampering at the time the collection of the customs on wool, for in May 1331 orders were drafted to prevent the export of wool, hides and woolfells from all such places where evasion might be possible, and to replace the existing weighers of wool by others likely to prove more diligent in the service of the king.[9]

So active did Roger Norman become in the business of the crown, 'having for no small time found at his own charges divers ships of war and armed men both on land and sea for the king's service in defence of the realm against foreign attack in the wars now imminent', that he and his men were exempted by royal order, on 2 May 1338, from 'guarding the sea coast or finding men-at-arms, hobelers or archers for such custody during the said wars, to wit, in the counties of Southampton, Wiltshire, Gloucestershire, Essex and Suffolk, with the commonalties of the counties where his lands are'.[10] Nor was this mixture of military and commercial involvement unfamiliar to other leading burgesses of Southampton at the time. Rather over a decade before, Thomas de Byndon had lost to the king's use at Hull a valuable cargo of wines. When he failed to obtain payment, he petitioned the king for his money, promising in return to furnish him with a good ship and forty well-armed men, to serve for forty days in the royal campaigns in Scotland, entirely at his own expense.[11]

Like many of the more substantial of his contemporaries in the town, Thomas de Byndon was deeply involved in shipping. In 1324 he controlled no fewer than four large ships, *La Juliane*, *La Rose*, *La Gracedieu* and *La Jonette*, with each of which he traded to the king's dominions overseas and to Flanders.[12] At least one of his ships was of 160 tons, for in 1327 the king requisitioned four vessels of that tonnage in the port of Southampton to carry his treasure to Aquitaine. One was the property of Thomas de Byndon, another of Hugh Sampson, his near-neighbour, with whom, in the previous year, he had been associated in a commission to muster a small fleet for the king.[13] Not content to share cargoes in hired vessels, as lesser men usually did, burgesses of the standing of Thomas de Byndon, Hugh Sampson and Roger Norman might frequently both own and freight a ship for themselves. Over a decade or more, Roger Norman's *La Seinte Mariecog* plied the Gascon route, no doubt contributing substantially to his fortune.[14] But while the profits of trade on this scale were considerable, the risks were proportionately high. Neither Hugh Sampson nor Thomas de Byndon escaped unscathed. The two of them, in 1329 and 1330 respectively, were complaining that their ships, carrying wine from Gascony, had been arrested on arrival in Flanders. Hugh Sampson's *La Katerine*, of Bayonne, had been loaded at Libourne with a cargo of 180 tuns of wine, the property of Gascon merchants. But Thomas de Byndon was himself on board *La Rose* when he and the ship were arrested, and the cargo was probably his own.[15] Piracy in Breton waters, together with confiscation in Flanders, led Hugh Sampson in 1329 to reckon his losses in ships and merchandise at a total of £786. 6*s*. 8*d*. And Thomas de Byndon's reversals, similarly, did not stop short at Flanders. Within a few years, he suffered the total loss of his ship *La Jonette*, pirated by Bretons on its return journey from Bordeaux. It had left Southampton with a cargo of corn and other victuals for Aquitaine, had discharged at Bordeaux and re-loaded with a valuable cargo of wines. Its loss, to three ships of subjects of the duke of Brittany, cost Thomas de Byndon something in the region of £260.[16]

Whereas Thomas de Byndon might bear such losses and survive them, most of his fellow burgesses preferred to spread their risk more widely. William le Smale (d. 1334), a Southampton burgess of considerable fortune, owned no more than part-shares in three vessels, *La Gracedieu*, *La Juliane* and *La Barthelmew*.[17] Of these, the first two may well have been the same vessels that Thomas de Byndon was handling in 1324; the third, almost certainly, was the ship of which John Hokele owned a quarter-share on his death in 1348/9.[18]

Increasingly, as war risks grew and as the trade became more specialized, the emergence of prominent seafaring families, in particular the Burches and the Hurnes, points to a separation of function between those who handled and captained the ships, and those who only freighted them. In 1326, William atte Hurne was master of *La Gracedieu*, William atte Burche of *La Seinte Mariecog*.[19] William atte Burche was master of *La Jonette* in 1343; Richard atte Hurne of the king's ship, *La Isabele*, in 1349.[20] Exceptionally, Roger atte Hurne was both patron and master of the ship *La Trinite*, employed in the export of wools in the late 1330s. On the same commission, Roger Norman's *La Seinte Mariecog* was captained by Nicholas Spark, Nicholas Sampson's *La Barthelmew* by Richard Bolde, whereas Robert atte Burche, master of *La Margarete*, had Henry Isembard (Imberd) and Walter atte Burche, a relative, as patrons.[21] Although neither the Hurnes, with the exception of Roger, nor the Burches held major offices in the days of their prominence in the port, they were yet men of substance, knowing each other well. In the thirties and forties of the century, William atte Burche lived on the east side of English Street, in the parish of St Lawrence. He had married Isabelle, widow of a fellow seafarer, William atte Hurne.[22]

Such clear stratifications in society, within which personal associations were close, undoubtedly served to isolate still further, whether in their own eyes or in those of others, that small group of wealthy burgesses which for so many decades continued to dominate the town. Interdependent originally in prosperity, they supported each other in adversity when it came. In 1339, the conviction of Nicholas de Moundenard for extensive customs frauds, followed by his bankruptcy in 1348, might have been a much more considerable disaster had his friends not rallied to support him. Roger Norman, his next-door neighbour, stood mainprise for him in July 1339, and secured his release from the Tower.[23] In 1350, at the nadir of his fortunes, he was yet named one of the four *echevins* of the town, sharing the distinction with Henry le Fleming, son of a former neighbour, Nicholas Sampson and John Fysmark, all considerable men.[24] In 1352–3, what remained of his former properties, appropriated in 1348 by the crown, was in the hands of Nicholas le Taverner, son of an old associate, John le Taverner, with whom he had worked in 1338.[25] It is possible that Nicholas was leasing the properties on behalf of the old man, for in 1357 he was remembered generously in Nicholas de Moundenard's will, almost alone, outside the family, to be so.[26]

In another way, and in more prosperous times, the members of Nicholas de Moundenard's immediate circle had demonstrated solidarity in the completion of an important public work. These were the years of the construction of the friary conduit, bringing fresh water from Nicholas de Barbflete's spring at Shirley down to their end of the town. But this was also the time when Holy Rood church was rebuilt on a more convenient site, east of the line of English Street. The two enterprises were not unconnected. The first moves in each were made in the last decade of the thirteenth century, and one of the few water-houses along the line of the conduit was sited where the original church had been, on English Street itself. In 1291, the year following Nicholas de Barbflete's gift of the spring to the friary, Adam le Horder granted a shop and curtilage to Walter atte Hall. It was on the east side of English Street, and faced the east end of the old church at Holy Rood. Subsequently, it was from Walter atte Hall that Thomas de Byndon acquired the means to improve the siting of the church.[27] Following much the pattern of the conduit works, it was not until April 1320 that proceedings were initiated to transfer this property, now Thomas de Byndon's, to St Denys Priory, to which the advowson of Holy Rood belonged. On 28 December the enquiry was held, meeting before a jury of notable burgesses, among them, Henry de Lym, Richard de Barbflete, Thomas Nostschilling, John Forst and Richard Bagge. The existing church, it was argued, was inconveniently sited, to the no small loss of the burgesses. It was also dilapidated and badly in need of repair. Two days later, on 30 December, the licence was granted, enabling Thomas de Byndon to alienate the property in mortmain to the prior and convent of St Denys. The formal transfer was enacted on 1 August 1321.[28] The plot, now vacant, measured 140 feet in length by 120 feet in breadth; it was to include a churchyard, or cemetery, of some kind. Within a decade, the best part of the work was completed. It was accomplished with the help of the leading parishioners, Thomas de Byndon, Roger Norman, Henry de Lym and Hugh Sampson, to whom, in recognition of their services, the right of burial in the new church was granted in December 1333.[29] Their neighbour Nicholas de Moundenard, almost a quarter of a century later, was to prefer burial in the friary church, near the bodies of his father and his first wife, Margery. But he still remembered Holy Rood with special affection in his will, to the neglect of other parochial institutions in the town.[30]

It was indeed no accident that the leading burgesses of their generation should have been brought together in support of the works at Holy Rood. They had, of course, long since learnt the advantages of co-operation in affairs both public and commercial. But what united them in this instance need have been nothing more complex than their knowledge of each other as neighbours. They were all, at the time, substantial landholders in the southern part of the town. And their messuages adjoined each other in what must have been an impressive display of burgess solidarity and wealth. Interestingly, they grouped at the south-west end of English Street, opposite the friary, where Walter le Fleming, their distinguished forerunner, had himself chosen to live. Walter le Fleming's house had been sited on the junction of English Street and Broad Lane, the lane lying immediately to the north. In due course, John le Fleming inherited the property, living there until his death in 1336. His son Walter, to whom it passed, must have sold it almost immediately to the ageing Henry de Lym, the occupant of the tenement in 1340 and already the owner of land in the vicinity. To the south, and probably next-door, was the tenement of Nicholas de Moundenard. It adjoined a house of Roger Norman's, to the south again, beyond which was the great messuage of Thomas de Byndon, next to the south gate and the shore.[31] Hugh Sampson, although not of this group, lived at West Hall between French Street and Bull Street, a few yards to the west of the English Street messuages. Despite a recent partition, it must still have been one of the major properties of the borough.[32]

By a happy coincidence of documentary and material survivals, it is still possible at least to suggest the form that these remarkable buildings took. Of the group as a whole, West Hall alone stands out as exceptional in design, but it is also very much the best documented. It had begun life in the last decades of the twelfth century as the capital messuage of the mighty Gervase le Riche. As the home, successively, of great men of the town, it continued to be extended and modified by later generations until, at the opening of the fourteenth century, its buildings straggled generously over a large site, bounded on the east by French Street, on the south by Rochelle Lane, and on the west by Bull Street. So miscellaneous, indeed, was the accommodation it offered, that it is not easy to see how it was planned. On the west of the site, shops with their attached solars fronted on Bull Street, and there were other stone buildings and cellars on French Street and Rochelle Lane. But for the rest, the precise siting of the buildings must remain largely conjectural. Probably, they were set about one large courtyard, with the great hall on the west, adjoining the rear of the Bull Street shops and solars. A garden would have occupied some part of the enclosure, separating the hall from the noise and bustle of the great gate on French Street, opposite the parish church of St John's. An important 'painted' chamber, with adjoining garderobe, was sited on the south of the court; a 'long' chamber, on the north. Both the chambers, as also the garderobe, were set over cellars of their own. There was another chamber called 'la Oriolle', over the gate; stables were attached to individual buildings in the court; a kitchen and bakehouse adjoined the southern end of the hall. There was a spring, or well, on a vacant plot towards the south of the enclosure.

Thomas le Halveknight and Christina, his wife, had lived at West Hall at the end of the thirteenth century, and in 1303/4 it was partitioned clumsily among their heirs. To John, the first-born, was assigned the painted chamber and garderobe, the great gate, garden and well. The second share fell to Thomas le Halveknight. It consisted of a stone house and cellar on French Street, with a stable and 'la Oriolle', over the gate. Roger le Halveknight, third in line, took a stone house and cellar, with attached bakehouse and stable, on the southern flank of the site; with these, went the cellar under 'la Garderobe'. The fourth share, allotted to Walter le Halveknight, comprised the southern half of the great hall and its adjoining kitchen, with a shop and two solars on Bull Street, immediately to the west. The northern half of the hall, together with another solar and shop on Bull Street and the cellar beneath Walter's second solar, made up the fifth share, assigned to William Bassingrom and his wife, Petronilla, daughter of Thomas and Christina le Halveknight. Their daughter, Matilda, had already acquired some years before the long chamber north of the hall, with its underlying cellars and the two adjoining vacant plots. It had been bequeathed to her by Master John le Fleming, a former occupant of West Hall. In the partition, the right to draw water in the well, and access to the court through the gate on French Street, were guaranteed to Roger, Thomas and Petronilla. Walter, whose portion was sited conveniently at the south-west angle of the enclosure, on Bull Street, presumably could do without such facilities.[33]

A settlement which carried so many built-in causes of dispute could not have been expected to survive for long. Already in 1314, 'in their great necessity' and with the consent of their daughter Matilda, William and Petronilla Bassingrom leased their family inheritance to a fellow burgess for the term of seven years. It would have included the whole north-west segment of the site, and took in the share of their daughter.[34] Within a few years of the partition, John and Thomas le Halveknight had sold their shares to John of Shirley, who for so many years at the beginning of the century was collector of customs jointly with Henry de Lym. Roger le Halveknight's share went to the same purchaser in 1327. By September 1331, Hugh Sampson, who already owned important properties immediately to the north, had acquired the portion of Walter le Halveknight, quit-claimed to him by Walter's widow, Joan.[35] He was subsequently to purchase from Felicia of Shirley the shares of Walter's brothers, John, Thomas and Roger. The Bassingrom inheritance, still the largest individual part of the mansion, came, by purchase or descent, to Walter of Brackley, mayor in 1326.[36]

In the sixteenth century West Hall, still among the greatest houses of the town, would be a perfectly conventional four-square structure, set about a courtyard with central fountain. It resembled many of the contemporary country residences of the gentry, and certainly excited admiration at the time, perhaps as the result of the continued improvements of successive Italian tenants.[37] But the jumble of buildings characteristic of the site before the general destruction of the French raid of 1338 was of no readily classifiable form. It comprised a complex of unrelated structures, the product of time and personal eccentricity, serving a multitude of purposes and obeying few architectural conventions. Very different were the tenements on English Street, south of Broad Lane. At an early date, the valuable English Street frontage had been divided into short individual sections, behind which narrow plots ran back in an east or west direction, sometimes to a considerable length. A wealthy merchant might absorb several of these plots, as had John Horn in the middle years of the thirteenth century, perhaps purposing to build across their limits. But his house, even so, would probably have followed the pattern of his property. It would be long, like the plot, and narrow. It would be placed gable-end to the street, and would conform, as likely as not, to the style of the well-known three-part hall-house, common to many English boroughs of the period.[38] In Southampton certainly, and frequently elsewhere, such a house would be built on a substantial semi-basement stone vault, entered independently from the street and serving, perhaps, as a shop and warehouse on its own. It would be characterized, above ground-level, by an open hall, centrally placed, with two-storey chamber blocks at either end. Facing the street, the lower of the chambers might have served as a shop. Above it was the solar, or private apartment and bedchamber of the burgess. At the far end of the hall, reached by a gallery, was another upper chamber, overlying a kitchen or buttery. Outhouses in the yard behind might hold other service rooms, including, frequently, the kitchen. Usually, a substantial stone-lined rubbish-pit was sited close by the kitchen door, in the yard at the rear or at the side of the house. It received the kitchen and other refuse of the household, and was cleaned out regularly while in use.

By the time that Peter James, early in the fifteenth century, acquired the corner property on Broad Lane and English Street formerly of Walter le Fleming, John le Fleming and Henry de Lym, it covered two plots at least. It was described as a 'great corner tenement with two vaults underneath', solars above, a kitchen at the rear, curtilage and garden.[39] The house, of course, has gone, and the vaults, while certainly still present in mutilated form, remain to be excavated. But adjoining them on the south is a remarkably fine surviving vault (Plate 10), in all probability the original undercroft of Nicholas de Moundenard's tenement. Recently skilfully restored, it is characterized by a ribbed barrel-vault, an entrance on the street front, and a pair of fine windows, next to the door, finished with good roll mouldings. Measuring overall 20 feet by 50 feet, it compares closely in scale with another great undercroft to the south, now known as 'Quilter's Vault'. Probably formerly a part of Thomas de Byndon's messuage, Quilter's is barrel-vaulted, like its near-neighbour, and is supplied with an entrance on the street with adjoining single-light, square-headed window. An entrance at the far end, on the west, would seem to have been a later insertion, perhaps belonging to the period, later in the Middle Ages, when the vault was divided in two, a central stone-built partition making two approximately equal shops, workshops or stores of what had formerly been one great undercroft.

Excavations to the north of these tenements, taking in a part of the north wall of Walter le Fleming's messuage, the line of Broad Lane, and the three plots immediately to the north, have recently made possible a reconstruction of the plans of a trio of medieval town houses (Fig. 5), closely similar to those lying south of the lane.[40] In

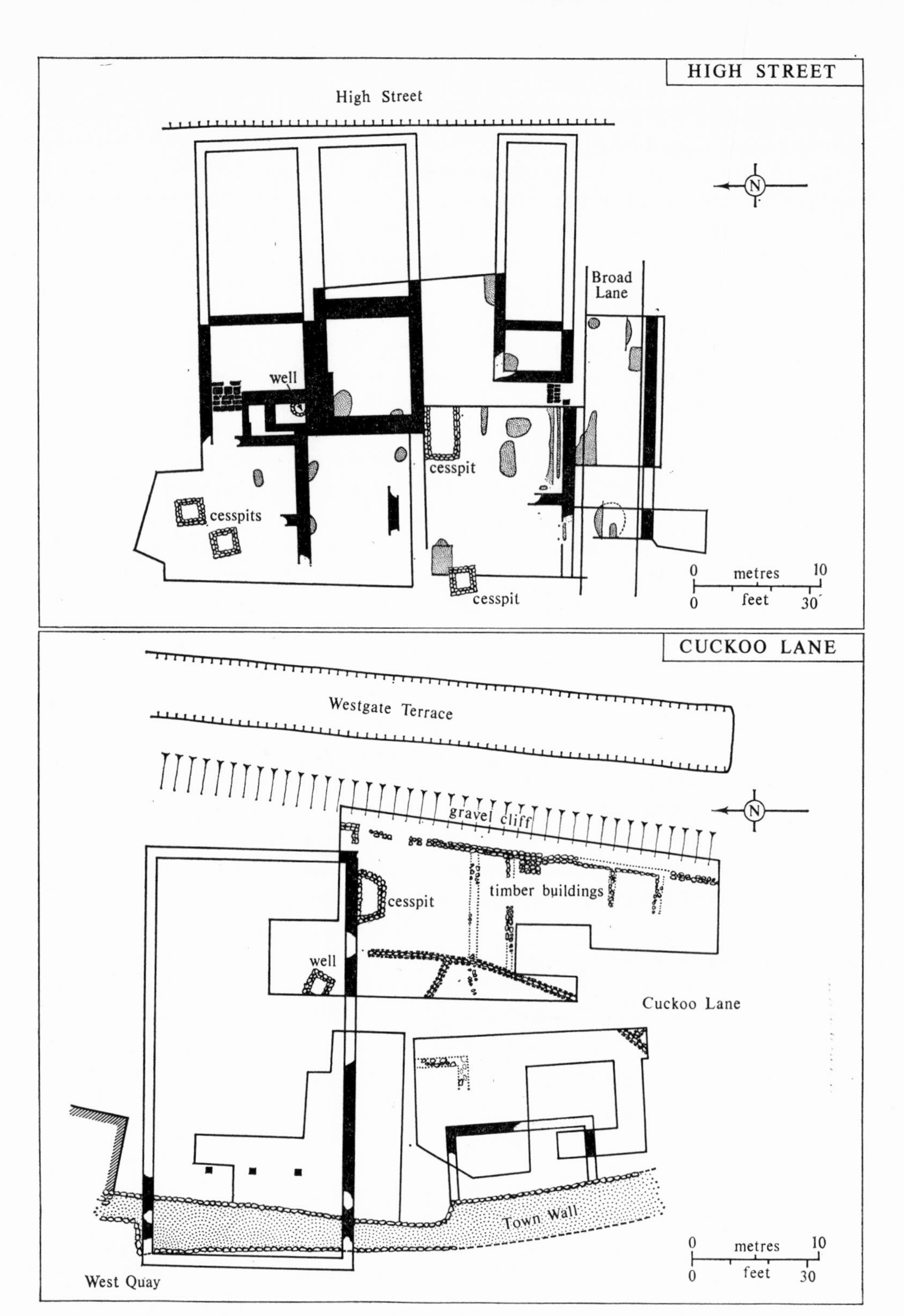

Figure 5 Block plans of recently-excavated burgess houses on the High Street and Cuckoo Lane; pre-1200 features on the High Street site are shown stippled

sequence of building, the central house is the earliest. It may be dated archaeologically to the turn of the twelfth and thirteenth centuries, and belongs to the class of house already described on Porters Lane, Cuckoo Lane and the western shore. A massive internal wall, originally bonded into the external walls of the tenement but later demolished and replaced, would suggest that the undercroft was divided from the beginning. There are no traces of vaulting corbels in any of the walls, and it seems clear that the roofing of the undercroft would have been contrived with the pillar-and-beam structure already noted as characteristic of the stone-built houses of this early generation. At some 23 by 68 feet, it is certainly the largest of the three houses. But it is exceeded slightly in width by the adjoining house, built up against it on the north. This house, again of thirteenth-century date, measures approximately 25 by 58 feet. It preserves a good part of its simple, but massive, barrel-vault, and had remained continually in use until comparatively recently. As at Quilter's, to the south, a late partition wall had been inserted to divide the vault in two. But the entrance at the north-west corner of the vault, undoubtedly original, belongs to the first period of building; it was modified, but not destroyed, in later years. Immediately behind the house, a finely constructed well-chamber, or cistern, dates, probably, to the fourteenth century or before. The third house, an altogether slighter structure, adjoins Broad Lane to the south. There is no satisfactory evidence of dating, but the house overlies twelfth-century material and is likely to belong to the next century at latest. It had been shortened in the eighteenth century at the rear, perhaps on the collapse of the original west wall, ill-founded like the others. Originally, it had measured some 14 by 60 feet, and would probably have been supplied with a vaulted undercroft, or cellar.

Each house, on construction, would have been sited at the head of a long plot, running westward from its English Street frontage. In addition, the earliest of the three houses was supplied with a small yard to the south, resembling in this the contemporary building on Cuckoo Lane. Through the years, the yard was used for the disposal, by cesspit, of domestic refuse of all kinds, remaining open until at least the turn of the sixteenth and seventeenth centuries. In contrast, the open yards and gardens at the back of the houses were sub-divided some years before the end of the fourteenth century. Timber buildings, set on light stone footings, were inserted to cross the lines of the earlier property boundaries and to front on Broad Lane to the south. These flimsier structures, demolished already by the seventeenth century, were replaced by a succession of brick-built warehouses and dwellings. But the earlier stone buildings on the valuable English Street frontage remained throughout the centuries consistently in use, transformed above ground to suit the taste of successive generations, substantially unaltered below.

At 58 French Street, within a few paces to the west, a surviving fourteenth-century house, now lightly disguised behind a seventeenth-century façade, may serve to illustrate their form. It is a stone-clad timber structure, measuring internally some 16 by 50 feet, set over a substantial stone vault of the conventional pattern. (Fig. 6). The hall, its central feature, is of two bays, originally open to the roof. At either end, there were two-storey flanking chamber blocks, linked on the first floor by a gallery. A door, with windows on each side, gave access to the street at the east end of the undercroft. Above it, an open shop-front was approached by way of a gallery and short stair. Both the shop and the undercroft were designed as distinct units, capable of being let independently of the main part of the dwelling into which they were incorporated. In this form, the house made excellent, and economic, use of the restricted site on which it was placed. It is a classic example of the three-part hall-house of the period: the pattern to which the majority of the English Street tenements undoubtedly belonged.[41]

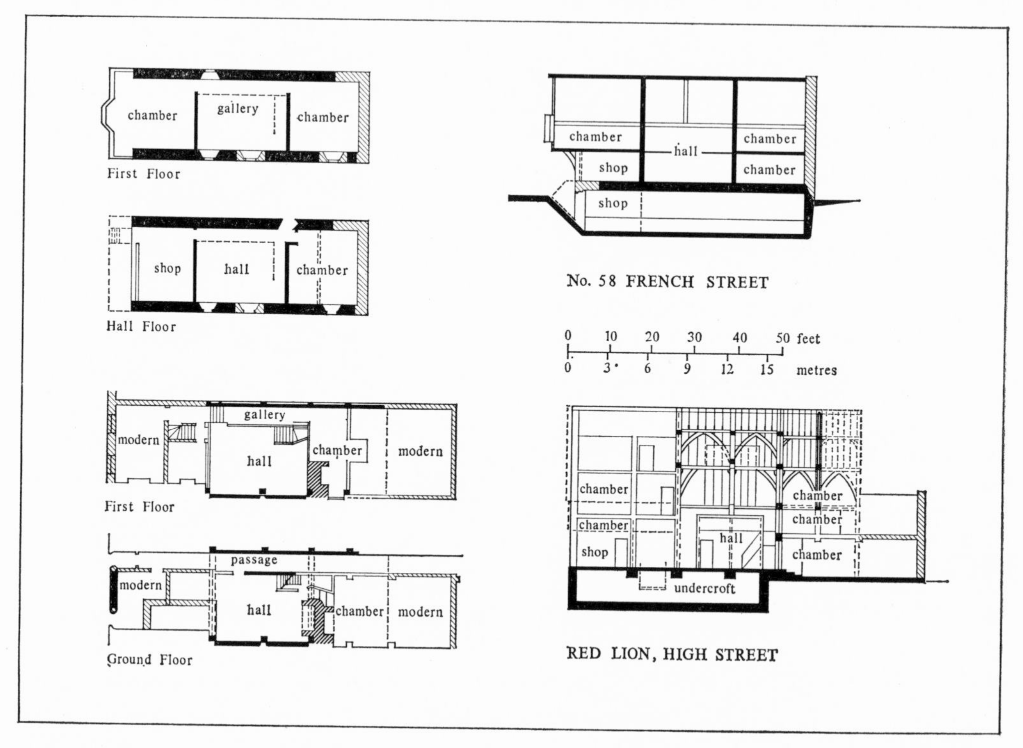

Figure 6 58 French Street and the Red Lion, High Street: burgess housing of the fourteenth and fifteenth centuries

A well-to-do Southampton merchant, comfortably established in just such a house as this, could afford many luxuries. Among the bequests listed in a will of 1349 were silver vessels, silk, lengths of fine cloth, carpets, bed-hangings, feather-beds and chests, with an assortment of doublets of the new fashion, as well as tunics and robes of the old.[42] And already, particularly in the sphere of fashion, there were indications of the extravagance so frequently chastised by later critics. Both men and women had begun to wear close-fitting garments, cut to mould the figure and to reveal its contours. The modest, all-enveloping styles of the thirteenth century were giving place to the doublet and hose of men, the low-necked, body-hugging kirtle and cote-hardie of women. The change would not go unremarked. If Richard Rolle (d. 1349) was undoubtedly an eccentric, he nevertheless voiced the opinions of many of the more sober-minded of his generation. 'Both men and women in their vanity wear clothes carven in the newest mode, and they pay no heed to what beseems nature, but to what the last rumour of vanity has introduced, at the devil's prompting.'[43]

Something of this spirit is recalled by the archaeology of the period. In the houses themselves, every opportunity was taken for display. A mason, drawing out a pattern for his customer, might contrive a fanciful design. In the fashioning of door frames and of windows, the mouldings had become elaborate, intricate and costly. Roof furniture, gable-ends, ridge-tiles and louvres would never be more flamboyant. Floors were paved in picturesquely patterned tiles, now as much a feature of the merchant's dwelling as of the church or cloister of the neighbouring religious house. In furnishings and other essential trappings, domestic fashions followed the same trends. Seldom content only with the products of their native pottery industry, the wealthier Southampton burgesses imported their wine-jugs and even some of their kitchen wares from south-west France. Polychrome and other vessels from Saintonge, north of Bordeaux, are frequently found in the rubbish pits of the early-fourteenth-century town (Plate 11). There are lustres from Spain, and the occasional ornate wine-jug from Rouen (Plate 12). Glass was not the luxury it once had been. Already, in the last years of the thirteenth century, Venetian and other fine imported glass was known in Southampton, to become familiar in the fourteenth. There was music and gaming in the town; a bone flute, a wooden pipe, a gaming counter and dice have been found in late-thirteenth-century contexts. And there is evidence also of that popular piety which might lead to the purchase and display of devotional objects in the home. A ceramic crucifix, in the form of a wall plaque, was once a part of the decorations of a great tenement north of Broad Lane. It is one of a group of such objects found in archaeological contexts in the town.[44]

Had it not been for the fortunate discovery of his seal in one of the most prolific rubbish pits in the medieval town, little might have been discovered of Richard of Southwick, burgess of Southampton, except that he owned properties in the south-west quarter of the town and in the northern suburb, and that, on his death in *c.* 1290, his wife and two daughters survived him.[45] As it is, we know that at some point in his life, probably in his later years, he lived in a great stone tenement on Cuckoo Lane (see Fig. 5), built almost a century before, from which he operated as the associate, or host, of a Norman merchant, Bernard of Vire, whose seal was recovered with his own. When, during the period of his occupation, a fire caused the collapse of the rear of the building, the debris filled to the top an adjoining stone-lined cesspit, effectively preventing its re-use. The pit remained thereafter waterlogged and undisturbed for another seven centuries, a near-perfect container for the preservation of a range of domestic and commercial waste unparalleled by the product of any other single-dated context in the town.

Richard was not, certainly, the wealthiest burgess of his generation, but he lived extraordinarily well. In addition to pewter and fine imported glass, his habitual tablewares included some of the costliest ceramics of Spain and south-west France. A selection of Spanish lustres, among the earliest to be recognized in England, accompanied the boldly-painted claret-jugs of Saintonge (Plate 11). They had spoilt his taste for local wares, for he imported, in large part, even the plainer vessels daily in service in his household, and where he did possess a fine product of the Sussex kilns, it was painted with a white slip on the inside of the rim, in clear imitation of the lighter products of the south. Wooden plates and bowls were otherwise the basic equipment of his table; several were recovered from the cesspit. With them were knife handles, one of wood, the other of polished horn, and a variety of clues to his diet. Beef and mutton, fish and eggs, oysters and mussels, had all left identifiable remains. There were the shells, stones and pips of a range of fruit and nuts, some of which must certainly have been imported: grape and fig, wild strawberry, raspberry, cherry and plum, hazel-nut and walnut. Of spices, understandably, there was nothing, but Richard must undoubtedly have had them at his table. A divided condiment dish, or saucer, was among the vessels recovered from the pit. It is of a local ware: a minor concession to the pottery industry of the region.

In late-thirteenth-century Southampton, a successful man of business handled many varieties of trade. Richard dealt in wine, wool and victuals, and his interests may have run to pottery and haberdashery as well. The remains of a small barrel were found in the pit; there was a box and a quantity of tally-sticks, discarded after use. Woollen cloth, of varying thickness and quality, was present in cuttings from the bales, as was also a single piece of silk. It is likely that some sewing, and possibly some weaving was done by the women of Richard's household. They had thrown away, shortly before the final filling of the pit, some of the waste and trimmings from their work; a large bone bodkin, also recovered from the fill, is more likely to have been used in the warehouse below, for the rougher work on the sacks.

As was no more than fitting to his rank, Richard dressed with care and some display. His shoes, or those of his household, were of several fashions, blunt-ended or finely pointed, adorned on occasion with pierced leatherwork. He wore a belt studded with pewter, carried a dagger in a sheath of intricately embossed Spanish leather, and would sometimes have taken with him a good sword, with pommel and belt-buckle of bronze. Very much a creature of his times, he had made a pilgrimage to Canterbury. He had bought there two *ampullae*, devotional souvenirs embossed with portraits of the saint, which he would have worn hung round his neck. He enjoyed gaming, playing dice and a type of chess or draughts, and was fond, it is obvious, of pets. There were cats, of course, in his household, essential on the rat-ridden quays. But he kept, in addition, a diminutive African monkey, which he must have bought off some sailor in the port. Like his dogs, it may have accompanied him on some of his errands in the town.[46]

Richard of Southwick, a near-contemporary of Roger Norman, Thomas de Byndon, Henry de Lym and their associates, must have shared many of their habits and tastes. In due course, we may anticipate, their own personal possessions will be excavated from the pits at the rear, and to the side, of their important English Street tenements. But already, on the site to the north of Broad Lane, the stone-built rubbish pits of their immediate neighbours have yielded a harvest of fine earthenwares and glass second only to the product of Richard's great pit on Cuckoo Lane. In one pit, in particular, the best work of the local pottery industry has been found in association with both fine and coarse wares from south-west France, with a handsome jug from Rouen, and with magnificent table glass, much of it very probably of Mediterranean origin or inspiration. A Southampton burgess of Richard's generation could well afford the luxuries of his own international trade. Seldom were commercial openings so plentiful, or extravagant tastes so easy to indulge. But the eve, the moralists might have said, accords nothing with the morrow; for 'after great heat cometh cold: let no man cast his cloak away'.

Notes

1 Davies, p. 171 (corrected); Appendix 1a below.
2 The affair is discussed by Alwyn Ruddock, *Italian Merchants and Shipping*, chapter vii. There is a further mention, without detail, of a 'great split' at the mayoral election of almost exactly a century before (*Cal.Inq.P.M.*, xv: 187–8).
3 *Cal.P.R. 1301–7*, pp. 185, 187.
4 Ibid., *1327–30*, p. 216.
5 *Cal.C.R. 1327–30*, p. 243.
6 P.R.O. C47/60/6/184; *Cal.C.R. 1327–30*, pp. 147, 256; *Cal. Memoranda R. 1326–7*, pp. 93, 274.
7 See, for example, *Cal.C.R. 1307–13*, pp. 275–6, 386, *1327–30*, pp. 69–70, *1337–9*, pp. 304–5, 361.
8 Ibid., *1330–3*, p. 138.
9 Ibid., pp. 283, 318.
10 *Cal.P.R. 1338–40*, pp. 56, 252.
11 P.R.O. SC8/324/E.625.
12 *Cal.P.R. 1324–7*, p. 33.
13 *Cal.C.R. 1327–30*, pp. 14, 434; and *Cal.P.R. 1324–7*, p. 317.
14 *Cal.P.R. 1324–7*, p. 95; also P.R.O. E372/194, m. 18.
15 *Cal.C.R. 1327–30*, pp. 466–7, 545, and *1330–3*, pp. 147–8; also P.R.O. SC8/273/13620.
16 P.R.O. SC8/237/11828. Breton pirates were a particular hazard on the route to the south. In 1319 Richard Bagge had already lost a cargo of Bay salt off the Breton coast, the value of which, with his ship *La Seint Denis*, he set at £661 (*Cal.C.R. 1318–23*, p. 209).
17 Bodleian, Queen's College MS. 1075.
18 P.R.O. E326/9321.
19 *Cal.C.R. 1323–7*, p. 611.
20 *Cal.C.R. 1343–6*, p. 129; P.R.O. E372/203, m. 29.
21 P.R.O. E372/194, m. 18.
22 P.R.O. E210/9312, E326/9325, 9332 and 9341.
23 *Cal.C.R. 1339–41*, p. 241.
24 *Oak Book*, ii: 130–1; P.R.O. E372/194, m. 2. Nicholas de Moundenard's debts exceeded £500.
25 P.R.O. E122/137/14, and *Cal.C.R. 1337–9*, pp. 395–6.
26 S.C.R.O. D/LY/23/3 and D/CJ/24. But the terms of the will, with its generous pious bequests, suggest a substantial recovery of the Moundenard fortunes following the bankruptcy proceedings of 1348.
27 *Cat.Anc. Deeds*, ii: B3437, B3443.
28 P.R.O. C143/140/19, E326/4491; also *Cal.P.R. 1317–21*, p. 535.
29 Davies, p. 353.
30 S.C.R.O. D/LY/23/3 and D/CJ/24. His bequests included the provision of 10 marks yearly to maintain a chaplain at Holy Rood.
31 Bodleian, Queen's College MS. 339, 340.
32 S.C.R.O. SC4/2/404, and Bodleian, Queen's College MS. 4G10.
33 P.R.O. E327/163; also St Denys Cart. 242; God's House Deeds 476, and S.C.R.O. SC4/2/396.
34 B.M. Add.Ch. 685.
35 S.C.R.O. SC4/2/398–401, 403, 404.
36 Bodleian, Queen's College MS. 4G10; and Davies, p. 171.

37 Alwyn Ruddock, *Italian Merchants and Shipping*, pp. 244–5. The main gate, curiously, by this date opened on to Bull Street.
38 The type, with examples in Chester, Exeter and Bristol, is discussed by W. A. Pantin, 'Some medieval English town houses', in *Culture and Environment, Essays in Honour of Sir Cyril Fox*, eds I. Ll. Foster and L. Alcock, pp. 458–73.
39 P.R.O. E326/11799, 11800 and 11804.
40 *Southampton Excavations*, forthcoming.
41 The house is discussed by P. A. Faulkner in *Southampton Excavations*, forthcoming; see also his 'Medieval undercrofts and town houses', *Archaeological Journal*, 123 (1966), pp. 125–7.
42 P.R.O. E326/9359.
43 Quoted by Margaret Deanesley in her introduction to *The Incendium Amoris of Richard Rolle of Hampole*, p. 43.
44 *Southampton Excavations*, forthcoming.
45 God's House Deeds 594; St Denys Cart. 260; S.C.R.O. SC4/2/8. See also Appendix 1a for a biographical note.
46 The objects on which this account is based are fully described and illustrated in *Southampton Excavations*, forthcoming.

Chapter ten

The French raid, 1338

When hard times came, introduced by the raid of October 1338 and consolidated a decade later by the plague, they did not come unheralded. Seventeen years before, almost to the day, the men of Winchelsea had appeared off the port in strength. In arms ostensibly to control the seas, they had taken advantage of the king's weakness and of current civil disorders to terrorize the entire south coast.[1] Their thirty ships were more than a match for Southampton. On 30 September 1321 they landed to burn fifteen ships drawn up on the strand, contemptuously rejecting the burgesses' offer of two good ships, fully equipped, to help them in the policing of the Channel. The next day, two more ships were destroyed and the marauders sailed off leaving damage estimated, six years later, at over £8,000.[2] Almost certainly Southampton's loss was exaggerated, nor was the incident alone in an already long history of disputes with the men of the Cinque Ports. But the experience could not have failed to revive the alarms endured, two years before, on the occasion of the Venetian affray of 1319.[3] It reinforced the native distrust of foreigners, and must surely have contributed to the rough reception given to the Genoese merchants lodging with Henry de Lym in 1322.[4] More usefully, it brought into being a new sense of military urgency in the town, enabling fresh efforts to be made, before the end of the reign, to complete the defences of the borough. On the instructions of the king, the burgesses began a programme of works on their enclosure and their quays. In 1326, petitioning the king for support, they claimed to have spent heavily already on the work, and to be unable to continue on their own. To this end, Edward II, on 18 March, conceded a custom of a penny on every pound's worth of goods brought into, or taken out of, the town. In the first instance the tax was granted for a seven-year term, but it was to be confirmed and extended for many years thereafter.[5]

Some such action was undoubtedly needed, but the implementation of the new policy was at best half-hearted; certainly it came too late. The king, for his part, had longed dragged his feet over the maintenance of his castle in Southampton. The last major works at the castle had been completed as far back as 1272/3; in 1286 it was reportedly in ruins.[6] There were orders, in 1307 and 1308, to fortify the castle and to guard it. And instructions had been given, back in 1282, to divert at least a part of the murage moneys to castle repairs.[7] But at no time could the sums directed to the work have been considerable, and there is little evidence of new projects undertaken, whether on the castle or on the town defences, before Edward II's initiative in the final years of his reign. In particular, no more than the barest precautions were taken to secure the sea frontages to the south and west of the town. The streets, we know, were barred. There were gates towards the end of Bull Street and French Street before 1330, and others protected the approaches from the line of the western shore.[8] But the castle was in no condition to give more than nominal protection to the waterfront, whilst those same motives of trading expediency that had kept the quays unguarded in the thirteenth century preserved them so in the fourteenth.

Many of the *maiores* of the town, those same men who had offered the Winchelsea marauders two ships to take themselves off in peace, held important properties by the sea. Thomas de Byndon, in addition to his great tenement at the southern tip of English Street, had a valuable house situated on the quay below French Street.[9] Between his properties, Robert le Barber, in the last years of the thirteenth century, had owned a large tenement known as 'La Chayne'. It descended, via his widow, Isabella, to his daughter, Matilda, the wife of Gaillard de Moundenard.[10] On the quay beyond French Street, to the west, Thomas Stout had three houses, described as 'outside the gate of Bull Street on the quay, which extend from the said gate to the gate on French Street'. One of these was to come to Thomas Nostschilling, on his marriage to Florence, Thomas Stout's widow and heir.[11] Hugh Sampson, with extensive interests at West Hall, north of Rochelle Lane, held property also at West Hithe, in the lee of the castle, where Thomas Sampson owned a quay.[12] And Richard of Southwick, a generation before, had lived at, and traded from, the great tenement, already antique in his day, on the sea front to the south of Ronceval. To each of these important individuals, it was essential that access to his house should be preserved. On Cuckoo Lane, where Richard had lived, the houses were never rebuilt following the raid of 1338. Their sites became garden plots shortly after the town wall in that quarter was completed. Ronceval, likewise, although more happily situated on Westgate Street, clearly lost its attractions as a private residence once the wall was built. Significantly, a note made in 1397 of property to the north, by Pilgrims' Pit and Simnel Street, described the plot as vacant and of no yearly value.[13] Within the walls, and bordered by them, it had ceased to have any real function.

Reluctant both by reason of cost and for fear of a deterioration of property values to seal the town within a wall, the burgesses had been searching already some years before the raid of 1338 for some more acceptable alternative. They were aware, as indeed the men of Winchelsea had taught them, of the vulnerability of their seaward defences. As a part of the programme of works initiated by Edward II, they built themselves a timber barbican 'towards the sea'. And in 1336, planning to replace it in stone, they secured from the king an extension of a customs levy, now to be known as 'barbicanage', to support the work.[14] But a barbican alone, while it might help outflank the enemy, could do little to prevent a landing. Evidently it failed to do so in 1338. Nor could it ever have been truly effective so long as the waterfront remained otherwise unprotected. If the burgesses, for good reasons of their own, continued hesitant, the king, after the bitter lesson of the raid, was to see clearly the need for immediate action. By March 1339, he had required a 'stone wall to be built forthwith towards the water', and was moving himself to further the work.[15]

Preparations for war had long been in hand. Already, in September 1337, the provision and adequate manning of warning beacons on the hill tops had been ordered by the king, and Hampshire, generally, was put in a posture of defence.[16] There is even a story that a French attack on the havens along Southampton Water was successfully repulsed in 1335.[17] But a full-scale assault, when it came in the first days of October 1338, found the burgesses in little heart to resist it. Inevitably, narratives of the raid vary, and there is even some doubt about the date.[18] But the story, as Froissart tells it, is that Hugh Quieret and his Genoese allies took the town by surprise on Sunday morning, while the people were at mass. Meeting little resistance, they slew many burgesses, violated their womenfolk and made off with considerable plunder on the next tide.[19] Although strong in circumstantial detail and enriched with appropriate patriotic embellishment, the narrative of John Stow, the sixteenth-century antiquary, is substantially the same:[20]

> The fourth of October, fiftie Gallies well manned and furnished, came to Southampton about 9 of the clock, and sacked the towne the townesmen running away for feare: by the breake of the next day they which fled, by helpe of the countrey thereabout, came against the Pyrats, & fought with them: in the which skirmish were slaine to the number of three hundred pirates, together with their Captaine, a young soldier, the king of Sicils sonne. To this young man, the French king had given whatsoever hee got in the kingdom of England: but hee being beaten downe by a certaine man of the countrey, cried Rancon, notwithstanding the husband-man laid on with his club, till he had slaine him, speaking these wordes: yea (quoth he) I know well enough thou art a Francon, and therefore shalt thou die, for he understood not his speech, neither had he any skill to take gentlemen prysoners, and to keepe them for their ransome: wherefore the residue of those Gennowaies, after they had set the Towne afire and burnt it up quite, fled to their gallies, & in their flying certaine of them were drowned. And after this the inhabitants of the town compassed it about with a strong and great walle.

Stung by the ease of the assault, which he took as an insult to himself, Edward III's reaction was immediate. Within a few days of the event, he commissioned Richard fitz Alan, earl of Arundel, to enquire into the circumstances of the raid. He suspected treachery on the part of the keepers of the coast and arrayers of men in the county, who 'knowing that the attack was to be made, not only neglected entirely to provide for the defence of parts threatened but basely fled with the men of the said town [Southampton] on sight of the enemy'. It had been reported to the king that 'the said keepers and their deputies permitted the men appointed to stay to guard the coast at the charges of the said county and of the counties of Berkshire and Wiltshire and of some other places, for money and other gifts received for this purpose by the keepers and deputies, to go home, and did not find the men-at-arms, archers and others for whom they had levied divers other sums of money in the said counties and places'. Richard fitz Alan was commanded to discover 'through whose default the town of Southampton was taken, how the keepers and arrayers bore themselves when the galleys came in sight and at other times, the names of the men of Southampton and others who fled from the enemy or adhered to them and all other particulars of the disgraceful neglect of duty in this behalf'. He was to 'punish such as are most guilty by imprisonment in the Tower of London or elsewhere as may be expedient'.[21]

The king's anger cooled, but it could scarcely have had time to do so before it was discovered that looting on a considerable scale had followed the departure of the raiders. On 18 October, five days after the issue of his original commission, Richard fitz Alan was instructed to seek out the names of the men of Southampton, Wiltshire and Berkshire who 'both before the king's enemies entered the town and afterwards, carried away his wool there'. It had been reported that a part only of the king's wool, brought to Southampton before the raid, had been burnt by the enemy, and that 'a great quantity unburned by them has since been carried away by men of the town'. There were reports, too, of looting of the king's wines, and complaints of Spanish merchants visiting the port, who had suffered loss the same way.

The enquiries, initiated in October and November 1338, continued through a good part of the ensuing year.[22] The king was seeking a scapegoat, and it may well have been this that brought Nicholas de Moundenard to the Tower of London in July 1339. But if Nicholas was carrying more responsibility than he deserved, the crimes of which he was accused were no more than might be expected of his circle. While collector of customs at Southampton in the years before the raid, he had allowed the lading of wool and other goods without due payment of customs; he had held back a portion of his receipts; he had sold ships to the king's enemies in Spain; he had misappropriated, on a considerable scale, the wools properly belonging to the crown. In the company of others, it was further alleged, Nicholas had converted to his own use the moneys collected, by authority of the king and his father, for murage, quayage and barbicanage in the town.[23] If the fall of the town were not blamed on him directly, it can only have been because there were others at least as guilty as he.

Wherever the fault might lie, there could be no doubt of the extent of the catastrophe. While they did little to identify the culprits, the king's enquiries showed that, of his wools assembled at Southampton, all but 29 sarplars and 50 cloves had been seized or burnt by the enemy. In total, he had had 270 sarplars, 136 sacks, 40 cloves and 5 pounds of wool at the port.[24] His wines had suffered as badly. Of a special purchase of 194 tuns of red wine, awaiting shipment at Southampton, only two tuns survived the raid. On the day of the landing, 152 tuns were on board *La Nicholas*, loaded and ready for dispatch; the remaining 42 tuns were stored in different houses through the town.[25] The king's financiers, the Florentine firms of Bardi and Peruzzi, had chosen Southampton as a loading-point for their wools, to by-pass the French fleet guarding the straits of Dover. Such were their losses in the raid that they transferred their business in succeeding years to Bristol, returning to Southampton only in the summer months of 1341.[26] For a full year after the raid, there were no wool exports recorded at Southampton, nor did the totals recover until the Italians came back to the port.[27] Trade of all kinds was almost at a standstill. In the four months of martial law, from 10 November 1338 to 15 March 1339, customs receipts, tolls and perquisites of the courts totalled together a bare £7. 19*s*. 11½*d*. For the six months following, despite a return to more normal conditions of government, Nicholas Sampson (mayor) and Richard Imberd (bailiff) could collect from the same sources no more than £8. 18*s*. 8½*d*. With regard to the receipts from Portsmouth, for which they should also have accounted, they declared on oath that no customable goods whatever had passed through the port, because of the war at sea.[28]

In Southampton, and Portsmouth too, the scene was one of desolation. The raiders had made a bonfire of the town. They had destroyed, or carried away, its instruments of government; they had burnt houses, even churches, to the ground. Rentals of 1340 and 1342 record properties still waste from St Michael's and Holy Rood, on the south, through the central parish of St Lawrence to All Saints, on the north.[29] But, inevitably, the greatest damage was done in the southern parishes, fired as the raiders retreated. Archaeologically, it is attested on several sites in the old town, perhaps most obviously at the junction of English Street and Broad Lane. Here great pits had been dug following the raid, to take the destruction debris it had caused. They held burnt tile and slate, with a little of the pottery of the period. In many cases, they were sealed deceptively by a layer of clean clay, the original spoil from the digging, and had become bell-shaped in section, quite distinct from the more normal rubbish pits scattered throughout each site.[30] Certainly, the destruction in these areas, on other evidence, is likely to have been unusually complete. Nicholas Sampson, who lived on the west side of French Street, parish of St John, was mayor at the time of the raid. In obedience to the borough ordinances, he would have kept at his house the common chest of the town, in which were stored its moneys, charters and seals.[31] There had clearly been no opportunity to salvage them. Within a few days of the raid, on 23 October 1338, the king ordered the cutting, with differences, of a new seal for the recognizance of debts at Southampton, the old one having been carried off by 'pirates of certain galleys'. It was ready by 16 November, when Robert de Stretfeld was appointed its custodian.[32] The documents, also, had suffered. The most important (because the latest) statement of the rights of the burgesses, Edward III's own confirmation of their liberties, 'by chance was burnt'. An exemplification was granted, at the request of the borough, on 4 April 1340.[33] Across the street, to the east, the Weigh House was looted. The weights and the weigh-beam were removed, and the customs seals carried away.[34] At the far end of Broad Lane, Henry de Lym had lost his copy, burnt in the raid, of letters patent granted to him on 23 October 1334 in pardon of his outlawry. He had them confirmed on 16 January 1341.[35]

Thomas de Byndon, his near-neighbour to the south, had to move out of the tenement he held from St Denys before the 'burning of the town'. He had lost a wine tavern and other adjoining properties in the fire.[36]

Undoubtedly among those worst affected were the religious foundations whose income depended in some part on rented property in the borough. Shortly after the raid, Gilbert de Wiggeton, once a royal clerk and now master of God's House, endeavoured to rescue his hospital by an astute personal arrangement with the king, his former employer. The king, it was agreed between them, would keep half the proceeds of a collection of rental arrears owing to the hospital, some of them accumulated before the raid, provided that he collected them himself. This half would go to the defence of the town, the other would support the brethren.[37] But it was easier said than done. In the circumstances, nobody could pay his rent, and on 22 March 1344 the custody of God's House, 'much depressed' by the raid, was granted in a salvage operation to the provost and scholars of Queen Philippa's new hall at Oxford. It was noted, on the occasion of a grant of relief from taxes and tolls, dated 18 November 1347, that 'the hospital in great part and its charters of liberties and other muniments have been burned by certain alien enemies'.[38]

The sad repercussions of the raid were felt at St Denys for another half-century at least. The prior and convent of this small Augustinian house joined with their fellows at Southwick in 1339 to seek a respite from the payment of tenths, by reason of 'houses and other buildings burnt and waste'.[39] The relief was extended in later years, and on 1 June 1347, in part compensation for its losses, the priory was permitted to absorb the assets of the leper hospital of St Mary Magdalene, to the north of the town defences.[40] But the debts of the house continued to mount. In 1385, the poor state of the priory's finances was still said to be the result of the heavy loss it had sustained to its possessions, 'burned and destroyed by the French and other enemies'.[41] And, thirty years later, the position had scarcely improved. When licence was granted to the prior and convent, on 4 April 1405, to appropriate the churches of Holy Rood and St Michael, it followed their plea that 'a great part of their lands, rents and possessions within the town of Southampton and elsewhere are waste and their charters and muniments are torn and burned by the French'.[42]

The conflagration, most destructive at the southern end of the town, left many of the leading burgesses homeless. It made government, on the old pattern, temporarily unworkable. To halt further looting, and to anticipate renewed threats from abroad, the king had little alternative other than to impose some form of martial law on the town. He made a virtue of necessity by using the occasion to demonstrate his extreme displeasure. When John de Scures and Thomas Coudray were appointed keepers of the borough on 12 October 1338, to hold it 'during pleasure' for the king, it was made clear that Edward III had been brought to this point by the disgraceful behaviour of the burgesses themselves, abandoning their defences to the dishonour of the crown and the peril of the realm.[43] In the event, neither Scures nor Coudray, both busy elsewhere, could accept the charge. But on 10 November two others, John de Boklond

Plate 10 94 High Street, a late-medieval vault recently restored

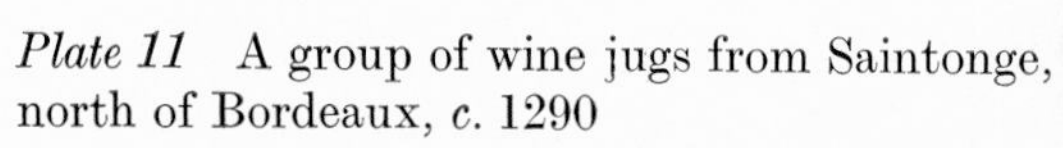

Plate 11 A group of wine jugs from Saintonge, north of Bordeaux, *c.* 1290

Plate 12 A thirteenth-century wine jug from Rouen

and John de Palton, took their place, bringing with them a garrison described, optimistically, as of 'no small number', although probably numbering no more than six men-at-arms and twelve archers.[44] During the four months of their stay, they accomplished little beyond the repair of the king's houses at the castle, where, presumably, they lodged, and the ordering of the royal gaol, burnt, with the castle, in the raid.[45] But there might, indeed, have been few opportunities to do more. A winter of exceptional severity set in, after an unusually wet autumn. Both seasons held up, and might even have halted, the work of clearance and repair. 'In this year', it was said,[46]

> from the beginning of October to the beginning of the month of December there fell such rains that the ground was rendered quite saturated, and in England, due to this, there was no sowing. And in the beginning of the month of December came a very hard frost so that the whole of the saturated ground was completely frozen and the whole earth was seen to be like ice. This frost lasted twelve weeks, whence the whole of the winter sowing was as if dead, so that in March, April and May, almost nothing appeared, especially in the fruitful valleys and other good grounds.

As the frost cleared and the weather generally improved, the king's concern for the safety of the port increased. Already, late in December, there had been rumours of another planned onslaught, and Roger Norman was commissioned to send a ship to sea to spy out the dispositions of the French fleet.[47] On Sunday 21 February 1339, Richard Talbot entered the town to take charge of the guard. He brought with him a small army of 50 men-at-arms and 100 archers.[48] By the middle of March, the king himself was at Winchester, visiting Southampton in person during his stay in the locality, and consulting with his council how best to protect it.[49] A flurry of activity, at last purposefully directed, accompanied the presence of the king. Arrangements were made to pay Richard Talbot and his men; the Winchester clergy, the bishop, the prior of St Swithin's and the abbot of Hyde, were instructed to send him reinforcements; two small boats were assigned to the defence; and the armaments of the town, the springalds, engines, arbalests, lances and armour, with stocks of iron and of lead, were delivered to Richard's charge.[50] On 15 March, the government of the town was restored to its elected officers, with Nicholas Sampson again mayor. The burgesses, by reason of the losses they had sustained in houses, goods and chattels, 'lately burned by the king's enemies', were granted temporary relief from taxation.[51]

On their excursion to the town, the king and council had decided that its defence would require the completion of the circuit of its walls. At once, an order went out to the sheriffs of Wiltshire and Southampton to recruit such carpenters, smiths, masons, plasterers and other workmen as might be necessary 'for enclosing the town of Southampton and the neighbouring parts with a wall of stone and lime'.[52] The next day, on 16 March, the king instructed the sheriff of Southampton to see that proclamation was made in the town to the effect that all burgesses should rebuild their houses, 'according to their faculty'. There were some, he had heard, who, because of their losses in the raid and the expense of rebuilding and fortification, had already left the town, to the manifest prejudice of its defence. Wherever they had settled, they were to return, or they would find their lands forfeit to the king.[53] By the last weeks of March, repairs to the walls and additional works on the enclosure were well in hand. Robert atte Barre, currently receiver for the king, accounted before the end of the month for £66. 13*s*. 4*d*., obtained for that purpose from the Exchequer. In the three months between 12 May and 11 August, the large sum of £206. 0*s*. 4¼*d*. was spent on the manufacture and repair of springalds and other engines of war, on the quarrying and transport of stone for wall-building, on the purchase of lime, iron, lead, timber and nails, and on the wages of the workmen.[54] Through August and September, the detailed accounts of Nicholas atte Magdaleyne, Robert atte Barre's successor, record regular payments to a large force of masons, carpenters, sawyers, labourers and carters, busy on the defences of the town. In the second week of August, for example, there were twelve carpenters and a smith working, under the direction of an expert sent down by the king, on the construction of a great new mangonel, or catapult. At the south end of English Street, next to the sea, the gate and its approaches required considerable attention. Further, a large item in the account, entered in the fourth week in September, was the cost of clearing a length of nineteen perches along the town ditch, immediately east of the friary. In its finished state, the ditch measured twenty-four feet in width, twelve in depth.[55]

While the works progressed, a permanent garrison was stationed partly in the town itself and partly at St Denys, on the Itchen. From April into July, Edmund de la Beche, banneret, headed a force of four knights, fifteen men-at-arms, forty foot-soldiers and fifty archers. They were paid the standard 'wages of the king accustomed in war': 4*s*. daily for the commander himself, 2*s*. for a knight, 12*d*. for a man-at-arms, 8*d*. for a foot-soldier, and 3*d*. for an archer.[56] In April, the king sent munitions to the town; in May, he ordered springalds, arbalests, quarrels, bows and arrows, lances and breastplates to be delivered there immediately.[57] Throughout the region, requisitions went out for supplies and additional men. Philip of Thame, prior of the Hospitallers in England and himself later commander at Southampton, was asked to furnish thirty men-at-arms. Men were summoned from the establishments of the religious houses at Romsey, Hyde, Beaulieu and Abingdon, and others requested from the sheriffs of Southampton, Hampshire, Oxfordshire and Berkshire.[58]

Few, in the event, responded to the call, and some had good reason to resist it. On 18 April, it was the abbot of Beaulieu who was supported in his plea that his contribution should be restricted to the provision of two archers for the garrison and a sum of money towards the enclosure of the town. He could afford no more.[59] Nearer home, at St Mary's, the precentor argued that as his church and dwelling were, in any case, outside the walls of the town, he should not be expected to find men for watch duties on the defences, beyond the two foot-soldiers and four archers he had already undertaken to provide. On 6 June, Edmund de la Beche and his associate keepers, Richard de Penle and Stephen de Bitterle, were ordered to desist from pressing their demand for more.[60] Exactly a week before, the six men-at-arms promised by the abbot of Hyde had been diverted to the defence of Portsmouth, then thought by Richard fitz Alan, earl of Arundel and keeper of the maritime lands, to be in greater danger than Southampton.[61] It was not an opinion shared by the custodians of Southampton itself. As recently as 20 May, Edmund de la Beche had complained that, despite the danger of another attack, 'daily imminent', the abbot of Abingdon and others were hanging back on their obligation to furnish the town with men and supplies of victuals.[62] By the time the earl of Warwick took charge of the town, late in July, the situation had deteriorated still further. On 29 July, he wrote complaining that he could discover no more than ten men adequately armed in the town. Of the absentees, it was the men of Berkshire and those of the Hospitallers who were particularly singled out for blame.[63]

As much, clearly, had been suspected when the earl obtained his original letters of appointment on 13 July 1339. His commission, granted under the great seal, carried with it the duty to 'muster the men-at-arms and archers of the prior of the hospital, and the men-at-arms of Berkshire, and others who shall be sent to aid in the keeping of the said town; and to punish them at such time as default shall be found; and also to constrain by force the people who used to be inhabitants of the said town, and who have now retreated, to return and live therein perforce according to their ability, and in case they will not do it, to seize their houses, rents and other possessions, and all their goods and chattels, in the same town, into the hand of our said lord the king'. Further, it was arranged that the earl should take with him to Southampton a considerable force of his own, to supplement the garrison he found there. 'The same earl shall have with him for the same custody one hundred men-at-arms, of which he shall have of his own people fifty men-at-arms, the earl himself, one banneret, and ten knights. . . . And shall have also with him for the said guard one hundred and twenty archers, of whom the said earl shall have of his own men, forty'.[64]

Allowing for the deficiencies of local recruitment, it is unlikely that the earl, through the thirty-two days of his residence in the town, could have had at his disposal many more than the fifty men-at-arms and forty archers of his own personal retinue. His replacement, Philip of Thame, who arrived on 29 August, four days after the earl's departure, brought with him a much smaller retinue of twenty men-at-arms and ten 'armed men', or foot-soldiers. But he also had assigned to him, on the direction of Edward, duke of Cornwall, an additional force of five knights, fifteen men-at-arms and forty archers. On 15 September, soon after the prior's arrival in the town, the errant men of Berkshire were reminded once again of their obligations. Yet their response was limited. Through October and early November, there was a notable fall in the numbers of the garrison at Southampton. Besides the prior's personal retinue, which remained with him until he gave up the charge of the town, the wages of a single knight and twelve men-at-arms were all that were accounted for at the Exchequer for the period 29 September to 8 November.[65] The crisis had passed some months before. On 24 June, Edward III's victory in the great sea battle at Sluys had shattered the French fleet, and the immediate danger of another full-scale assault on the English coast was over. There are other indications of a more relaxed climate at

Southampton. On 15 September, at his own petition, Thomas atte Marche was allowed to go about his business in the realm. He had been restricted, like all his fellow burgesses, to the vicinity of the town itself.[66] In November, the men of Southampton, reluctant though they might be to assume it, were entrusted once again with the care of their own defences. Although Philip of Thame did not leave the town for some weeks, the decision to remove him had clearly been taken at the beginning of the month. On 6 November, he was ordered to deliver the armaments in his charge to Arnold of Exeter, John Forst, Nicholas Lony and Henry Imberd. He listed them as 3 springalds, 33 arbalests, 9 arbalest belts, 62 lances, 31 bows, 49 sheaves of arrows, and assorted ammunition (quarrels) for the springalds and two sizes of arbalest. Arnold and his associates put off accepting the charge as long as they could. But the prior left the town before the end of the month, and on 10 December they were ordered to receive the weapons forthwith, or suffer imprisonment if they refused.[67]

No record survives of further royal garrisons at Southampton, and in future years it was the burgesses themselves who were arrayed to meet each fresh crisis as it came. New invasion scares marred the summer of 1340, 1342 and 1346.[68] But there was now at least some pattern to determine the limits of personal responsibility in the borough. An agistment of men-at-arms for the town, dating probably to 1341, has survived among the public records. It lists armed men who, it states, exceeded 120, and defence charges exceeding 200 marks. Of the many burgesses cited, Thomas de Byndon was to provide £5, and must serve himself with three men-at-arms; John Forst, £4, himself and two men-at-arms; Henry de Lym, £3, himself and two men-at-arms; Henry Fleming, £3, himself and two men-at-arms; Nicholas Sampson, himself and an archer. Roger Norman, perhaps the wealthiest burgess of his generation, was excused altogether from service. Presumably he chose to claim exemption by virtue of the special privileges he had earned in the royal cause. But he had already been exceptionally active in defence work immediately following the raid.[69] Among Southampton burgesses generally, the climate of opinion had changed. When Robert Marlebrew drew up his will in 1349, he bequeathed three shops to the borough, 'to the maintenance of the walls round the town of Southampton'. Two of them were sited on the sea front.[70] At another vulnerable point next to the sea, the warden of God's House made his own personal provision against raids. In his chamber at the hospital, inventoried in 1362, arms and armour were an important element in the otherwise sparse furnishings of the apartment.[71]

Notes

1 Rymer, *Foedera*, ii:456; *Cal.C.R. 1318–23*, pp. 486, 490.

2 William Stubbs (ed.), *Chronicles of the reigns of Edward I and Edward II*, i:298; *Rot. Parlm.*, ii:413; and P.R.O. SC8/17/833.

3 *Cal.C.R. 1318–23*, pp. 159, 696; *Cal. State Papers Venetian, 1202–1509*, pp. 5–6; *Cal.P.R. 1321–4*, p. 276, and *1324–7*, p. 195. The incident is discussed by Alwyn Ruddock, *Italian Merchants and Shipping*, p. 25.

4 *Cal.P.R. 1321–4*, pp. 250–1, 450, 453, and *1324–7*, pp. 225, 315; also Ruddock, op. cit., p. 26.
5 *Cal.P.R. 1324–7*, p. 252, *1327–30*, p. 64, *1334–8*, pp. 240–1, and *1340–3*, p. 136. A 'new wall of the town', on its south-eastern quarter where the properties of God's House lay, is mentioned already in the hospital accounts of 1323–4 and 1325–6 (*R.C.H.M.*, 6th report, pp. 566, 567).
6 P.R.O. E372/117, m. 3; *Cal.P.R. 1281–92*, p. 229.
7 *Cal.C.R. 1307–13*, pp. 29–30, 50; *Cal.P.R. 1281–92*, p. 13.
8 S.C.R.O. SC2/6/2, no. 1; *Cat.Anc. Deeds*, ii:B3396.
9 Bodleian, Queen's College MS. 339, 340.
10 Win.Coll.Mun. 17761, 17762.
11 S.C.R.O. SC2/6/2.
12 Bodleian, Queen's College MS. 339; *Cat.Anc. Deeds*, ii:B3396.
13 Cal.Inq.Misc. *1392–9*, pp. 196–7.
14 *Cal.P.R. 1334–8*, pp. 240–1.
15 Ibid., *1338–40*, p. 237, and *Cal.C.R. 1339–41*, p. 101.
16 Rymer, *Foedera*, ii:996. For a discussion of the royal defensive strategy on the south coast, see A. Z. Freeman, 'A moat defensive: the coast defense scheme of 1295', *Speculum*, 42 (1967), pp. 442–62.
17 V. H. Galbraith (ed.), *The Anonimalle chronicle, 1333 to 1381*, p. 5.
18 The chroniclers agree, and Froissart's version depends upon it, that the landing took place on the Sunday morning, 4 October 1338. But within a few months of the event the king was told that the town had been plundered on the following Monday, to be burnt before the sailing of the galleys the next day (*Cal.C.R. 1339–41*, p. 143).
19 J. A. C. Buchon (ed.), *Les chroniques de sire Jean Froissart*, i:72–3.
20 Edmund Howes, *Annales, or, A Generall Chronicle of England, begun by John Stow*, p. 235. For another sturdily patriotic version of the event, playing down the degree of the disaster, see the ballad in Thomas Wright (ed.), *Political poems and songs relating to English history*, i:64.
21 *Cal.P.R. 1338–40*, pp. 180–1.
22 Ibid., pp. 179, 183, 184, 283, 286.
23 *Cal.C.R. 1339–41*, pp. 119, 241, and *Cal.P.R. 1340–3*, pp. 312, 326. Customs frauds were a phenomenon of the times: the product as much of confusion as of criminal intent. In 1336 the king heard that several Southampton merchants had caused their ships to be unloaded before inspection by the collectors in the port (*Cal.C.R. 1333–7*, p. 680). Widespread evasions, in Southampton and elsewhere, would be suspected in 1340, and there was a general post of collectors in January 1341 (Ibid., *1339–41*, pp. 627, 628, 663). Henry Fleming, John Forst, Nicholas Sampson and others were to be implicated in further alleged customs frauds in 1341–2. Accusations would be brought against them in 1344, and heavy fines imposed in 1345 (P.R.O. E372/190, m. 27; accusations and rejoinders are discussed by Henry S. Cobb, *Local Port Book, 1439–40*, pp. xiii–xiv).
24 *Cal.C.R. 1339–41*, pp. 550–1. A sarplar contained about 2½ sacks of wool; a clove, seven pounds.
25 Ibid., p. 143.
26 Alwyn Ruddock, *Italian Merchants and Shipping*, pp. 32–5.
27 E. M. Carus-Wilson and Olive Coleman, *England's Export Trade, 1275–1547*, pp. 45–6.
28 P.R.O. E372/184, m. 17d.
29 Bodleian, Queen's College MS. 339, 340; see also, for the churches, *Cal.C.R. 1339–41*, p. 104. It should be said, however, that H. T. Riley, on the basis of these same rent rolls, considered contemporary accounts of the destruction vastly exaggerated. Of the 108 tenements of the hospital, he points out, only 29 had been burnt, none of these in the suburbs. Properties burnt included 1 of the hospital's 17 tenements in Holy Rood, 4 of the 18 in St John's, 17 of the 37 in St Michael's, 4 of the 6 in St Lawrence's, and 3 of the 9 in All Saints within the Bar (*R.C.H.M.*, 6th report, p. 555).
30 *Southampton Excavations*, forthcoming.
31 *Oak Book*, i:46–9. For the siting of Nicholas Sampson's capital tenement, see S.C.R.O. SC4/2/57.
32 *Cal.C.R. 1337–9*, p. 548; *Cal.P.R. 1338–40*, p. 162.
33 *Charters*, i:10–21, and *Cal. P.R. 1338–40*, p. 453.
34 Rymer, *Foedera*, ii:1070; *Cal.C.R. 1339–41*, pp. 7, 375.
35 *Cal.P.R. 1340–3*, p. 79.
36 St Denys Cart. 235; also *Cat.Anc. Deeds*, ii:B3406.
37 *Cal.P.R. 1338–40*, p. 275.
38 God's House Deeds 316 and 318; *Cal.P.R. 1343–5*, p. 215; *Cal.Ch.R. 1341–1417*, p. 70; *Cal.C.R. 1381–5*, p. 627.
39 *Rot.Parlm.*, ii:111; *Cal.C.R. 1339–41*, p. 104.
40 *Rot.Parlm.*, ii:114; *Cal.P.R. 1340–3*, p. 579, *1345–8*, pp. 298–9.
41 *Cal.P.R. 1381–5*, p. 556; royal custody of the house and its possessions was extended, at two-year intervals, in 1387 and 1389 (Ibid., *1385–9*, p. 277, *1388–92*, p. 8).
42 Ibid., *1405–8*, p. 26.
43 *Cal. Fine R.*, v:97.
44 Ibid., v:102; *Cal.C.R. 1339–41*, p. 18.
45 P.R.O. E372/184, m. 17d.
46 E. M. Thompson (ed.), *Adae Murimuth:*

continuatio chronicarum, pp. 88–9, quoted by C. E. Britton, *A Meteorological Chronology to A.D. 1450*, p. 139; see also J. Titow, 'Evidence of weather in the account rolls of the bishopric of Winchester, 1209–1350', *Ec.H.R.*, 2nd series, 12 (1959–60), pp. 396–7.

47 *Cal.P.R. 1338–40*, p. 171.

48 *Rot.Parlm.*, ii:108.

49 *Cal.P.R. 1338–40*, p. 275.

50 *Rot.Parlm.*, ii:108–9.

51 *Cal. Fine R.*, v:124; *Cal.C.R. 1339–41*, p. 102.

52 Rymer, *Foedera*, ii:1077, and *Cal.C.R. 1339–41*, p. 55.

53 *Rot.Parlm.*, ii:108; *Cal.C.R. 1339–41*, p. 101; Rymer, *Foedera*, ii:1077.

54 P.R.O. E101/22/11.

55 P.R.O. E101/22/7, 12; *Cal.C.R. 1339–41*, p. 202. Robert atte Barre, the former receiver, had died in July (Ibid., p. 175).

56 P.R.O. E101/22/11; *Cal.C.R. 1339–41*, p. 166.

57 *Cal.C.R. 1339–41*, pp. 64, 83.

58 Ibid., pp. 67, 114, 215, 218, 233; Rymer, *Foedera*, ii:1079.

59 *Cal.C.R. 1339–41*, p. 67.

60 Ibid., p. 215.

61 Ibid., p. 218.

62 P.R.O. E101/561/17, SC8/172/8598.

63 P.R.O. SC1/41/171.

64 *Sign Manuals and Letters Patent*, i:46–7.

65 P.R.O. E101/22/10; *Cal.C.R., 1339–41*, pp. 260, 305.

66 *Cal.P.R. 1338–40*, p. 316.

67 P.R.O. E101/22/6 and 17; *Cal.C.R. 1339–41*, pp. 288, 304–5, 340.

68 *Cal.P.R. 1340–3*, pp. 12, 476; Rymer, *Foedera*, ii:1210, iii:78, 86.

69 P.R.O. C47/2/39/42. For Roger Norman's exemption, see *Cal.P.R. 1338–40*, p. 56. On 30 May 1339, following the raid, he had obtained an exemplification of these letters patent. It is possible that he, like Henry de Lym his near-neighbour, had lost documents and other properties in the fire (Ibid., p. 252).

70 Bodleian, Queen's College MS. 1077, and P.R.O. E326/9359.

71 Bodleian, Queen's College MS. 230, quoted by Richard Harris, 'God's House, Southampton, in the reign of Edward III', Southampton M.A. dissertation, 1970, p. 33. The God's House requirement in the agistment of 1341 consisted of the warden himself, two men-at-arms and two archers.

Chapter eleven

Recession

There was probably nothing exceptional in Thomas atte Marche's determination to resume trade as soon as possible after the disaster. But in the borough as a whole, the recovery of pre-war levels of trade was slow and desperately uncertain. It was not, primarily, the raid that was at fault, although the burgesses were accustomed to blame it for their troubles. Rather, the recession stemmed from a profound, and very general, crisis of business confidence, the product of endemic war compounded by plague. At Southampton, in the wake of the raid, an effort was made at reconstruction. Provision for the rebuilding of two houses in St Lawrence, to the west of English Street, was included in a lease negotiated in June 1341, to which a saving clause was also attached against further enemy attack.[1] The Florentines were persuaded to return to the town in the summer of 1341, and in the following season there was a spectacular, if temporary, recovery of denizen wool exports.[2] But although the issues of the town climbed steadily from £19. 6*s*. 5*d*. in 1339–40 to £41. 0*s*. $2\frac{1}{4}$*d*. in 1340–1, and to £65. 18*s*. $5\frac{1}{4}$*d*. in 1341–2, the growth could not be sustained. A generation later, in the seventies, for lack of alien merchants to pay the tolls, the issues had fallen back to nearer £40. The foreigners, upon whom the town was becoming increasingly dependent, had been frightened off, like the Bardi and Peruzzi before them, by the war.[3]

The placing of the economy on a wartime footing, and the transition, inevitably painful, from one kind of trading situation to another, temporarily destroyed the borough finances. When prosperity returned again to the town, late in the century, it was the consequence less of local initiatives than of the renewed activity of alien merchants, principally Italians, who might favour the town or withdraw from it, precisely as they chose. Yet it took many decades to achieve even this. In the meantime, there was little life in the economy of the region. The ancient cloth industry of Winchester was bankrupt; alien merchants avoided the ports; the king's war machine drained more resources from the boroughs than it could possibly return. In 1360, Winchester, Southampton and Portsmouth were associated in an exemption from further military taxation in the immediate future, 'for the poverty which they are undergoing in these days'.[4] And this was the condition which, in Southampton at least, had persisted already for two decades.

Starting with the initial exemption from taxes, granted on 15 March 1339 as an interim measure following the raid, there was little break in the long succession of pleas, advanced by the burgesses to the king, for the reduction, or remission altogether, of their farm. In response to one such plea, the king that November ordered his collectors in the county to visit the borough and to assess for themselves the degree of relief to which its burgesses ought to be entitled.[5] But by July the following year, the queen, to whom the farm belonged, was complaining that she had received nothing from the burgesses since the raid, and arrangements had to be made, both then and in 1342, to compensate her.[6] Effectively, the town's expected payments were reduced to £100 in 1342. But three years later the tax liability of the burgesses, computed at the Exchequer in November 1345, had come to total £1,810. 8*s*. 6*d*., well beyond all hopes of repayment.[7] Other smaller obligations, in the interim, remained unmet. For two centuries, the abbot of Cormeilles, in Normandy, had drawn a pension of £9. 5*s*. 0*d*. from the revenues of Southampton. Latterly, it had been collected for him by his proctor, the prior of his Gloucestershire cell at Newent. But in 1344, and again in 1347, it was recorded that nothing had been received from the town.[8] The abbot of Lyre, entitled to an identical sum, suffered the same experience. In 1347 he complained likewise, through his priory at Carisbrooke (Isle of Wight), that he had received no payments since the raid.[9]

The accumulated obligations of the town, recorded in detail at the Exchequer, could never, of course, be met. But it took another calamity, hard on the heels of the first, to persuade the king finally of the unreality of the farm. In the last months of 1348, just ten years after the raid, the Black Death visited Southampton. It had made its first appearance in the Mediterranean in 1347, had spread over most of southern and central France by June 1348, and reached Southampton before the end of the year.[10] Henry Knighton, the Leicester chronicler, held that it was at Southampton that the plague first penetrated England. But whether there or, as others maintained, at Bristol, the infection, once contracted, spread rapidly.[11] In the warmer weather of the spring of 1349, as the plague fleas emerged from hibernation, mortality rose. Little is known at Southampton of the progress of this 'wretched, fierce, violent' pestilence, at the conclusion of which only the 'dregs of the populace live to tell the tale'.[12] But Alice Kempe and Robert Marlebrew drew up their testaments at the height of the epidemic, within a day of each other early in April 1349. And Alice Barnabe, wife of Walter, had anticipated them both on 7 January that year.[13] John Hokele, a wealthy merchant and ship-owner, may have been another victim of the pestilence.[14] While at Holy Rood, through the worst weeks of the epidemic, no fewer than three vicars were presented separately to the cure, the first on 12 March, the second on 22 April, the third on 20 September.[15]

By 1351, the plague, whatever its toll, was counted among the principal causes of the borough's impoverishment: a reason for the halving of the farm.[16] Epidemics had been known before, and in due course, as they became familiar, a routine was developed in Southampton, as elsewhere, to isolate the victims and to prevent contagion wherever possible. But the great pandemic of 1348–9 had struck with unparalleled ferocity, and few had the courage to resist it. In 1352, when the Black

Death had reached as far as Novgorod in the distant north, the chronicler recorded it with resignation:[17]

> The same year there was a great plague in Novgorod; it came on us by God's loving kindness, and in His righteous judgement, death came upon people, painful and sudden, it began from Lady Day till Easter; a countless number of good people died then. These were the symptons of that death: a man would spit blood and after three days he was dead. But this death did not visit Novgorod alone; I believe it passed over the face of all the land; and whom ever God commanded, that man died, and whomever he saved, him he admonished and punished, that the rest of our days we may live in the Lord virtuously and sinlessly.

Even for the survivors, horizons had narrowed and prospects dimmed. From Michaelmas 1351, the release for eight years of £100 of the borough farm heralded the opening of another era of extended military activity in the town and of sluggish, even stagnant, trade. Over the next half-century, the export of raw wool, everywhere in decline as the demands of the home-based cloth industry rose, rarely reached more than half its pre-war figures in the port, and was usually very much less. Cloth exports at Southampton, although certainly expanding in the fifties, showed no permanent increase until the last two decades of the century.[18] Meanwhile the commerce in wine, the other major trading commodity of the port, reacted badly both to the war and to the pestilence. Imports of wine were never to sink as low again as they had done in 1348–9, following the visitation of the plague at Bordeaux. But at no point within the century did the number of tuns imported even so much as approach the totals of the beginning of Edward III's reign, still less those of a decade before.[19] It would be a sad comment on the altered face of trade that the safe arrival, in 1381, of a fleet of ships at Southampton, loaded with spices and wine, should be a matter for nation-wide remark.[20]

The war, which had cut back wine production at Bordeaux, and which was everywhere forcing up prices, touched Southampton at many points. Much of the fighting took place in Gascony, and Southampton's existing links with that province made it the natural embarkation point for expeditions in support of the English interest. Already, before the plague, Henry, earl of Derby, had mustered his troops at Southampton in the summer of 1345, in preparation for his Gascon campaign; while William de Bohun, earl of Northampton, at the neighbouring harbour of Portsmouth, gathered his forces for Brittany.[21] A Southampton ship, *La Trinite*, had been seized off the Isle of Wight and its cargo forcibly unloaded, to help transport the earl of Northampton's men.[22] For many weeks that summer, and this was to be a recurring experience, troops had gathered in the area, allowing malefactors, under cover of the preparations for Gascony, to collect there still, late in November.[23] The next year, in July, the king himself was at Portsmouth, embarking with a large army for Normandy at the start of his victorious Crécy campaign. And exactly three years later, at the height of the pestilence, twelve ships were arrested in the port of Southampton to make ready for the king's service overseas. Sailors, surely, were in short supply, and orders were given to scour the counties of Southampton, Dorset and Devon for mariners sufficient for the crews.[24]

It was the plague, no doubt, that further held up work on the defences. Murage grants, at what had become the standard rate of a penny in the pound, had been allowed by the king in 1345 and 1347.[25] But an inquisition into the condition of the defences, ordered in 1353, revealed that the rampart and wall on the east side of the town was in poor condition, its bank eroded and its poplar-board parapet 'destroyed by wind and rain to the danger of the town'.[26] There had been no looting of timber, it was reported, whether on the parapets or on the engines-of-war stationed about the town. And the two great mangonels and smaller 'tripoget', constructed in 1339, were presumably still in working order. But the work on the walls, as recent excavations have shown, had been shoddy, completed with greater haste than skill. It would have been expensive to maintain. The foundations, of little more than three courses of un-mortared masonry, were inadequate. Above them, the wall rose against the face of the pre-existing rampart to a width of no more than 2 feet 6 inches. Its core, piled up against the bank, was of loose, un-mortared rubble, and it had been cheaply finished with a face of thin, mortared ashlar, roughly hewn to shape.[27] When required, probably as a result of the inquisition, to set about the completion and repair of their wall, the burgesses appealed to the king for support. Edward recognized that they could not hope to finish it for themselves. On 28 June 1355, perhaps spurred on by the danger of another French attack from the sea, he granted them murage for ten more years. Little more than a week later, he was warning them that the attack was on the way.[28]

The expected assault never came. However, Edward's decision to press home his advantage after the Black Prince's victory at Poitiers the following year resulted in a temporary escalation of the war. On 8 April 1360, in the name of the child regent, Thomas of Woodstock, a second inquisition was ordered into the state of the borough defences. It should be seen in the context of the king's winter campaign of 1359–60, which had kept him for many months overseas; it was also the product of the new alarms that had alerted the entire south coast in March. At Southampton, there had been reports already of defective walls, of lean-to buildings and orchards obstructing the existing defences. The recommendations of the jurors, delivered on 9 May, were exhaustive. All the lesser gates of the town, including Pilgrims' Gate on Simnel Street and the postern of John Wytegod's cellar on West Hithe, were to be walled up. A fighting platform or gallery (*garite*) was to be built between each pair of towers. Where the wall was not yet complete, on the western shore, the doors and windows of the houses on that quarter were to be blocked, to a thickness of three feet or more. Within the walls and immediately behind them, a roadway, twelve feet wide, was to be cleared for the use of the defenders. Beyond, the gardens and houses in the exposed Newtown suburb were to be swept away, and a double ditch made 'round the town from end to end', fed with water from the spring at Houndwell in the northern suburb.

The recommendations were accepted and the work ordered immediately. But such drastic measures, inevitably, were to prove unpopular, and within a few weeks Sir Henry Peverel, keeper of the town for the king, was to write eloquently to the regent, pleading either for release from his charge or for more explicit support in the action he was taking against the opposition of the townsfolk, among them the most prominent of their time.[29]

> My lord, the town of Southampton is well repaired since you were there, the moats dug out and faced, some of the ditches scoured, and several turrets and breastworks made, but twelve more are needed. I have begun to cut down apple trees and pear trees outside the town. I have viewed the people in arms, and there are 30 well-armed, 30 others armed, 30 archers, and others with clubs up to 200; but if the town is to be well guarded in time of war, there should be 100 men-at-arms and 100 archers. John le Clerk was grievously angry on account of his garden which was to be destroyed and threatened the people and said he would break their heads, and made a great disturbance and bade them go into the town, saying that the king's commission did not order the destruction of gardens outside the town. A writ came to me *sub pede sigilli* with the copy of the inquest of Suthampton, commanding me to do all things contained in the said copy which had not been done by my negligence. I therefore pray that you will order a commission that the gardens and houses on the ditches may be removed to the width of 300 royal feet, and that no apple tree or pear tree may be therein so high that a ladder of 10 or 20 feet can be made thereof. Adam Inwes, mayor of the town, and John Fismark, burgess, came to me and prayed that I would suffer the garden of John le Clerk to be taken away without cutting anything, which I granted on condition that he would pull down the walls and trees on the ditches to the width of two carts till he could sue before my lord and you for a *supersedeas* within nine days; and they agreed to bring me one. The people of the town are very angry because of what has been pulled down, and their condition; and the other people want a ditch round the town on the land side. Pray let me know your pleasure, my lord, if you will be pleased to believe what the bearer hereof will tell you from me concerning the town and myself. If it please you, discharge me of this office and appoint others in my place, as I can no longer endure the labour; and if it please you that I should remain, let me have wages for myself and two squires and other people.

Some of the recommended works may have been completed promptly enough. Certainly, on the western shore the blocking of the doors and windows of the seaward-facing houses is still plainly visible to this day (Fig. 7). But in John le Clerk the keeper had come up against a formidable opponent, the trusted servant, and within three years the pensioner, of no less a person than the Black Prince himself.[30] Adam Inweys and John Fysmark, his associates for many years, had clannishly rallied to his support.

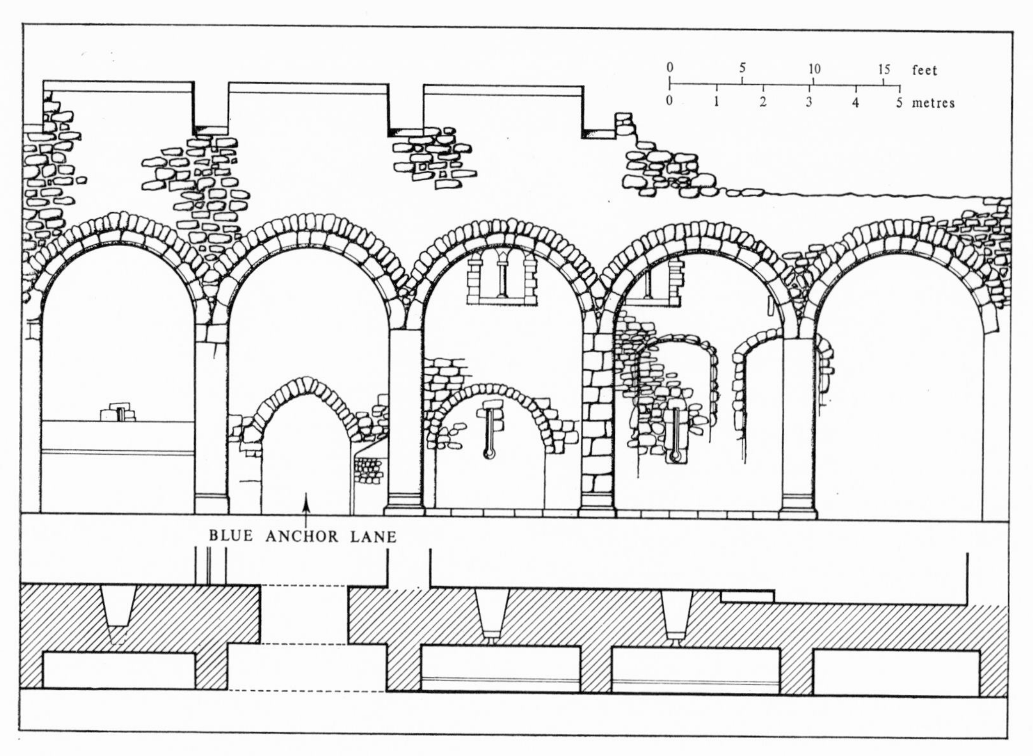

Figure 7 Late-twelfth-century quayside houses incorporated in the fourteenth-century defensive arcade by Blue Anchor (Wytegod's) Lane; the inverted keyhole gunports are important early examples of their kind

And the opposition is likely to have been joined by the other great figure of the time, John Wytegod, whose access to the shore would be blocked if his postern were sealed, and whose property might deteriorate in value.

No record survives of a settlement, but at least the quarrel was not long-lasting. When, after a decade of service in the town, Sir Henry Peverel felt the need to settle his affairs, he appointed John Wytegod one of his executors. Like his knightly successors, Sir John de Montague and Sir John Popham, both of whom held property on English Street in the parish of Holy Rood, Sir Henry had put down roots of his own in the town. He owned two houses, one of them in Bull Street. And in his will, dated 15 December 1361, he directed that, should he die in the town, his remains should be interred at the friary, to which he made appropriate bequests.[31] He belonged, patently, to that older generation which had seen Southampton through the difficult years immediately following the French raid and the pestilence. Adam Inweys, John le Clerk, John Fysmark and John Wytegod had each held office in the forties; through the fifties and early sixties, they shared the mayoralty between them.[32] But by 1369, on the renewal of war, a fresh generation was ready to replace them. Ruling the town for almost three decades, its dominant figures were John Polymond and William Bacon Wytegod, an associate of the original John Wytegod of the generation before. Significantly, they were at least as much royal servants as traders. With John Flete, five times bailiff while Polymond was mayor, they saw to the victualling of the king's castles and his armies overseas; they supervised the building and repair of his ships; they controlled, and accounted for, the new works on the walls and on the castle; and they assembled in the process, sometimes by dubious means, considerable fortunes of their own. As early as 1371, John Polymond was acquiring valuable tenements and shops on English Street, next to properties still held by John le Clerk and John Wytegod.[33] In 1374, he absorbed the Nostschilling lands in English Street, French Street, East Street and the northern suburbs.[34] In 1377, he could find the resources to grant a short-term mortgage, costing him £63. 6*s*. 8*d*., on the new tenement recently built by Nicholas Sherwynd on the site of Nicholas de Moundenard's great messuage north of the friary, once the home of the Barbfletes and a victim, very probably, of the raid of 1338.[35] Polymond himself lived on the other side of English Street, in the great tenement then called 'Ongerisplace'. Although the tenement was the property of the priory of St Denys, Polymond clearly made it very much his own, for in 1454, a full two generations after his death, it was known still as 'Polymond's Hall', its earlier name forgotten.[36]

In the trying circumstances of renewed, and unsuccessful, war, such a fortune as this, slight though it might still be in comparison with those collected by fellow burgesses earlier in the century, could not be built exclusively on trade. At Southampton, exports of raw wool touched new depths in the seventies. The figures for cloth exports, although missing for the greater part of the decade, are unimpressive where they survive. The wine trade, particularly affected by the troubles, suffered perhaps worst of all in a war which damaged production at least as much as sales.[37] John Polymond and William Bacon both reported severe losses by piracy in the trade to the south.[38] And it is scarcely surprising to find them associated, with John Flete and others of the town, in forestalling and similar devices, and in the taking of excessive profits. This was in 1376 and 1377. Six years later, on 28 May 1383, the king revoked an earlier grant of the farm of the new subsidies on wine and other merchandise, which he had already demised to William Bacon for a down-payment of 400 marks. He did so because 'it appears by an account already rendered by John Polymond and himself of 3*d*. in the pound that he has profited enormously, in fraud of the king, by the said demise'.[39]

Scruples, in such circumstances, were unrealistic. Nor would the king, in his own cause, hesitate to ride roughshod over the tenderer susceptibilities of his subjects. In 1369, as war approached, the letters of appointment of Hugh de Escote and Emery de S. Amand, captains and keepers of the town from 12 June and 15 August respectively, leave little doubt as to the wide range of their powers, both civil and military. Hugh de Escote was to have 'full power to chastise and punish all men of the town found rebellious against the king or the governance of the town and disturbers of the people or the peace, as well as vendors of victuals, regrators and servants and labourers found by inquisition or otherwise to be delinquent against the form of the ordinance and statute relating to such, and do all other things necessary for the better salvation and governance of the town and the punishment and bridling of the malice of the said evil-doers'. And Emery de S. Amand was to see to the 'ruling, chastising and doing justice on all men of the town and the suburbs, as well as men-at-arms, armed men, hobelers and archers coming to the town'. Already, on 26 April 1369, the mayor and bailiffs had been commissioned to require all those holding property in the town to contribute, 'each according to his state and faculties', to the repair of the defences, or suffer imprisonment in default. The following year, on 30 June, sailors arrested in Southampton for refusing the king's service were ordered to be transferred to the gaol at Winchester, there to await the royal pleasure. And a commission of array, dated 22 August, instructed Hugh de Escote and John Polymond, acting in concert, to muster 'all men dwelling in the said town and its suburbs who are able in body, and to compel by amercements or otherwise all who are not able in body to find arms and armour for those who are, each according to his estate and means, so that they be ready to resist the king's enemies of France if they presume to attack the town and suburbs'.[40] There is nothing, perhaps, unusual in the phraseology of the king's commands. But when Sir John Arundel took up his appointment as keeper in July 1377, greater care was taken to define the limits of his juridical authority, probably as a consequence of the disputes which the earlier commissions had caused. He was empowered, on 20 July, to do speedy justice in all disputes, 'for the securer government of that town'. But he must summon the mayor to hear the case and do justice with him, wherever one of the parties was a townsman.[41]

Edward III had resumed his claim to the crown of France on 3 June 1369, and many of the preparations for the threatened war, including the appointment of the keepers at Southampton, anticipated by some months Charles V's formal confiscation, on 30 November, of the Plantagenet lands in his realm. A cause for immediate concern had been the condition of the coastal defences. As far back as March, the king had alerted endangered towns with the command to array all fencible men. On 9 May 1369, the mayor and bailiffs of Southampton were required to forbid henceforth the departure of all men with property in the town, and to secure, within the space of eight days, the return of such as had absented themselves already. In June, repairs at the castle were hastened by the grant of a hundred oaks, and a military commander was appointed.[42] Initially, Hugh de Escote's garrison was small. For the first two months of his stay, it remained at eight squires and two archers. But Emery de S. Amand, taking office later in the summer, either attracted, or brought with him, considerable reinforcements. For a month, from 17 September, there were 47 men-at-arms, 39 hobelers and 172 archers stationed at the town.[43] It is improbable that such a large force could have been kept there very much longer. But at least twice in the next decade, similar armies mustered at Southampton. Through most of the summer of 1372, the retinue of John, Lord Nevill, lingered in the port, awaiting transport for France. And there were similar delays attending the departure of Sir John Arundel's ill-fated fleet in 1379. It sailed, eventually, early in December, to be dispersed almost immediately by a storm. The loss of lives, which was considerable, included that of Arundel himself.[44]

In an atmosphere of repeated military alarms, aggravated by the disturbing presence of soldiery in the vicinity, work on the Southampton defences gathered momentum. The heavy expenses on the enclosure absorbed the moneys of the farm, but in 1371 the king was persuaded to pardon arrears on the farm totalling £402. 6*s*. 4*d*., built up in the previous two years; for the remainder of his reign, he continued to excuse the burgesses their payments.[45] In a programme which included the completion of the walls, the digging of ditches, and the building of towers and *garites*, the friars finished their own *garite* on the east wall, next to their house, by September 1373. It measured 26 feet in length and 21 feet in breadth, and commanded a postern giving access to the friary gardens in Newtown, beyond the wall and ditch to the east. A specially-built ambulatory, at a height of 14 feet over the road now known as 'Back of the Walls', connected *garite* and friary dormitory.[46] Three years later, despite the general effort, a great part of the enclosure yet remained to be completed. Many former burgesses had fled the town. Those who were left, by their own account, had spent £1,000 over and above their farm on the works. In 1376 they implored the king to take the town into his own hands, and to see to its defence for himself.[47] Predictably no such action was taken. But in the next reign there was a steady flow of similar petitions for relief, met by the king by concessions on the borough farm.[48] Progress in the work may well have been substantial. For although the remittance on the farm was extended for another three-year period in 1382, it was reduced that year by half. And, once the new term had expired, there was no further mention of concessions.

The years of Richard II's personal rule were characterized by truces, culminating in the peace of 1396. But his accession in the summer of 1377 coincided with the renewal of French and Castilian raids on the coast, assaults on the Isle of Wight and on Yarmouth, and the burning of Rye and Hastings. Sir John Arundel, a soldier of standing and the leader of the luckless expedition of 1379, was appointed to the keepership of Southampton on 30 June 1377, in one of the first decisions of the new reign. On 9 July, perhaps harking back to Sir Henry Peverel's recommendations of nearly two decades before, he was commissioned to take 100 men-at-arms and 100 archers to the town.[49] In fact, he seems to have exceeded his quota. The castle garrison stood at 20 men-at-arms and 20 archers. Sir John brought with him an additional force of some 120 men-at-arms, 120 archers, 20 crossbowmen, 8 gunners and 2 engineers. At the end of September, the garrison of the town was to be allowed to run down to no more than 40 men-at-arms and 40 archers. But John Polymond, in the meantime, had been engaged in a concentrated programme of works on the walls. He had spent, between 13 July and 29 September, the large sum of £202. 10*s*. 0*d*. on the defences, including in the work, very probably, the completion of the rebuilding of the crucial tower at the north-west angle of the town, still known as the 'Arundel' tower.[50]

It may well have been Sir John Arundel's reports, supported by the rumour, current in December 1377, of another impending French attack on Southampton, that decided the Council to launch a fresh campaign of works at the royal castle in the town.[51] For many years, the rebuilding of the castle had been postponed. It was already over a century since any considerable sum had been spent on its repair. And it must have been clear that there could be no question on this occasion of yet another patching operation. Instructions, given in March 1378, unequivocally directed Henry Yevele, the architect, to advise on the building of a new tower: in effect, the total reconstruction of the keep.[52] Clearly, the Council attached great importance to the work. On 7 May, Henry Yevele was joined by William de Wynford in a commission to initiate the building, thus bringing together two of the most distinguished architectural talents of their generation.[53] And Yevele's design, indeed, was striking. He made use of the existing mound of 'Old Castell Hill', packed solid over the years and about 200 feet in diameter, to found a great cylindrical keep, eventually topped with four turrets. There was a mantlet to retain the mound, a barbican to defend the outer gate, a ditch, twelve feet deep or more, bridged at the gate, and two inner gates, each with its portcullis.[54] When completed, the new tower stood bold above the roof-tops of the town, transforming its appearance from the sea. 'The Glorie of the castelle', as John Leland would remark, 'is yn the dungeon [keep], that is both larg, fair, and very stronge, both by the worke and the site of it'.[55]

The construction by 1382 of the main bulk of the keep, within four years of the start of operations on the site, must have owed much to the organizing talents of John Polymond and William Bacon 'of Bristol', to whom direct charge of the work had fallen as early as 6 April 1378. They had the help of John Thorp, a clerk of Winchester diocese, whose efficiency would later be tested in other works at Lyndhurst and in the victualling of the royal garrison at Cherbourg. And it was William de Wynford himself who took charge of the masons on the site, remaining there, from 26 July, for a total of 399 days. Together, they made extensive purchases of building materials and tools. They bought stone at Portland and Beer, at Purbeck and on the Isle of Wight. They gathered stocks of timber, nails, mortar and plaster of Paris. For the use of the craftsmen working on the site, they purchased a windlass for raising timber, lead and 'other necessaries'; they bought carts, barrels, trays, and hods, rakes, sieves, chisels, hammers and wedges, a stone-saw, picks, shovels and smelting-ladles. Early in the day, they purchased the castle bell 'with full apparatus weight 70 lbs'.[56]

The details of the surviving accounts suggest an ordered haste. The king, on the advice of his Council, had commanded the tower to be 'quickly made'.[57] And by the time that William de Wynford gave up his charge, its walls must largely have been in place. Already by Christmas 1379, the bulk of the expenses on the keep, totalling £1,193. 6*s*. 5*d*., had been incurred. In the next ten months, to the following November, expenses on the work were still high. But even allowing for stock-piling of materials and tools, the drop in subsequent expenditure is striking. John Polymond, accounting for the period between November 1380 and February 1382, recorded costs at only £141. 1*s*. 6¼*d*.[58] From June 1383, additional works on the castle, on the mantlet and the pavement round the tower, became the charge of John Thorp and William Bacon 'the elder'.[59] Thorp rendered accounts for works completed between June 1383 and December 1384, and again for the period between then and Michaelmas 1388. But his final account recorded that the work was finished, and in November 1390 he handed over the surplus equipment and materials to Thomas Tredington, chaplain and keeper of the king's new tower since July 1386. Included with the other items in his charge was the castle bell, still unhung.[60]

It was at the end of 1388, just as the castle works were completed, that the first moves were made towards a negotiated peace with France. The death of Charles V in 1380 had left the French kingdom divided, and had removed some of the purpose of the war. But it had taken a further eight years of unsuccessful fighting to sap the aggression of the English, in particular of the king's uncle, Thomas of Woodstock. And it was not until after the crushing Scottish victory at Otterburn, on 5 August 1388, that the duke of Gloucester and his fellow appellants were brought to the point of negotiation. In the meantime, Southampton suffered annual invasion alarms. On 22 June 1383, the king alerted the sheriff of Southampton to array all fencible men in the county and to take them to Southampton for its defence. A French fleet was reported on its way to besiege the town and sack the surrounding countryside. The next year, in September, the king's enemies were again at sea, threatening the safety of the wine fleet as it mustered for the journey to Bordeaux. Later that year, perhaps on the return of the fleet, there was evident disarray at Southampton, for on 29 January 1385 the king required the mayor, bailiffs and burgesses there, 'under pain of forfeiture', to put their town 'under good and sufficient ruling'. He had been informed by Thomas de Holand, earl of Kent and non-resident keeper of Southampton and its castle, that there was danger of a scattering of the burgesses if discipline were not quickly applied.[61] On 28 June 1385, another invasion fleet was said to be on its way from France. And the next summer, Sir John Sondes, keeper by delegation of the town, was associated with the mayor, John Polymond again, in a commission to survey the defences of Southampton, to repair the walls and ditches, and to arm and array the burgesses 'against the threatened invasion of the French', considered at the time to be imminent.[62] At least one further invasion scare, in June and July 1387, intervened before the beginning of the truces.[63]

There is nothing to suggest that these recurring alarms ever came to anything. But the unrelenting condition of emergency which characterized the two decades following the renewal of war in 1369 undoubtedly disrupted the economy of the borough. Cloth exports rose in the eighties, but the rise was almost exclusively the work of alien merchants at the start of well over a century of foreign domination of the trade.[64] The commerce in wines, at a low level at the beginning of fighting, survived the war years only through the organization of convoys: an efficient but cripplingly expensive method of conducting each new vintage in safety back to the home ports from Bordeaux. Some idea of the cost, as well as of the system which required it, may be obtained from the king's published arrangements for the convoys of 1372:[65]

> Know ye that by the advice of our Council we have ordained that fifteen ships and five barges furnished for war, of which five ships and one barge are of Bayonne, and ten ships and four barges are of England, shall, for the security and safe passage of all merchants who at this time of vintage are minded to set forth for Gascony, there to buy wines to be brought to our realm of England, sail with the merchants as often as they wish to make the voyage out or home, in company with our well-beloved and trusty Admirals at sea, Philip de Courteney and William de Nevill; (And we) desiring that the owners of the said fifteen ships and five barges should, by way of recompense for their labour and the expenses they incur in performing such convoy duty, have and receive for every tun of wine that is thereby safeguarded, and under this convoy comes to our realm of England, when the wine arrives safely in any port of our realm, (the sum of) two shillings.

In 1381, reflecting the high cost of safe transportation of the wine, freight charges on the long haul between Bordeaux and Southampton stood at 20*s*. a tun, more than twice the charge common at the beginning of the century. They remained high throughout the following decade, and contributed to the substantial increase over pre-war levels in the prices charged for wine.[66]

In the final resort, sagging trade figures and the increasing intrusions of alien merchants delivered Southampton, for at least a quarter of a century, into the embrace of the military. Royal assignments of one kind and another occupied its leading figures through the better part of their public lives. Sir John de Montague, at various times commander in the port, may stand for that combination of military officer and local landowner so characteristic of conditions of endemic war. His first appointment at Southampton dated from July 1373.[67] Five years later, while commander of the garrison in the town, he bought John atte Barre's great corner tenement, on the junction of Broad Lane and English Street, formerly the property of Henry de Lym, of John and of Walter le Fleming.[68] On his death, he bequeathed to Margaret, his widow, at least six messuages in the town.[69]

Those military preoccupations which had kept Sir John at Southampton were reflected even in the character of the town's clergy. When Philippe de Mézières, former chancellor of Cyprus, specified the aggressive postures of the clergy in his well-known attack on the violence of the English, he was thinking, principally, of Henry Dispenser, bishop of Norwich.[70] But his words would have found a target at Southampton just as easily. In 1373, the bishop of Winchester had arrayed his clergy, on the king's command, to meet an expected attack on Southampton.[71] At least one of his clerks, John Thorp, held important office in the control of the king's works in the town.[72] Thomas Tredington, appointed in July 1386 to celebrate divine service in the new tower at Southampton, held conjointly for many years the office of keeper of the armour, artillery and victuals therein, 'because skilled with guns and artillery'.[73]

Notes

1 S.C.R.O. SC4/2/67 and 68.
2 E. M. Carus-Wilson and Olive Coleman, *England's Export Trade, 1275–1547*, p. 46, and Alwyn Ruddock, *Italian Merchants and Shipping*, p. 35.
3 P.R.O. E372/185 (m. 19), 186 (m. 44), 187 (m. 35); SC8/86/4263.
4 *Cal.C.R. 1360–4*, p. 90.
5 Ibid., *1339–41*, p. 297.
6 *Cal.P.R. 1340–3*, pp. 4, 572.
7 *Cal.C.R. 1343–6*, pp. 620–1.
8 *Cal.P.R. 1343–5*, pp. 268–9; *Cal.C.R. 1346–9*, p. 195.
9 *Rot.Parlm.*, ii: 188–9.
10 Élisabeth Carpentier, 'Autour de la peste noire: famines et épidémies dans l'histoire du XIVe siècle', *Annales*, 17 (1962), map facing p. 1071.
11 J. R. Lumby (ed.), *Chronicon Henrici Knighton*, ii: 61. For Bristol as the point of entry, see V. H. Galbraith (ed.), *The Anonimalle chronicle, 1333 to 1381*, p. 30, dating the arrival of the plague to the beginning of August, and E. A. Bond (ed.), *Chronica monasterii de Melsa*, iii: 68.
12 These words were used of the plague in the well-known inscription at Ashwell church, Hertfordshire (V. Pritchard, *English Medieval Graffiti*, pp. 181–2).
13 Bodleian, Queen's College MS. 1077, 1081; Win.Coll.Mun. 17811.
14 P.R.O. E326/9321.
15 Davies, p. 368.
16 *Cal.P.R. 1350–4*, p. 56; P.R.O. E372/196, m. 32. As one of the few administrative references to the plague, this confirms Élisabeth Carpentier's prediction that little is likely to emerge from such records, reflecting the unbroken continuity, despite the plague, of the administrative processes (op. cit., p. 1092).
17 Robert Michell *et al.* (eds), *The Chronicle of Novgorod, 1016–1471*, Camden Society, 3rd series, 25 (1914), p. 145.
18 E. M. Carus-Wilson and Olive Coleman, *England's Export Trade, 1275–1547*, pp. 130, 148.
19 Margery James, 'The fluctuations of the Anglo-Gascon wine trade during the fourteenth century', *Ec.H.R.*, 2nd series, 4 (1951), p. 194; Yves Renouard, *Bordeaux sous les rois d'Angleterre*, pp. 364–5.
20 Edward Maunde Thompson (ed.), *Chronicon Angliae, ab anno domini 1328 usque ad annum 1388*, p. 281.
21 Rymer, *Foedera*, iii: 44; *Cal. C.R. 1343–6*, p. 573.
22 P.R.O. C47/6/6/2 and 3.
23 *Cal.C.R. 1343–6*, p. 674.
24 *Cal.P.R. 1348–50*, p. 386.
25 Ibid., *1343–5*, p. 467, *1345–8*, p. 279.
26 *Cal.Inq.Misc., 1348–77*, p. 38.
27 *Southampton Excavations*, forthcoming.
28 *Cal.P.R. 1354–8*, p. 254; *Cal.C.R. 1354–60*, p. 214.
29 *Cal.Inq.Misc. 1348–77*, pp. 154–5.
30 *Register of Edward the Black Prince, 1351–65*, pp. 143, 504.
31 Bodleian, Queen's College MS. 1083; Peverel was dead by May the following year (*Cal.Inq.P.M.*, xi: 324).
32 Davies, pp. 171–2.
33 S.C.R.O. SC2/6/3.
34 Win.Coll.Mun. 17779.
35 S.C.R.O. SC4/2/115 and 116.
36 God's House Deeds 417 and 426; S.C.R.O. SC13/1; later names for the property included Wall's House and Hampton Court.
37 E. M. Carus-Wilson and Olive Coleman, *England's Export Trade, 1275–1547*, pp. 130, 148; Yves Renouard, *Bordeaux sous les rois d'Angleterre*, p. 411.
38 P.R.O. SC8/136/6767, SC8/290/14487.
39 *Cal.P.R. 1377–81*, p. 81, *1381–5*, p. 281.
40 Ibid., *1367–70*, pp. 229–30, 270, 304, 471, 474.
41 Ibid., *1377–81*, p. 8.
42 *Cal.C.R. 1369–74*, pp. 18–19, 20, 26; Rymer, *Foedera*, iii:863, 865, 866.
43 P.R.O. E101/29/34.
44 J. W. Sherborne, 'Indentured retinues and English expeditions to France, 1369–1380', *E.H.R.*, 79 (1964), pp. 725–7, 730–1.
45 P.R.O. E372/216–222.
46 S.C.R.O. SC4/2/109.
47 *Rot.Parlm.*, ii:346.
48 P.R.O. E372/222, 228, 231, SC8/86/4263, 4264, SC8/140/3640, SC8/141/7046; *Cal.P.R. 1377–81*, pp. 76, 448, *1381–5*, p. 184.
49 *Cal.P.R. 1377–81*, pp. 4, 12.
50 P.R.O. E364/10/F, E364/12/E. The equivalent tower on the north-east corner bears the name 'Polymond's Tower'.
51 *Cal.P.R. 1377–81*, p. 80.
52 H. M. Colvin (ed.), *The History of the King's Works*, ii: 842. For a good summary of the works at the castle in the following decade, see pp. 842–4.
53 *Cal.P.R. 1377–81*, p. 199; John Harvey, *English Medieval Architects*, pp. 312–20, 307–10.

54 For recent excavations on the castle mound and ditch, see *Southampton Excavations*, forthcoming.
55 L. Toulmin Smith (ed.), *The itinerary of John Leland in or about the years 1535–1543*, i: 277.
56 P.R.O. E364/13/G.
57 *Cal.P.R. 1377–81*, p. 466.
58 P.R.O. E364/14/C, E364/15/B; see also Colvin, op. cit., p. 843.
59 *Cal.P.R. 1381–5*, pp. 280–1, 334.
60 P.R.O. E101/485/7, E364/20/B, E364/22/B; Colvin, op. cit., pp. 843–4.
61 *Cal.C.R. 1381–5*, pp. 314, 480, 502.
62 Ibid., *1385–9*, p. 6; *Cal.P.R. 1385–9*, pp. 177, 258.
63 *Cal.C.R. 1385–9*, pp. 327, 329.
64 E. M. Carus-Wilson and Olive Coleman, *England's Export Trade, 1275–1547*, pp. 148–9.
65 R. G. Marsden (ed.), *Documents relating to law and custom of the sea, A.D. 1205–1648*, Navy Records Society, 49 (1915), pp. 92–4.
66 Margery James, 'The fluctuations of the Anglo-Gascon wine trade during the fourteenth century', *Ec.H.R.*, 2nd series, 4 (1951), p. 188.
67 Rymer, *Foedera*, iii: 988.
68 P.R.O. E326/11787, 11805. The purchase is dated 7 September 1378, and between 30 July and 3 October that year Sir John was accounting to the Exchequer for the wages of himself, two knights, seventeen men-at-arms and twenty archers and crossbowmen, 'staying in Southampton for its safe custody against the king's enemies' (P.R.O. E101/38/11, E364/12/F).
69 P.R.O. C47/60/3/65; *Cal.C.R. 1389–92*, p. 193.
70 G. W. Coopland (ed.), *Le songe du vieil pelerin* (Philippe de Mézières), i: 402.
71 Rymer, *Foedera*, iii: 988.
72 P.R.O. E101/485/7.
73 *Cal.C.R. 1385–9*, pp. 162–3.

Part IV

1400-15

Chronological table IV

1400 Warlike preparations and incidents in France; Henry IV invades Scotland

1402 Percy defeat of Scots at Homildon Hill

1403 Percy rebellion crushed at Shrewsbury; the Bretons attack English wine convoys and land a force near Dartmouth

1407 Commercial agreement with Flanders halts shipping raids

1408 Percy defeat at Bramham Moor

1400 Danger of invasion; Southampton to be guarded day and night (*Cal.C.R. 1399–1402*, p. 58)
£200 granted annually towards fortification and repair of the defences (*Cal.P.R. 1399–1401*, p. 240)

1401 Charter of Henry IV extends local judicial powers; burgesses to be JPs (*Charters*, i:40–51)

1402 Merchants of Genoa obtain exemption from scavage on goods brought to London by road from Southampton (*Cal.P.R. 1401–5*, p. 179)

1403 Threat of attack; arrangements to be made for the defence of the town against the king's enemies; should it fall, the whole region would suffer (*Cal.C.R. 1402–5*, pp. 82, 288; *Cal.P.R. 1401–5*, p. 286)

1404 French raid the Isle of Wight: Southampton alerted (*John de Wavrin*, ii:95; *Cal.P.R. 1401–5*, p. 506)

1406 The burgesses compound with the bishop of Winchester for the right to buy and sell at Southampton during St Giles Fair (*Letters Patent*, ii:150–3)

1407 Enquiry ordered into the expenditure of murage moneys at Southampton (*Cal.P.R. 1405–8*, p. 356)

1407–10 Orders to restore rents to God's House and St Denys; St Denys completes the appropriation of the parish churches of which it already holds the advowsons (*Cal.C.R. 1405–9*, pp. 124, 158, 178–82, 466–7, *1409–13*, pp. 132–3; *Cal.Pap.Reg., Papal Letters*, vi:202; *Cal.Inq.Misc. 1399–1422*, pp. 213–14; *Cal.P.R. 1405–8*, p. 26)

1408 Enemy fleet at sea; no ships to leave the port until further notice (*Cal.P.R. 1405–8*, p. 421)

	1410–11 Dispute with the men of Salisbury, Winchester and elsewhere concerning wharfage payments at the new Watergate quay (*Cal.Inq.Misc. 1399–1422*, p. 228; *Cal.P.R. 1408–13*, pp. 283, 310; Bird, *Black Book of Winchester*, p. 30)
	1412 The fleet musters at Southampton (*Cal.C.R. 1409–13*, p. 273)
1413 Death of Henry IV; accession of Henry V	
1413–14 Sir John Oldcastle's rebellion	
1415 The Scrope conspiracy; Henry V invades France; capture of Harfleur and French defeat at Agincourt	1415 Henry V's expeditionary force assembles at Southampton; the Scrope conspiracy is unmasked there, and the conspirators are tried and executed in the town (*Cal.C.R. 1413–19*, pp. 162, 214; *Cal.P.R. 1413–16*, pp. 344, 407, 409; *Rot.Parlm.*, iv:65–7) The burgesses petition successfully for relief on their farm; they acquire also the right to purchase property for the town, to the value of £100 annually in rents (*Rot.Parlm.*, iv:53; *Cal.P.R. 1413–16*, p. 284; P.R.O. E372/264)
1416 Peace deliberations and overtures	1416 A French fleet is driven off; the king summons his forces to Southampton, and remains there some time himself; work begins on the building of the *Gracedieu* (*Gesta Henrici Quinti*, pp. 80–3; *Cal.C.R. 1413–19*, p. 365; P.R.O. E364/57/I)
1417 Henry invades France again	1417 Troops and shipping muster at Southampton; the king embarks there for France (*Gesta Henrici Quinti*, pp. 109–11; *John de Wavrin*, ii:234; *Cal.C.R. 1413–19*, p. 428; *Cal.P.R. 1416–22*, pp. 109–10)
	1417–18 The king allows £100 from the customs collected at Southampton for repairs to the castle keep and for works at God's House Gate (P.R.O. E364/55/F, E372/265)
1419 The French find allies in Scotland and Castile	1419 A Spanish fleet threatens the king's shipping lying at Southampton and Portsmouth (*Cal.P.R. 1416–22*, p. 209; *Cal.C.R. 1413–19*, p. 526)
1420 Treaty of Troyes: Henry V recognized as the regent and heir apparent of France	1420 John Benet leaves money to the town to take over and restore the friars' conduit (S.C.R.O. SC4/2/238)
1422 Death of Henry V; accession of the infant Henry VI	
	1425 The friary and the rector of St Mary's in dispute over burials in the friary cemetery (*Cal.Pap.Reg.*, *Papal Letters*, vii:409)

1427–9 English defeats in France

1429 West Hall is purchased for the town (*Stewards' Books*, i:10–11, 30–3) Cardinal Beaufort crosses to France from Southampton with 4,000 men (*John de Wavrin*, iii:190)

1430 Joan of Arc captured at Compiègne

1431 Joan of Arc tried and burnt

1435 The Burgundians abandon the English alliance

1437 Anglo-Scottish truce

1439 Anglo-Burgundian truce

1444 Anglo-French truce at Tours

1444 An enquiry is ordered into customs evasions concerning Spanish and Italian ships at Southampton and elsewhere (*Cal.P.R. 1441–6*, p. 272)

1445 Henry VI marries Margaret of Anjou

1445 Margaret of Anjou joins Henry at Southampton, conducted there by William Soper (*Wars of the English in France*, i:448)
Henry VI grants a charter of incorporation to Southampton (*Charters*, i:54–69)

1447 Southampton becomes the 'town and county of Southampton', acquiring a sheriff of its own (*Charters*, i:70–81)

1448 Renewal of the fighting in France and in Scotland

1450 Jack Cade's rebellion

1450 The men of Romsey riotously descend on the town, threatening the Lombards; they are imprisoned (S.C.R.O. SC5/1/7, f. 22)

1451–2 Bordeaux falls and is recaptured

1451 Henry reissues his earlier charters and amends them (*Charters*, i:82–97)
Genoese merchants and their goods are attacked in Southampton harbour; they obtain the special protection of the king for their alum trade, based on the port (*Cal.P.R. 1446–52*, p. 442; *Rot. Parlm.*, v:216)

1452 The king orders his justices to stop interfering in disputes occurring within the borough boundaries (*Oak Book*, ii:122–7)

1453 Bordeaux surrenders to France

1453 Troops, proceeding to France, muster at Southampton (*Wars of the English in France*, ii:2:483–4)

1454 A terrier of properties in the town is compiled to apportion responsibility for the repair of the defences (S.C.R.O. SC13/1)

1455 Battle of St Albans: beginning of the Wars of the Roses

1456–7 Anti-Italian rioting in London

1457	French raids on the south coast	1457	Threat of attack at Southampton; watch to be kept day and night (*Cal.P.R. 1452–61*, p. 371)
		1458	Talk of traitors in the town, and of a threatened descent of the French (*Letters*, pp. 12–13)
1459	Yorkist rising and defeat at Ludford Bridge; attainder of Richard of York	1459	The men of Kent and Sussex are said to be at Southampton with the earl of Warwick and Edward, earl of March, later Edward IV (*R.C.H.M.*, 5th report, p. 493)
1460	Battles of Northampton and Wakefield; Richard of York killed	1460	Ships are arrested at Southampton to serve the king against Warwick; the town is warned against a threatened attack by Richard of York; a riot at mayor-making leads to the election of Robert Bagworth, a member of John Payne's faction (*Cal.P.R. 1452–61*, pp. 602, 606, 639, 654)
1461	Battles of Mortimer's Cross and Towton; Henry VI deposed; accession of Edward IV	1461	Edward IV confirms the town's charters, with extensions (*Charters*, i:98–119)
1463	Anglo-French truce	1463	John Payne is deposed from the mayoralty by order of the king (Davies, p. 174)
1464	Peace with Scotland		
1469	Battle of Edgecote: Edward IV defeated	1469	Edward IV grants the corporation an export licence to ship wool free of customs, the proceeds to be used to repair the town defences (*Cal.P.R. 1467–77*, pp. 154–5)
1470	Edward escapes to Flanders; Warwick restores Henry VI		
1471	Battles of Barnet and Tewkesbury; Edward IV restored; Henry VI murdered	1471	The countess of Warwick comes to Southampton to meet Margaret of Anjou; she learns there of the defeat and death of her husband at Barnet, and takes refuge herself at Beaulieu Abbey (*John de Wavrin*, v:664)
		1473	William Overy translates the ancient gild ordinances, presenting his translation to the town in 1478 (*Oak Book*, i:85–100)
1474	Anglo-Burgundian alliance; settlement with the Hansa at Utrecht leads to confirmation of Hansa rights in the steelyards at London, Boston and King's Lynn		
1475	Edward IV invades France; peace concluded at Picquigny	1475	The king's army musters at Portsdown and at Southampton (*Cal.C.R. 1468–76*, pp. 377–8; S.C.R.O. SC5/1/15, f. 15)
		1477	The corporation obtains a further export licence on wool to support work on the defences (*Letters Patent*, ii:56–63)

	The king listens favourably to a petition from the corporation to require householders in the town to contribute to the cost of paving the streets (*Rot.Parlm.*, vi:180–1)
	1478 The king grants £40 yearly for seven years, to be a charge on the customs, towards repair of the walls; this is to replace his grant of 1469 (*Cal.P.R. 1476–85*, p. 76; *Cal.C.R. 1476–85*, p. 109)
	1480 The king publishes an order re-granting the issues of local courts to the mayor etc. of Southampton, because the previous grant, of 1461, had proved 'not good in law' (*Charters*, i:122–9)
1481 Anglo-Scottish war	
	1482–3 Southampton and Winchelsea are at odds concerning the pirating of goods at Winchelsea and their sale at Southampton (*Sign Manuals and Letters Patent*, i:14–15; *Black Book*, ii:142–3)
1483 Death of Edward IV; accession of Edward V; usurpation of the throne by Richard of Gloucester, becoming Richard III; rebellion of the duke of Buckingham and abortive attempt of Henry Tudor to land at Poole	1483 Richard III asks Southampton to send him a troop of horse to join him at Coventry against the duke of Buckingham; William Overy and three other Southampton men are attainted for treason, this judgment being reversed by Henry VII in 1485 (*Sign Manuals and Letters Patent*, i:17; *Rot.Parlm.*, vi:246)
1484 Anglo-Scottish truce	
1485 Richard defeated and killed at Bosworth; accession of Henry VII	
1486 Anglo-French truce	
1487 Rebellion and defeat of Lambert Simnel	
1488 Anglo-French and Anglo-Scottish wars renewed	1488 Venetian galleys, on the way to Southampton from Antwerp, are attacked by pirates and pursued into the harbour (*Cal. State Papers Venetian, 1202–1509*, p. 176)
	1490 The well, watering-place for horses and wash-house at Houndwell are rebuilt (S.C.R.O. SC5/3/1, f. 9)
1491 Anglo-Scottish truce at Coldstream	1491 Thomas Overy publishes his reforming regulations (*Oak Book*, i:151–60)
1492 Anglo-French treaty at Étaples	1492 By royal patent, the staple of metals is established at Southampton (*Cal.P.R. 1485–94*, pp. 383–5; *Letters and Papers, Richard III and Henry VII*, ii:373)
	1493 Henry VII gives £50 towards the cost of repairs to the town wall on the west (S.C.R.O. SC5/1/23, f. 45v)

1496 Henry joins the Holy League against France

1497 Perkin Warbeck's rebellion; Henry welcomes the Observants to England

1498 Peace of Étaples renewed

1495 Venetian galleys are attacked in Southampton harbour by the French; certain leading Venetians are carried off (*Cal. State Papers Venetian, 1202–1509*, pp. 224–5, 231)

1496 Grant of a fair to be held annually at Holy Trinity Chapel, parish of St Mary (*Letters Patent*, ii:88–9)

1497–8 The Franciscan friary at Southampton becomes an Observant house (*Monumenta Franciscana*, ii:182)

Chapter twelve

Recovery

The military tutelage of the borough of Southampton did not end with the change of regime at the turn of the century. The usurpation of Henry Bolingbroke and the death of Richard II brought an almost immediate renewal of the war, to be followed by another two decades of warlike preparations in the town. But of the old generation, John Polymond and William Bacon were dead, and, with them, something of the accustomed order had gone. Broadly, the men who lived through the renewed alarms of Henry IV's unhappy reign, were those also who profited from the notable victories of his son. With few exceptions, they survived to take advantage of the revival of trade in the borough. And, indeed, there is more than one point of resemblance between the group of energetic men which handled the affairs of the town in the first decades of the fifteenth century and its prosperous equivalent, exactly a century before. Thomas Middleton, a great property-holder in the town for several decades, was perhaps the most important figure there at the turn of the century, with Richard Bradway and Thomas Armorer in support. But the men who came to matter most in the new generation, sharing authority within a group larger than any that had held control in the town for many years, were William Soper, Peter James, William Nicholl, Walter Fetplace, the Chamberleyns (especially William and John), Nicholas Banastre, John Emory, John Benet, Walter Lange and John Mascall. Of these, all but the last, who was probably the son and heir of Roger Mascall, himself the son-in-law of Nicholas de Moundenard, would seem to have come fresh to the leadership of the town. Little is known of their origins, but it is likely that many of them were immigrants. The Chamberleyns came from Grampound, in Cornwall; Thomas, the founder of the line, first leasing extensive properties in Southampton from John Botiller, then mayor, as late as December 1400.[1] It may be that the Nicholl family was of Cornish origin as well, for it was being pestered, later in the century, by a man of Bodmin, claiming to be a relative.[2] John Benet, mayor on three occasions and a notable benefactor of the town, is likely to have had relatives in Botley, a village a few miles to the east; while Walter Lange was probably of Weymouth stock.[3]

The French reluctance to comply with Henry IV's request for a marriage treaty on behalf of his son revived the threat of war within months of the beginning of the new reign. There was a general warning of the danger of another invasion in January 1400, and by the end of the month a new appointment had been made to the keepership and governorship of Southampton. Ivo Fitz Warin was to have full powers to 'fortify the town with walls, towers, loups, gates, garrets, ditches and other defences with the advice of the mayor with all speed and to cause the inhabitants to contribute according to their means'.[4] The mayor at the time was William Ravenston, and considerable stocks of material and equipment were collected during his mayoralty. But it was Thomas Middleton, mayor for three years in succession from 1401, who supervised the best part of this fresh programme of works on the walls. He began accounting himself in the mayoralty of John Botiller, his immediate predecessor in office. The works, limited to six years by the terms of the royal grant-in-aid, were completed in the late summer of 1405, under the direction of his successor, Henry Holwey.[5] John Benet, mayor in 1418–19, accounted for the next noteworthy expenditure on the fortifications, at least a part of which was incurred during his mayoralty. There were repairs and alterations to be made at the king's new tower and at God's House Gate, at the south-east angle of the town. Benet spent £100 on stone, on timber, on lead, on the materials for mortar (chalk, sand and gravel), and on wages. He paid Bartholomew, the mason, and ten stone-cutters, 'called hewers', for their work over fifty-four days. John Shadyngton and eight other stone-workers 'called leggers' (stone-layers), worked on the job for thirty-five days. There were seven carpenters, eight labourers and two plumbers.[6]

Both Middleton and Benet, when they worked for the king, no doubt had considerable reserves of experience to draw on. Their names certainly stand out in the record of public works in the town. It was Thomas Middleton, very probably, who built the great warehouse at the southern end of Bull Street, long known as the Wool House, later the Alum Cellar and now the Maritime Museum. For a brief period, this or another very similarly placed building was used to house the king's weigh-beam for the assessment of customs on wool and other commodities passing through the port. In 1406, the royal customs officials and collectors of the subsidy on wines petitioned for the removal of the weigh-beam to a more convenient site, from which they might oversee the transactions taking place at the Wool Bridge. There was nowhere more convenient than Thomas Middleton's new warehouse. An inquisition, held on 25 July 1407, declared unequivocally in its favour.[7]

> A new house of Thomas Midlyngton, situated on a sufficient site, is of all the houses in Southampton the most suitable for the weighing of wool, both for the king's advantage and for the convenience of merchants coming there for wool, cloths and other merchandise, and less injurious to the king and the merchants, because of all the merchant-houses in the town it is the largest and strongest and so near the said bridge [the Wool Bridge], which it is opposite, that whoever are customers during the weighing of wool and customing of cloths and other merchandise can see that nothing enters or

> goes out by the bridge without their sight and knowledge. For these reasons the wool-beam was lately placed in this house by the customers and collectors of the subsidy in the port by virtue of the king's letters patent [of 29 November 1406], and there it remains. The house of the West Hall, where the beam used to hang, is by no means so fit for the weighing of wool, because of its distance from the said bridge and its crooked and unsuitable site and also because of the sinister suspicion of stealing the custom and subsidy, as is said to have been usual before now at the times when the customers were occupied in weighing wool therein.

These were good arguments, but they could not withstand tradition. Roger Appleby, in possession of John Polymond's rebuilt Weigh House on French Street, north of Broad Lane and opposite West Hall, had been granted, on 22 August 1401, the custody of the weigh-beam for life. Although for some years in the recent past the beam had had no fixed abode, Appleby successfully petitioned in the summer of 1410 for it to be returned to its antique resting place on French Street. There could be no question, for all its inconvenience, that this was the place 'accustomed of old time' for the tronage of wool. On 4 July 1410, judgment was delivered to the effect that the letters patent granted to the former customers and collectors in 1406 had expired with their office. The beam was to be restored to Appleby.[8]

Meanwhile, not many months before, Thomas Middleton had completed another major project, designed to provide adequate port facilities at the Watergate, within a few yards of the Wool House. He had built, or at least largely financed, a new quay, supplied with a crane of its own. Once Middleton himself had received his due in the issues of wharfage and cranage for life, the quay was to become self-financing, an important asset to the town. Initially, the charges seemed high, arousing the immediate complaints of the merchants of Winchester, Salisbury and elsewhere. They had been accustomed to unload their goods on the hard by the gate, without use of a crane and at much less cost. Towage and scavage together had totalled only 2*d.* on each tun of wine or oil unloaded. Now a new charge would have to be added to this, the extra 5*d.* on every tun covering wharfage, cranage and lighterage at the quay. Anticipating 'grave harm' to their interests, the merchants of Winchester resolved not to have anything to do with the new charges. But the king, two months later, in letters patent dated 28 March 1411, authorized the levy at Southampton. Customs abuses had long been present in the town, as the attempt to re-site the weigh-beam had recently shown. The quay, it was claimed, had been designed as much to prevent these as to ease the lot of merchants coming to the town with their merchandise; its detractors took the line they did, because guilty of evasions of their own. Wharfage and cranage were to be payable by all in Southampton, as was customary already in London and elsewhere, provided that the wharf and crane were maintained by the borough in a state of adequate repair.[9]

The contribution of John Benet to the welfare of his fellow burgesses was scarcely less remarkable, although it came, in his case, as a final gesture to the town of his adoption. The friary water conduit, in the century since its construction, had fallen into serious disrepair. 'For many reasons', on the admission of the warden and convent, it had been poorly maintained over a long period of time. John Benet, mayor in the year before his death, must have been well aware of its defects. In 1420, by the terms of his will, his executors were empowered to set aside a sum of money sufficient to restore the conduit, converting it to the public service by the construction of a new water-house and cistern at the west end of Holy Rood Church. The warden and convent of the Franciscan friary, out of the 'particular affection which we bear to the mayor and community of the town of Southampton', were glad to transfer responsibility for the conduit to the borough, shedding the burden of its maintenance. On 3 October 1420, in the mayoralty of John Mascall, the deed of transfer was delivered. It provided that the mayor and burgesses, at the expense of the executors, should take up all the lead pipes from the conduit head at Hill to the wall of the friary churchyard, at the south-east angle of English Street. The pipes would then be re-cast, to be re-laid along the line of the original conduit. In a new stone building, to be set up against the west end of Holy Rood Church, the water was to be allowed to rise in a large lead pipe, branching into two separate pipes of identical diameter. One of these would be led off to the south, to serve the friary as before; the other would feed into a cistern, fitted with stopcocks of its own, for the benefit of the townsfolk. A key of the new water-house was to be retained by the friary, which would also preserve in its sole charge the conduit head at Hill, the stone superstructure of which survives to this day in the grounds of Nazareth House, Hill Lane. All other expenses were to devolve on the borough, to appear frequently in later years in the accounts prepared annually by the steward.[10] Four centuries later, when Sir Henry Englefield made his tour of Southampton, the conduit, although altered in some respects, was still in use.[11]

> The conduit which stands opposite the church [Holy Rood], is a modern and ugly building. The springs which supply it are excellent: they rise in the hill north of the town about a mile, and unite at an ancient stone conduit-house just under the Polygon [near St Peter's Church, Commercial Road], whence the water is brought to the town by a leaden pipe. This conduit is as ancient as the eighteenth year of Edward I, and was made for the use of the house of Friars Minor, situated in the south-eastern part of the town. The water was formerly brought in earthen pipes, formed in lengths of about eighteen inches, and fitting into each other with a shoulder or flanch. They are still not unfrequently dug up in the repairs of the pavement.

This record of public works in the town, unparalleled for another century at least, suggests not without reason the return of a modest prosperity to Southampton. To be sure, after a decade of renewed invasion alarms and military requisitions, the burgesses were brought to complain again of the poverty and depopulation of their town. But their grumbles in 1414 were to be concerned at least as much with the

Plate 13 Catchcold Tower and the west wall in the nineteenth century

Plate 14 The Watergate (watercolour by Edward Hawkes Locker, 1777–1849)

poverty of the municipality as with any failure of private wealth. The return on tolls, on which payment of the farm depended, had fallen drastically in recent years, principally as a result of the war. It was the king's view that the danger of the town's situation and the extreme peril of those who remained there justified the release of 140 marks annually on the farm, almost half of the total due. But his supplementary grant to the municipality of the right to acquire property yielding rents to a total of £100, demonstrates that he knew very well exactly where the real trouble lay. In effect, what the town most needed was an additional source of income to make up the deficiencies on its tolls.[12] Within a generation of the burgesses' complaint, Humphrey, duke of Gloucester, had cause to write to the king on the theme of the wealth of Southampton, 'the best port of youre royaume'.[13] He was exaggerating the position, of course, the better to establish the misdeeds of Cardinal Beaufort. But the recovery of the borough finances undoubtedly was real. And it had begun as much as half a century before.

Indeed, in nothing is this more evident than in the beginnings of rebuilding in the town. Rebuilding leases had characterized the years immediately following the raid of 1338.[14] But the pestilence and the continuing crisis of the war held back the processes of reconstruction. Nicholas de Moundenard's great tenement, on a particularly choice site north of the friary, remained waste after the raid for nearly forty years, to be rebuilt at considerable cost towards the end of the seventies.[15] A tenement and shops, carrying a rent of £10, had been newly built on the east side of English Street by 1381.[16] And we know that John Botiller, mayor in 1400 and bailiff at least twice in the preceding decade, 'built anew' two adjoining tenements on the west side of English Street, in Holy Rood. They had gardens at the back, shops on the ground floor at the front, and cellars below.[17] But standards of accommodation in the town had changed; not always for the better. There could be no return to the tradition of stone-building that had characterized the wealthy thirteenth-century borough. A house of the new style might re-use, as certainly happened on one occasion in 1504, the existing stonework of earlier foundations.[18] It might, and frequently did, incorporate a thirteenth-century stone cellar. But it would be built predominantly of timber. And its frame, where there was no earlier stone structure to support it, would rest on a low masonry base, frequently of mediocre workmanship.

In such conditions, the sub-division of plots was common, sometimes cutting across former property boundaries. And speculative building, or 'development', was certainly not unknown. In the autumn of 1411, Simon Mone, a carpenter by trade, developed a vacant plot on the east side of French Street, a property of the hospital at God's House. He seems to have found room there to put up at least three houses.[19] And there were many more houses cramming the lots south of Broad Lane in 1454 than ever appeared in the rentals of a century before. Even the friary cemetery was not held sacrosanct by the developers. With what one must imagine as the full co-operation of the friars themselves, William Soper, a great patron of the house, 'caused to be built' a pair of adjoining messuages, set over a cellar, in the churchyard of their house, shortly before he drew up his will in November 1458. He would have done it to assist their tottering finances; perhaps also to give them some entry into what, for others, was proving a boom.[20]

The sub-division of plots and development of vacant sites was matched, understandably enough, by the partitioning of existing accommodation, both above and below the ground. When, in 1411, John Benet 'of Botley', very likely a relative of the alderman of that name, failed to find a purchaser for his tenement on English Street, north of the castle, he divided the property in two. It was probably already a building of distinct structural parts, for it was described, in a not uncommon phrase, as having 'two roofs'. But it overlay a vault, perhaps of an earlier building on the site, which would have had to be divided with the remainder of the tenement in the north-and-south partition negotiated in January 1412.[21]

Just such processes of sub-division, both of the plots and of the tenements themselves, have been observed in the archaeology of the town. On the High Street site, at the junction of the former English Street and Broad Lane, it is evident that, after the removal of the debris of the raid, rebuilding on the garden plots behind the stone houses on English Street had followed within the century. A deliberate re-planning of the site, to make use of several garden plots at once, had enabled the developers to insert there a succession of long, narrow tenements, running north from a Broad Lane frontage. The timber-built houses of the period, resting on insecure stone foundations which frequently subsided into pre-existing pits, had not the staying-power of the earlier stone structures on English Street, to the east. They had disappeared by the seventeenth century, at the latest. But it is noticeable that even the larger and solider buildings they adjoined had been exposed to sub-division of some kind. At the north-east corner of the High Street site, a great stone vault, which had run back towards the west from English Street, was found to have been divided in two. Like the Benet property on the same side of the street, to the north, and Quilter's Vault to the south, it came to serve the needs of two owners.[22]

Yet there was nothing necessarily irreversible in a process such as this. Tudor House, fronting on St Michael's Square, which became the home of a wealthy Southampton capitalist late in the fifteenth century, would absorb in its growth a group of earlier tenements, identifiable now only in what remains of their cellars. Nor is it to be doubted that the great merchants of the early Lancastrian town were at least as ready as their Tudor equivalents to set themselves up in style. Perhaps inevitably, it was precisely those houses south of Broad Lane which had been the homes of Henry de Lym, Nicholas de Moundenard, Roger Norman and Thomas de Byndon a century before, that were re-occupied at this time by Peter James, by the Mascalls (Roger and John), by Walter Fetplace and William Soper. Peter James lived in the best-documented tenement of them all, on the southern corner of Broad Lane and English Street. It had been, in previous generations, the house of Sir John de Montague, John atte Barre, Robert Beverley, Henry de Lym, and the Flemings. It would remain in his family for almost a century.[23] Immediately to the south, Walter Fetplace had followed Roger and John Mascall in the occupation of the great tenement once of their relative, Nicholas de Moundenard,[24] whilst, for a quarter of a century or more, William Soper either owned or leased all the property south of Fetplace's tenement, as far as, and including, the tenement later used as a Customs House on Porters Lane. A large part of this property had once been the capital messuage of Thomas de Byndon.[25] Along Porters Lane, to the west, William Nicholl had taken possession of a group of adjoining tenements formerly the property of John Polymond.[26] And to the north, on the far side of Broad Lane, were the two adjoining tenements of William Chamberleyn, to which Sir Henry Plesyngton had conceded his rights in 1429.[27] John Chamberleyn, a goldsmith by trade, lived higher up English Street, on the same side. He was a man of position and of property, and his tenement was large in proportion. It had three 'roofs' and two vaults.[28]

A fifteenth-century urban community was united by many personal ties. It was to be Thomas Chamberleyn, the son of John, whom William Soper selected to administer an obit endowed by himself in the church of the Friars Minor. With Joan, Soper's second wife, Thomas Chamberleyn would be named joint executor of his will.[29] Walter Fetplace, recorded among the witnesses to the document, was the kinsman and heir of the great merchant of that name. In his turn, Walter would serve as an executor of the will of John James, probably the son of the Peter James who had been the former neighbour of Walter Fetplace 'senior'.[30] An important charge on the James estate was an obit at the parish church of Holy Rood. At the same church there were other obits to be observed, endowed in the names of Margery Mascall and of William Nicholl 'junior'.[31] Holy Rood, in effect, had become a genuine neighbourhood church for the leading families of the town. Earlier in the century, it had been the setting of the baptismal ceremony of Catherine James, daughter of Peter James, born on 10 August 1416 and baptized the same day. Thomas Halughton, then vicar of Holy Rood, officiated, and there were a number of the James's neighbours present on the occasion. Among them, Walter Fetplace 'senior' was named godfather of the infant Catherine. Isabel and Catherine, the wives respectively of William Soper and William Nicholl 'senior', were the two ladies chosen as godmothers.[32]

Catherine James was born to exciting times. The burgesses and their wives who attended her baptism had lived only recently through one of the most dramatic episodes in the history of their town. Through the spring and early summer of 1415, troops had mustered at Southampton in great numbers, preparing to embark for France in support of the young king's resurrected claim to the French throne. The fleet sailed, eventually, on 11 August, at the start of what was to be the victorious Agincourt campaign. But a few days before, a treasonable conspiracy had been brought to light, fostered by the confusion of the muster and active in the last weeks of July. Of its principal figures, three at least were at Southampton, waiting to embark with the army. They were headed by Richard, earl of Cambridge, the brother of the duke of York. But Henry Lord Scrope of Masham (Yorkshire) and Sir Thomas Gray of Heton (Northumberland) were as deeply implicated as the earl. Betrayed by Edmund de Mortimer, earl of March, a key figure in the conspiracy to whom they had revealed their plans, the earl of Cambridge and his associates were imprisoned by order of the king at Southampton Castle, under the guardianship of Sir John Popham, then keeper. On Friday 2 August 1415, a local jury, hastily collected for the purpose, met in the town. Sir John brought his prisoners before it to hear an indictment to the effect that they had conspired in the town on 20 July that year, as well as at other times in other parts of the country, to overthrow the existing government, to murder the king, his three brothers and 'other lords, magnates and faithful lieges', and to set up the rightful claimant, Edmund de Mortimer, in Henry's place, proclaiming him king in Wales where the memory of Richard II was still held in loyal affection.

The conspirators freely admitted the charges, only one, Henry Lord Scrope, submitting a defence. He had been a party, he confessed, to all the preliminaries of the plot, but he had never planned the murder of the king or of his brothers, intending, if he could, to prevent it. Both the earl and Scrope himself could delay a verdict by requesting trial by their peers. They were removed by Sir John Popham to the castle to await it. But Sir Thomas Gray could claim no such privilege, and his sentence took immediate effect. Condemned to be drawn, hanged and then beheaded, he was pardoned the first two penalties by the king. Through the crowded main street of the town, he was led on foot from the Watergate, on the south, to the Bargate, on the north; there to be executed, an example to the assembled burgesses and military. His head, when justice was done, was despatched to the north, to be put on public display at Newcastle upon Tyne, to the terror of the men of his county.

It was not difficult, with so many noblemen already at Southampton in the army, to find a jury competent to declare on the treachery of the earl of Cambridge and Lord Scrope. It met on Monday 5 August. The guilt of the earl stood already self-confessed, and Scrope's defence broke on the fact that he had done nothing to reveal the intentions of the other conspirators to the king. Both, after 'full deliberation' and with the unanimous consent of their peers, were declared guilty of treason. They were sentenced, as Sir Thomas had been before them, to be drawn, hanged and beheaded, and, like him, they forfeited all their possessions to the crown. But they avoided the savager penalties of their sentence: the earl most particularly because he was of the blood royal, Scrope because of his membership of the order of the Garter. It is probable that Cambridge, on the intervention of his brother who was present at the trial, avoided at least some of the public display of the execution. He was buried at the diminutive chapel of St Julian at God's House, where his grandson, Edward IV, would later see that his remains were appropriately respected. But Scrope made the same public procession as Thomas Gray before him, up through the length of the town. His head was sent to decorate one of the gates of York. His possessions, such as he had brought with him on campaign, were dispersed among the servants of the king. The record of a few of them has survived. They included coats of woollen cloth and velvet, scarlet, green and black, lined with tartarin (a rich silk) and furred with marten and minever. He had packed twenty-four pairs of sheets for the journey, and had with him six old cloths of red and black worsted and six pieces of old napery, 'much worn'.[33]

In the two succeeding years, Henry V twice made use of Southampton as a point of muster and embarkation for his forces. Perhaps it recalled agreeably his late decisive action in the suppression of a dangerous conspiracy. Certainly, it had pleasant associations with the opening of the successful Agincourt campaign. Furthermore, the shifting focus of the Anglo-French war from Gascony back to Normandy again had returned to Southampton a military potential it had not enjoyed since the days of King John. Naval activity, in particular, brought to the port a fresh measure of prosperity and a valuable boost to local employment. William Soper, for many decades a leading spirit in the borough and one of its wealthiest burgesses, began his long association with the king's navy in 1414. He learnt the skills of a ship-builder in the reshaping of the *Holy Ghost of the Tower*, a work begun in February that year. Within months of its completion, he turned his hand to the construction of the mighty *Gracedieu*, an unlucky monster which began and ended its days in the Solent.[34] Created clerk of the king's ships while the building of the *Gracedieu* was in progress, he was appointed keeper and governor of the ships from 1423, drawing a fee of £40 per annum for himself and a clerk to assist him. He continued in office for nearly twenty years, surrendering it only when the work itself was slight, in the spring of 1442.[35]

The years of crisis and of war had brought, in the final event, distinct compensations. A relationship of mutual confidence and profit had been established once again between the king and leading burgesses of Southampton. It was demonstrated fittingly in later years by the choice of William Soper to meet Henry VI's bride, Margaret of Anjou, at Rouen, from there to conduct her in safety to the king, with whom a rendezvous had been arranged at Southampton for April 1445.[36] But the partnership had local roots far deeper than this, owing much to the personal friendships which knit together in continual association the more substantial men of the borough. Nicholas Banastre and William Soper had co-operated in the building of the *Gracedieu*; they were brought together again in the sale of ships of the king's navy, the result of retrenchment at the opening of the reign of Henry's infant son. Banastre, the controller of the king's ships, was the neighbour of Soper, their keeper and governor. They both held important properties in Holy Rood, south of Broad Lane, and shared a taste for the acquisition of extensive country estates, the one at 'Banastre Court' in Shirley (now 'Banister's Park', the county cricket ground), the other across the water at Fawley.[37] John Chamberleyn, a close associate in public office and trade, served as clerk of the king's works at Portsmouth, and was long in receipt of a royal pension of 6*d*. a day, granted to him initially by Henry IV and subsequently confirmed by his son.[38] When the labours of Thomas Armorer, many times bailiff of Southampton, were rewarded by a grateful king and borough in the grant of sweeping exemptions from further service of any kind, men of comparable stature in the town were present to honour their fellow. They included John Mascall, John Benet, William Nicholl and Walter Fetplace 'senior'.[39]

To an appreciable extent, as other burgesses before them, such men had built their fortunes in partnership with the king. Thomas Armorer himself would shortly reappear as the purchaser of surplus stores, shoring-posts, piles and stakes, on the launching of Soper's *Gracedieu.*[40] In 1437, while building the *Little Jesus of the Tower*, William Soper was able once again to put some business in the way of a friend. It was from Peter James, fellow-parishioner, near-neighbour and long-time associate, that he chose to make his purchases of ropes, pulleys and oars, with a boat-cover and other nautical gear.[41]

Notes

1 *Black Book*, i:56–61.

2 *Letters*, pp. 6–10.

3 *Black Book*, i:128–9; S.C.R.O. SC4/2/112, 120. A similar pattern of immigration is observable in late-medieval London, although it has proved quite as difficult to trace to source (Sylvia Thrupp, *The Merchant Class of Medieval London*, pp. 206–10).

4 *Cal.C.R. 1399–1402*, p. 58; *Cal.P.R. 1399–1401*, p. 186. The gift of as much stone as the burgesses needed from the king's quarries on the Isle of Wight followed almost immediately, on 17 February 1400 (Ibid., p. 239).

5 P.R.O. E364/37/B, E364/36/G, E364/36/H, E364/39/D, E364/40/D, E372/247 (m. 40), 248 (m. 41), and E352/197 (m. 34). Initially, the grant, dated 17 March 1400, had been made 'during pleasure'. In the first year, it had consisted of an appropriation of £100 from the subsidy of wools in the port, with the allowance of another £100 on the farm. Subsequently, if the burgesses contributed an annual £100 of their own, they would be excused the whole of their farm, to make a total of £300 available for the defences each year. On 2 September 1401, back-dating to the previous Michaelmas, the period of the grant was limited to six years (*Cal.P.R. 1399–1401*, pp. 240, 535).

6 P.R.O. E364/55/F.

7 *Cal.Inq.Misc. 1399–1422*, pp. 186–7; *Cal.P.R. 1405–8*, pp. 279, 352. For the identification and siting of the house, see S.C.R.O. SC4/2/210. For the placing of the Wool Bridge, see Davies, p. 96; also L. A. Burgess, 'A topographical index of Southampton', typescript deposited at Southampton City Reference Library.

8 *Cal.C.R. 1409–13*, pp. 45–6. John Polymond's rebuilding of the original Weigh House, perhaps damaged in the raid of 1338, must have been completed shortly before November 1384 (*Cal.P.R. 1381–5*, p. 476).

9 The incident is discussed at length by Henry Cobb, *Local Port Book, 1439–40*, pp. xxvi–vii.

10 S.C.R.O. SC4/2/238, and John Speed, *History of Southampton*, pp. 24–31. Of the many entries in the Stewards' Books relating to repairs on the conduit, the more explicit include those of 1441–2 (SC5/1/6, f. 15v), 1461–2 (SC5/1/10, f. 15), 1467–8 (SC5/1/11, f. 11v), 1470–1 (SC5/1/13, f. 41v), and 1485–6 (SC5/1/21, fos 27–27v). A small private cistern, fed from a well and maintained in excellent repair, was recently uncovered in excavations on the High Street site. Associated pottery dates it not later than 1300 (*Southampton Excavations*, forthcoming).

11 Henry C. Englefield, *A Walk through Southampton*, p. 37.

12 *Rot.Parlm.*, iv:53; P.R.O. E372/264, m. 33; *Cal.Ch.R. 1341–1417*, p. 482. Recent alarms and expenses had included the cost of building and fitting out a barge, required by the king for the defence of the realm in 1401 (*Cal.C.R. 1399–1402*, p. 238); an invasion threat in the autumn of 1403 (Ibid., *1402–5*, pp. 82, 288; F. C. Hingeston (ed.), *Royal and Historical Letters during the Reign of Henry the Fourth*, i:167–70; *Cal.P.R. 1401–5*, pp. 286, 289); a similar scare the following October, causing the arrest in the port of ships of forty tons burden or over (P.R.O. C47/2/49/19–21; *Cal.P.R. 1401–5*, p. 506); and a restriction of shipping to the port in February 1408, while the French fleet remained at sea (*Cal.P.R. 1405–8*, p. 421).

13 Joseph Stevenson (ed.), *Letters and papers illustrative of the wars of the English in France*, ii:2:443. Duke Humphrey's letter was written in 1440.

14 God's House Deeds 565; S.C.R.O. SC4/2/68; Win.Coll.Mun. 17809.

15 S.C.R.O. SC4/2/115, 116. Described as 'ruinous' in 1350 and 1358, the building and plot together were valued at only 40*d.* (P.R.O. SC6/981/26, 27).

16 God's House Deeds 428.
17 *Black Book*, i:120–5.
18 God's House Deeds 693.
19 Ibid., 570–1.
20 *Black Book*, ii:102–3.
21 Ibid., i:128–36.
22 *Southampton Excavations*, forthcoming. There is no means of dating the partition, but the apparent absence of brick in the dividing wall at least suggests a date before the sixteenth century.
23 P.R.O. E326/11789, 11799, 11800, 11802, 11804.
24 P.R.O. E326/11787, 11799, 11804, 11805; S.C.R.O. SC4/2/126, 129, 132, 133; *Black Book*, i:68–71. The property is said to have consisted of two adjoining tenements, with shops at the front, overlying a vault.
25 S.C.R.O. SC13/1; Win.Coll.Mun. 17835.
26 S.C.R.O. SC4/2/164, 165, 193.
27 S.C.R.O. SC13/1; *Cal.C.R. 1422–9*, p. 454. These tenements were excavated in 1967–9 (*Southampton Excavations*, forthcoming).
28 S.C.R.O. SC4/2/269, SC13/1; P.R.O. E372/278, m. 45.
29 *Black Book*, ii:112–15, 122–5.
30 Ibid., iii:26–7; *Letters Patent*, ii:50–1.
31 P.R.O. E301/52.
32 *Black Book*, ii:58–9.
33 *Rot.Parlm.*, iv:65–7; William Hardy and Edward L. C. P. Hardy (eds), *A collection of the chronicles and ancient histories of Great Britain*, ii:182–3; H. T. Riley (ed.), *Ypodigma Neustriae, a Thoma Walsingham*, pp. 456–7; *Cal.P.R. 1413–16*, pp. 378, 384, 386, 409, *1461–7*, p. 116.
34 Work on the *Gracedieu* began in the autumn of 1416. Royal ship-building at Southampton in the first decades of the century is discussed by Mrs W. J. Carpenter Turner, 'The building of the *Gracedieu, Valentine* and *Falconer* at Southampton, 1416–1420', and 'The building of the *Holy Ghost of the Tower*, 1414–1416, and her subsequent history', *The Mariner's Mirror*, 40 (1954), pp. 55–72, 270–81.
35 *Cal.P.R. 1422–9*, p. 64, *1441–6*, p. 58.
36 Joseph Stevenson (ed.), *Letters and papers illustrative of the wars of the English in France*, i:457.
37 *Cal.P.R. 1422–9*, pp. 57, 64. Nicholas Banastre's Broad Lane tenement lay south of the lane and to the rear of Peter James's corner house (P.R.O. E326/11785). He acquired 'Suttones place' in Shirley in 1420 (*Cal.C.R. 1419–22*, p. 62); it was probably this property that had been re-named 'Banaster Court' by 1493 (*Cal.Inq.P.M. Henry VII*, i:368–9). For William Soper's Fawley residence, see *Black Book*, ii:122–5.
38 P.R.O. E122/140/13, E364/55/F, E372/272, m. 37d.
39 *Black Book*, ii:2–5.
40 W. J. Carpenter Turner, 'The building of the *Gracedieu, Valentine* and *Falconer* at Southampton, 1416–1420', *The Mariner's Mirror*, 40 (1954), p. 62.
41 W. J. Carpenter Turner, 'The *Little Jesus of the Tower*, a Bursledon ship of the early fifteenth century', *Proc. Hampshire Field Club*, 18 (1953–4), p. 176.

Chapter thirteen

Trade, distribution and supply

It has been said with much truth that the prosperity enjoyed by Southampton in the fifteenth century was deceptive: that its trade was in the hands of foreigners, and that it had no industry of its own.[1] But the borough had never been a centre of production on any considerable scale; it scarcely ranks as such today. Then, as now, it earned a living by the provision of services and by the distribution of merchandise. For the majority of its burgesses, trade was one interest alone, among many. Peter James, ship-chandler for the season of the building of the *Little Jesus of the Tower*, used his great tenement on Broad Lane to house foreign merchants visiting the town.[2] He took his share of the profits of hosting and acting for aliens, even while he engaged in trading ventures of his own. With Walter Fetplace, William Soper, Ralph Chamberleyn, William Nicholl and John Emory, he was importing and exporting merchandise while John Pole was royal searcher in the port (1423–7). Peter James had a ship of his own, and he dealt, frequently in co-operation with his neighbours, for the most part in cloth and in wines. Like them, he was guilty repeatedly of minor customs frauds.[3]

To be sure, there was to be no Robert Sturmy nor any William Canynges in fifteenth-century Southampton, and the tradition of merchant venturing in the borough was never as strong as it became in contemporary Bristol. But the individual Southampton burgess, for all his many preoccupations in the service of aliens or the king, was far from ignorant of trade and no more reluctant than anybody else to seek it for himself. Much later, in the sixteenth century, Richard Mershe, a wealthy Southampton mercer, thought it fitting to bequeath his 'shippe chest' and his lute to his grandson, Richard Eston 'the younger'.[4] The bequest, with its flavour of seafaring days and of the lost freedoms of youth, must have echoed the shared experience of many Southampton men.

Indeed, throughout their most active years, the leading figures in the town can be shown freely to have engaged in trade. Whether they went there in person or not, both William Soper and Walter Fetplace traded to the Mediterranean, no doubt receiving thereby some return on the favours they had themselves bestowed on Italian merchants visiting their town.[5] William Soper, acting for himself as much as for the king, helped his neighbours, Walter Fetplace and Peter James, by hiring them the royal *Petit Holy Gost de Suthampton* for a trading excursion to Portugal.[6] Some years earlier, Soper himself might have been found acting with William Nicholl in the chartering of a vessel to bring wine home from La Rochelle. And in 1426, in partnership with William Payne, he had sent a ship loaded with salt and with wine to Ireland, to effect an exchange for fresh salmon and for hides.[7]

Just as Soper and his contemporaries recur repeatedly in the trading record of their community, so they appear in another capacity in the agency business, acting as the hosts of foreign merchants who came with their goods to the port. In the six years following the Hosting Act of 1439, the hosting returns for the town are especially complete. Taken with the views of merchandise compiled by each host, they show the principal burgesses of Southampton not merely finding house-room for their visitors but also competing actively for their goods. Frequent hosts in these years were John Bentham, William Nicholl, John Emory, William Soper, Peter James, John Fletcher, Robert Aylward and Nicholas Bilot. They housed merchants of Brittany and western France, of Italy, Spain, Flanders and the north. Recording the sales of their guests, they noted that Walter Fetplace had made big purchases of the wines of La Rochelle, of iron from Spain and of sweet wines from the Mediterranean. John Emory, Robert Aylward and Peter James, each of them hosts themselves, had also bought quantities of wine. Peter James again, William Soper, William Fletcher, William Nicholl, Nicholas Bilot and John Payne bought iron. William Nicholl, John Payne and Walter Fetplace sold cloth.[8] By 1447, the king was moved to remark that, as he understood it, Southampton 'abounds in merchants, sailors and mariners who flock from distant parts to that town with an immense quantity of cargoes, galleys, and ships plying with merchandise to the port there'.[9] At Michaelmas 1449, there were at least fifty aliens resident in the borough. Of these, forty-one came from Flanders, Holland, Zeeland and Picardy; the remainder, from Genoa and Venice.[10]

It was the return of the Italians in particular, long delayed by the war, that brought new purpose to the town. As early as 1379, a visiting Genoese grandee had proposed to make of Southampton the centre of his city's trading activities in the country. He had envisaged siting the headquarters and store of his countrymen in the royal castle, just then in the process of reconstruction.[11] And although the jealousy of the Londoners brought him to his death and his scheme to nothing, the Genoese merchants trading in England retained a particular affection for Southampton. In 1402, to avoid the payment of the due known as 'scavage' at the capital, they successfully petitioned the king for permission to unship at Southampton, bringing their goods by road to London.[12] After further decades of war, when peace and a commercial alliance were concluded between England and Genoa in 1421, they were ready to step up immediately their shipments through the port, thus opening a new era of frequent commercial exchanges, in which the Florentines and the Venetians soon came also to play their part.

In almost any year, after 1421, the great Italian carracks and galleys might have been found lying-up at Southampton during at least part of the winter, usually between January and March. The schedule of ports-of-call of the Florentine galley fleet of 1447 listed Port-de-Bouc, St Felix de Guixols, Majorca, Valencia, Javea, Villajoyosa, Denis, Alicante, Almeria, Malaga, Cadiz, Lisbon, Corunna and Sluys, before the fleet split to visit Sandwich and Southampton in England.[13] And by the time a typical fleet had got as far as the English ports, its crews were ready for their shore-leave. Conditions on board even the largest of the Italian ships were cramped. On the galleys, in particular, the crews' quarters were brutally exposed to the elements. Few preferred to remain afloat when there were comfortable lodgings available on dry land. Within reason, the burgesses themselves liked it that way. When Luca di Maso degli Albizzi, captain of the Flanders galleys, brought his fleet safely to Southampton in the first days of January 1430, he met the mayor and his officers within three days of anchoring to discuss measures to control his galleymen. He found the mayor entirely co-operative, speaking, as he judged, with 'much kindliness and discretion'. The town's requirements, after all, were modest. Only Luca's officers were to bear arms within the walls; no Italian was to climb up on to the defences of the town, or to damage the orchards that surrounded it; all were to carry lights after dark. The next day, Luca had these conditions announced on board his galleys.[14] A generation later, with the galleys again in the port, the town steward's accounts showed a payment of 2*d.* to the public crier of Southampton. He had been hired to cry through the streets that no stranger should bear a weapon, and that everyone not of the town should take to his lodgings in good time after night fall.[15]

Primarily, it was the rich trade in English cloths and wool that had brought the galleys back in force to Southampton. If convenient for London, Southampton was also admirably sited for easy access to the resources of the major cloth-producing region in the country. Its own best regional customer was Salisbury, the nodal point of the flourishing Wiltshire cloth industry. And it drew from there what was quickly becoming the richest single commodity of its trade. A very typical transaction of the period was the exchange negotiated in 1417 by Walter Fetplace. For the sweet wine offered by Antonio Duodo, a Venetian, he promised a quantity of narrow cloths, called 'Osetys', with western blankets to make up the balance on the deal.[16] But he was almost as likely to be concerned in the old-fashioned wool trade as he was in the more modern handling of cloths. Wool exported direct to the Mediterranean by way of Southampton could legitimately by-pass the Staple at Calais. In May 1440 Fetplace obtained a licence to cover the shipping of a hundred sacks of wool by carrack or galley to Lombardy.[17] He would, with reason, have anticipated a good profit on the deal. Later in the century, an Englishman calculated the likely costs and receipts on each sack of wool transported to Italy in this way. The cost to a Venetian of wool landed and ready for sale totalled about £14. 11*s.* 0*d.* per sack. The initial purchase price in the Cotswolds, depending on demand, was something in the region of £8. A sack loaded on the galley at Southampton had already incurred additional charges of £3. 6*s.* 8*d.*, covering road transport, handling and port dues, and customs. Freight might have added another £3. 4*s.* 4*d.* to the bill. The anticipated sale price at Venice, showing a very comfortable margin of profit, was nearer £20.[18]

In the cloth trade also, easy sales and handsome profits had received a further boost in recent years on the collapse of Flemish competition. To supplement the already rich Italian market, English cloth might now expect to penetrate, on an ever-increasing scale, many continental centres dominated hitherto by the Flemings. In south-west France, for example, traditional trade links with Southampton helped secure first place for English products in the local market for cloth.[19] And at home, cloth took its place alongside the ancient staples of overseas trade, the wine and wool of the traditional exchange. Cloth and the essentials of its manufacture, henceforth, were likely to take a prominent place in any large shipments to or from the port. Walter Fetplace and his 'companions' reappear, in 1440–1, as the purchasers of a large consignment of alum, a mordant commonly employed in the fixing of dyes. With other cargo, including green ginger and cotton, it had been imported in a great carrack of Venice, one of several Italian vessels to visit the port during the year. Of these others, a Genoese carrack had brought woad, to be despatched to London and to Winchester. Two Venetian galleys had loaded great cargoes of finished cloths, western dozens and kerseys.[20]

Just the year before, for which the record of his transactions is unusually complete, Walter Fetplace emerges as a dealer in woad and in alum, a specialist in the supply of dyes and mordants to the cloth-manufacturing industry of the region. He handled other commodities as well, among them wine. But there is no doubt of the nature of his specialization, nor of the area within which he chose usually to conduct his business. At the turn of June and July 1340, he purchased a total of 154 balets (77 bales) of woad from the Italians, most, if not all, from the Genoese. And he had already made other purchases of woad within that accounting year, totalling 79 balets. In November and April, he had made use of coastal shipping to transport 17 balets of woad and two bales of alum. However, the greater part of his distributive business, showing a ceaseless round of activity with few intermissions even in the worst months of the winter, was done by road, mainly by cart, or very occasionally by pack-horse. It was to Salisbury that his carts went most often. With woad, alum and teasels for the local cloth industry, they took wine, soap, oil, silk, white herrings and salmon. Woad and alum, likewise, were despatched on his behalf to the cloth-manufacturing centres at Winchester and Romsey (Hampshire), Frome (Somerset), Wimborne Minster (Dorset), Wilton (Wiltshire), Reading (Berkshire), and Henley-on-Thames (Oxfordshire). With the exception of Reading, to which he sent additional loads of oil, wine, cumin and raisins, and Henley-on-Thames, with its loads of wine, salt, fruit, saffron, canvas and millstones, the bulk of Fetplace's business lay to the west. His connections were overwhelmingly with Salisbury, to which he sent almost as many loads as to all the other centres put together. But his interest in the cloth industry took him as far west as Frome and Wimborne Minster, and, on occasion, he departed so much from his routine as to direct a consignment of oil to Warminster, of fruit to Guildford, or of cloth, presumably for finishing, to London. Meanwhile his neighbour, Peter James, dealt principally in wines, choosing to trade usually to Oxford. When the wine fleets were in, he sent carts there twice in December, three times in January, and once, very much later in the season, in August. Serving approximately the same area, some wines of his went to Burford in January, others to Gloucester in the same month, still others to Worcester early in September. A specialist, like Fetplace, in a single commodity, he had yet no objection to a certain diversification of interests. He had sent his usual wine and some fruit to Salisbury on 31 December 1439, to the order of the cathedral clergy. The following April, it was woad that he despatched there in two cartloads.[21]

In the wholesale and the agency business, the cultivation of a good connection in a particular town, or region, was at least as important as the acquisition of some special expertise. At home in Southampton, Peter James sought the good will of the Italians by standing pledge regularly for their payment of local customs. At Oxford and elsewhere, he secured his position with individual merchants by accepting their commissions and by consigning them goods to order. Such connections, built up over the years, were a valuable asset within the family. In 1443–4, the part Peter James himself would play in the overland trade was small. He sent only one cart out of Southampton that year, loaded with wines for Oxford. But Andrew James had since taken up the connection. Andrew despatched wine and raisins to Oxford in February, April, May and July 1444; he sent other loads to Abingdon, again raisins and wine, in March and June. In the family tradition, he maintained an interest at Salisbury, to which he consigned a cartload of iron in May and two of woad in September. But with the exception of one other local commission, a single consignment of iron to Winchester, his business in the immediate locality was slight. It compared not at all, for example, with that of his contemporary, Nicholas Holmhegge, just then making his way as a considerable figure in the town. Holmhegge dealt chiefly in victuals, trading to Winchester, to which he made regular consignments of wine, herrings and salmon, with some iron. But he had other, lesser, connections at Salisbury, Poole and Newbury. To the first, he sent three carts in March, May and August, with loads of herrings, oil and garlic; to the second, he made a single consignment of two packs of kerseys in February; it was probably from the third that he obtained a load of wheat in October, returning wine and herrings by cart the following March.[22]

It was perhaps inevitable that as long as trade in general remained exposed to the hazards of tempest and of war, no individual Southampton merchant could afford to be exclusive in his interests. But the specialisms already detectable in the overland distributive trade of the fifteenth century, had themselves developed naturally enough out of the character of the merchandise reaching the port by sea. Neither in Fetplace's generation nor in its immediate successors was there a sound market outside the capital for the luxuries characteristic of the Italian trade: the spices, cloth-of-gold and other fine weaves, silks, glass-wares, armour and precious stones of Venice, Genoa and Florence. The Italians, with resident agents both at Southampton and London, were as well equipped as anyone to handle the trade, and they reserved it almost exclusively to themselves.[23] Yet the bulk commodities for which there was a demand in the provinces, the dyestuffs and mordants, wine, salt, iron, fish and building materials, not all of which derived from the Mediterranean, were best distributed by local men, each with his speciality and each with at least one regional contact of his own. In victuals and dyestuffs, as much as in luxuries, the balance of advantage in the traffic to London remained consistently with the Italians. In the provincial trade, it was the English merchants, among them the burgesses of Southampton, who were usually in the lead. Walter Fetplace, in 1439–40, had been a big man in the handling of Genoese woad and in its transport to various provincial centres. But his dealings in the capital were slight, and, of the two carts he sent there, only one carried the mixed merchandise that could reasonably have included some luxuries. His contemporaries among the Southampton burgesses were still more reluctant to compete in the London trade. That same year, Peter James had sent a barrel of apples to London, no more. Andrew James and Nicholas Holmhegge, three years later, sent nothing to London at all.

There were good reasons for keeping clear of the capital. The luxury trades, handling exotic and costly materials, required a combination of expertise and financial backing beyond the reach of the average provincial merchant. Profits on a completed sale might very well be great, but bills were often left unpaid, not least by the king. And an outsider, without influence and protectors in the capital, risked ruin if he traded on his own. Furthermore, at its peak the Italian trade could be relied upon to bring regular shipments of woad, alum, sweet wines, currants, soap and fruit to the port, much of which might go direct to London in the consignments of the resident Italian agents, the Catanei, De Negri, Spinelli and Morelli, but all of which were also in demand, to a greater or lesser degree, in the provinces as well. There was much there already for the local men to handle. In addition, there were cargoes of iron, wax, oil, leather and oranges from Spain; wine, wax, figs, currants and other fruits from Portugal; wine and woad from Gascony; salt from the Bay; canvas from Brittany and the Channel Islands; hides from Ireland; hemp, linen, walnuts, onions, Rhenish wines, tiles and building materials from Flanders; herrings, pitch, tar, bow-staves and timber from the Baltic (Fig. 8). Of all this, beyond doubt, the Italian trade remained the richest in Southampton. But increasingly, on all but the Mediterranean routes, and sometimes even on these, native shipping took over the role formerly shared by alien carriers. Inevitably, it brought business direct to the English merchant, reducing the role of the alien factors resident in the provincial ports.[24] These, too, had always had their problems. Through most of the century, there were men of Brittany, Ireland and the Channel Islands, of Zeeland, Holland and Brabant, either resident at, or visiting, Southampton. They needed the services of local men, brought new trading opportunities, and paid handsomely for the privileges they obtained.[25]

In the circumstances, there was already plenty to be done, and good profits to be made, in the distributive trades alone. Nor were these without a developed expertise of their own. Some of the dispersal of imported goods, and much of the collection at Southampton of the bulkier exportable commodities, was done by coastal shipping. Woad, alum and wine were frequently re-distributed by sea. And coastal shipments to

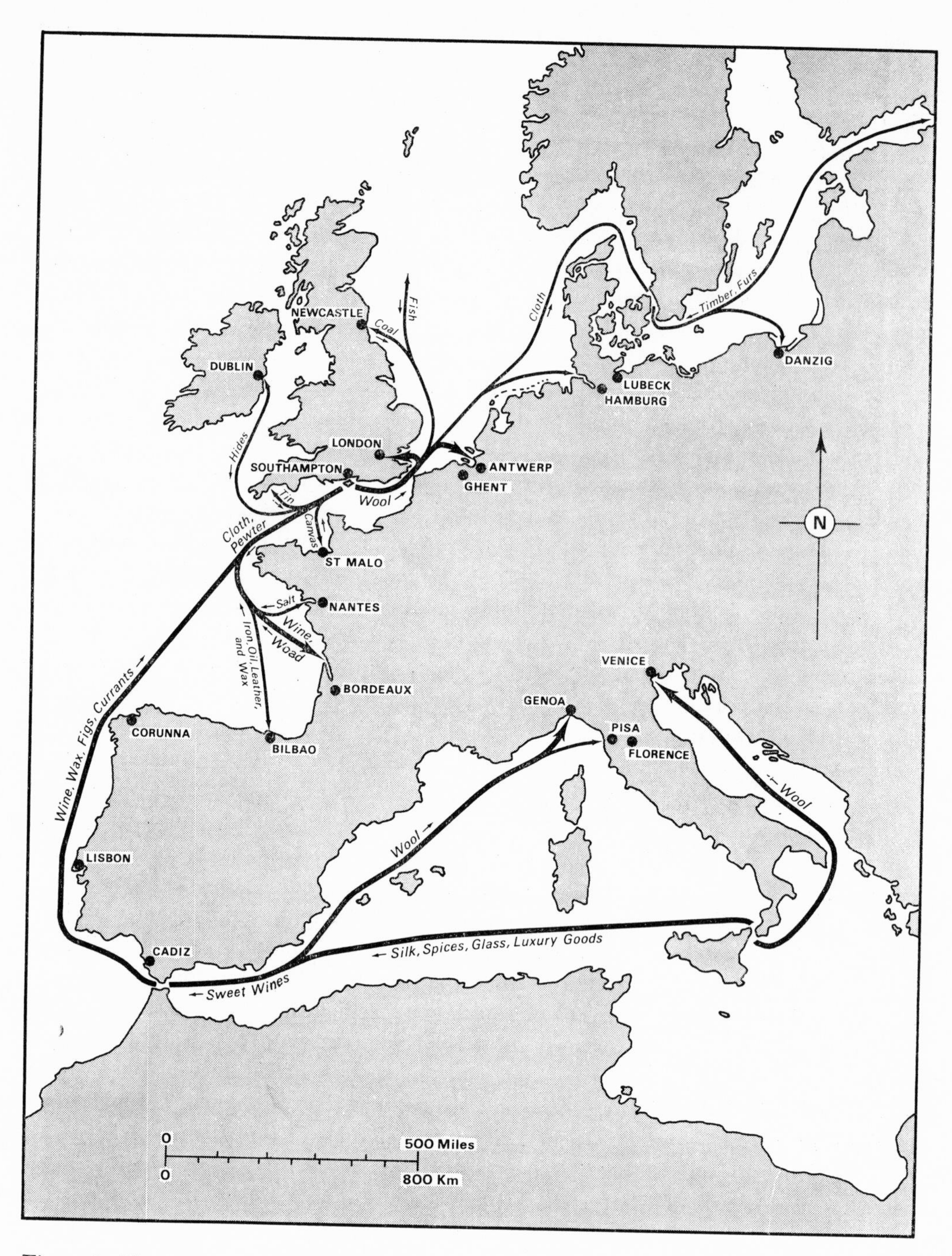

Figure 8 The overseas trade of Southampton in the fifteenth century

Southampton included tin from Cornwall for re-export by the Italians, slates from Devon, sailcloth from Dorset, linen and canvas from the Channel Islands, wheat and malt from Sussex, and fish from East Anglia.[26] Nevertheless, it was a common experience for piracy and war to place intolerable risks on shipments through the Narrow Seas, and although, doubtless, it would have been cheaper to send bulk shipments of wine and woad from Southampton to London by sea, there were yet many occasions during the century when road transport dominated, or even absorbed, the trade.[27] Well-established carting routes, radiating from Southampton, carried every variety of trading commodity through all four seasons of the year. To London, the route went by Alresford, Alton, Farnham, Guildford, Ripley, Cobham and Kingston. To Bristol, it took in Salisbury, Warminster and Bath. Northwards, there were routes by Andover, Newbury, Abingdon, Oxford and Banbury; by Salisbury, Marlborough, Burford, Stow-on-the-Wold, Chipping Campden, Stratford and Warwick; and by Basingstoke to Reading. To the west, the inland route followed the way from Salisbury to Shaftesbury, Sherborne, Honiton and Exeter; alternatively, a lengthy passage, characterized by numerous ferry crossings, took in Ringwood and Poole, Weymouth, Lyme (Regis), Exmouth, Teignmouth, Dartmouth, Salcombe, Plymouth, Saltash, Looe, Fowey, Truro and Helford.[28]

Within a day's cartage, there and back, Southampton functioned precisely as any market-centre might have done. In return for supplies of victuals and malt, locally grown, it sent out small consignments of imported commodities to the villages and manor houses of the vicinity. Carts laden with wine went to Shirley, Botley, Durley, Brockenhurst, Sherfield and Bishopstoke. There were consignments of wine and iron to Bishop's Waltham; iron and coal to Twyford, Hursley and Nursling; coal to Stoneham and Michelmersh. Wine, black soap and wax went to Southwick, perhaps to supply the needs of the Augustinian canons at Southwick Priory; iron, oil, salt, oxhides, soap, grindstones and salt-fish to Alresford; woad, alum, iron, white soap, wax, salmon and herrings to Fordingbridge. Trade, at this level, was handled almost exclusively by local men. And although the Italians and other enterprising outsiders intruded where they could, it was broadly local men again who monopolized the richer regional markets at Winchester, Romsey and Ringwood. Of these, Winchester was far and away the most important. The needs of its religious houses and of its weaving and cloth-finishing industry absorbed the greater part of the short-haul carrying trade from Southampton. Large consignments of fish and wine went there, especially in Lent. There was a demand in the monastery kitchens for garlic and almonds, onions, figs and oranges, cider, vinegar, salt and oil. Repairs and improvements on the fabric required the supply of paving-tiles and slates. Iron, soap, grindstones and napery found their way to Winchester with the raw wool, woad, madder and teasels needed in the manufacture of cloth. Much the same conditions obtained at Romsey, the home of one of the most important Benedictine nunneries in the country. The nuns took consignments of hake and salmon, stockfish and red or white herrings. They bought garlic for seasoning, onions, and wine for the table; silk for fine vestments, coal for heating, iron and freestone for repairs. A flourishing cloth industry existed alongside them, attracting regular consignments of woad, alum, madder and fuller's earth. Ringwood, with no such ecclesiastical foundation to stimulate demand, rated a poor third to the others. In 1443–4, Winchester had attracted 370 carts from Southampton, Romsey 213, and Ringwood only 30. They brought woad and madder for the dyers, with iron and a selection of victuals and household goods.[29]

Inevitably, the greater the market and the further it was sited from the port, the less the average Southampton burgess might expect to take a part in it. Already, both at Winchester and Romsey, local merchants rivalled the Southampton man even for aliens, there had been the openings to secure a proportion of the trade. Still more, then, at London and at Salisbury, the two principal markets for Southampton merchandise of every kind, the Southampton burgess, if not positively excluded, could make but little impact. Just as the London market continued to be dominated by the Italians, whose agents commonly handled over 80 per cent of the loads consigned there, the Salisbury trade fell principally to the men of Salisbury itself. Precisely as at Winchester and Romsey, they were meeting the needs of a large ecclesiastical establishment. But the importance of Salisbury, and the reason for the crucial role it played in Southampton trade, lay rather in its choice situation at the hub of a prospering textile industry and at the junction of the main roads to the west. With a wine order that seldom fell below 250 pipes throughout the century, Salisbury received important consignments of dyestuffs and mordants, in particular of woad. These were to be added to a list of goods, every one of which was carried by road from Southampton, monotonous in its length. There was alum, madder, fuller's earth, teasels, flax, soap, canvas and shears for the cloth industry; almonds, dates, figs, raisins, garlic, pepper, ginger, aniseed and oil for the victuallers and spicers; mulwell, hake, sprats, salmon, red and white herring, and salt-fish for the fishmongers; timber, wainscots, nails, paving-stones, paving-tiles and slates for the builders; mercery and household goods, fustian and silk, napery and haberdashery, bolsters, featherbeds, pots and pans of brass and earthenware, candlesticks, cauldrons, washbasins and grindstones. In 1443–4, it required over a third of the outward journeys from Southampton to carry the Salisbury trade. Not all of it, of course, was destined only for Salisbury. There were men of the west country trading through the city: of Taunton and Yeovil, Bruton, Frome, Shepton Mallet, Glastonbury and Mere. Others had come from Warminster, Bradford-on-Avon and Bristol. There were even those who had preferred Southampton to important markets closer at hand, making the long journey down by road from centres as remote as Ludlow, in Shropshire, or Coventry, in the midlands.

Excluding the London trade, exceptional throughout the century in its emphasis on high-priced luxury goods and spices, the pattern of distribution out of Southampton followed its own clear rules (Fig. 9). Sales of certain bulkier commodities (coal, in particular, and building materials) were strictly local. Iron, with many purchasers in the region, was consigned usually to destinations within Hampshire, seldom travelling far even into the adjoining counties, Wiltshire, Berkshire, Dorset and West Sussex.

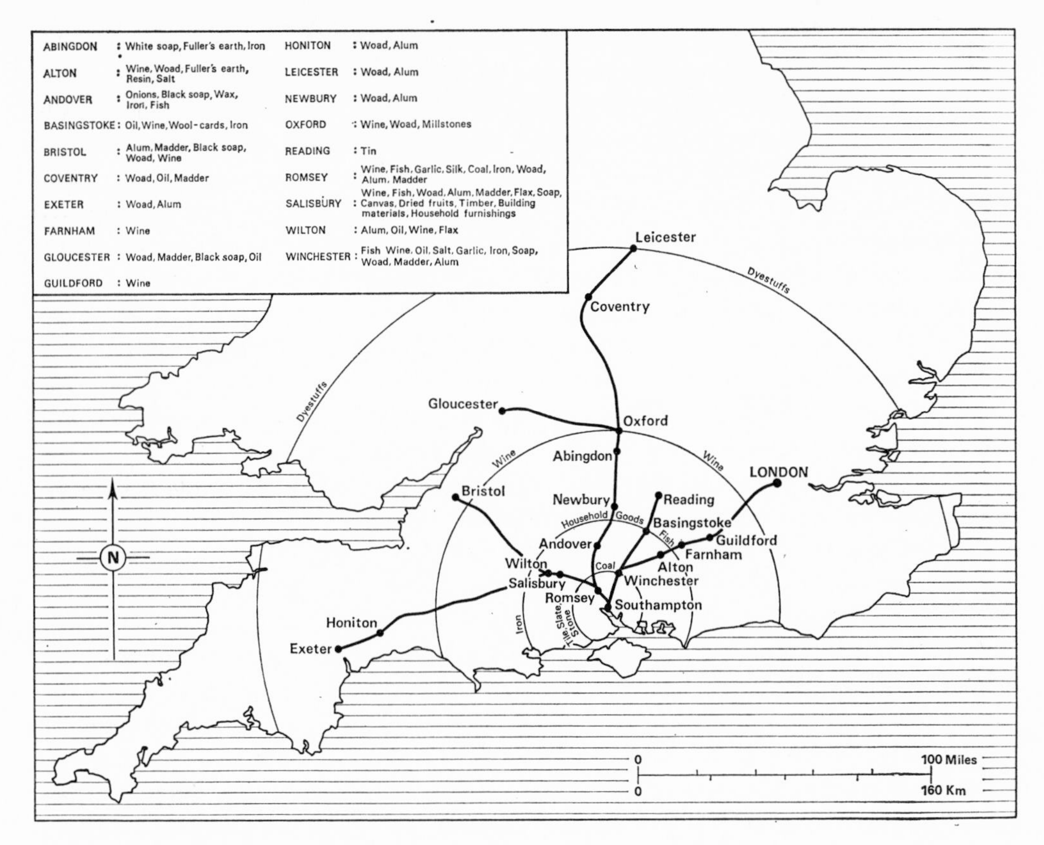

Figure 9 The inland trade of Southampton, *c.* 1440

Household goods, including earthenware pots, were similarly restricted in their sales. They were sent, usually, to Winchester, Romsey and Salisbury, although some might go further: to London, for example, or Cirencester. Fish, distributed in quantity throughout Hampshire, reached Wiltshire, west Dorset and south Berkshire, no further.

Value, equally with bulk, determined the range of sales. Both wines and dyestuffs, for example, travelled far. Oxford, a big purchaser of wines, took woad and even millstones from Southampton. On the way, sales of onions, black soap, wax, iron and fish might be made to the men of Andover; Newbury took woad and alum; Abingdon, white soap, fuller's earth and iron. On the road to London, Alton, Farnham and Guildford were each purchasers of wine; at Alton, still within easy reach of Southampton, there were buyers for woad, fuller's earth, resin, salt and bowstaves. To the north, Reading took tin for the pewterers of London, while at Basingstoke, along the same road but nearer to Southampton, there were sales of oil, wine, wool-cards and iron. Wine might travel as far as Gloucester and Oxford, to the north, or Frome, to the west. But it was more usual for long-distance hauls to be commissioned primarily for dyestuffs. Coventry, a particularly good customer for Southampton woad, bought also some oil and madder; Leicester took woad and alum; Gloucester bought woad, madder, black soap and oil. Similarly, it was the cloth industry that dominated the long haul to the west. On the way, Wilton, Blandford, Frome, Honiton and Exeter were all purchasers of woad. In addition, Wilton, the nearest, took some alum, oil, wine and flax; Blandford, some madder; Frome, some oil, wine and wool; Honiton and Exeter, some alum.

The business, taken as a whole, might be small. But the direction that it took – primarily to the cloth centres of the Cotswolds, the midlands and the west – will serve to emphasize the prolonged dependence of Southampton trade on just two basic exportable commodities, wool and cloth. During an ordinary year, it was mainly in the late autumn and early winter, from October to December, that the wool carts reached the town. Their loads were weighed and assessed for custom, sealed and loaded on the ships waiting for the wool fleet to depart. As the wool arrivals reduced to a trickle, the cloth carts and pack-horses took their place. They came throughout the winter and spring, braving the worst conditions on the roads. But arrivals did not reach their peak until well into the summer. Typically, a cart, arriving with wool or cloth, departed with dyestuffs or wine. And it was precisely this simple exchange of primary products that remained the basis of Southampton's trading economy through the best part of the later Middle Ages. However, there were other interests also, of course not unrelated to the exchange, to keep the town alive. One of the very few commodities, apart from wool, cloth, victuals and hides, to reach Southampton by road, was rope from Bridport in Dorset. The quantities involved were never significant. Nevertheless, they point to another major quality of Southampton's working life: the supply and servicing of shipping, constantly in the port.

Indeed, it was a part of the life of every considerable burgess in Southampton to be expert in a variety of trades. If, that is, Southampton merchants often compare unfavourably in the business they handled with their contemporaries in Salisbury or London, it should be remembered that they chose also to serve as ship-chandlers and repairers, as agents and as hosts to foreigners. It was a common experience throughout the century, particularly when the trading fleets were in, for Southampton to swarm with alien mariners: they 'abounded' in the port, to repeat Henry's words, having 'flocked' there from many different parts. To many of the men of the borough, to artisans, victuallers, taverners and small shopkeepers, as much as to the greater merchants who controlled them, they brought a comfortable livelihood, often contingent on their coming. In 1406, at the beginning of the new era, the craft of tailors, seeking to set some limit on alien competition in their town, had explained that the 'greatest commodities and profits wherewith they maintain and sustain their poor estate . . . were wont to arise from the alien folk coming into the port of the said town in carracks, galleys, ships of Spain, Portugal, Germany, Flanders, Zealand, Prussia, and others, who at their arrival there were wont for their use to have their cloths cut out by the tailors of the same town'.[30] And although the rivalry of foreign craftsmen remained a grievance of the trades throughout the century – coopers, drapers and shearmen were to complain of it – there can be little doubt that the visitors, whatever their faults, continued to bring to the town more business than they ever took away.[31]

As it was, much of the victualling in the port, and a good deal of the supply of ropes and other equipment to the shipping, profited Southampton men. Repairs to visiting carracks and galleys were a source of finance to the municipality.[32] In the victualling trades, good profits might be made, for example, in the supply of ships' biscuits. Certainly, they were enough to tempt a small group of bakers, in 1519, to corner the market for themselves.[33] And if foreign business lagged or failed, there were the king's ships to fit-out and provision. In 1486, at the beginning of the year, the *Mary of the Tower* was made ready for service. Certainly, it was a Bridport man who supplied the rigging, and there were Londoners concerned all along in the supply of materials and skilled labour. But a local man, Vincent Tye, found the canvas and twine for the sails; another, Lawrence Haynes, provided an anchor and a mast; from a third, Philip Loker, a smith, the king's agents purchased serpentines and gunpowder, with iron plate, spikes, bolts and nails.[34] The previous year, for the space of some weeks, the *Governor* had lain off the port. A Southampton butcher had been among those selected to provision the crew.[35]

Clearly, it was in business such as this, at least as much as in trade, that the roots of the borough's economy were bedded. Ultimately, as the burgesses themselves well recognized, this too would depend on the maintenance of a brisk exchange of merchandise through the port. And it is for this reason that the incidence of trade at Southampton can be taken as no bad index to the degree of prosperity in the borough. Nevertheless it should be said that the true economic situation of a town like Southampton is not to be measured by trade alone, whether handled by natives or by aliens. Nor yet can it be assessed on the evidence of frequent, almost routine, complaints of municipal poverty, the product not of a falsely-based economy but of frozen local taxes and dues. In the next century, the young king, Edward VI, would find the town 'handsome', with as fair houses, in proportion to its size, as London itself could offer.[36] It had not become so overnight.

Notes

1 Olive Coleman, 'Trade and prosperity in the fifteenth century; some aspects of the trade of Southampton', *Ec.H.R.* 2nd series, 16 (1963–4), pp. 9–22.
2 For example, between 1441 and 1445 (P.R.O. E101/128/31, 35, E179/173/110).
3 P.R.O. E122/184/3. Pole's testimony, however, is suspect. He was charged himself with customs frauds in 1433, and had been guilty of wrongful confiscation of goods, allegedly uncustomed (*Local Port Book, 1439–40*, p. lxvi).
4 H.R.O. will of Richard Mershe, 1558.
5 Alwyn Ruddock, *Italian Merchants and Shipping*, pp. 190–3.
6 P.R.O. SC8/111/5504.
7 S.C.R.O. SC4/2/223; *Cal.P.R. 1422–9*, p. 329.
8 P.R.O. E101/128/31, E179/173/105, 107, 110. Hosting in the borough in these years is discussed by Alwyn Ruddock, 'Alien hosting in Southampton in the fifteenth century', *Ec.H.R.* 16 (1946), pp. 30–7.
9 *Charters*, i:70–1.
10 P.R.O. E179/173/118.

11 Edward Maunde Thompson (ed.), *Chronicon Angliae, ab anno domini 1328 usque ad annum 1338*, pp. 237–8.
12 *Rot.Parlm.*, iii:491, 521; *Cal.P.R. 1401–5*, p. 179.
13 Michael E. Mallett, *The Florentine Galleys in the Fifteenth Century*, p. 90.
14 Ibid., p. 256.
15 S.C.R.O. SC5/11/8, f. 12b.
16 *Cat.Anc. Deeds*, vi:C6759.
17 *Cal.P.R. 1436–41*, p. 397.
18 Eileen Power, 'The wool trade in the fifteenth century', in *Studies in English Trade in the Fifteenth Century*, eds Eileen Power and M. M. Postan, p. 45.
19 Philippe Wolff, 'English cloth in Toulouse (1380–1450)', *Ec.H.R.*, 2nd series, 2 (1949–50), pp. 290–1.
20 P.R.O. E122/141/24.
21 *Local Port Book, 1439–40* and *Brokage Book, 1439–40*, passim. The details are taken from the accounts of the water-bailiff and Bargate broker respectively. For the trading interests of Fetplace, see also Barbara Carpenter Turner, 'The brokage books of Southampton. A Hampshire merchant and some aspects of medieval transport', *Proc. Hampshire Field Club*, 16 (1944–7), pp. 173–7; and Alwyn Ruddock, *Italian Merchants and Shipping*, pp. 191–2.
22 *Brokage Book, 1443–4*, passim.
23 The commodities of the Italian trade are discussed at length by Alwyn Ruddock, op. cit., pp. 71–93.
24 Dorothy Burwash, *English Merchant Shipping, 1460–1540*, in particular chapter V; G. V. Scammell, 'Shipowning in England, c. 1450–1550', *T.R.H.S.*, 5th series, 12 (1962), pp. 105–22; Yves Renouard, *Bordeaux sous les rois d'Angleterre*, pp. 547–59; A. R. Bridbury, *Economic Growth: England in the Later Middle Ages*, pp. 36–7.
25 Sylvia Thrupp, 'A survey of the alien population of England in 1440', *Speculum*, 32 (1957), pp. 262–73. See also, for the Breton trade, Henri Touchard, *Le commerce maritime Breton à la fin du moyen âge*, pp. 182, 244–5, and A. R. Bridbury, *England and the Salt Trade in the Later Middle Ages*, pp. 116, 121. For the Netherlands trade, see N. J. M. Kerling, *Commercial relations of Holland and Zeeland with England from the late 13th century to the close of the Middle Ages*, passim.
26 *Port Books, 1427–30*, pp. xix–xxii. A single re-shipment of goods at Southampton, destined for Seaton (Devon) although pirated on the way, included ten bales of alum, two bales of madder, 84 balets of woad, a pipe of white soap, a butt of Rumney, and six measures (*sorts*) of fruit (*Cal. P.R. 1446–52*, p. 271).
27 *Brokage Book, 1443–4*, i:xxix–xxx, ii:321–7.
28 Olive Coleman, 'Trade and prosperity in the fifteenth century; some aspects of the trade of Southampton', *Ec.H.R.*, 2nd series, 16 (1963–4), pp. 12–13; *Brokage Book, 1439–40*, pp. xxvii–ix; H. B. Wheatley and E. W. Ashbee (eds), *The Particular Description of England, 1588 (William Smith)*, pp. 69–70.
29 These and the ensuing particulars of the carting trade out of Southampton are derived from Olive Coleman, op. cit., pp. 9–16; also *Brokage Book, 1439–40* and *Brokage Book, 1443–4*, passim.
30 *Black Book*, i:98–9; also *Book of Remembrance*, i:5.
31 *Black Book*, ii:146–7; *Letters*, pp. 30–2; *Book of Remembrance*, i:19.
32 S.C.R.O., Stewards' Books, passim.
33 *Third Book of Remembrance*, p. 30; for sales of biscuit, see also *Books of Examinations and Depositions*, p. 26.
34 M. Oppenheim (ed.), *Naval accounts and inventories of the reign of Henry VII*, Navy Records Society, 8 (1896), pp. 12–20.
35 Ibid., p. 27.
36 J. G. Nichols (ed.), *Literary Remains of King Edward the Sixth*, Roxburghe Club, 1857, i:81, quoted by Robert Douch, *Visitors' Descriptions of Southampton, 1540–1956*, p. 9.

Chapter fourteen

Incorporation

It may very well be that the finances of the municipality were slow to benefit from the renewal of trading activity in the port. But the wealth of individual burgesses, and their familiarity with the routines of borough government, equipped them early in the day to seize the initiative in forwarding, by a series of well-judged moves, the self-determination of their borough. The incorporation of Southampton belongs to what has been termed the 'classic age' of incorporation, and although Southampton was among the leaders of the field, there is no reason to claim any peculiar priorities for the town.[1] Nevertheless, what was achieved in the fifteenth century, in Southampton as elsewhere, was a workable structure of local government in the borough and a highly-prized independence from the county.

It was in 1401, near the beginning of Henry IV's reign, that the first important step was taken. On the petition of the burgesses, Henry allowed the mayor and bailiffs of Southampton a major extension of the judicial powers to which, at the expense of the sheriff, they had already enjoyed some claim since 1256. He did it, he said, for the 'betterment and fortification of the aforesaid town, notoriously situated in front of our enemies, and also that our liege subjects may the more eagerly resort to and come to inhabit the said town, the more they shall see the burgesses of the town aforesaid strengthened by greater privileges and grants'. It was to be open to the mayor and bailiffs to take cognizance of 'all pleas, real, personal and mixed, both those held by Assizes and certifications and of all others whatsoever concerning all tenements and tenures existing within the town and liberty, also of all manner of offences, debts, accounts, conventions, and other contracts whatsoever, arising or done within the same town and liberty both on land and sea, namely, to be held before them in the Guildhall of the town aforesaid, and there to be fully determined by the same mayor and bailiffs'. In a happy adaptation of the system already well tried in the counties, Southampton was to have its own justices of the peace, chosen from among the aldermen and 'discreet' men of the community, under the leadership of the mayor. The justices would have full power to hear and terminate all causes falling within their purview, saving cases of felony to the crown.[2]

The principal purpose of the new measures had been to exclude the interference of the county authorities in borough affairs, and this interference remained an issue up to, and even beyond, Southampton's achievement of county status in 1447. However, in the meantime the burgesses had secured for themselves a charter of liberties exceeding anything they had had from the king since the granting of the fee farm by King John. So long, that is, as the borough remained without a well-defined corporate identity, its officials were personally liable before the law for its debts and other failings. Formally, though not so obviously in fact, it lacked the elements of a corporate voice: the perpetual succession of legally-appointed representatives, the power to sue and be sued in the name of the town, the right to hold lands and other revenue-producing properties, to employ a common seal and to issue by-laws of its own. Antique custom and particular grants had anticipated the crown's eventual concession of some, at least, of these rights. Nevertheless, the incorporation charter of 1445, one of the earliest to be granted in the country, went several stages further, proposing for the municipality a precise legal status such as would be essential in any contest for authority. In the words of the king, 'the town shall be for ever incorporate of one mayor, two bailiffs and the burgesses'. These and their successors 'shall be one perpetual community, incorporate in word and deed by the name of the mayor, bailiffs and burgesses of that town, and shall have perpetual succession'. They might plead, or be impleaded, as a corporation in the courts; they might hold lands, notwithstanding any statute to the contrary; they might elect officers without delay to fill gaps in the ranks of their representatives, created in between the usual election times by death or deposition. The mayor, holding the offices of escheator and clerk of the market, would be protected against the intervention of powerful royal officials: the king's Clerk of the Market, the Constable, the Earl Marshal and the Lord High Admiral. A new staple, created in the town by the terms of the charter, formalized the already ancient exclusion of foreigners from the retail trade. The proceeds of outlawries, declared against members of the community, were henceforth to be absorbed by the town funds. And there was to be protection for the town against arbitrary requisitions of foodstuffs by the provisors of the crown.[3]

The charter of 1445 brought something to everybody. But, as an early example of its kind, it suffered from faults of drafting and had to be amended many times. There were gaps still in the barriers that the burgesses had erected against the interventions of the county authorities. And it was to plug these that a new 'county of the town of Southampton' was created in 1447, to exist henceforth alongside the 'county of Southampton', as Hampshire until quite recently was known. There was now to be a sheriff of Southampton, elected from among their number by the burgesses; there would be quarter sessions and assizes at the borough.[4] The terms of the separation had provided unambiguously that 'no other sheriff of our realm or bailiff or officer of any sheriff of the same realm, except only the sheriffs of us and our heirs of the said town and their bailiffs or officers, shall in any wise enter the same town, precincts or ports aforesaid [including Portsmouth] to pursue or execute anything which pertains or may pertain to their office, nor in any wise shall intrude in the same'. But the clash of jurisdictions had gone beyond opposition to the sheriff, and it remained difficult, even after 1447, to reserve the town's affairs to itself. In 1451 another redefinition of powers was attempted. Alleged to be necessary in view of the 'crafty ways and artful guise of certain of our officers who unjustly exercise their office within the said town', the new charter repeated the terms of the charters of 1445 and 1447, to develop still further the powers of the mayor. Clearly, it had not been enough simply to exclude verbally the interventions of the Steward, the Marshal and the Admiral in the borough. In place of the 1445 directive, the new charter vested the powers of these officers in the mayor, to hold 'without contradiction of us, our heirs and successors soever, as freely, peaceably and wholly as any seneschal or marshal of our household or admiral of England does, exercises or shall have executed in any way his offices or any of them, and all and everything that pertains to those offices or any of them'. In effect, it did for these offices what had already been done for that of the Clerk of the Market.[5] The following year, in October, while the scope of jurisdictions remained unclear, the burgesses secured a re-statement of their own juridical rights, contested by the justices of the neighbouring county. They had had difficulty recently in making good their claim even to the oversight of retailing in the borough. But the king supported them in a clear instruction to the justices not to meddle in the affairs of the town. The burgesses had always enjoyed, he acknowledged, the 'power of rectifying the assize of bread and beer there, when broken, and the fines and amercements of shoemakers, tanners, dyers and other artificers exercising their trades within the liberty of the said town unduly, and also of butchers, fishmongers, publicans, regrators, and others who within the said liberty sell victuals at an excessive price or in any other undue manner, to the prejudice of our people in those parts'.[6]

By the middle of the century, successive charters had effectively established the right to self-government of the burgesses. But a certain tidying up of administrative arrangements within the borough remained to the Yorkist king, Edward IV, to be confirmed as a token of his special favour. In a lengthy charter, dated 16 December 1461, within a few months of the beginning of his reign, Edward re-stated the juridical rights of the burgesses, 'considering the faithful and laudable submission with which they have shewn themselves hitherto grateful in all things to us and to our ancestors of famous recollection and memory, lately kings of England, and especially ready in late years for the expenses, costs, labours, burdens and perils, and these not small'. Confirming the scope of the borough court in civil law actions, Edward recognized what was probably already the regular practice of a weekly meeting in the Guildhall, over the Bargate. He added a recorder, 'a certain man skilled in law', to the panel of justices of the peace, and gave power to a quorum of justices, in each case to include the recorder, to investigate felonies committed within the borough limits.[7] An important additional provision had assigned fines arising in the court to the benefit of the town funds, in support of payment of the fee farm. But in time this was to be adjudged 'not good in law', and it required a further charter, conceded nearly two decades later, to over-ride the objections of the Exchequer. From August 1480, it became lawful on all counts for the mayor, bailiffs and burgesses and their successors, to annex all such fines to their own use and profit, 'without account of rendering any thing to us or our heirs, and without demand, molestation or impediment of us or our heirs, of the justices, escheators, sheriffs, or of any other officers, or servants of us or our heirs whatsoever'.[8]

In clearing old impediments to their freedom, just as in the assembly of new resources in revenue, the burgesses were active in many directions. The bishop of Winchester's fair at St Giles had for centuries imposed a pause on normal trading in the town for the fortnight it was held each September. It was a grievance as ancient as the dispute with the sheriff. The settlement negotiated in 1254 had gone substantially the way of the bishop, limiting trade in the borough for the duration of the fair to the sale of victuals alone. Yet, by the fifteenth century, the fair and its institutions were in decay, and by 1406, if not before, the men of Southampton had begun to contract out of their ancient obligations, arranging for a small composition payment to be made in lieu of attendance at the fair.[9] They had, in any case, acquired a fair of their own. And while there is no saying how old the fair at Trinity Chapel may have been, it is certain that, from the fifteenth century onwards, it was being held annually 'at and about' the chapel, next to the Itchen and due east of the mother church at St Mary's. Gathering on Trinity Sunday and the three following days, the fair was still an important occasion in Sir Henry Englefield's time:[10]

> From the church-yard [St Mary's], a road not very wide, and bordered on either hand by a deep and muddy ditch, leads to the ancient mill called the Chapel mill. In this road, inconvenient as it is, an annual fair is held on Trinity Monday, Tuesday and Wednesday. This fair is opened by the mayor and bailiffs, with much ceremony, on the preceding Saturday afternoon. The mayor erects a pole with a large glove fixed to the top of it, near the miller's house; and the bailiff then takes possession of the fair, as chief magistrate in its precinct during the fair, and invites the mayor and his suite to a collation in his tent. He appoints a guard of halberdiers, who keep the peace by day, and watch the fair by night. During the fair, no person can be arrested for debt within its precincts. On the Wednesday at noon, the mayor dissolves the fair, by taking down the pole and glove, or rather ordering it to be taken down; which till lately was done by the young men of the town, who fired at it with single balls, till it was destroyed, or they were tired with the sport. Probably it formerly was a mark for the less dangerous dexterity of the young archers.

In the matter of the fair, as in so much else, antique conflicts were resurrected and successfully resolved. The men of Southampton, in the new circumstances of the fifteenth century, continued to buy their freedom cheaply from the bishop. Their victory over the county authorities was complete. In correspondence with another ancient rival, the Cinque Ports, a fresh arrogance emerges, appropriate to the prosperous condition of the town: 'we understonde not that your seid lettres yeveth us eny suche auctorite ne that we be bounden by the lawe to obey eny suche writynges or commaundementes from you'.[11] It was a mood that attracted new business to the port, bringing the Staple of Mines in 1492, in circumstances very different from those that would promote the gift of the monopoly of sweet wines rather more than half a century later. Philip and Mary were to confer the latter on the town in an effort to make good its failing economy. But when the Staple of Mines was established at Southampton, in the reign of Henry VII, it came not so much as a life-saver to a failing community, but rather as a compliment to the acknowledged energy of the burgesses:[12]

> Forasmuch as the King our sovereign lord, considering that the mines within this realm of England and other countries adjoining bearing gold, silver and tin, copper, lead, and other metals, for lack of diligent labour be left unsought and unwrought, and so the commodities and riches in the same mines turn no manner to profit:
>
> His highness therefore hath granted and licensed an incorporation to be had, of a mayor and a certain fellowship of merchants of the Staple of all manner of metals, to the intent that they shall not only cause the said mines to be occupied and much idle people to be set over in work for the approvement of the commodities therein, but also shall cause all the metals hereafter to be found in the said mines to be uttered for a reasonable price, to the great wealth of his said highness and of his realm and of his subjects of the same; and thereupon hath ordained certain Staples of metals to be set and kept in divers places within this his said realm, that is to say, at Southampton, so that no tin nor lead, after the feast of St Michael the Archangel next coming, be shipped nor carried out of the said realm but it be first brought and stapled at one of the said Staples, and the customs and duties to his said highness thereof due be to him there contented and paid; upon pain of forfeiture of all such lead and tin, that one half thereof to his said highness and that other half to the finder of the same, according to the tenor of our said sovereign lord's letters patent thereupon made.

It was in this reign, furthermore, that the volume of trade passing through Southampton reached new heights. And if, as always, the increase benefited chiefly the individual merchant in the town, there had yet for some time already been encouraging signs of the dawning of a new era even in borough finances. As far back as 1415, specifically to relieve them, a licence had been granted to the town by Henry V to acquire property, against the conditions of the statute of mortmain, to an annual value of £100.[13] The borough authorities had held properties before, among them a tenement on French Street noted in 1408; and the first recorded town lease, relating to a tenement and curtilage on East Street, is dated 25 November 1378.[14] But the major purchases of municipal lands belong rather to the fifteenth and sixteenth centuries, building up a new endowment for the town to supplement its traditional resources in the profits of petty customs and tolls.

None is better recorded than the purchase for the town of the great tenement at West Hall, originally built for Gervase le Riche at the beginning of the borough's prosperity. The negotiations, which were lengthy and expensive, were completed during the mayoralty of Peter James, in 1428–9. The mayor himself, William Chamberleyn and John Fleming, a member of a local family almost as old as the Hall itself, conducted the business between them. With their five servants, they rode to Salisbury to treat with Robert Lange, the other principal in the transaction. They remained there for four days, claiming expenses from the town at thirty shillings. Shortly after a price had been agreed, Robert Lange and the other feoffees of the tenement made the journey to Southampton to deliver seisin to the mayor. Robert Lange alone had come with no fewer than twelve servants in attendance, and it cost the town a large sum both to bring him to Southampton and to maintain him and his retinue during their stay. In addition, there were other charges to be met. Peter James, William Chamberleyn and John Fleming again made a journey, this time to Lange's country seat. They had to pay the expenses of William Westbury, a king's justice, who met them there, and themselves charged the borough for the purchase of three cloaks 'for riding on the said journey', for green ginger and pepper, presumably taken as gifts, and for the hire of six horses, additional to their own. On a purchase price of £120, conveyancing charges alone totalled £13. 15*s*. 9*d*. Other expenses, which included £16. 9*s*. 4*d*. spent on essential repairs, exceeded £50. Paolo Morelli, a wealthy Florentine commission agent, took West Hall from Michaelmas 1429. The rent, which he paid in advance, was agreed at £10.[15]

Everywhere, the fashion in housing had changed. In 1457, the men of Winchester welcomed the opportunity to lease their 'grete old mancyons' to Italians seeking a quieter base than London.[16] Equally, at Southampton, as the rebuilding of the town gathered pace, the cumbersome tenements of an earlier age were sold off readily to any willing purchaser. Among the buyers, the corporation headed the list. In due course, it came to own Le Vernecle, later to be the workhouse, on French Street north of West Hall. It bought the antique mansion at Ronceval, on the western shore, and acquired at least a share in La Chayne, on Porters Lane.[17] The Italians, in the event, had not taken up the houses at Winchester. But they were obviously better suited at Southampton and, so long as they remained there, good tenants were not hard to find. For many years, from the last decade of the fifteenth century, the Marini were tenants of West Hall.[18] Galley patrons, soon after the acquisition of Ronceval by the town, hired it for a store.[19] There were Italians at Bull Hall and at the newer Polymond Hall in the mid-century.[20] And La Chayne was to be held by two, at least, of the more notable Italian-born merchants in Southampton: Gabriel Corbet and Christopher Ambrose, both of whom obtained denization in the kingdom, to become active in the politics and the trading of the borough.[21]

By 1637, revenues from corporation lands would come to total nearly £300.[22] Undoubtedly, substantial progress had been made in the previous two centuries towards the supply of an alternative source of revenue for the town. However, there were new charges to be met as well, reflecting new standards in the promotion of the health and well-being of the burgesses. There might be little difference in detail between the street-cleaning provisions of the ancient gild ordinances and their equivalent in the Modern Laws of the fifteenth-century borough. Both provided against the littering of the streets with kitchen or butchers' waste; both forbade pigs to be let loose in the street; and both required that dung-hills, piled outside street doors, should not be left there longer than two days.[23] Nevertheless, there is evidence of an increasing concern on the part of the fifteenth-century municipality to maintain certain standards of cleanliness and hygiene in the borough. As was already not uncommon elsewhere, public latrines were provided and maintained by the corporation, where possible next to the water. One of these, at Southampton, was sited on the West Quay.[24]

Anticipating the appointment of a town scavenger, for whom a contract of 1561 has survived, a workman was being paid a few pence in 1433–4 to clean English Street from the friary gate, and to carry the refuse to the sea.[25] Unquestionably his task would have been made somewhat easier by the first paving of the streets, a municipal improvement recognized at the end of the previous century by the successive pavage grants of 1384, 1391 and 1398.[26] Repairs to the pavement and to the central drainage channels in the streets, as the new century advanced, became an increasing burden on municipal finances.[27] And it is not surprising that, when a large-scale programme of repair became necessary again, the borough authorities should have tried to share their responsibilities. In 1477, seeking an order from the king to compel each burgess to take his part, they noted that the town was 'full febly paved'. It was proving, especially in the main thoroughfares – English Street, French Street and Bull Street – 'full perilous and jepardouce to ride or goo theryn'. Henceforth, every householder in the streets most affected was to repair the paving in front of his own tenement, as far as the middle of the street. For three centuries the arrangement held good, until upset in 1769 by 'some few strangers . . . seiz'd with the Epidemical Madness of New Paving'. It was made more workable in 1482 by the appointment of a salaried town paviour, employed to survey the state of the paving and to undertake repairs at the cost of the householders.[28] His duties would certainly have included the exclusion of heavy carts with iron-shod wheels, 'thowght to be a great annoyance to the towne in breakinge the payments of the same, which hathe byn and is daylye chargeable to the inhabitants thereof'. It was the brewers, particularly, who were at fault, and an order excluding them, subsequently copied almost verbatim into the Modern Laws, was published on 9 September 1562.[29]

In putting forward their claim, in 1477, to be relieved of the charges of paving, the mayor and his associates in office had reported that they had 'no Londes nor Tenementes, Rentes nor other yerly revenus in Common' with which to meet the anticipated costs. And although they were arguing, as was their style, rather for effect than from truth, it may very well have been the case that such resources as they had were already fully deployed in the care and maintenance of the defences. These, through the century, had persisted a heavy charge on the town. On the waterfront, especially, erosion was a perpetual problem. While Peter Grew was steward, a great wind stripped the roof off West Hall and did much damage to the quays and the defences.[30] And it was erosion and the 'force of the sea' that, throughout the century, was the most often repeated explanation of the poor condition of the walls.[31] Furthermore, bad workmanship in the past and skimped repairs had left even the landward defences inadequate. The draft of a letter complaining of this survives in the corporation records. It was written in or about 1460, and may have been the product of the alarms which characterized that year, while the town was threatened with the anticipated assault of Richard of York, the earls of Warwick and Salisbury, and the 'king's adversaries of France'.[32] Addressed to the lords of the Council, it sought aid against the malice of the king's enemies, 'whiche with all theyre wittes power & cursed ymagynacions long & contynually hath labored & yet laboreth to prevayle and opteyne ayenst this seide poure place'. It reported the walls on the landward side to be 'so feble that they may not resiste ayenst any gonnes shotte, and so thynne that no man may well stond upon them to make eny resistence or defence'. Following continual expense on scaffolding platforms and earth countermuring, which 'yerely wastith & consumyth by force of wetheryng', the burgesses despaired of maintaining the walls for themselves. Furthermore, there were other serious weaknesses in the defences. Short of calling on the help of aliens resident in the town, 'whiche we dar not trust unto', there were not enough men arrayable in the borough to defend the considerable circuit of its 'feble & olde wallys'. Even the castle was in poor condition, its well blocked and its seaward wall sadly decayed. To the town's existing armament of twenty-five guns 'grete & smalle', at least another sixty pieces would need to be added if an adequate defence were intended.[33]

Within the limits of their own strained resources, successive kings did whatever they could to help the town. Edward IV, in 1469 and again in 1477, conferred on the municipality licences to export wool free of custom, to an annual maximum of fifty sacks, in return for a guaranteed expenditure of £135 on the fortifications and quays in each year that the grant took effect.[34] The next year, on the surrender of the 1469 letters patent, he allowed the town an additional £40 yearly out of the receipts of custom in the port, to be put to the same use.[35] Henry VII, early in his reign, gave £50, which was spent immediately, towards the repair of the seaward wall on the west.[36] In 1511, his son repeated the device of an export licence on wool, doubling the permitted maximum. And shortly afterwards he was to allocate a further £100 out of the customs to the cost of scouring the ditches of the town.[37]

Yet the king's efforts, significant though they were, paled before the outlay required of the town itself in meeting the charges of its own defence. As with the costs of paving, as much as possible was done to spread the load. In the maintenance of the walls, the terrier of 1454 shows the system in action. Under the direction of the alderman of his ward, each householder was allotted, in respect of his tenement and with strict regard to its size, a stretch of the town wall to repair.[38] Traditionally, upkeep and repair of towers fell to important individual burgesses, religious institutions, and to the trades acting in concert. The Watergate Tower (Plate 14), for example, was leased in succession through the century to William Ravenston, William Soper, Roger Kelsale and Richard Palshid, each of whom was expected to restore and maintain it.[39] Similarly, the Augustinians at St Denys shouldered the burden of the vital Polymond Tower, at the north-east angle of the town;[40] whereas the opposing Arundel Tower, at the north-west corner, with its neighbouring 'little tower' towards the east, had become, by the sixteenth century, the charge of the shoemakers, curriers, cobblers and saddlers. East Gate Tower and the little tower to its north were assigned to the goldsmiths, blacksmiths, locksmiths, pewterers and tinkers; the tower by the warehouse on Porters Lane, to the mercers; St Barbara's Tower and the neighbouring Corner Tower, to the brewers and bakers; the tower next along to the north-west, 'behind Bull Hall', to the coopers; and the three towers on the west shore between the West Gate and Pilgrim's Gate, just south of the castle, to the vintners, mariners and lightermen, to the weavers, fullers and cappers, and to the butchers, fishmongers and chandlers respectively.[41]

On every burgess, likewise, there fell the obligation to take his part in the watch, to furnish himself with hand-arms, and to answer the summons to the muster. The first surviving orders for the watch, although they are of sixteenth-century date, probably repeat in all but detail a long-standing arrangement in the town:[42]

> Provision for the watche within this towne & libertie of the same. Hit is agreed the viith day of November [1522] that there shall nyghtly be vi men watchyng within the towne, wherof all weis ii to kepe ye walles and the other iiii to walke within the towne and oftymes to walke upp to the the castill hill and there to have good respect to the sea and every quarter of the towne for fyre & other daungers; and that every man, when the watche comyth to his hous, be redy at the walls yn proper person or a sufficient person being no aliaunt [alien] for hym, uppon peyn to lose xiid for every tyme making defaute. And from All Halowen day to Candilmas it is agreed that every watcheman shall have for every nyght iiid, and afterward till the fest of All Seynts iid, and that no watcheman depart from the watche before Candilmas day before vi a clok yn the mornyng, uppon peyn of imprisonment and ferther ponysshment as shalbe thought for his desert, and fro Candilmas to the fest of All Seynts befor v a clok.
>
> Item that there shalbe iiii watchemen nyghtly above barre & Seynt Maris, kepyng there walks to Our Lady of Grace [Trinity Chapel] & by the see side to Godds Hous yate & so upp to Bargate the post ageynst Arundells tower, and the other ii to walke above barre & upp to the crosse [Padwell Cross, at the north end of London Road] by hether Rokkysden lane [Rockstone Lane] and some tyme down Gossewellane [Goswell Lane] to Hilbrig [formerly Achard's Bridge, at the base of Hill Lane] & so by the se side upp to Bargate.
>
> Item the tething of Portswood to kepe nyghtly ii men watchyng
>
> And this to endure as aslond as shalbe thought necessary, every watcheman to kepe his watche & have like wages as abovesaid.

In general, although forever short of manpower, the town authorities, by the end of the Middle Ages, had contrived a relatively effective system of local defence, independent of such further resources as the king, in times of crisis, might feel able to supply. Again the load was spread. Every male inhabitant of the town, over the age of sixteen and under sixty, was liable for military service on call. At regular intervals, he was summoned to a general muster on Houndwell Field, to assemble with the others of his ward for counting and military exercises. Totals of up to 421 able-bodied men were recorded at such musters in 1556, 1573 and 1580. Of these, the majority were billmen, or halberdiers, but there was also a fair force of archers and a few gunners. They had all brought their weapons to the musters, to be counted with themselves. The hand-guns, of which more than half belonged to men of the wealthy parish of Holy Rood, totalled twenty in 1556.[43]

Heavier armaments, in particular the guns, remained the responsibility of the borough. Of course, the great mangonels and other stone-throwing engines of the fourteenth-century defensive system had gone. The site of the 'Magnell', next to the West Gate, was already vacant by 1454, and many years had passed since there was talk of repairs to the engines-of-war.[44] In contrast, the stewards' accounts, throughout the fifteenth century, return constantly to the theme of the municipal guns. And the exceptionally early inverted-keyhole gunports (Fig. 7) in the town walls, thought to be of late-fourteenth-century date, suggest that the preoccupation was by no means a new one.[45]

Stephen Palmer, at the end of his stewardship in 1468, was to draw up an illuminating inventory of the corporation's armaments, for the guidance and information of his successor. In the Guildhall, over the Bargate, had been gathered a brass gun 'chawmbered of himself', two other guns on trestles with their six chambers, or breech-blocks, and two chamberless guns, usually placed in the two towers between the Bargate and Polymond Tower. At Polymond Tower itself, known to Palmer as 'St Denys tower', there was another gun without its chamber. A great gun on a wheeled carriage, which formerly had stood at the Bargate, was now placed at the door of the king's Custom House, next to the Watergate. Its chambers, Palmer noted, were kept in the general armoury at God's House Tower. To the west of the Bargate, in the next tower, there were two guns fitted with their chambers. There was a gun with three chambers at Pilgrim's Gate, at the base of Simnel Street; another gun, without its chamber, lay in the tower next to the public latrine on West Quay; and a third, with three chambers, was kept at the Watchtower, immediately east of the Watergate. The defence of the landward wall, on the east, evidently depended largely on the battery over the tide-mill at God's House. But there were two guns, with three chambers, in the next tower northwards from God's House Gate, and another two guns, with six chambers, in a tower further up the east wall. God's House Tower itself was used as an armoury and store, housing a miscellaneous collection of armaments, many of them imperfect. There was a broken gun there, two good guns and a serpentine, a collection of eleven chambers for guns and serpentines, and the nineteen chambers of the guns known as the 'organs', given to the town by a benefactor some years before. Two banners, one of linen painted with the arms of the king, were housed in the same great chest with the 'organ' chambers. There were a few halberds, gun-stones 'of divers sorts', three-quarters of a barrel of gunpowder, and some broken and rusty armour. Next door, in the battery over the tide-mill, the guns were set in their embrasures. There were guns in at least two of the 'windows', with two other guns on carriages of their own, the 'organs', a great gun, and another placed on trestles, 'chambre of himself'. Six gun-chambers and some gunpowder were kept there also, with a 'great broken chamber that served for a gun called Thomas', no longer in the town's keeping.[46]

If, then, the fifteenth century had seen an increase in the scope of local government in the borough, it had seen it also in matters of hygiene and military organization, each bringing new powers and responsibilities to the municipality. This being the case, for as long as the control of borough affairs was retained by a self-perpetuating minority, tensions were bound to grow. In 1460, the riot at mayor-making is unlikely to have been an isolated incident. Nor can it be explicable simply in terms of immediate personalities. Rather was it the product of grievances accumulated over many years of unchallenged domination of borough politics by a small group of men: by the Walter Fetplaces, 'senior' and 'junior', by Peter James, Robert Aylward, Nicholas Holmhegge and their associates. In their hands, the prosperity of the town had grown on a policy of steady encouragement of alien trading. They had been committed, and it scarcely matters that it was in their own interest as much as in that of anybody else, to the support and protection of foreign merchants conducting their affairs in the borough. Others not so inclined were perhaps the less judicious. But it is hard, at this distance in time, to decide who was in the right. Both the ruling oligarchy and its opponents could distort justice in the interest of a friend. And both, as the Yorkists triumphed at a major turning-point of the civil war, took advantage of local disorders in 1460–1 to jettison, for the moment at least, any pretence of legality in their actions.

Broadly, the opposing parties in the borough divided themselves between those who supported the old order – Walter Fetplace 'junior', Robert Aylward, John Emory and Nicholas Holmhegge – and those who, in taking the side of John Payne, followed him not merely in opposition to the establishment but also in an outright hostility to foreigners, in particular to Italians. In such a small society, divided allegiances were inevitable. Andrew James, probably the son of Peter James, a typical establishment figure, became, on his second marriage, the son-in-law of John Payne, leader of the opposition and father-in-law also of Thomas White. In the fifties, still in support of Peter James, Andrew joined with him and with John Fleming, then his father-in-law, in an all-out attack on Thomas White, whom, for a while, they were successful in depriving of his burgess-ship.[47] But by 1460 Andrew James had switched his allegiance to his new father-in-law's faction, joining that year with Thomas, Payne's brother, and John, his son, in the leadership of the rioters at mayor-making, to force the election of Robert Bagworth, their candidate, in place of either Walter Fetplace 'junior' or Nicholas Holmhegge, the nominees of the outgoing mayor.[48] Complex conjunctions of anti-alien sentiment and civil war tensions underlie the events of that and of the immediately succeeding years. But the story has been told very fully elsewhere,[49] and it need only be said that neither side by any criterion was guiltless. If Payne twisted justice in a merciless pursuit of the Italians, he got his deserts when his opponents enlisted the help of the king in engineering his deposition from the mayoralty, some months before the expiry of his term, on 13 May 1463. Nor was his replacement in office, Walter Fetplace 'junior', so much less guilty of action inimical to the law. Within a short space of the fall of Payne, Fetplace was said to be using his mayoral authority to protect an alien merchant lodging with himself, sheltering him from the due process of the courts.[50]

At Southampton, as in the larger field of contemporary national politics, it had become abundantly clear that the 'law goes as it is favoured'. Certainly, few could have preserved any illusions as to the impartiality of justice in the borough. For the outsider, conditions were harsh. A plaintiff at Chancery, a stranger himself at Southampton, reported that he had been unjustly arrested at the borough at the suit of one who had 'great acquaintance there'. A resident of London, with few friends in Southampton, feared that judgment would go against him in the borough court. An Italian complained of a corrupt jury in the court of piepowder in the town; another alleged that an attempt had been made to rush an action through that court 'in derogation of Chancery', where the case was pending. As long as John Fleming was recorder in the town, the provost and fellows of the Queen's College, Oxford, could expect to obtain no justice there, as 'no one will gainsay him'.[51] Yet it might be said, in mitigation, that the burgesses, in the prevailing contempt of law, at least expected no better from others than they themselves were prepared to give. The steward's accounts of 1433–4 record a gift of wine to a number of jurors in Winchester. It had been arranged by William Chamberleyn, 'lest at any time they should be bitter against any of our comburgesses'.[52] Nor would the corporation shrink, in later years, from despatching a pipe of wine to the renowned chief justice of the king's bench, Sir John Fortescue, 'that he should be friendly and favourable to the town'.[53]

Furthermore, the arbitrary conduct and receding responsibility of the magistracy did not pass uncriticized within the borough itself. The reforming ordinances of Thomas Overy, mayor for three years from 1488, although clearly very little observed, point hopefully to the persistence of some remnant of respect for democracy in the borough. Overy published his new code in 1491 in response, he said, to 'divers grevous compleyntis' made to himself, which, if they were not remedied, would result in the 'utter distruccion of this seid gode towne, the which god defende'. It had been ancient practice, long since perverted, for twelve jurors to be appointed at the common assembly of the town to decide the nomination of borough officials: sheriffs, bailiffs, stewards and others. These were again to be chosen by the 'comune vois of the hole Assemble', not 'by election of the bench only'. At the same time, wealthy burgesses, perhaps living themselves on country estates outside the borough limits, had joined with the borough officials in evasion of the duties of the watch. Henceforth, they were to take their part in it like everybody else. Some officials, including magistrates and the clerk of the market, had neglected their duties, failing to appear

Plate 15 A group of local and imported wares, *c.* 1550

Plate 16 Tudor House Museum, St Michael's Square, formerly the house of Sir John Dawtrey and later of Sir Richard Lyster

in the courts. They were to resume them, sitting in judgment 'as the law in all such offices requirith'. It had been noticed that 'divers persons' lately had made encroachments on borough property and had blocked ancient passages and rights-of-way. They were to make full restoration to the town. General ordinances protected the ancient gild regulations, market and retailing statutes, and the exclusive position of the crafts. They were to be supplemented by a new machinery of financial control and government, carefully outlined by Overy. Auditing procedures were revised, tariffs upgraded, and the unauthorized appropriation of moneys forbidden. Regular quarterly inspections of town property were provided for, and an annual terrier of borough rents, beginning that very year, was to be compiled. It would require, Overy was careful to provide, the consent of the common assembly of the town before any one of these ordinances were altered. Furthermore, four new officers, to be known as 'conservators' and to be chosen equally from the ruling élite and the burgess commoners, were to be appointed by the jurors at mayor-making to assist in the enforcement of the ordinances.[54]

It was, perhaps, an over-optimistic assessment of the situation, for the elements of oligarchy would not take long to reappear. In a neat reversal of Overy's intentions, vitiating immediately much that he had tried to achieve, another hand, almost contemporary in style, corrected the town's copy of his ordinances. At every point in the text where the word 'conservator' had been used, 'alderman' was substituted in its place. It was an amendment, clearly, very much to the taste of the establishment.[55]

Notes

1 The incorporation of Southampton is discussed by Martin Weinbaum, *The Incorporation of Boroughs*, pp. 70–2; for a summary of the main principles of incorporation, see also his *British borough charters, 1307–1660*, pp. xxiii–viii.

2 P.R.O. SC8/73/3625; also, for an enrolment of the borough's judicial rights, see E372/249, m. 41; *Charters*, i:40–51. As Mr Welch has recently pointed out, Weinbaum's misreading of the entry in Gidden's *Charters* led him erroneously to claim priority for Southampton in the appointment of municipal JPs (Edwin Welch, *Southampton City Charters*, p. 12).

3 *Charters*, i:54–69.

4 Ibid., pp. 70–81.

5 Ibid., pp. 82–97. Gidden, mistakenly, dates the charter 1452.

6 *Oak Book*, ii:122–7.

7 *Charters*, i:98–119.

8 Ibid., pp. 122–9.

9 *Letters Patent*, ii:150–3; S.C.R.O. SC4/2/200.

10 Henry C. Englefield, *A Walk through Southampton*, pp. 75–6. The fair is first mentioned in a charter of 2 Henry IV, now no longer in existence. Letters patent confirming the fair were granted to the mayor etc. by Henry VII on 19 July 1496 (*Letters Patent*, ii:88–9; *Cal.P.R. 1494–1509*, pp. 61–2). See also O. G. S. Crawford's brief note 'Trinity Chapel and Fair', *Proc. Hampshire Field Club*, 17 (1949–52), pp. 52–3.

11 *Black Book*, ii:142. Named burgesses of Southampton had been accused of doing damage to men and goods of the Cinque Ports, and a request had followed for justice in the mayoral court. The previous year, in 1482, a Breton ship had been cut out from its anchorage at Winchelsea, and its goods dispersed illegally at Southampton (*Sign Manuals and Letters Patent*, i:14–15).

12 Paul L. Hughes and James F. Larkin (eds), *Tudor Royal Proclamations*, i:28–30; *Cal.P.R. 1485–94*, pp. 383–5.

13 *Rot.Parlm.*, iv:53; *Cal.P.R. 1413–16*, p. 284; *Charters*, i:38–9; *Letters Patent*, ii:2–7.

14 *Black Book*, i:104; S.C.R.O. SC4/3/1.

15 *Stewards' Books*, i:8–11, 30–3. The trading activities of Paolo Morelli are discussed by Alwyn Ruddock, *Italian Merchants and Shipping*, pp. 98–105.
16 J. Gairdner (ed.), *The historical collections of a citizen of London in the fifteenth century*, Camden Society, new series, 17 (1876), p. 199; cited by Ruddock, op. cit., p. 168.
17 For Le Vernecle, an acquisition of the sixteenth century or earlier, see S.C.R.O. SC13/1, and the town rental of 1637 (B.M. Add. Ch. 17449). Ronceval must have been acquired before 1482/3 (S.C.R.O. SC5/1/17, f. 4v). For the corporation's interest in La Chayne, see S.C.R.O. SC4/1/2, SC4/3/71.
18 Alwyn Ruddock, op. cit., pp. 234–54.
19 S.C.R.O. SC5/1/17, f. 10.
20 Alwyn Ruddock, op. cit., p. 131.
21 *Black Book*, ii:72–3; Win.Coll.Mun. 17763–4, 17799, 17800, 17840. For denization as a relatively common practice in medieval England, particularly in the mercantile classes, see Alice Beardwood, 'Mercantile antecedents of the English naturalization laws', *Medievalia et Humanistica*, 16 (1964), pp. 64–76, and C. T. Allmand, 'A note on denization in fifteenth-century England', *Medievalia et Humanistica*, 17 (1966), pp. 127–8.
22 B.M. Add. Ch. 17449.
23 *Oak Book*, i:52–3, 130–1.
24 S.C.R.O. SC13/1, and, for repairs there, SC5/1/8, f. 13, and SC5/1/11, f. 6. At Leicester, the public latrine was sited next to the Soar (Mary Bateson (ed.), *Records of the Borough of Leicester*, ii:60–1). London latrines, and sanitary regulations in general at the capital, are discussed by Ernest L. Sabine in three papers published in *Speculum*, 8 (1933), 9 (1934) and 12 (1937).
25 *Stewards' Books*, i:58–9; *Third Book of Remembrance*, ii:79–81.
26 *Cal.P.R. 1381–5*, p. 448, *1391–6*, p. 2, *1396–9*, p. 317. A small contribution towards the cost of the 'new' paving in the town already featured in the God's House internal accounts of 1382/3 (Bodleian, Queen's College MS. 264).
27 For example, S.C.R.O. SC5/1/10, f. 12v and SC5/1/15, f. 24v, both of which mention a 'chanelle'. Open gutters of this kind were a common feature of English towns of the period (H. E. Salter, *Medieval Oxford*, p. 85; Angelo Raine, *Medieval York*, p. xii).
28 *Rot.Parlm.*, vi:180–1; *Third Book of Remembrance*, i:26–7; John Speed, *History of Southampton*, pp. 39–42; Davies, pp. 119–20.
29 *Third Book of Remembrance*, ii:87; *Oak Book*, i:145. At York, a special tax had been imposed in the fifteenth century on all such traffic through the town. It was lifted early in the sixteenth century (Angelo Raine (ed.), *York Civic Records*, Yorkshire Archaeological Society, Record Series, 106 (1942), p. 66).
30 S.C.R.O. SC5/1/9, fos 14, 15v, 17v, 19v, 22v–23.
31 *Black Book*, ii:81; *L. & P. Henry VIII*, i:1:385.
32 *Cal.P.R. 1452–61*, pp. 602, 654.
33 *Letters*, pp. 21–2.
34 *Cal.P.R. 1467–77*, pp. 154–5; *Letters Patent*, ii:56–63. The licences were subsequently sold to ready Italian buyers (Alwyn Ruddock, *Italian Merchants and Shipping*, p. 195).
35 *Cal.P.R. 1476–85*, p. 76.
36 S.C.R.O. SC5/3/1, f. 12, and SC5/1/23, f. 45v.
37 *L. & P. Henry VIII*, i:1:385; *Third Book of Remembrance*, i:10–11.
38 S.C.R.O. SC13/1. Now published in the most recent volume of the Southampton Record Series.
39 S.C.R.O. SC4/3/2, 4, 6, 7, 7a, 14; *Black Book*, ii:79–87, 170–1.
40 S.C.R.O. SC13/1.
41 S.C.R.O. SC13/2/1, fos 4–6.
42 *Third Book of Remembrance*, i:35–6, ii:19–20; *Oak Book*, i:141.
43 S.C.R.O. SC13/2/2, 4, 5a.
44 S.C.R.O. SC13/1.
45 For recent comment on the gun-ports, see B. H. St J. O'Neill, *Castles and Cannon, a Study of Early Artillery Fortifications in England*, pp. 6–14; A. R. Dufty's review of this work in *The Archaeological Journal*, 119 (1962), pp. 367–70; D. F. Renn, 'The Southampton arcade', *Medieval Archaeology*, 8 (1964), pp. 226–8; and A. D. Saunders, 'Hampshire coastal defence since the introduction of artillery', *The Archaeological Journal*, 123 (1966), pp. 136–71. The accounts of Michael Luke, steward in 1450, record the payment of 3*d*. to a mason for the driving of a hole through the wall at the Bargate 'for a gunne' (S.C.R.O. SC5/1/7, f. 25v).
46 S.C.R.O. SC5/1/11, fos 17v–18. For the gift of the 'organs', see SC5/1/7, f. 25.
47 P.R.O. C1/16/352.
48 *Cal.P.R. 1452–61*, p. 639.
49 Alwyn Ruddock, *Italian Merchants and Shipping*, chapter vii, and the same author's 'John Payne's persecution of foreigners in the town court of Southampton in the fifteenth century', *Proc. Hampshire Field Club*, 16 (1944–7), pp. 23–37.
50 P.R.O. C1/29/435.
51 P.R.O. C1/64/2, C1/294/83, C1/59/39, C1/64/222, 312, C1/106/57.
52 *Stewards' Books*, i:64–5.
53 S.C.R.O. SC5/1/9, f. 34.
54 *Oak Book*, i:xli–ii, 151–60.
55 Aldermen, commonly ex-mayors, might be

expected to be the least enthusiastic for reform. They already belonged to a small, exclusive group. In 1573, another reforming mayor, William Capelin, would publicly remark the tendency for all offices in the town to be restricted to such burgesses 'as do use and occupie sciences & faculties', to the exclusion of those 'men of occupacions, artificers and handie crafts men, who seldome or never attaynethe within this towne to that welthe and abilitie to beare the said offices'. It was an ancient abuse, and Capelin, even if it could have been done at all, was not in office long enough to change it (*Third Book of Remembrance*, ii: 148). For a discussion of the reforming intentions of Thomas Overy and William Capelin, see Caroline E. Boden, 'The borough organization of Southampton in the sixteenth century', London M.A., 1920.

Chapter fifteen

Borough society

The society that the burgesses of Southampton, in their different ways, struggled to protect, had much, after all, to recommend it. Foreign visitors commonly deplored its violence, its chronic insularism and its frequently tasteless display. They discovered qualities of cunning, of treachery and of ruthless avarice in their hosts. But all acknowledged that the English lived remarkably well, and, furthermore, that they knew it – 'there are no other men than themselves, and no other world but England'.[1] They noted the clean houses and rich tables of the English; the display of silver plate and pewter; the fashionable and costly clothing of the burgesses. The food, they agreed, although not always of the highest quality, was invariably abundant. There were many wines to choose from, all of them imported. And even to a Venetian, the local beer and ale seemed 'most agreeable to the palate, when a person is by some chance rather heated'. English cooks were the acknowledged masters of fine roasts. English salmon, delicate in flavour and highly prized by native and alien alike, was one only among the many varieties of fish freely available on the market. And if Englishmen were not greatly given to learning and the 'studies of humanity', they shared an ingenuous affection for 'great noises that fill the ear, such as the firing of cannon, drums, and the ringing of bells', with a true appreciation of the niceties of choral music, of motets and other polyphonic compositions, for which they were justly famed. Further, they were unusually courteous by disposition; they drank less than the Germans and ate with more style than the French; they excelled in dancing, and had the attractive habit of greeting all comers with a kiss. In matters of the heart, it is true, the same Venetian would find them unduly reserved, concluding 'either that the English are the most discreet lovers in the world, or that they are incapable of love'. But their womenfolk, then as now, enjoyed an international reputation both for beauty and for warmth: qualities, it must be said, better appreciated abroad than at home.

No society can count itself immune from injustice, and there were many in fifteenth-century England who lived and died in poverty and distress. But, broadly, the lot of the burgess was a happy one, and he was glad to share his comforts with his wife. Accustomed to a sterner regime at home, a sixteenth-century merchant of Antwerp, long resident in England, found his adopted country a 'Paradise of married women'. He had evidently heard many English husbands recommending to their wives the industry of their sisters in Germany or the Netherlands. But usually, he observed, the women persisted in their customs, leaving their husbands to find servants in their place for tasks about the house and in the shop:[2]

> They go to market to buy what they like best to eat. They are well-dressed, fond of taking it easy, and commonly leave the care of household matters and drudgery to their servants. They sit before their doors, decked out in fine clothes, in order to see and be seen by the passers-by. In all banquets and feasts they are shown the greatest honour; they are placed at the upper end of the table, where they are the first served; at the lower end they help the men. All the rest of their time they employ in walking and riding, in playing at cards or otherwise, in visiting their friends and keeping company, conversing with their equals (whom they term *gosseps*) and their neighbours, and making merry with them at child-births, christenings, churchings, and funerals; and all this with the permission and knowledge of their husbands, as such is the custom.

Van Meteren's portrayal of the burgess wives of sixteenth-century England conveys pleasantly the relaxed self-indulgence of a mature society. But it would be a mistake to conclude that the gossip's ease made her any the less houseproud. It was the opinion of Levinus Lemnius, a contemporary Zealand physician, that it was precisely the wholesome living and 'exquisite meate' of the English that preserved them in such evident good health. On a visit to England which impressed him in almost every way, Lemnius remarked the 'neate cleanlines, the exquisite finenesse, the pleasaunte and delightfull furniture' of his hosts. 'Their chambers and parlours', he wrote, 'strawed over with sweete herbes, refreshed me; their nosegayes finely entermingled wyth sundry sortes of fragraunte floures in their bed-chambers and privy roomes, with comfortable smell cheered mee up and entirelye delyghted all my sences'.[3]

It may be that the minute care taken on behalf of a great nobleman to furnish and sweeten his privy were still alien to the conventions of medieval urban living. Not for the burgesses were the cushions, hand-basins, towels and cloths 'to wipe the nethur ende' of Humphrey, duke of Gloucester.[4] Nevertheless, those improved standards of municipal hygiene that have already been noted in the fifteenth-century town can have proceeded only from similar demands in the home. Few were yet able to contrive a private supply of piped fresh water such as John Fleming negotiated with the corporation in 1515, in return for the gift of a spring.[5] But, as the archaeology of the late-medieval town abundantly illustrates, the wealthier burgesses of Fleming's and of earlier generations were fully prepared to meet considerable costs in the provision of good drainage or adequate cesspits at their tenements. Stone-lined drains, carefully sited to take advantage of the natnral fall of the land, have been found at Cuckoo Lane (Fig. 5) and Winkle Street. At Cuckoo Lane, a thirteenth-century drain served at least three outlets, taking kitchen waste and sewage to the sea. Whereas at Winkle Street a well-fashioned channel, running down from the north-east corner of the tenement, was equipped with another entry, built skilfully into the thickness of the roadside wall and clearly designed to serve an overlying privy. It had been finished with care, and, like the many stone-lined cesspits of the time, had been designed to facilitate regular cleaning. Near by, on the High Street site, a sixteenth-century cesspit, at the rear of a Broad Lane tenement, was found to have been constructed with a vaulted stone roof of its own. Abandoned some time in the middle years of the sixteenth century, it held the waste of a lavish household, its members the purchasers of ornate glass and exotic painted ceramics from the Mediterranean, of stoneware beer tankards from the Rhineland, and of the characteristic amber-glazed kitchen wares of the Netherlands (Plate 15).[6]

Outwardly at least, Southampton by the sixteenth century had more than recovered the prosperity it had lost some two centuries before. John Leland, on a visit to the town in the 1530s, found English Street 'one of the fairest streates that ys yn any town of al England . . . welle buildid for timbre building'.[7] And among the houses he would have noticed there was one, on the east side of the street, in Holy Rood, that stands virtually intact to this day. Now the Red Lion, a public house, it is a fine survival of the common 'right-angle' type of hall-house, with the hall running back from the street (Fig. 6). Overlying the usual stone vault, the house is of a fifteenth-century timber-frame construction, incorporating a ground-floor side-passage, and making remarkably efficient use of a strictly limited site: in effect, of the long, narrow house plot that had come to be characteristic of the fully developed late-medieval English town.[8] Originally, it was equipped with a shop on the ground-floor street frontage, underlying another two storeys of chambers. Behind it, there was a hall, extending to the full height of the building. Behind that again, another three-storey chamber block completed the main structure of the tenement. An internal gallery, against the north side of the hall, gave access to the first level of upper chambers in both chamber blocks. From it, flying staircases served the attic levels.[9]

In making skilful and effective use of a limited site, the plan adopted at the Red Lion was probably repeated up and down the length of the main street of the town, as well as elsewhere within the walls. Certainly, it employed an entirely traditional scheme unaltered in its essentials since the thirteenth century or earlier, well-suited to the requirements of urban living. But where plots were larger, or the individual burgess could afford to build on two or three together, the plan naturally varied to take advantage of such extra space as became available, in particular to improve the lighting of the hall. No early specimen of such a house survives in Southampton to compare, for example, with the fourteenth-century Balle's Place, in Salisbury, or Tackley's Inn, in Oxford.[10] But among the houses that Leland admired, finding it 'very fair', was one which had been reconstructed on an earlier core by Sir John Dawtrey, royal victualler and customer in the town, at the corner of Blue Anchor Lane and St Michael's Square. A late-fifteenth-century timber-framed structure, it has since become the Tudor House Museum, the most notable surviving early-modern building in the town (Plate 16). At Tudor House, as at Tackley's Inn, which it closely resembles in plan, the medieval hall had been set longitudinally behind a row of shops, these facing the market square. Dawtrey had the shops converted into parlours. He inserted a ceiling in the hall, and built attics between it and the roof. Another range, built to hold the buttery, pantry and kitchen, ran back along the line of Blue Anchor Lane to the rear of the hall. Over the service rooms there were bedchambers, as there were also over the parlours on the street front. Attics covered the whole.[11]

In houses such as these, the standard of furnishings reflected the solid bourgeois prosperity of their owners. Harrison, writing late in the sixteenth century, found the household effects of his countrymen 'growne in maner even to passing delicacie'. And what he said, he was careful to make clear, applied not only to the wealthier classes. In his day, he alleged, even an artisan might purchase silk or tapestry bed-hangings, might fill his cupboard with pewter and furnish his table with fine linen. Everywhere, pillows and feather beds had replaced straw pallets, pewter tableware had taken the place of wood.[12] No doubt Harrison exaggerated, and what he said was certainly no more than a part of the truth. Nevertheless, at Southampton surviving inventories of the sixteenth century point to a high level of material well-being, in men of middling condition as equally among their betters. Typically, the apartments for which the furnishings were listed included a hall, a parlour, two or more chambers, a kitchen, buttery and shop. Thomas Goddard, a man of wealth, kept two shops, a great and a little, in his tenement at Holy Rood. At St Lawrence, Richard Mershe, a lesser man, kept only one, which he stocked with green and white kerseys, with russets, scarlets and lengths of cotton. The inventories of the effects of Goddard and Mershe, drawn up within three years of each other in the 1550s, illustrate usefully the differences in standing between them. Goddard kept his parlour as a sitting-room, and furnished it with painted hangings, a table, chairs, cushions and carpets. But for Mershe, as for many of his condition, the parlour had to do service as a bedchamber, to be equipped with the familiar furnishings of such an apartment: the bedsteads, feather mattresses and bolsters, the cupboard, table and hangings. For both, the hall held tables, benches and cupboards, and was hung with painted cloths or tapestries, but Goddard could afford to soften the effect with cushions and tapestry carpets, with a fair display of candlesticks in addition. And it was in plate and linen particularly, as Harrison observed a generation later, that wealth was commonly displayed. Mershe's buttery was adequately but not excessively furnished with an old cupboard, a set of pewter plates and a charger, a basin and ewer, two porringers, a dozen saucers, six quart and two pint pots, two salt-cellars and seven candlesticks. In his closet, he had fifteen pairs of sheets, six tablecloths, two dozen napkins, two table-towels, and six pillows with their cases. In contrast, the buttery at Goddard's establishment held a cupboard, a press and a trestle table; there were bread-bins, candlesticks large and small, pewter platters and dishes of all sorts, basins, ewers and cruets; there was a colander, probably of brass, and a set of jugs with their covers, possibly of the imported Rhenish stoneware by now commonly in use in the town. Of linen and napery, similarly, there was no lack. With twelve pairs of linen sheets, Goddard had another sixteen pairs of 'canvas' sheets and eight pairs of pillow-cases. His napkins, table-cloths and towels were to be counted rather in dozens.[13]

The inventories, of course, fail us where there were few possessions to disburse. And although cottages are mentioned in the corporation terriers of the time, there is little else to tell us how the poorer classes were housed. Nor has Southampton archaeology yet produced anything to compare with the row of diminutive single-cell cottages excavated on the Lower Brook Street site at Winchester in 1966–7, a one-period development perhaps comparable, on a lesser scale, with the speculative building of artisan housing at St Martin's Row, Coney Street, York, or to the terrace of more substantial cottages on Spon Street, Coventry.[14] Yet in 1454, when the first comprehensive terrier was taken in Southampton, there were cottages and small tenements scattered through the length of the town, frequently adjoining, or even attached to, the larger messuages, and filling up whatever vacant spaces there might be. Whether as single-bay units or joined in multiple-bay terraces as at Winchester or York, these cottages can seldom have held more than one basic chamber. Within this, light partitioning of cob, reinforced with stakes, might distinguish the living from the sleeping areas, these to be loosely described in primitive inventories as the 'hall' and 'parlour' of the cottage. In Leicester, in the sixteenth century, such a cottage could be built for less than £5. It would have been of timberframe construction, in-filled with wattle and daub. Slate was readily available at Leicester as at Southampton. In both towns it was the usual material for roofing.[15]

While nothing, perhaps, could ever transform the lot of the unskilled labourer without influence or position in the town, there can be little doubt that the standard of living of the average artisan had risen substantially by the fifteenth century, accompanying an unprecedented rise in the real value of his wages.[16] Already, in 1335, the six dwellings of the St Martin's Row terrace development at York had been planned with attention to comfort. Each cottage had its door and window on the lane; each, a hearth, mantel and chimney of its own; each, a jettied upper storey carrying the bedchamber, with a window facing the churchyard at the rear.[17] If this were adequate accommodation for the journeyman, the tradesman and small shopkeeper could expect better. A contract of 1410 survives for the building of three small adjoining houses on Friday Street, London. On the ground floor, they were to be equipped with shops. Over these, jutting over the street, the first floor would carry a hall, larder and kitchen. On the second floor, there was to be a principal chamber, retiring-room ('drawyng chaumbre') and privy. A somewhat different arrangement, concentrating the accommodation on two floors, was contracted for at Canterbury at the end of the century. Each of the four houses of the new terrace was to be supplied with a shop and buttery on the street front, with a hall and kitchen behind them. A chamber, reached by a stair from the hall, occupied the jettied first floor.[18]

Indeed, in many material respects the condition of the average tradesman and artisan had decidedly improved, to the erosion of antique social distinctions. Where it had been possible to distinguish class by dress, 'it is now harde to discerne and know a tapester, a Cookesse, or an hostellers wyffe ffro a gentilwoman, if they stonde in a rowe'.[19] Interest in fashion was general. To the mixed fascination and repulsion of contemporaries, styles in gowns and in headwear for women, in jerkins, doublets and hose for men, changed repeatedly through the fifteenth century.[20] At Southampton, tailors off the Italian carracks brought Mediterranean fashions to the town, one such 'carackeman' cutting a doublet of silk for William Overy, translator of the gild ordinances and a relative, perhaps the father, of Thomas Overy, the reforming mayor.[21] Overy may have intended to wear it on Sundays, for then, as now, the holiday was an occasion for particular display. Among the many bequests of Richard Mershe, draper of St Lawrence, was one addressed to his brother. It conveyed to him, in a pleasant gesture of affection, Richard's 'Sundayes rayment hole as I am accustomed to go in'.[22]

The men, and the women too, who enjoyed dressing up on a Sunday, welcomed diversions of any kind. On an ordinary day, hours of work were long. A man might begin in the summer at 4 a.m., to work through till seven that evening; in the winter, he started at daybreak, leaving off only at dusk.[23] But religious festivals were plentiful, and they were freely supplemented by occasions of civic celebration. In particular, Christmas was an opportunity for relaxation and merriment. In the Christmas week, there was a noticeable falling-off of cart traffic reaching and leaving the town.[24] And shortly afterwards there might be a civic banquet, or gild feast, such as was held at the Guildhall, over the Bargate, on 13 January 1434. Large stocks of drink and foodstuffs were laid in for the occasion. The steward's accounts record purchases of wine and beer, of beef, pork, sucking pig, capons and rabbits. There were cooks and servingmen to be hired, rushes, fuel and a set of twenty wooden cups to be bought. Other supplies included bread and flour, eggs and cheese, lard, salt and vinegar, with small quantities of pepper, mace and saffron, currants, raisins and dates, the spices and luxury fruits beloved of medieval gourmets.[25] A Venetian who, in the line of duty as an envoy from the doge, attended two such civic banquets in London, remarked the sumptuous entertainment, the display of plate, the long duration of the meals, and the 'infinite profusion of victuals'. Certainly, there were longer pauses between the courses than he had been accustomed to at similar functions at home. But what struck him chiefly as remarkable was the 'extraordinary silence of everyone', so different from the style of his compatriots.[26]

It is perhaps true that, in a small provincial centre like Southampton, the range of winter entertainments was restricted. It might include dice, chess and card-play, tavern society and the stews. But the summer brought opportunities for all. Few games, Chaucer had maintained, could draw him from his books, even on holidays. But:[27]

> whan that the month of May
> Is comen, and that I here the foules synge,
> And that the floures gynnen for to sprynge,
> Farewel my bok, and my devocioun!

For the Southampton burgess, overtaken by a similar mood, there was tennis on a vacant site just south of Le Vernecle, handball on a plot west of Bull Street, and archery at the butts, by the moats east of the Bargate; on the friary site, immediately following the Dissolution, Thomas Welles was to set up his bowling alleys, to the scandal of many contemporaries.[28] Plays and minstrelsy, bull-baiting and displays of wild beasts, caught the attention of the idle and the curious.[29] Characteristically, the burning of the timbers of the old Watergate, on 28 June 1471, was made the occasion of a civic entertainment.[30] There would be salvoes of guns to greet a wedding, or to salute a royal visitor. And few events of national importance might pass unnoticed in the borough. Church bells and criers announced and commemorated each victory. A procession of clergy and solemn *Te Deum* celebrated, by command of the king, the birth of his son, Prince Arthur.[31]

That procession, late in September 1486, recalls appropriately the special relationship which, particularly in the immediately preceding generations, had been allowed to develop between the local secular church and the borough. No civic ceremony was complete without the ministrations of the mayor's personal chaplain. Obits, memorial masses and funerary devotions preoccupied the borough officials. At St Michael's, the clock was a charge on municipal funds. At Holy Rood, the parish clerk rang the day-bell and curfew of the town.[32] Parish fraternities, societies for mutual aid, had made their appearance in the churches. There were fraternities of St Thomas, St John and St Leonard at Holy Rood, another of St Barbara at St Michael's.[33] But perhaps most characteristic of the religious tastes and instincts of the century was the chantry, or obit, the perpetual endowment of memorial masses, limited in range only by the wealth of the donor. It was well suited to the mood of a society haunted by pestilence and exposed to the eschatological vision of its divines. For familiarity had made of death a cult, its symbol the *danse macabre*, and while no man, as the preachers were quick to point out, could expect to escape it, many might hope to soften the blow.[34]

At Southampton, chantries had been known since the thirteenth century at least. Walter le Fleming and his son-in-law, Robert Bonhait, had endowed chantries of their own, the one on five-year terms at St Mary's and Holy Rood, the other at St Michael's in perpetuity.[35] Likewise, some such intention no doubt moved Henry de Lym's grant, in 1330, of five messuages, lands and rents to Barton Oratory, on the Isle of Wight.[36] Nevertheless, the bulk of chantry foundations can be said to belong, rather, to the fifteenth century, coming to cover a wide range of individual endowments, from the straightforward obit to elaborate provision for the setting up of a permanent chaplaincy. For a wealthy man, there were few limits to the preparations he might make. Anticipating his final illness by several years, William Soper entrusted his country estates at Eling, Dibden and Fawley to his friend, Thomas Chamberleyn, to support an obit, worth forty shillings, at the friary.[37] By the time he came to draw up his last will and testament, in November 1458, Soper had built himself a fine marble tomb in the south aisle of the friary church. He provided for lavish gifts to the poor (specifying married men and women, the decrepit, blind and lame) on the day of his burial, and arranged for thirty days of 'solemn services and requiem masses' at the altar next to his tomb. For the future, in perpetuity, the profits of his considerable English Street properties were to be employed to support an obit at the friary. Every day, at morning mass, a penny was to be given to the collection in his name. On both the eve and the day of his anniversary, the parish clerk at Holy Rood was to receive a fee to ring the assembly bell. Similarly, the crier, suitably rewarded, was to proclaim, in the 'customary places', the manner of Soper's anniversary. A requiem mass was to be sung next to his tomb. Immediately afterwards, the town clerk would read publicly the terms of Soper's will, and there would be a distribution of pennies to the needy. Soper, for all his two marriages, died childless. The bulk of his wealth, in consequence, could be deployed for the benefit of his soul.[38]

It may be that William Soper's motives were selfish. But it cannot be doubted that the occasion of a well-endowed anniversary was of great moment to the poor of the town. Obligatory attendance at the memorial mass was a small price to pay for the gifts of money, drink and victuals commonly provided for on the foundation. Ale, bread, cheese and spiced buns accompanied the distribution of pennies to the needy. For the mayor, priests and 'other magnates' present, there was wine, in addition to the customary fees. Such occasions, further, were an important source of supplementary revenue to every parish priest, or clerk, in the borough. No anniversary foundation neglected to offer suitable rewards to the clergy present at the devotions. At the church appointed for the ceremony, the fees and expenses of the officiating priests were invariably generously covered. Even where the endowment extended to the support of a full-time chantry priest, the rights of existing incumbents were most particularly protected. Nor were the needs of the poor neglected in these cases, for anniversary charitable distributions were as much a part of the expensive perpetual chantry foundations as of the more familiar obits. Little is known of the important Nicholl chantry at St Mary's, except that it continued to support for at least a century the salaries of two chantry priests of its own.[39] But William Nicholl had further endowed an obit at Holy Rood, his parish church, the accounts of which, merged with the obits of Richard Thomas and Thomas Payne at the same church, have survived in the borough terrier of 1495/6. The joint obits were celebrated on 25 April each year. On this occasion, there had been payments of two shillings each to the mayor and to the steward, and of twopence to the bedeman. The vicar of Holy Rood had received twenty pence for 'himself and for his wax', and there had been the other customary fees to the clergy: twopence to the vicar's clerk, eightpence each to the other four curates in the town, and sixpence to their clerks. The victuals were simple but abundant. Four hundred 'white' buns and three hundred spiced buns had been provided, with saffron, butter and cheese. There were four 'dozens' of good ale and a dozen and a half of penny ale. For the priests and borough officials, a gallon of Romney had been bought, with a 'potell' of Gascon wine.[40]

It was the association of the mayor and his officers in the administration of these sometimes quite complicated bequests that accounts for the presence of contemporary transcripts of the wills of William Gunter and Joan Holmhegge in the so-called 'Black Book' of the town. So careful, indeed, was William Gunter to ensure recognition of his wishes, that he used the opportunity of his own mayoralty in 1493–4 to enrol his will, originally drawn up the previous year on 1 August 1492. His desire was to be buried next to the tomb of his wife's former husband, John James, at the mother church of St Mary's. But his chantry was to be established at his own parish church at Holy Rood, which he would have attended by virtue of his two tenements in the parish, one of them the 'Dolphin'. To Alice, his wife, with a reversion to the town, he left his two tenements on the east side of English Street, with a third property in Salisbury. From the revenues of these, a 'discrete' priest was to be found, competent to hold divine service daily at the high altar for the souls of Gunter, his mother and father, John James, his friends and all the faithful departed. Carefully, Gunter apportioned the profits. A stipend of £6 was set aside for the priest. Of the remaining revenues, calculated at £2. 13*s*. 4*d*., the sum of £1 was reserved to cover the cost of an anniversary obit. The remaining 26*s*. 8*d*., surplus to immediate needs, was to be reserved for essential repairs on the tenements, the responsibility of the landlord. Failing these, it would go to the purchase of an ornament for the church at Holy Rood. As had been the case with William Soper, there was no surviving son to be provided for. Agnes, Gunter's first wife, had been buried at Andover. In her memory, a silver chalice and paten were to be presented to that church. The second wife, Alice, had the charge of the distribution of the residue of Gunter's estate. She was to do it 'as shall seem to her to be the most expedient to please God and to profit my soul, and as she wishes to answer therefor before the highest Judge in the day of judgement'.[41]

William Gunter had neglected to specify in detail the duties of his chantry priest. But he might almost have taken them for granted. A full generation before, Joan Holmhegge, widow of a former mayor, had established a very similar chantry at St Mary's. Towards its endowment, she had assigned a total of eleven messuages, situated in St Michael's and Holy Rood, to the mayor, burgesses and commonalty of the borough. An anniversary distribution of 26*s*. 8*d*. was to be made from the profits. But the principal part of the anticipated revenues was to be assigned to the stipend of a priest, at the rate of £6. 13*s*. 4*d*. annually. In the directions to the executors concerning the duties of the priest, little was left unsaid. The chaplain appointed was to conduct the anniversary service at St Mary's:[42]

> Also I will that my chaplain aforesaid, immediately after my death, shall celebrate mass daily, no lawful impediment hindering him, in the church of the blessed Mary aforesaid. And likewise he ought to be present on every Sunday and feast day at prime, vespers, matins, high mass and second vespers, and other canonical hours of the day from the beginning to the end. And henceforth he shall not be absent without lawful hindrance or leave from the aforesaid precentor [of St Mary's] or his successors.

> Provided always that the said chaplain shall once in a week say services and commemorations for my soul, etc., and in like manner a requiem mass on the day following with a special collect, mentioning my name, to wit, Joan, in the same collect. And that the said chaplain be admitted by the aforesaid precentor and his successors; provided always that the said chaplain be examined by the said precentor and his successors as to learning and character, and that he be admitted if he be altogether capable; and if incapable, be rejected.

When, nearly a century later, the chantries in Southampton and elsewhere were examined by order of Edward VI, John Baker was the current incumbent of the Holmhegge chantry, having no other living. His stipend, at £6. 13*s*. 4*d*., showed no change on that of his predecessors in the chaplaincy. Over and above that and the cost of the obit, also unchanged, there was 20*s*. 8*d*. surplus on receipts, to be spent on the repair of the houses assigned by Joan Holmhegge to the endowment. No plate or other ornaments attached to the chantry. At Holy Rood, William Gunter's chantry, still in existence, had suffered a decline. Its value now stood at an annual £7. There is no mention in the chantry certificates of an obit in Gunter's name; £6 continued to maintain a priest, and only £1 remained to cover repairs on the chantry tenements.[43]

It had been to Andrew Arthur, her personal chaplain, that Joan Holmhegge had assigned her chantry in the first instance. And she can scarcely have been alone in the employment of a household priest. Already in 1420, Thomas Middleton had obtained permission from the Curia at Rome to keep a chapel, or oratory, in his house. His contemporary, William Chamberleyn, while securing the same right for himself, seems to have thought it additionally worth the expense to purchase a plenary indulgence for his deathbed. It had been William Soper who had initiated the move to obtain these permissions from Rome, a few months in advance even of Thomas Middleton. Certainly, it is very likely that Soper had a chapel through most of his life at his capital messuage in Holy Rood. He built one, additionally, at his country house on the far side of Southampton Water, for it was there that Luca di Maso degli Albizzi, captain of the Flanders galleys, attended vespers on 2 February 1430, at the insistence of his generous host.[44]

A locally-recruited clergy, frequently in private employment, was closely bound by ties as much social as economic to the borough community it served. Few priests active in the ministry could have been without long-term friends and associates among their flocks. They had grown with them to maturity, and came, as often as not, from the same leading families in the borough. A boy such as Richard Bishop, son of an ex-mayor and studying at Oxford in 1513 for what his father quaintly called the 'degree of priest', was clearly expected to return to the ministry at home. One of a family of three sons, he was to be allowed, on the completion of his studies, a 'sufficient house, with all the furniture belonging to it'. In the meantime, in the event of his father's death, he was to be supplied by his mother with a 'sufficient maintenance to enable him to apply himself to letters at Oxford'.[45] And there were always other important Southampton families, through the centuries, with representatives of their own in the priesthood. In 1305, Thomas le Barber was rector of the church at All Saints; at St Michael's, Thomas Banestre was presented to the cure on 19 February 1557.[46] Of the two sons of Richard Mey (d. 1392), Ralph was a chaplain, as was Richard atte Marche, the son of Thomas and Joan.[47] There was to be a Brother William Chamberleyn, warden of the friary, among the beneficiaries of William Soper's will.[48]

Such, clearly, were the conditions that fostered local interest in the churches. Tithes, undoubtedly, were frequently neglected. They might be made up, occasionally, by the conscience-money of defaulters.[49] But if Southampton lacks the record of parish collections, such as were commonly levied elsewhere to support major improvements to church buildings, it may be remembered that the rebuilding of Holy Rood had been the work of a group of wealthy parishioners, co-operating to complete it in the first decades of the fourteenth century.[50] Similarly, gifts for the repair of the fabric at one, or all, of the parish churches, are rarely omitted from fifteenth-century Southampton wills. Very occasionally, a single important donation might answer the particular need of a church. Wall-paintings in the chapel of Our Lady, Holy Rood, were financed, at the cost of £13. 6*s*. 8*d*., by a bequest of Gabriel Corbet, a naturalized Venetian and parishioner of Holy Rood.[51] Four years later, in 1467, the little church of St John's, French Street, situated in an area of the town much favoured by alien merchants, acquired a set of tapestry hangings of its own. They were the gift of the captain and patrons of a visiting fleet of Florentine galleys, and of the Florentine mercantile community at that time resident in the port.[52]

Regrettably, no complete inventories of Southampton church goods survive to recall the generosity of its parishioners. The process of dispersal of church plate, vestments, books and other furnishings began in the forties of the sixteenth century, not long after the formal break with Rome. It anticipated, and was influential in calling forth, the enquiries and catalogues of the royal commissioners, appointed in 1548 to inventory the remainder and to stem, if they could, the flow.[53] By the time the commissioners reached Southampton, stirred on in 1551 by further reports of embezzlement, many of the movable assets of the churches had been sold to meet the cost of the defences, or to bridge financial crises of the town. At the church of St Lawrence, for example, no more than a bare minimum survived. There was a chalice and paten of silver-gilt, a cope of red velvet, another of white damask and a third of rose-coloured silk, a black pall, two altar cloths and three surplices. A few years before, church ornaments and plate to the value of £41. 14*s*. 1*d*. had been sold at the order of the earl of Southampton, then lieutenant of the shire. The money was spent on the purchase of a 'piece of brass' for the town's defence.[54] At All Saints, the position was scarcely better. Within the space of the previous decade, plate, vestments and ornaments worth £32. 16*s*. 8*d*. had been sold to meet the needs of the town. Two silver chalices, with their patens, had been preserved, as had a silver pyx, another chalice with stem and paten of copper-gilt, and a small collection of miscellaneous vestments, altar cloths, palls, hangings and cushions.[55] A matter of months before the survey, conducted in 1552, the wealthy church at Holy Rood had been stripped of plate to the value of £60. 7*s*. 4*d*., probably with the connivance of the mayor, to whom it was delivered for the purposes of the town. A great processional cross and staff in silver-gilt had been preserved in the keeping of the parish. But it was not long to remain a parish asset. The following year, surplus plate above the minimum requirements of each parish was called in, by royal command, to the Jewel House. The cross and staff alone would have made up more than half the total yield from the borough.[56]

Although not of Southampton, the inventory of church goods at St Ewen's, Bristol, compiled for the proctors in 1445, may serve to point the contrast between what we know to have survived the Reformation at Southampton and the probable splendour that preceded it. St Ewen's was a small parish, not especially well-endowed and certainly no wealthier than the Southampton parishes at St Lawrence or All Saints. But its church furnishings, by any standard, were lavish. A full set of service books, of the Salisbury rite, included mass books and grails, psalters, hymnals, processionals and antiphoners. Vestments ranged from lavish ceremonial copes, embroidered and richly coloured, to the simple white linens of Lent. There were surplices for the use of the parson, rochets for the parish clerk and servers. Of the plate, the most important was a newly-made processional cross of the same general type as, although significantly smaller than, the great cross of Holy Rood, Southampton. Further, there was a good chalice of silver-gilt, another 'little' chalice also of silver, an embossed silver-gilt cup set with precious stones, and an ivory box, silver-bound. Of the three altar crosses, one was of gilded copper, another of latten and the third of wood; there were lamps and candlesticks of latten, a censer of the same metal, sacring bells, a copper cup, and a set of pewter cruets, these last for wine and water at the mass. The high altar, beneath the image of St Ewen, was of alabaster, sculptured at the base with gilded figures of Our Lady and the twelve apostles. With the corporals and paxes of the mass, it was equipped with fine towels and altar cloths and might be hung, as were the other three altars in the main body of the church, with painted cloths or tapestries. Banners decorated the aisles and the rood screen; images, richly-costumed, were set above the altars. At St Ewen's, as at other parish churches of its generation, much of this splendour came directly from the gifts of individual parishioners. One such had provided the best chalice, $30\frac{1}{4}$ ounces in weight, and had had his name inscribed on the base; others bought costumes for the images, and banners to the honour of favourite saints. The fraternity of St John Baptist, of the craft of tailors, had made a chantry chapel of the entire south aisle of St Ewen's. The brethren screened and protected it from the rest of the church, and furnished it entirely at their cost.[57] At Southampton, similarly, it was probably the fraternity of St Barbara, keeping a chaplain of its own, which maintained the chantry chapel attached externally to the south chancel aisle at St Michael's. The north aisle, traditionally the 'Corporation Chapel', was used, among other purposes, for the swearing-in of mayors.[58]

Notes

1 C. A. Sneyd (ed.), *A relation, or rather a true account, of the island of England*, Camden Society, 37 (1847), pp. 20–1. The material below is derived from this text, from W. D. Robson-Scott's *German Travellers in England, 1400–1800*, pp. 4–16, and from W. B. Rye's *England as seen by foreigners in the days of Elizabeth and James the First*, passim.
2 W. B. Rye, op. cit., pp. 72–3.
3 Ibid., pp. 78–9.
4 Directions for keeping the privy clean are included in John Russell's *Boke of Nurture*, a mid-fifteenth-century manual prepared by the duke's marshal (F. J. Furnivall (ed.), *The Babees Book*, Early English Text Society, 32 (1868), pp. 179–80).
5 S.C.R.O. SC4/2/334, and John Speed, *History of Southampton*, pp. 33–5.
6 *Southampton Excavations*, forthcoming.
7 Lucy Toulmin Smith (ed.), *The itinerary of John Leland in or about the years 1535–1543*, i:278.
8 Good examples of the plan are cited by W. A. Pantin in 'Medieval English town-house plans', *Medieval Archaeology*, 6–7 (1962–3), pp. 228–31. The same examples, from Chester and Exeter, are discussed by the same author at greater length in 'Some medieval English town houses', in *Culture and Environment, Essays in Honour of Sir Cyril Fox*, eds I. Ll. Foster and L. Alcock, pp. 460–70.
9 The house is discussed by P. A. Faulkner in *Southampton Excavations*, forthcoming.
10 Helen Bonney, '"Balle's Place", Salisbury: a 14th-century merchant's house', *The Wiltshire Archaeological and Natural History Magazine*, 59 (1964), pp. 155–67; W. A. Pantin, 'The development of domestic architecture in Oxford', *Antiquaries Journal*, 27 (1947), pp. 123–7.
11 *Southampton Excavations*, forthcoming; W. A. Pantin, 'Medieval English town-house plans', *Medieval Archaeology*, 6–7 (1962–3), pp. 219, 222–3.
12 F. J. Furnivall (ed.), *Harrison's Description of England in Shakspere's Youth*, i:238–40.
13 H.R.O. will and inventory of Thomas Goddard, 1555, and will and inventory of Richard Mershe, 1558.
14 Martin Biddle, 'Excavations at Winchester 1967. Sixth interim report', *Antiquaries Journal*, 48 (1968), pp. 265–6; Angelo Raine, *Medieval York*, pp. xiii, 151; *V.C.H., Warwick*, viii:147.
15 W. G. Hoskins, 'An Elizabethan provincial town: Leicester', in *Studies in Social History, a Tribute to G. M. Trevelyan*, ed. J. H. Plumb, pp. 56–7.
16 For wage rates and the purchasing power of wages, see the important papers of E. H. Phelps Brown and Sheila V. Hopkins in *Economica*, new series, 22 (1955), pp. 195–206, and 23 (1956), pp. 296–314.
17 L. F. Salzman, *Building in England down to 1540*, pp. 430–2, and Angelo Raine, op. cit., p. 151.
18 L. F. Salzman, op. cit., pp. 483–5, 554–6. Jutting upper storeys as a common feature of late-medieval town houses are discussed by Margaret Wood, *The English Medieval House*, pp. 219–22.
19 Charlotte d'Evelyn (ed.), *Peter Idley's instructions to his son*, p. 163. The 'instructions' date to *c*. 1450.
20 The abundant, and highly critical, sermon literature on this theme is discussed by G. R. Owst, *Literature and Pulpit in Medieval England*, pp. 390–411, and by J. W. Blench, *Preaching in England in the late Fifteenth and Sixteenth Centuries*, pp. 241–3.
21 *Assize of Bread Book*, p. 43, cited by Alwyn Ruddock, *Italian Merchants and Shipping*, p. 154.
22 H.R.O. will of Richard Mershe, 1558.
23 A. F. Leach (ed.), *Beverley Town Documents*, Selden Society, 14 (1900), p. 56.
24 *Brokage Book, 1439–40*, p. 73; *Brokage Book, 1443–4*, p. 66.
25 *Stewards' Books*, i:104–7. For an entertaining discussion of cooking styles, see W. E. Mead, *The English Medieval Feast*, passim.
26 C. A. Sneyd, op. cit., p. 44.
27 The lines are taken from the opening of 'The legend of good women'.
28 S.C.R.O. SC4/2/351, SC5/1/17, 18, 21; *Book of Remembrance*, iii:42–3; P.R.O. E315/165, f. 5.
29 C. E. C. Burch, *Minstrels and Players in Southampton, 1428–1635*, passim; S.C.R.O. SC5/1/29, f. 22v; *Stewards' Books*, ii:90–1.
30 S.C.R.O. SC5/1/13, f. 46v.
31 S.C.R.O. SC5/1/31, f. 22; SC5/1/32, f. 19v; SC5/1/35, f. 18v; *Book of Remembrance*, iii:53.
32 For a good list of such charges on the corporation accounts, see S.C.R.O. SC5/1/17, f. 42.
33 Davies, p. 376; H.R.O. will of Richard

Winson, 1517, and will of Thomas Bayly, 1515. The parish fraternity is discussed by George Unwin, *The Gilds and Companies of London*, pp. 108ff.

34 Jean Leclercq *et al.*, *La Spiritualité du Moyen Age*, pp. 577–9; E. F. Chaney (ed.), *La danse macabre des charniers des Saints Innocents à Paris*, passim.

35 God's House Deeds 517, 1071. Chantries, generally, became popular only in the thirteenth century. They had been known before, but were not widely supported by the pious (K. L. Wood-Legh, *Perpetual Chantries in Britain*, p. 5).

36 P.R.O. C143/210/28.

37 *Black Book*, ii: 122–5. The arrangement probably confirms an earlier agreement, dated 15 August 1452, for daily masses and an obit at the friary (S.C.R.O. D/LY/7/25).

38 *Black Book*, ii: 98–115. Soper's will was proved at Winchester on 20 November 1459.

39 P.R.O. E301/52.

40 The accounts of eight obits are included with the terrier (S.C.R.O. SC4/1/1). Similar accounts, although not usually in such detail, feature regularly in the Stewards' Books (e.g. *Stewards' Books*, i: 73, 131). And records of the terms of the obits of Robert Florice (1443), Richard Grime (1487) and John Shropshire (1495) are preserved in the *Black Book*, ii: 138–9, 180–1, iii: 16–19. For closely comparable obits at Leicester, see Mary Bateson (ed.), *Records of the Borough of Leicester*, ii: 424–5, iii: 39.

41 *Black Book*, ii: 152–61.

42 Ibid., iii: 2–9. The deed is dated 6 May 1462. The duties commonly assigned to such a chaplain are discussed by K. L. Wood-Legh, op. cit., pp. 271–302; see also Douglas Jones, *The Church in Chester, 1300–1540*, Chetham Society, 3rd series, 7 (1957), p. 107, for the directions at Robert Parys's chantry, specifying most exactly the form of service to be followed.

43 P.R.O. E301/51, 52.

44 *Cal.Pap.Reg., Papal Letters*, vii: 303, 337, 342, 562; Michael E. Mallett, *The Florentine Galleys in the Fifteenth Century*, p. 260.

45 *Black Book*, iii: 64–9.

46 Davies, pp. 393, 400.

47 *Black Book*, i: 26–9; God's House Deeds 428.

48 *Black Book*, ii: 110–11; for the similar experience of Chester, see Douglas Jones, op. cit., pp. 25–6.

49 P.R.O. E326/11798, E327/775; H.R.O. will of Richard Vaughan, 1546.

50 Parish collections in aid of the founding of a new bell and the construction of a spire are recorded in fourteenth-century Bridgwater archives (T. B. Dilks (ed.), *Bridgwater Borough Archives*, Somerset Record Society, 48 (1933), pp. 65–7, 159–64). The routines of fund-raising, with particular reference to earlier work on cathedral and monastic buildings, are discussed by C. R. Cheney, 'Church-building in the Middle Ages', *Bull. John Rylands Library*, 34 (1951–2), pp. 20–36.

51 Win.Coll.Mun. 17799.

52 Alwyn Ruddock, *Italian Merchants and Shipping*, p. 132.

53 A rare list of the goods sold before the official inventory of 1551 was preserved at the church of St Maurice, Winchester. It included some plate and brass-ware, chasubles, albs, copes, 'broken images', altar cloths and hangings, books, a cupboard, coffer, chests, cushions and boxes (J. Hautenville Cope, 'Church goods in Hampshire, A.D. 1552', *Proc. Hampshire Field Club*, 8 (1917–19), pp. 32–3).

54 P.R.O. E326/12001.

55 P.R.O. E315/47, p. 18 (printed by J. Hautenville Cope, op. cit., pp. 37–8).

56 P.R.O. E117/11/3, 29, E326/11355; *Letters Patent*, ii: 110–16; J. Hautenville Cope, op. cit., p. 39. The arrangement with the mayor had been that the sale price of the plate, required for the 'town's necessity', should be returned to the parish over the years to meet the cost of repairs to the fabric. There appears to be no surviving inventory of the church goods at St Michael's; for the St John's inventory, see P.R.O. E315/45, p. 147.

57 Betty R. Masters and Elizabeth Ralph (eds), *The church book of St Ewen's, Bristol, 1454–1584*, Publications of the Bristol and Gloucestershire Archaeological Society, Records Section, 6 (1967), pp. xix–xx, 1–11.

58 Davies, pp. 387–8; H.R.O. will of Thomas Bayly, 1515, and will of Rawlinus Grete, 1512.

Part V

1500-1600

Chronological table V

1501 Prince Arthur marries Catherine of Aragon

1502 Death of Prince Arthur

1509 Death of Henry VII; accession of Henry VIII

1511 Anglo-French war

1513 Henry wins an action at Guinegate against the French; Scots defeated at Flodden

1514 Anglo-French peace

1500 The first salt-marsh riot: a confrontation between the burgesses and God's House, the encloser; in 1504, the king requires an end to the dispute (S.C.R.O. SC4/2/314–5, 316–32; *Sign Manuals and Letters Patent*, i:34)

1501 Preparations are made at Southampton to receive Catherine of Aragon, but she lands instead at Plymouth (*Letters and Papers, Richard III and Henry VII*, ii:103–5; *Letters*, p. 33; *Cal. State Papers Spanish, 1485–1509*, pp. 121, 129, 137, 138, 226, 255)

1502 A dispute with Hastings is resolved (*Book of Remembrance*, i:13–15)

1505 The mayor is granted an annuity of £10, in return for waiving other rights to payment (*Black Book*, ii:60–2)

1507 A dispute arises with Lymington over petty customs levied there (*Letters Patent*, ii:90–5)

1511 The corporation is granted a licence to export 100 sacks of wool free of customs, to support repairs to the walls (*Charters*, ii:6–9)

1512–14 The king and his army are at Southampton; preparations are made there for an expedition to France; threats of attack; heavy expenditure on the defences, including £100 from the king towards the cost of scouring the town ditches (*L. & P. Henry VIII*, i:1 and 2, passim; *Assize of Bread Book*, p. 60; S.C.R.O. SC5/1/30)

1514 Charter obtained to restrict buying and selling retail in the town to burgesses (*Charters*, ii:10; S.C.R.O. SC5/1/31, f. 36v)

	1515 Toll agreement with Guernseymen to attract their trade from Poole (*Third Book of Remembrance*, i:27–8)
	1517 The second salt-marsh enclosure riot, directed against the mayor (*Sign Manuals and Letters Patent*, i:35–7; *Third Book of Remembrance*, i:20–6)
1518 Peace of London	1518 Henry VIII visits the Venetian galleys at Southampton; Cardinal Wolsey later complains of the poor quality of the merchandise brought by the Venetians (*Cal. State Papers Venetian, 1509–19*, pp. 445–7)
	1519 Rebuilding of the Audit House begins (*Book of Remembrance*, iii:88–9)
	1519–20 Richard Palshid supervises the building of a new Customs House (S.C.R.O. SC5/3/1, f. 45)
1520 The emperor Charles V visits England; Henry VIII meets Francis I at the Field of Cloth of Gold; Henry VIII and Charles V conclude a secret treaty at Calais	
1522 Charles V again visits England; Anglo-French war	1522 Charles V embarks at Southampton; the town gates are dressed and the guns fired in salute (*L. & P. Henry VIII*, iii:2:1009; S.C.R.O. SC5/1/32, f. 19v) Henry VIII addresses a commission of array to the mayor, etc., of Southampton (*Letters Patent*, ii:104–9)
1525 Anglo-French peace	
1527 Anglo-French alliance at Amiens	
1528 War declared on Charles V	
1529 Charles V and Francis I conclude the Peace of Cambrai; Henry VIII accedes to it; fall of Cardinal Wolsey	
	1531 The town petitions successfully for release from the forty mark supplement to the fee farm (*Statutes of the Realm*, iii:351–2)
1533 Henry VIII marries Anne Boleyn and declares his earlier marriage to Catherine of Aragon void; Thomas Cromwell appointed Secretary	1533 The town complains of reduced receipts on petty customs and difficulties with the fee farm. Merchant strangers 'arriving here in galleys and carracks . . . do not come as they have done' (*L. & P. Henry VIII*, vi:676)
1534 Act of Supremacy	1534 Gabriel Pecock, warden of Southampton friary, speaks out against the king; Austin friars replace the Observants at Southampton (*L. & P. Henry VIII*, vii:185, 377)
1535 Thomas Cromwell appointed Vicar-General	1535–6 The town writes to Cromwell seeking the cancellation of its debts and promising repairs to the defences if

1536 The smaller religious houses are dissolved

1539 The greater religious houses are dissolved; Henry VIII makes military preparations to warn off possible invaders

1540 Thomas Cromwell executed

1543 Henry VIII allies with Charles V against France

1544 English invasions of Scotland and France

1546 Anglo-French Peace of Ardres

1547 Death of Henry VIII; accession of Edward VI; Scots defeated at Pinkie

1549 First Act of Uniformity; Anglo-French war

1550 Peace of Boulogne with France and Scotland

1552 Second Act of Uniformity

1553 Death of Edward VI; accession of Mary I

1554 Thomas Wyatt's rebellion; marriage of Mary to Philip of Spain; England reconciled with Rome

this were done (*L. & P. Henry VIII*, viii:338, x:203)

1536 St Denys Priory dissolved (P.R.O. SC6/3326, SC12/33/27). Orders published for the regulation of begging in the town 'for asmoche as a grett nomber of beggars of late have resortid unto this towne & dayly doo resort' (*Third Book of Remembrance*, i:52–3)

1537 French ravaging shipping in the area, customs receipts are badly down as a result; Antonio Guidotti suggests bringing Italian craftsmen to the town to start a silk industry there; moves are made to attract the Cornish tin trade (*L. & P. Henry VIII*, xii:1:210–11, xiii:1:206; *Third Book of Remembrance*, i:60–1)

1538 Southampton friary is dissolved (P.R.O. E36/115)

1539 Preparations for war at Southampton; a fleet is mustered at Portsmouth (*L. & P. Henry VIII*, xiv:1:335, 369, 498)

1542 Southampton complains of poverty and inability to pay the fee farm (*L. & P. Henry VIII*, xvii:71)

1544–5 Rumours of a French plan to invade England through Southampton (*L. & P. Henry VIII*, xix:1:343, xx:2:63)

1552 Southampton farm reduced to £50 (*Charters*, ii:12–29)

1552–3 The remaining church goods are inventoried, to be removed, for the most part, to the Jewel House (P.R.O. E117/11/3, 29, E315/45/147, E326/11355, 12001; *Letters Patent*, ii:110–16)

1553–4 Foundation and endowment of the grammar school (B.M. Add. MS. 14265; S.C.R.O. SC4/2/409; *Black Book*, iii:154–65)

1554 Philip lands at Southampton; grant of the sweet wine monopoly to the town (*Cal. State Papers Venetian, 1555–6*, p. 535; *Cal. State Papers Spanish, 1554–8*, p. 8; *Charters*, ii:36–9)

1555 Persecution of Protestants; Latimer and Ridley burnt at Oxford; foundation of the Muscovy Company

1556 Execution of pirates at Southampton 'for the terror and example of others' (*Third Book of Remembrance*, ii:55–6; *Cal. State Papers Venetian, 1555–6*, p. 620)

1557 Anglo-French war

1558 Loss of Calais; death of Mary I; accession of Elizabeth I

1559 Act of Supremacy; break with Rome

1561 The entry fine for a burgess-ship is raised to £10 (*Third Book of Remembrance*, ii:82–3)

1562 Huguenot Wars begin; Elizabeth concludes a treaty at Hampton Court with the Huguenots

1564 Anglo-French peace; England and Spain begin a trade war

1564 An order is published at Southampton enforcing the regulations governing alien trading in the town (*Third Book of Remembrance*, ii:90–1)

1564–5 Foundation and endowment of Richard Butler's almshouse (*Black Book*, iii:121–5)

1565 A report is compiled on the state of the port; the Italian trade is said to have gone, but the port facilities are still in good repair and well able to handle a revival of trade (B.M. Add. MS. 25460)

1566 Protestant unrest in the Netherlands begins

1567–8 Abdication, defeat and flight of Mary Stewart, queen of Scots

1567 Walloon artisans settle at Southampton (*Cal. State Papers Domestic, Addenda, 1566–79*, pp. 31–2)

1569 Dispute, resolved in 1574, concerning tolls payable by Channel Islanders at Southampton, particularly in the linen and canvas trades (B.M. Lansdowne MS. 11/24; *Black Book*, iii:166–7)

1570 Huguenots obtain a general amnesty at the Peace of St Germain

1570 The old open market by St Lawrence church door is moved to a new building in Holy Rood (*Third Book of Remembrance*, ii:110–12)

1572 Massacre of St Bartholomew at Paris; Dutch war of liberation begins

1572 Norman 'rebels and heretics', escaping persecution in France, land at Southampton (*Cal. State Papers Spanish, 1568–79*, p. 432)
An argument is drafted for the corporation against the proposal for a separate customs house at Portsmouth (*Letters*, pp. 88–9)

1573 The mayor, William Capelin, proposes reforms in the town government (*Third Book of Remembrance*, ii:145–52)

1576 Sack of Antwerp	
1579 Foundation of the Eastland Company	
1581 Foundation of the Levant Company	1581 Southampton is in financial difficulties, not being able to pay even the revised farm; all foreign wools, alum and currants are to be imported through Southampton (*Cal. State Papers Domestic, 1581–90*, p. 7)
1582 Sir Humphrey Gilbert founds the Newfoundland colony	1582 Southampton men play a role in the expeditions of Fenton and Gilbert (*Cal. State Papers Colonial, East Indies*, ii:79, *America*, ix:14–17) An anonymous local writer comments on the current state of Southampton, listing what he supposes to have been the causes of its decay and suggesting reforms (P.R.O. SP12/156)
	1583 Lawrence and William Sendy endow their charity at St Lawrence Church (Win.Coll.Mun. 17888)
1585 Open war with Spain; Leicester is sent to the Netherlands to assist the Dutch	1585 A survey of the castle at Southampton reveals it to be in a condition of decay (P.R.O. E178/2031)
1586–7 Trial and execution of Mary Stewart	1586 Hawkins departs from Southampton (*Cal. State Papers Spanish, 1580–6*, p. 642)
1587 Drake raids Cadiz	1587–8 Military preparations in the town: invasion expected (*Letters*, pp. 121–37)
1588 The Spanish Armada is defeated	1588 The town complains of poverty; it cannot supply ships to meet the Armada (P.R.O. SP12/209/48, 97; *Cal. State Papers Domestic, 1581–90*, pp. 471, 477; *Letters*, pp. 134–5)
	1589 Southampton supplies four ships and 151 mariners for the Drake and Norreys expedition to Spain (P.R.O. SP12/222/97–8)
	1592 Southampton warned of a hostile fleet threatening the coast (*Letters*, pp. 205–6)
1595 Franco-Spanish war	
1596 The English sack Cadiz, allying with the French and the Dutch against Spain	1596 It is thought that the Spaniards may attempt an invasion by way of Southampton, Portsmouth and the Isle of Wight (*Cal. State Papers Domestic, 1595–7*, p. 303)
1597 A second Armada is destroyed by storms	
	1599 Invasion threat: Southampton to send out pinnaces as scouts; but Calshot Castle makes the town itself a hard place to take (*Letters*, p. 215; *Cal. State Papers Domestic, 1598–1601*, p. 179)

Chapter sixteen

Central government and the Dissolution

Tudor society, in Southampton as elsewhere, was not for the faint in heart. An endemic instability of national policy had given the advantage to men of an unscrupulous disposition. They were to be found in every community in the small, but dominant, official class, self-perpetuating, usually interrelated and always infinitely accommodating, on the conscience of which there was room enough to turn 'eight oxen and a wain'. At Southampton, such men had not been unknown before. Nor were they, at any time, uninvolved in the day-by-day affairs of the borough, to which many of them devoted their lives. But the group that began to make its appearance soon after the accession of Henry VII was distinguished by an unusual cohesion, to be expressed partly in continuity of personnel, partly in its unchanging objectives.

To successive generations of burgesses, a royal customership at Southampton had appeared a worth-while prize. From 1486, the post of controller of customs was held by Thomas Thomas, a Welsh adventurer in the train of Henry Tudor, who settled at Southampton on his appointment, to become a burgess there and prosper. His son, Sampson Thomas, made his career in the borough through some of its most turbulent decades. Controller of customs, like his father, in the 1540s, he had already been sheriff in 1519–20, and mayor on two occasions, in 1523–4 and 1535–6.[1] Richard Palshid, who, as recorder and town clerk, had assisted Thomas Thomas in his property transactions in the borough, and who, in 1508, was designated executor of Thomas's will, became a royal customer in his turn. In 1519–20, it was he who supervised the building of the new Customs House, 'with a gallery over', at the southern end of English Street, next to the Watergate.[2]

In John Dawtrey, Thomas Thomas had an exact contemporary with ambitions very similar to his own. They both held customerships at Southampton; they both set themselves up in expensive establishments in the town; they were both succeeded by sons whose names and fortunes in the borough were at least as substantial as their own. In addition, the subsequent marriage of Dawtrey's widow, Isabella, to Richard Lyster, later chief justice, linked the Dawtrey interest with that of another substantial Southampton family, prominent in the borough through the first half of the sixteenth century. Thomas Lyster was sheriff in 1514–15, mayor in 1517–18, 1527–8, 1536–7 and 1544–5. Richard himself, despite his interests elsewhere, never deserted Southampton. He lived at Dawtrey's residence on the corner of Blue Anchor Lane, now the Tudor House Museum. He was buried, in some state, at St Michael's Church, just across the square, where his tomb and effigy may still be seen, re-sited at the west end of the north aisle.[3]

Each of these men, Thomas, Palshid and Dawtrey, invested heavily in property, choosing traditional locations. They lived, like the majority of their wealthy predecessors, in the fashionable parishes of St Michael's and Holy Rood. Dawtrey, early in the 1490s, built himself a fine house in the new mode, extravagantly timbered and jettied (Plate 16).[4] It has been greatly admired ever since. Palshid, a few years later, purchased the lease of the great tower over the Watergate, built originally at the expense of William Soper. He modernized and extended it with a range of additional chambers, and lived there for rather more than two decades.[5] Thomas Thomas chose to concentrate his investment, in large part, on the two great properties immediately to the south of Broad Lane, on the west side of English Street. During the term of his customership, Thomas leased and then bought from John Ludlow, an ageing ex-mayor, the property next-but-one to the lane, formerly of Nicholas de Moundenard and Walter Fetplace. It cost him £100 in 1499, still a considerable price. Seven years later, in 1506, he bought the adjoining tenement, to the north, for £60. He acquired it from William Justice, recently mayor, who had got it himself from Henry James only a couple of years before.[6] For centuries already, it had been the home of the greatest men in the town. Beginning with Walter le Fleming, its occupiers had included John le Fleming, Henry de Lym, Robert Beverley, John atte Barre, Sir John de Montague and Peter James. After Peter James, it had descended to his son William, and then to his grandson Henry.

In part, at least, the wealth which supported these costly acquisitions must have proceeded from the new interest that the king himself was beginning to take in the facilities offered by the borough, in particular by its port. Henry VII visited Southampton at least twice early in his reign, to be loyally received by his burgesses. In August 1499, the queen was at Southampton. And it was for Southampton that Henry planned the reception of Catherine of Aragon, the Spanish princess whose marriage to Prince Arthur was to cement the alliance with Ferdinand II.[7] In the event, the princess never came. She landed unexpectedly at Plymouth, to the cruel loss of all those who, further along the coast, had invested in her welcome.[8] But in 1504, preparations were in hand to receive the king once again, and Henry's second son, whether to supervise military operations or to make private purchases from the Venetians, came regularly to the port when king.[9] Early in the young king's reign, the obligations of the Spanish alliance brought renewed war with France, and for a few years Southampton was the scene of intense military and naval activity, at the centre of which stood Dawtrey, victualler, customer and trusted agent of the king. A great expeditionary force, under the command of Thomas Grey, marquis of Dorset, mustered at Southampton in the spring and early summer of 1512. There were ships building in the harbour from early in the reign, and a fleet collected there in the summer of 1513.[10] Dawtrey had probably never been busier. As victualler, he handled great sums for the king: in June 1513, £16,000 in gold, with another £300 that September.[11] As one of the king's customers in the port, he was finding money for the building and repair of the king's great ships, the *Regent* and the *Sovereign*, to be delivered to Robert Brigandyn, clerk of the king's ships, and to be spent on the supply of timber and iron, of sails, twine, cables, shrouds, hawsers and pulleys, of streamers and standards, of compasses, tankards, dishes and lanterns.[12]

The king, as became a young man of military temperament, spent much time with his forces in Southampton. He would have known Dawtrey well, and it was to Dawtrey that he entrusted the remodelling of the town's defences, once again in a condition of decay. Over a period of two years, with the generous financial support of the king, Dawtrey supervised a programme of major works on Southampton's walls and ditches. His accounts cover the months between April 1512 and August 1514. During that time, he ordered and took delivery of bricks, 210,000 of them, from a local brick-maker at Portswood. He purchased straw from Northam and stone from the Isle of Wight. He found money to scour the ditches, to repair the walls, to patch the Guildhall and to restore the arsenal at God's House Tower. At the Watergate, new ironwork was paid for in part by the tenant, Richard Palshid. On the castle, a fire-pan was obtained to replace the original beacon. Gunpowder in quantity was stock-piled in the town magazine, and three new guns were bought, although these were subsequently to be re-sold to the king. To meet bills totalling nearly £450, Dawtrey, now become Sir John, drew his funds from three main sources, all of them originating in the king. In addition, that is, to making an outright grant of £100 to the cost of cleaning out the moats, Henry bought guns from the town valued at £42. 2*s*. 4*d*. Further, he granted the corporation a valuable negotiable licence to export a hundred sacks of wool free of custom. Purchased by Leonardo Frescobaldi, it brought to Sir John, after deductions, the substantial sum of £296. 13*s*. 4*d*.[13] With so much accounting expertise at his call, it is small wonder that Dawtrey, on at least one occasion, should have been able to set right even an experienced colleague like Palshid. As victualler, evidently, Dawtrey was not directly concerned in the fitting-out expenses of the ships being built or repaired in the port; although in his other role, as customer, he might have been expected to find some of the money to meet them. Palshid had delivered seventy tuns of beer to the dock for the victualling of the *Lizard* and the *Sovereign*. He sought to recover the money from Dawtrey, but was advised that it should show, rather, in the reckoning of Robert Brigandyn, clerk of the king's ships.[14]

It was precisely the support and practical aid of professionals such as Dawtrey that enabled the king to carry through successfully the major social revolution of his reign. Sir John himself never lived to experience Henry's Reformation. But Francis Dawtrey, his son, was to be among the principal lessees of the former monastic estates. And it was Henry Huttoft, former protégé of Sir John and his trainee in the customership, who handled locally the mechanics of the transfer and appropriation of lands. As the other names associated with the Dissolution in Southampton bear witness, the despoiling of the religious houses was to become strictly a family, or a party, affair. James Bettes, immediate successor to Dawtrey in the customership and a frequent correspondent of Thomas Cromwell's, was another patron of Huttoft. His own successor, Thomas Welles, was active with Huttoft and John Mille, recorder and town clerk in place of Palshid, in the administration of the forfeited lands. Huttoft's son, John, and Mille's son, Richard, both played important roles in the settlement. Just a little before, in October 1535, the three eldest sons had been admitted to burgess-ships: John Huttoft and George Mille together on 12 October, Thomas Bettes ten days later.[15]

At least initially, their task cannot have been too difficult. Over many years already, the prestige of the religious institutions of the town had been in the decline. At the friary and at the parish churches generally, old loyalties remained intact. But it had long been difficult to arrange a transfer of properties to the Church: John Nostschilling had wanted to do so, and had failed.[16] And the old-established religious foundations in the town had become increasingly greedy and oppressive in their poverty. Beyond question, the appropriation by St Denys of the ancient leper hospital at St Mary Magdalene, contrived in the mid-fourteenth century to restore losses sustained in the raid, had been an unpopular move in the town. Accusations of mismanagement were levelled at the priory, and it was probably this grievance, among others, that lay behind the common withholding of St Denys rents, of which many of the leading burgesses, early in the fifteenth century, were guilty.[17] At God's House Hospital, a very similar situation had arisen. Again as a consequence of the raid of 1338, the hospital, with all its lands and rents, had been appropriated by the Queen's College, Oxford. But while it should have been possible, on the recovery of their economy, for the burgesses of Southampton to renew the traditional payments of quit-rents owing on their properties, their enthusiasm for Gervase le Riche's foundation had been forgotten with their dues. It took thirty years of repeated inquisitions at the end of the fourteenth century and at the beginning of the next to secure full restoration of the rents.[18] A century later, on 28 December 1500, the first salt-marsh riot found the town and the hospital again bitterly at odds. It was the mayor himself who headed the two hundred 'riottouse and evill disposed persones' who cast down the hospital's enclosures on the marsh. The dispute continued for a full four years, with John Dawtrey serving among the attorneys appointed to represent the town. It ended only when the king, tiring of the matter, required an immediate settlement.[19] Significantly, whereas bequests to the religious houses and hospitals had been common in wills of the thirteenth and even the fourteenth centuries, they fell away sharply in the fifteenth century. Southampton burgesses of this period were to remember meticulously the friary and the parish churches in their wills. But they scarcely mentioned either St Denys or the hospital at God's House. Of the many chantry and obit foundations so characteristic of the late-medieval town, only one, agreed in 1371, helped support a canon of St Denys as its chaplain.[20] At God's House, the obit for which lands were granted on 6 June 1497 was endowed in the name of John Pearson, a clerk in minor orders. It compared very unfavourably in scale with the foundations of contemporary burgesses.[21]

While there is nothing to suggest corruption, or a decay of morals, at the religious establishments of the town, undoubtedly fashions had changed. The Augustinian canons of St Denys, in particular, were diminished by their crippling poverty, nor was there any immediate prospect of a turn of the tide in their favour. Yet despite this, they had managed to maintain a fair standard of discipline in their house. Bishop Fox of Winchester, conducting a visitation of the priory early in the sixteenth century, found little there to correct. The canons, perhaps, were over-fond of dining away from their own refectory, at Portswood or possibly Southampton. Some, even, may have been seen in tavern society. But in other respects the bishop's advices were conventional enough, giving support to the impression later formed by the king's commissioners on the occasion of the suppression of the priory in 1536 that the canons, as a group, were of 'good conversation', three of them worthy to continue in religion. It was not enough to save them. The priory had always been a poor one, and its income classed it well below the limit required for preservation. As it was, the church and claustral buildings, in the judgment of the commissioners, were in a condition of 'extreme ruin and decay'. The plate, jewellery and ornaments were of less worth than those of any of the parish churches of the town. In the priory woods, the good timber was 'very thin set'.[22]

At the friary, although the Observants had already been expelled in 1534, the position was very different. If reform had been desirable before 1498, the substitution in that year of brethren of the Observant persuasion in place of the old-fashioned Conventuals had brought the Southampton house into line with an austere, fundamentalist tradition, recently become fashionable on the Continent.[23] Something of this fundamentalism is displayed in the events that immediately preceded the suppression. In a series of outspoken sermons, Gabriel Pecock, warden of the Southampton convent, attacked the doctrine of royal supremacy in the English Church. One of these addresses in particular, delivered on Passion Sunday 1534 at Winchester cathedral, attracted the attention of Cromwell, and an order was made for his arrest. The support that, even in circumstances such as these, Pecock was able to muster in Southampton, is a testimony to the good reputation of his house. Both the then mayor, John Perchard, and Henry Huttoft, customer and leading merchant in the port, spoke out in his defence. In Huttoft's words, Pecock, since his arrival at Southampton, had been 'of a very good behavyor'; he had kept his convent in a 'right good order'. That summer, with the co-operation of the burgesses, Pecock was able to turn away a malicious visitation of his house. But the general expulsion of the Observants, later in the year, swept away the brethren at Southampton. Pecock, in the last notice that survives of him, had been removed to imprisonment at Lincoln.[24]

For another four years, Austin friars kept the religious life in being at the convent. They had come into the occupation of a fine building, well maintained. And in their care, both the church and the conventual buildings were preserved in 'good estate'.[25] No Observant house could have permitted the accumulation of wealth within its walls. But the furnishings of the Southampton friary, listed with the final deed of surrender of 6 October 1538, reveal a very fair standard of comfort in the house. In particular, the church was handsomely equipped. At the east end, in the choir, the high altar carried a fine retable, sculptured in alabaster with a 'fayer' scene of the Passion. Above it, the reredos was painted and gilt with a pageant of the same. There were 'proper' triple sedilia for the priest, deacon and sub-deacon, and a good set of double choir stalls, 'well and substancyally graveyn'. Three further altars, each with its sculptured retable, were set in the body of the church, which was furnished with seats for the congregation. As was to be expected in a Franciscan house, the vestments were 'honest' without being extravagant. They were kept in a 'goodly' press in the vestry, with the corporals, altar-cloths, towels and cushions required for the celebration of the mass. The domestic quarters, adequately furnished and hung with devout pictures and images, were distinguished above all for the unusual excellence of their plumbing. The friars, over the years, had learnt to make good use of their conduit. Outside the chapter-house, in the cloister, they had constructed a 'fayer' wash-place, furnished with running water. There was piped water also both in the refectory and the infirmary. In the kitchen and the adjoining wash-house, 'goodly' lead troughs had been supplied to hold the water.[26]

It was this privileged access to fresh running water that, in the uncertain years of imminent suppression, evidently caught the attention of Sampson Thomas, 'reputed by all his neighbours in Southampton as a very true man', but not above taking advantage of the current distress of the friary. Some years before, John Fleming, a contemporary of Sampson's father and a direct descendant of Walter le Fleming, had obtained for himself a private water supply, piped from the municipal water-house at Holy Rood.[27] Sampson Thomas, a neighbour of the friary, was understandably anxious to contrive a similar facility for himself. His opportunity came within months of the expulsion of the Observants. On 12 October 1535, in grateful recognition of his 'manyfold good acts done to and for the communewelth of the same towne', the corporation conferred on Thomas the right to pipe water direct from the final conduit-house, up against the friary, to his own tenement on English Street. By fitting a pipe of precisely the dimensions of the existing waste-pipe on the conduit-house cistern, he was to share with it whatever 'superabundance' of water there might be.[28] As a neighbour, his interest in the friary site was obvious. Already, the previous August, he had taken, on a long lease from the corporation, the square tower on the town wall to the east of the convent site, formerly maintained by the Franciscans. The next January, in a successful bid to improve still further the amenities of his house, he negotiated an agreement, extremely favourable to himself, with the resident Austin friars. For ninety-nine years, the contract specified, he was to have the tenancy of the friary washing-yard, complete with its existing water-supply. The rent agreed was 4*d*.[29]

The lease of the washing-yard, as was customary with all such arrangements entered into in good faith before the Dissolution, remained valid after the surrender of the friary. It was one of many similar transactions hurried through at the last minute while communities of religious yet survived to negotiate them. At Southampton, virtually every man concerned with the post-Dissolution settlement, had taken out some such insurance in advance of the departure of the monks. James Bettes, one of the royal customers, concerned himself with the farm of the chantry at St Mary's. By August 1535, he had contrived a settlement that gave possession of the crops and the tithes of the chantry to Thomas Cromwell.[30] It was Cromwell, again, who employed John Mille, only the year before the suppression of the Cistercian community at Quarr, to negotiate leases with the abbot for his nephew.[31] Nor was Mille himself unmindful of his own interest. On 31 October 1537, barely in advance of the dissolution of Beaulieu Abbey, he obtained a lease, on the maximum 99-year term, of the abbot's important town properties in Southampton. No doubt in the belief that it would help consolidate his claim, he set about instantly to develop them.[32]

By such cliff-hanging manœuvres as these, the crown was habitually defrauded. It may be that there was little truth in the rumour that Mille had been implicated, some years before, in the dishonest manipulation of a former abbot of Beaulieu's will.[33] But, evidently, neither he nor any of his colleagues was above taking advantage of his official position to cheat, or at any rate to anticipate, the king. Since 10 January 1535, the Milles had been major tenants of St Denys in Southampton, within the walls. The dissolution of the priory, the following year, left them in uncontested possession of their 90-year leases on these tenements.[34] Only the previous September, Thomas Welles had secured for himself the lease, on a 60-year term, of an important Netley Abbey tenement and garden on the west side of English Street, parish of Holy Rood.[35] Henry Huttoft, further afield, had obtained, on 12 June 1533, a 40-year lease on one of the Hampshire rectories of the Augustinian canons at Mottisfont.[36] His son, John, was a pensioner of the Benedictine nuns at Romsey, whereas Thomas Welles, in the fitting company of Cromwell's creature, Wriothesley, drew an annuity from the brethren at Hyde Abbey, Winchester.[37]

The association as annuitants at Hyde of Thomas Welles, burgess of Southampton, and Thomas Wriothesley, servant of the king, usefully demonstrates the very close contacts maintained throughout the Dissolution and its preliminaries between the central government and its provincial outposts. It was contact based partly on the long mutual acquaintance of the principals, partly on their willingness to co-operate in furthering each other's ambitions. By 1535, or so he claimed, Henry Huttoft had known Thomas Cromwell for a quarter of a century.[38] And when Wriothesley was received into a free burgess-ship of Southampton in 1538, he could call upon James Bettes, Henry Huttoft, Sampson Thomas, Thomas Lyster, Thomas Welles and John Mille to support him, in addition to the then mayor, Thomas Husee, and several other leading figures of the town.[39] In return for patronage at court, for loans and lucrative appointments, Southampton men were very willing to do what they could to assist the local projects of their protectors. At Titchfield abbey and then at Beaulieu, Wriothesley acquired important buildings which he proceeded to convert to his own use. He found his friends in the area very useful. Henry Huttoft, in 1537, was the Southampton agent to whom loads of Caen limestone were consigned for the new buildings and conversions at Titchfield. At one point, early in January 1538, Huttoft, Mille and Welles were at Titchfield together, consulting on the works and organizing, as a commercial proposition, the fishponds of the former Premonstratensian house.[40] Within a few months, Beaulieu also had been dissolved. Acting probably for Wriothesley, Huttoft had kept the monks in victuals for the last weeks before the surrender. He was there, on Wriothesley's business, in December 1539. The next year, it was his son, John, with Richard, the son of John Mille, who accounted for the Beaulieu estates.[41]

Arrangements of this kind were of value to both parties. For the local man, there was much to be gained from such a post as the custodianship of a former monastic estate. For the administrator, with commitments in the capital, the provincial agent offered an irreplaceable service. Sometimes, understandably, misunderstandings arose. One such clouded relations between John Mille and Thomas Cromwell in September 1538, even while Mille was organizing the removal of Wriothesley's household to Southampton.[42] But there were profits enough for both sides, and harmony was generally maintained. While Wriothesley, on the proceeds of forfeited monastic estates, endowed an earldom, the local men, Francis Dawtrey and William Bettes, made gentry of themselves as leaseholders of the St Denys demesnes. Together, Francis Dawtrey and Lord Chancellor Wriothesley held the constableship of Southampton Castle from February 1546. And both Dawtrey and Bettes, for all their burgess ancestry, would come to be classed as gentlemen of the county in their time.[43] On a less pretentious level, there were many also who made good use of their opportunities to convert pre-Dissolution leases into something more secure. By 1544, the Milles had bought the freeholds of their St Denys tenements and of their other ex-monastic holdings in the borough. It was John Mille who subsequently transferred to Thomas Welles the Holy Rood tenement which Welles had held originally from Netley.[44]

But a civil service capable of handling all these transactions without error would have needed exceptional talents. And the quarrel between Sampson Thomas and Henry Huttoft in the summer of 1538, reminiscent of an earlier dispute of thirteen years before, almost certainly concerned monastic property. Both were 'greete occupyers' in the town, and both would have had an interest in the approaching disposal of the friary site.[45] Curiously, too, it was over the friary site again that there occurred a celebrated local imbroglio, launching a period of deplorable uncertainty of tenure, and recalling the very common tension that everywhere existed between Londoner and local man, the one enjoying privileged access to the clerks of the Court of Augmentations, the other in effective occupation of the land. Initially, it had been to Henry Huttoft that the custody of the site had been entrusted. But it was Thomas Welles who paid the full rent for the friary in 1540–1, and it was Welles who, to his own considerable discomfiture, found himself ousted by a Londoner. By a contract negotiated at the Augmentation Office on 14 November 1541 and back-dated to the previous Michaelmas, William Gonston, of London, secured the friary for himself at the same rent as Welles. Evidently, Welles knew nothing of this. When told of the new situation and required to deliver the keys, he became violent, seized Gonston's agent by the collar and struck him in the face, 'swering by godes blode & wondes that yf it had not byn for shame he sholde never speke more'.[46] In the event, Gonston retained the crown lease of the site. But Welles was a man of great local influence, at that time collector of customs in the port. And by 1544, whatever the circumstances that decided him, Gonston had abandoned his lease, with eighteen years still to run. On 6 January 1545, back-dated again to Michaelmas, it was resumed by Sir John Pollard, a royal official, and William Byrt, a yeoman. They bought the friary outright on 7 April, but sold it almost immediately to Nicholas Bacon and William Breton, both Londoners, on 13 May.[47] For a brief period in the summer, the site came to William Knight, a Southampton man and the son, by an earlier marriage, of Margaret, wife of Thomas Welles. In October, however, Knight was to restore full ownership once again to the king, probably in exchange for some property better suited to himself.[48]

The dispiriting muddle at the friary, harmful to the interests of almost everybody concerned, clearly displayed at least one of the more unfortunate consequences of the Dissolution. Another rapidly became apparent when tenants, accustomed to make their way satisfactorily enough before the departure of the monks, found in their new landlords men of a markedly less sympathetic turn. On the St Denys estates, it was probably the personal prestige and conservative tastes of Sir Francis Dawtrey that, for his lifetime, held change in check. But even so the rights of his Portswood tenants to make use of the Southampton commons, seemingly unchallenged during his lifetime and accepted by earlier generations, were to be disputed soon after his death.[49] Further, Sir Francis himself had done little to improve the condition of his buildings on the St Denys estates. A fall in rentals, already depressed by the neglect of the canons, had followed on the 'great ruin & decay for want of reparations' of the 'most part' of the priory's houses. It became the clear obligation of the new tenant, William Bettes, who took up the lease on 20 January 1569, within months of Dawtrey's death, to do whatever he could to remedy this. But the considerable expenditure required of him could not be met without a reorganization of rents. Almost immediately, his tenants began to complain of persecution. A group of copy holders, each with no more than a cottage, small-holding or garden plot of his own, united in an appeal to the Court of Requests, the accepted instrument of a poor man's justice. They were being forced, they said, into new agreements, beyond their means to support.[50]

Such, indeed, was the confusion, and so frequently deleterious were the effects of long-term leases, that many local interests sustained permanent injury. As property of the provost and fellows of the Queen's College, Oxford, the lands and tenements of God's House had escaped appropriation by the crown. But the chronic uncertainty of tenure that affected all such estates in the vicinity, enabled at least one major tenant of the college to take unwarranted liberties with his lease. Upton, a few miles to the north-west of Southampton, was the site of a college estate of 210 acres. It had been leased to a local landowner, Nicholas Barnard, on an 80-year term, well before the beginning of the troubles. When the lease fell in, early in the seventies, the provost of Queen's discovered what he thought to have been a substantial fraud. Nicholas, he believed, had freely enclosed college property, incorporating it with his own. Boundaries, after so many years, had ceased to be remembered, and this had happened particularly where the college lands lay interspersed with others, or scattered through the common fields of the vill. Moreover, Francis Barnard, successor in the tenancy to Andrew, Nicholas's son, had sold college property with his own, to the great loss of the provost and fellows.[51] The accusations, of course, were denied, and counter-claims were made in their place. But it was troubles such as these, almost as much as the desperate cash deficiencies of the administration, that persuaded the crown, from a relatively early date, to encourage the conversion of many of its original leases to outright sales, at values to be determined by an agreed multiple of existing rents. Such sales, for example, took place at Southampton in the time of Philip and Mary. Treating former monastic lands and other crown properties, the contracts specified payment in ready money by a date fixed in either May or June 1557. Prices were agreed at terms that ranged from sixteen to twenty-eight years' purchase. Among the lands thus sold was the former capital messuage of Sampson Thomas, since become crown property and recently leased to William Knight, together with a corner tenement, once a monastic holding, that had been held by Thomas Welles. The purchaser was William Herbert, earl of Pembroke, already crown lessee of the friary site, to which, at last, Sampson Thomas's washing-yard and conduit head were re-united.[52]

Disillusion with the territorial settlement matched, and clearly aggravated, discontent at recent meddlings with the faith. A drabness had lowered on religion, to the shocked surprise even of those who had gained much themselves from the Reformation. At Southampton, Sir Richard Lyster, the chief justice, and Margaret Welles, wife of Thomas Welles and mother of William Knight, both incautiously voiced their support for Stephen Gardiner, bishop of Winchester, imprisoned in the Tower. It was said of Margaret, also, that she had spoken in the summer of 1550 of a 'sturre that shuld be in this Realme before Mighlemas next greater then the sturre of the last yeares'.[53] Parson Wigg, an ex-friar, had used language in the town the previous summer, apparently with impunity, 'of the limitation of the kinges majesties reigne nothing unlikely a traytour'. The warnings of friends enabled him to escape arrest.[54] Indeed, the conservatism of the burgesses, in particular of their leaders, was remarked by Thomas Hancock, a visiting preacher of the new reformist persuasion. Unable to preach himself as a result of the hostility of Sir Richard Lyster, he had the satisfaction of hearing his replacement in the pulpit making just those accusations that he himself had earlier intended. With Sir Richard and other borough notables in the congregation, he 'challenged him that he, being Chief Justice of the law, did suffer the images in the church, the idol hanging in a string over the altar, candlesticks and tapers on them upon the altar, and the people honouring the idol, contrary to the law'. With this, Hancock added, the preacher had spoken 'much other good doctrine'.[55]

He would have spoken it almost alone. To many burgesses still living, the wealth of the parish churches derived from the deliberate investment of their forebears. And if the town had undoubtedly anticipated the king in the disposal of the plate and other furnishings of its churches, it had surely done so less from reforming passion than out of the understandable desire to preserve whatever it could from outright confiscation by the crown. There was little, after all, to admire in the novel austerity of the communion table, the unique suit of vestments and lonely chalice: all that survived the collections of 1552 and earlier years. Swiftly, in better times, the burgesses took steps to restore something of the original display. Today, the surviving Edwardian and Elizabethan church plate in the town demonstrates something of this. At St Michael's, an Edwardian silver-gilt chalice and paten cover, bearing assay marks of 1551, may just have preceded the 1552 collection, to be preserved in preference to other earlier pieces as the most recent acquisition of the parish. At St Michael's too, until its recent sale, there came to be lodged a magnificent silver-gilt tazza of 1567, an unusual and important secular piece, beautifully chased and embossed. The St Lawrence church plate, now at Bitterne, included a silver chalice of 1562, engraved with an interlace pattern and foliated pendants at the lip.[56] Meanwhile, in the fine sculptured tombs of the period, there were other opportunities for display. Sir Richard Lyster's monument at St Michael's, a handsome memorial put up in 1567, over a decade after his death, carries a decorative canopy over the chest, supported on fluted columns. And Thomas Fasshon, drafting his will the previous decade, had clearly intended something at least as dignified for himself. His monument, he directed, was to bear his name, 'what I was and of what place and my picture to be made in the fourme of a merchaunte and of my two wyves and all my children behind them and me. That is to say v sonnes and vii daughters'.[57]

As he wrote, Southampton was enmeshed again in the old traditions, briefly restored with Mary. There were Franciscans once more in the town, seemingly in residence at the friary. It was in their church that Jane Rygges, in 1558, expressed the desire to be buried. And it was to them that Charles Harrison, a local physician, left his books that October, to inform them of philosophy, divinity and history, and to be preserved in their library for ever.[58] A month later, the death of Mary, followed quickly by the expulsion of the friars, effectively invalidated the bequest. Yet there were already few enough reasons for supposing that, even had the time available been longer, the restoration which Mary attempted would have come very close to success. Whether consciously or not, the role of the clergy was everywhere under examination. Everywhere, too, the hitherto predictable piety of wealthy laymen had significantly altered course. At Southampton, a proposal to be rid of the chaplains at God's House was made in the face of evidence that the parish of Holy Rood, in particular, was in need of a more numerous clergy.[59] And the new carelessness of obligation exhibited by the provost and fellows of the Queen's College, who would have done much to save a charge of £20 on their estates, is still more vividly displayed in the wording of contemporary wills. Thomas Huttoft, in June 1554, had been among the last to provide elaborately for the ceremony at his death. His careful directions for the siting of his tomb in the fraternity chapel of St Barbara at St Michael's, for the celebration of memorial masses, and for the reward of all concerned, belong to a respectable but a failing tradition. John Staveley's testament, prepared within the decade, is refreshingly free of such morbid preoccupations. The arrangements were to be left to the good sense of his wife and his friends. The one stipulation made was that they should not be 'over costely'.[60]

Notes

1 P.R.O. E326/11798; *Black Book*, ii:162; *L. & P. Henry VIII*, xxi:2:84; *Third Book of Remembrance*, i:64–5.
2 P.R.O. E326/11790, 11798; *Third Book of Remembrance*, i:66; *L. & P. Henry VIII*, iii:2:1041–2; S.C.R.O. SC5/3/1, f. 45.
3 S.C.R.O. SC5/3/1, f. 7; *Assize of Bread Book*, p. 60; *L. & P. Henry VIII*, iii:2:1041–2; *Third Book of Remembrance*, i:10, 64–5.
4 S.C.R.O. SC5/3/1, f. 15, and *Oak Book*, ii:170–1.
5 S.C.R.O. SC4/3/14, 19; *Black Book*, ii:170–1.
6 P.R.O. E326/11786, 11789, 11790, 11792, 11794, 11795, 11796.
7 *Book of Remembrance*, iii:54–6; James Gairdner (ed.), *Letters and papers illustrative of the reigns of Richard III and Henry VII*, i:111–12, ii:103–5. On Prince Arthur's death in 1502, his widow was betrothed to Prince Henry, still a boy. They were married on 11 June 1509.
8 *Letters*, p. 33.
9 *Book of Remembrance*, i:21–2, 48–9, 52–3; S.C.R.O. SC5/1/28, f. 29, SC5/1/29, f. 22, and SC5/1/31, f. 22; *L. & P. Henry VIII*, ii:2:1312; *Cal. State Papers Venetian, 1509–19*, pp. 445–6.
10 *L. & P. Henry VIII*, i:1:133, 527, 538, 543, 555, 567, 689, and 2:852, 854, 856, 879, 1118; *Cal. State Papers Venetian, 1509–19*, p. 89.
11 *L. & P. Henry VIII*, ii:2:1461–2.
12 P.R.O. E101/517/19.
13 S.C.R.O. SC5/1/30.
14 *L. & P. Henry VIII, Addenda*, i:1:4. It was Richard Palshid who drew up the accounts for the victualling of the *Regent* at Portsmouth in the summer of 1512, published by Alfred Spont (ed.), *Letters and papers relating to the war with France*, Navy Records Society, 10 (1897), pp. 13–16. Biscuit, beer and fish were bought at Southampton, to be brought round the coast by lighter.
15 S.C.R.O. SC3/1/1, pp. 66v, 67v.
16 Nostschilling's intention, on his deathbed in 1361, had been to leave his property initially to Agnes, his wife, in trust for many local religious institutions, including the churches at Eling and at Holy Rood, Southampton, the hospital at God's House, the priory at St Denys, and Winchester cathedral priory (P.R.O. E326/9381). But he neglected to obtain the necessary licence to alienate these properties into mortmain, and, on the death of his wife in 1373, they became forfeit to the crown (P.R.O. C143/376/19; Win.Coll. Mun. 17779; *Cal.Inq.P.M.*, xiii:272; *Cal.P.R. 1370–4*, p. 354).
17 P.R.O. C47/60/8/303, E364/32, SC6/981/28; *Cal.Inq.Misc. 1392–9*, pp. 63–4; *Cal.P.R. 1399–1401*, p. 505, *1396–9*, p. 443; *Cal.C.R. 1409–13*, pp. 132–3; S.C.R.O. D/LY/7/18. The priory's interest in the hospital was based, allegedly, on a confirmation of Pope Alexander III in 1179 (S.C.R.O. D/CJ/33).
18 *Cal.P.R. 1381–5*, p. 283, *1388–92*, p. 54, *1396–9*, p. 365, *1399–1401*, pp. 43–4, *1401–5*, p. 69, *1405–8*, pp. 149, 227; also *Cal.C.R. 1402–5*, p. 158, *1405–9*, pp. 124, 178–82, 466–7.
19 S.C.R.O. SC4/2/314–332; *Sign Manuals and Letters Patent*, i:34.
20 P.R.O. C143/376/20; *Cal.P.R. 1370–4*, p. 115. The prior of St Denys, in insisting on a licence before he 'dared' enter the property of Roger Haywode's endowment, clearly had in mind the likely fate of the Nostschilling bequests, currently being contested in the courts.
21 God's House Deeds 495.
22 Davies, pp. 441–2; P.R.O. SC12/33/27.
23 A. G. Little, 'Introduction of the Observant Friars into England', *Proc. British Academy*, 10 (1921–3), pp. 455–71, and 'Introduction of the Observant Friars into England: a bull of Alexander VI', Ibid., 27 (1941), pp. 155–66.
24 Alwyn Ruddock, 'The Greyfriars in Southampton', *Proc. Hampshire Field Club*, 16 (1944–7), pp. 143–5.
25 P.R.O. SC12/33/28.
26 P.R.O. E36/115 (printed by J. S. Davies, 'Dissolution of the Friary at Southampton',

Proc. Hampshire Field Club, 1 (1885–9), pp. 19–22). Dr Ruddock (op. cit., pp. 145–6) has used the same inventory, curiously, to illustrate the poverty of the house.
27 John Speed, *History of Southampton*, pp. 32–5. The arrangement is dated 1 June 1515. It followed the transfer to the Corporation of a spring to feed the conduit, sited on John Fleming's land beyond the walls.
28 P.R.O. E326/6957.
29 S.C.R.O. SC4/3/23; P.R.O. SC6/Henry VIII/7407.
30 *L. & P. Henry VIII*, iv:3:2649, vii:143, ix:26.
31 Ibid., ix:313.
32 P.R.O. SC6/Henry VIII/3340.
33 *L. & P. Henry VIII*, xiii:2:511.
34 P.R.O. E318/603.
35 P.R.O. E318/603, SC6/Henry VIII/3326.
36 *L. & P. Henry VIII*, xix:1:78.
37 Ibid., xiv:2:75.
38 Ibid., viii :346.
39 *Third Book of Remembrance*, i:61.
40 *L. & P. Henry VIII*, xii:1:287 and 2:274, xiii:1:6–7, 210, 282–3.
41 Ibid., xiii:1:253, xiv:2:263; P.R.O. E315/363, 442.
42 *L. & P. Henry VIII*, xiii:2:124.
43 Ibid., xiii:1:582 and 2:99, xxi:1:144; P.R.O. E310/24/131, fos 6, 25, SC6/Henry VIII/7415, 7417.
44 *L. & P. Henry VIII*, xix:1:281, xxi:1:352.
45 Ibid., xiii:1:430; *Third Book of Remembrance*, i:39–40.
46 B.M. Harleian Roll I.14; P.R.O. E315/165, f. 5, SC6/Henry VIII/7407; *L. & P. Henry VIII*, xvii:698.
47 P.R.O. E318/870, E326/8275; *L. & P. Henry VIII*, xx:1:301.
48 P.R.O. E326/5505, 6329.
49 *Third Book of Remembrance*, ii:113–14, 115–16, 125–6, 128–9, 130–4.
50 P.R.O. E310/24/131, fos 6, 25; Req. 2/279/51.
51 P.R.O. C3/135/73.
52 B.M. Harleian 606, fos 35v, 36, 118v; P.R.O. C1/1372/3; *Black Book*, iii:90–2. The sale and purchase of former monastic tenements became, almost immediately, a regular traffic in the town (Ibid., iii:74–9, 96–101, 102–3).
53 *Letters*, pp. 78–9. There had been serious risings in the west country and in East Anglia the previous summer. Regional disturbances continued through 1550 and 1551, provoked by religious reforms and enclosures.
54 Ibid., pp. 71–2.
55 Davies, pp. 383–4.
56 P. R. P. Braithwaite, *The Church Plate of Hampshire*, pp. 299, 301, 302–4 (with illustrations). The tazza was purchased by Southampton Corporation in 1969.
57 *Black Book*, iii:150. But Fasshon died a resident of London in 1558. His monument at St Michael's was never built.
58 H.R.O. wills of Jane Rygges and Charles Harrison, 1558.
59 P.R.O. E301/52, E321/30/62.
60 H.R.O. will of Thomas Huttoft, 1554; *Black Book*, iii:106.

Chapter seventeen

The economy transformed

There were five houses, in particular, that caught the attention of John Leland on the occasion of his visit to Southampton. The 'chefest' of these, in a town already remarkable for its 'many very fair marchauntes houses', was the mansion of Henry Huttoft, on the site of the ancient tenement at Bull Hall. Confessedly an extravagance, it was a fashionable quadrangular building, reminiscent of the country houses of the gentry and not unlike the corporation's re-modelled property at West Hall, a little down the street on the left. West Hall, another of Leland's selections, was still in the tenancy of Italians, the then tenant being Niccolo de Marini de Egra, of Genoese extraction, the close friend and business associate of Sampson Thomas. Recently, he had spent much on repairs and embellishments at the mansion, among these a turret over the entrance. In the other direction, higher up the street where it opened into the fishmarket before St Michael's, Leland noticed Sir Richard Lyster's tenement on the corner of Blue Anchor Lane. On English Street, in the parish of Holy Rood, he remarked the properties of John Mille, town clerk and recorder, and Antonio Guidotti, Henry Huttoft's enterprising Florentine son-in-law.[1] In Leland's record, the conjunction of these properties is a significant one. Henry Huttoft, John Mille and his near-neighbour Sampson Thomas, in addition to their connections with the government, were each of them deeply committed to what was left of the Italian trade. They were the last of their kind to be so, poised, at great risk to their fortunes, on the very brink of change.

One thing, though, is certain. These men, beyond question, were professionals. The many outside interests of John Mille appear to have affected little the efficiency with which he handled, over four decades, the affairs of the borough. He brought up his son, Thomas, to succeed him in the clerkship. Henry Huttoft and Sampson Thomas, each in his day a controller of customs in the port, were both active in property transactions in the borough and its environs, as well as daring in overseas trade. In a generation distinguished for the commercial enterprise that had driven the native carrying trade north into the Baltic and south into the Mediterranean, Henry Huttoft was an important shipowner. His great ship, the *Margaret Hart*, of 180 tons, was intended for the passage to Italy. It was one of several local ships to carry the merchandise of Southampton burgesses direct to the Mediterranean markets on the joint Anglo-Italian trading ventures in which Sampson Thomas, through his Marini connection, played an active part.[2] In Niccolo de Egra and Antonio Guidotti, both denizens and burgesses in their own right, the men of Southampton had able mentors, capable of imparting that commercial expertise essential to the penetration of the existing Italian monopoly. At West Hall, Niccolo de Egra's tenement was remarkable for its three counting-houses, or studies. There were shelves fitted to hold business papers in the principal study on the ground floor, with fixed benches for the use of the clerks. Guidotti, at Holy Rood, also had his study. There, under lock and key, he kept the tools of his trade, the 'account and reckoning books, bills of obligation, both current and past'.[3]

It was not only through the good graces of its Italian settlers that the borough was able to make regular use of imported talent. In common with most medieval urban communities, Southampton had long been the focus of the ambitions of many of the more energetic spirits of the locality. The draw, inevitably, would weaken as competition, particularly at London and at Salisbury, developed. But it was strong enough still in the first half of the sixteenth century to bring men of great ability to the borough. Thomas Thomas, a Welshman, had been attracted to Southampton by the offer of the controllership of customs. He remained there to his profit. But, in general, the birth-places of recruits to the burgess body were considerably more local than this. A major Southampton shipowner, Robert Reneger, was a native of Basingstoke. Thomas Beckingham, mayor in 1547–8 and a leading participant in the Italian trade, was of Salisbury extraction. Close contacts with the Channel Islands, long characteristic of the Southampton coastal trade, brought several islanders to make their fortunes in the town. One of these, Edmund Cockerell, became the son-in-law of Henry Huttoft. Another, Thomas Fasshon, the mayor's free burgess in 1531–2, was to be mayor himself in 1545–6, having been sheriff already in 1541–2.[4]

Yet, in all of this, there was weakness present as well as strength. Those civic loyalties that Southampton men of the current generation were coming to observe for themselves in Italy, had never taken such deep root in their own borough. Adversity in the sixteenth century led, precisely as it had done in the fourteenth, to desertion by both merchant and artisan. Of the many sad reports which, beginning already in the thirties, characterized the later years of the century, one, of 1588, remarked that numbers of artisans had left the town, that gentry refused to settle there, coming only for the winter season, and that the foreigners recently established at Southampton were not of the wealthier kind.[5] There was altogether too much truth in the complaint. The issues it touched upon were those that, over the space of just a few decades, had combined to bring the port to insignificance.

Important among these was the attitude of the burgesses themselves. Particularly in recent years, the social and economic draw of the capital had noticeably intensified. John Huttoft's appointment as a clerk of the signet in 1539, opening the prospect of a career at court, was the beginning of long absences from the town. The two Channel Islanders, Edmund Cockerell and Thomas Fasshon, after making their mark at Southampton, moved on once again to London.[6] But mobility, of social standing as much as of residence, had long been a characteristic of Southampton society, and that same rapid turnover of burgess families has been remarked on as commonplace elsewhere.[7] At Southampton, it was rare for a family, in the main line, to equal the three-generation continuity of Peter, William and Henry James. Although, frequently, a cadet line might remain in residence to continue the family tradition, the lure of the country, as often, was too much for the principal heirs. Whether in the building of large houses in the immediate vicinity of the borough, or in the purchase of more distant estates, a steady progression of the major families away from Southampton had long been observable. The Flemings, Chamberleyns, Banestres and Ludlows of the older generation, the Dawtreys, Milles and Bettes of the new, all made this comfortable transition. As long as the investment of surplus wealth remained a problem, no better outlet presented itself than land. Nor should the draw of a country retreat, as lively a temptation today, be underrated as a factor in the decision. William Soper, loyal burgess though he always remained, made use of his wealth, comparatively early in his career, to purchase a country estate on the edge of the New Forest, of which he was evidently very proud. It was there that he chose to entertain his Italian guests, the captain and patrons of the Florentine galleys, whom he had invited to join him for the holiday on Thursday 2 February 1430, the Feast of the Purification of the Virgin. At Soper's country house, a journey by water and land of some three miles from the borough, they sat down together to enjoy a 'very fine' lunch. Later, they went out hunting in the forest, accompanied by servants and dogs provided by their host. On their return, another meal of several courses awaited them, to be followed by a private celebration of vespers at Soper's own chapel, 'and thus he behaved towards us in the most courteous and informal way imaginable, not wanting us to leave'. Yielding to the persuasions of their host, the Italians stayed on until after midnight.[8]

Both in wealth and in experience of society, Soper, naturally, was the exception. But, in a burgess group always restricted in number and interdependent in so many ways, the tastes and habits of the leaders cannot have failed to influence the remainder. In the brief economic recovery that characterized the third quarter of the sixteenth century, an anonymous critic, writing in 1582 when a decline had already set in, noted the extravagant and imitative ways of his fellow townsmen:[9]

> Then beganne costly apparell: then downe with old howses, and newe sett in their places: for the howses where the fathers dwelt could not content their children. Then must everie man of good calling be furnished with change of plate, with great store fyne lynnen, rich tapistrie, and all other things which might make shewe of braverie. And who then but Hampton for fyne dyett and great cheare.

Further, as trading opportunities narrowed and men of independent enterprise saw fit to desert the port, the residue of the burgess body grew progressively more introverted and exclusive, guarding what was left of its privilege. By the seventies, it had already long been the case that men of humbler station were commonly excluded from municipal office. Nor is it without significance that when, earlier in the century, a fresh outbreak of violence had greeted the salt-marsh enclosures of 1517, it was the mayor, not God's House Hospital, who was the target. Seventeen years before it had been the mayor himself who had led the rioters in the same cause.[10]

The record of class rivalries remains obscure, but physical divisions had long existed in the town to distinguish the poor from the rich. From the twelfth century, if not before, wealth had tended to concentrate in the southern part of the town, first in the parishes of St Michael and St John, then increasingly in Holy Rood as well. By the sixteenth century little had changed, one consequence being that of the five houses especially admired by John Leland, not one was to be found north of the Holy Rood boundary with the small central parish of St Lawrence, itself a middle-class preserve. In general, the poor lived in the great northern parish of All Saints. They settled back-lots in the more fashionable parishes to the south, or spread through the inner suburbs, north of the Bargate and west of St Mary's. Through the centuries, the consistent imbalance of wealth is shown in the ecclesiastical taxations of the parishes.[11] It emerges in the subsidy accounts of Henry VIII and Philip and Mary, and recurs in corporation muster records of the same century, in which hand-gunners are shown to have concentrated in Holy Rood, St Michael and St John, whereas archers and bill-men were drawn equally from every parish, including St Lawrence and All Saints.[12]

Yet it was in Tudor society, in particular, that a high level of local unemployment, the product of increased population and an imperfectly understood price-revolution, brought an unwelcome confrontation between the classes. It may be that the evaporation of monastic charity forced the growth of contemporary concern with the problems of the idle poor. But there was more than this behind the publication, in 1536, of a new set of regulations for the control of begging in the town, recognizing that 'a grett nomber of beggars of late have resortid unto this towne & dayly doo resort, aswell men as wemen, and inhabite them selffs here intendyng to lyve only by beggyng, to the grett charge of all the dwellers wythin the said towne, and contrary to many good actes & statutes made for the same'.[13] Twenty years before, in keeping with the antique traditions of their gild, the town fathers had reacted very differently when one of their own number had come into reduced circumstances. On 2 July 1516, Robert Wright one-time steward and sheriff, and a town officer since the eighties of the previous century, was granted a forty-shilling pension out of town moneys, 'inconsideracion that he hath borne the office of shryvaltie wythin the said towne and also hath be an old serjaunt of the townes'.[14] As the critic of 1582 would caustically remark, 'you must understand that after a man hath borne anie good office in the towne, it is some discreditt unto him to goe any more to the seas, but must still tarie at home, keepe some state and countenance. This ease and state ys manie times dearly bought.'[15]

Indeed, by his day, 'ease and state' were harder than ever to come by. The century had opened well. The recovery of the wine trade and the restoration of some order on the seas began with the treaty of Picquigny in 1475. Exceptional economic advance characterized the reign of Henry VIII, pushing cloth exports up to new heights at the turn of the century, and keeping them there for something like two decades.[16] But too much, locally, depended on the London interest. The Italians, trading for themselves, were already less in evidence in Southampton. When the Londoners, in their turn, withdrew their capital from the port, little was left to sustain it.[17] Nor did local initiatives in trade offer any viable alternative. Lacking the support of wealthy trading companies, the individual Southampton burgess risked nothing less than bankruptcy in the hazardous Mediterranean exchanges to which his interest was briefly directed. Antonio Guidotti's failure in 1536, a crash on a disastrous scale, brought down also many of the ambitions of his father-in-law.[18] In similar circumstances, the humiliations that afflicted Henry Huttoft were shared by his close friends and business associates, James Bettes and John Mille.[19]

Where individual burgesses found themselves rebuffed in trade, 'tricked' by the cunning of foreigners they had trusted, the corporation faced deepening poverty. Ever since its inception, the agreed farm payable by Southampton had been met out of the return on local tolls. There were long periods, of course, of failure, but in the prosperous years of the fifteenth century, by now regarded with nostalgia, the visit of a single Italian trading fleet had been enough to raise receipts to a comfortable level and to guarantee the farm. Discouraged as much by their own internal politics as by the young king's renewal of war with France, the Italians had reduced their sailings. Their substitutes, the Londoners, although they temporarily kept the level of trading high, claimed extensive relief from tolls. Repeatedly, the townsmen petitioned the king and beseeched his ministers for their support. Merchant strangers, they claimed, came seldom to the port, or not at all. The receipts on petty customs no longer sufficed to meet the heavy charges of the farm. In 1531, to the accompaniment of a well-calculated distribution of presents, rewards and fees, John Mille negotiated the remission in perpetuity of forty marks of the farm, with small additional privileges designed to swell the revenues of the town.[20] It was something, perhaps, but obviously it was not enough. Within a few years, the near-total failure of the corporation to meet even its amended farm made it clear that more drastic reforms were necessary. Southampton was not unique in its troubles, and it was with evident appreciation of the difficulties of the boroughs generally that the crown, at the mid-century, embarked on a widespread revision of farms. In 1550, by order of the Privy Council, a large part of Southampton's accumulated arrears were remitted, the remainder to be paid by instalments. Two years later, on 4 April 1552, the lowering of the farm to £50, a mere quarter of the original requirement, came nearer to recognition of the borough's reduced estate.[21]

In quartering the farm, the king had provided for an upward revision of his receipts should the Italians again visit the port. And it was exactly this consistent refusal to recognize their departure as an accomplished fact, that pervaded economic thinking in Southampton for at least a century after the Italians had gone for good.

Still, in 1603, the burgesses were hoping for the resumption of their once 'lively' trade.[22] Its failure, for many years past, had been the principal substance of their complaints. Preoccupied as much with problems of defence as with economic advance, successive governments did what they could to remedy the borough's condition, if for no other reason than that its decay constituted a standing threat to the security of the south coast. But trading monopolies, the characteristic Tudor specific for most economic ills, while they did much to boost the dominance of the capital, proved largely unworkable in its outports. In the thirties, the tin trade which, since the turn of the century, had brought a fleet of Cornish coastal vessels regularly to the port, followed the Londoners to the Thames. The sweet wines monopoly, granted by Philip and Mary and recognized by Elizabeth, was even less successful in sustaining activity in the port. Immediately the subject of dispute, it became no more than the source of composition payments, payable to the corporation in lieu of the obligation to unload the wines at Southampton. Certainly, it did nothing to bring back Mediterranean shipping to the harbour.[23]

With the direction, in 1581, of foreign wools, alum and currants through the port, the dream of monopolies and special toll exemptions came to haunt local men in the eighties.[24] But the future, it was becoming obvious, lay with the great London-controlled trading companies, and these had begun already the routines of exclusion that would minimize the share of provincial merchants, even in markets traditionally their own. Furthermore, the loss of the initiative abroad had its effect on the distributive trades at home. By 1582, the regional distribution of canvas and other French products still imported through Southampton had been taken over very largely by the enterprising men of Salisbury, 'become great Merchants themselves of those commodities'. Similarly, woad, traditionally supplied by Southampton to a wide ring of cloth-producing towns, had been lost to the superior initiative of the 'western' men, of Lyme (Regis), Taunton and Bristol.[25] In the circumstances, there was little that Southampton could do except offer preferential tariffs and other special incentives of its own. Early in the century, it had had some success in tempting, by just such means, the Guernsey men from Poole. And through the next decades the Channel Islands trade, particularly in linen and in canvas, remained of great importance to the town.[26] The burgesses were less fortunate in re-asserting their claim to the tin trade out of Cornwall. There is nothing to suggest that it ever returned on any scale to Southampton following the departure of the Italians and the Londoners. Yet this, on the part of the Southampton authorities, was not for want of trying. In 1537, they nominated to a free burgess-ship the deputy to the receiver of the Duchy of Cornwall. He was the eldest son of Richard Capleyn, alderman and lately mayor, and could be expected to have the borough's interest at heart. Certainly, the terms of his nomination were unambiguous. The privilege was accorded him 'yn consideracon that he hath ben and may be hereafter occacon and cause to help that the trate of tynne, whiche hath ben with-drawen from this towne along tyme, may resort hether ageyn, which restith muche in the Resceyvor & his servant at shipping tymes, and also in consideracon that he is sworne to be true to this towne and to certifie the towne truly at every shipping the very true owners of the tynne to be shippid hether withowt color, so that the towne lose not there custume by coloring of other men as they have don'.[27]

Towards the end of the century, when Portsmouth attempted to shake off its dependence in matters of custom on Southampton, feelings understandably ran high. The break could scarcely have led, as its opponents suggested, to the 'utter undoing' of Southampton.[28] But few Southampton burgesses of that generation could remain unconscious of the ineluctable pressures that for years had been stripping their borough of its ancient and traditional roles. The draw of London, perhaps their greatest single affliction, was at least an experience shared equally with almost every provincial centre of note.[29] More galling were the competing claims of those, even within the region, who little by little were contributing to the erosion of the borough's economy. Southampton's decline was never absolute. Despite all the talk of utter decay and the pervading sense of irremediable disaster, it kept in being as a market town, a local industrial centre and minor port. But the international trade that for centuries had sustained it, had fallen to the merest trickle. Lieutenant Hammond, visiting the port in 1635, found in it much to admire. It was 'neat', in his opinion, 'providently governed' and 'strongly walled about'. But his explanation of Southampton's remnant prosperity recognized, perhaps unwittingly, the shrunken trading function of the port. From the walls of the ruined castle, Hammond looked out over the 'pretty, well compacted Streets, and Buildings' of the borough. In particular, the central sweep of English Street caught his flattering attention. There the 'Buildings both within and without, I meane the Fabrickes, and Inhabitants, are fayre, neat, beautifull, streight and hansome'. They had got that way, to his mind, by 'matching and Trucking with her fostering Neighbour Islands' [Jersey and Guernsey].[30]

If Hammond understood only a small part of the truth, the economic conditions he witnessed in the port had followed from a decisive break with the past, already a century old. When prosperity briefly returned to Southampton in the wake of the recession of the thirties, it did so only spasmodically, without pattern or prospect of permanence. The brief commercial revival of the sixties and seventies depended on fragile exchanges with Spain. It failed as the political situation deteriorated, and as the new London-based Spanish Company, founded in 1577, tightened its hold on the trade. Locally, the impact of the trading companies was immediate. By 1582, or so it was alleged in the town, the London companies of Muscovy, Antwerp and Spain had annexed to themselves the bulk of Southampton's overseas trade, so that 'only Ffrance is left free to our towne, a Contrie where no English comodities are in price or estimation'. The occasional visit of a Venetian wine ship had done nothing to revive the once flourishing Mediterranean trade. There is no mention of Italy among those countries to which Southampton ships continued to sail in the years that preceded the commercial collapse of the eighties. It is a significant omission in a list that includes Bordeaux for wine, La Rochelle for salt, St Malo and Rouen for canvas, Flanders for luxury goods and Newfoundland for fish.[31] Within the decade, the Spanish wars completed the transition. By 1588, the town which Sir Francis

Walsingham had known but recently as a 'place of great wealth & Traffique', was already wonderfully decayed and dispeopled. Although lately the home port of a considerable merchant fleet, it could now do nothing to assist the queen in her preparations to meet the Armada.[32]

But even as Southampton adjusted to its new role, minor developments in the economy helped accommodate its burgesses to the change. Promoted by the war at sea with Spain, numerous privateers, among them the *Saucy Jack* of Thomas Heaton and Richard Goddard's *Gift of God*, made their headquarters in the Solent. Their presence encouraged ship-building and repairs on the slips to the north of West Quay; their activity brought profit to individual ship-owners in the town.[33] But privateering was likely to flourish only at such times as trade itself was dead. In the long run, it was the small textile industry, developed by the Walloon refugees since their settlement in the borough in the late sixties, that was of more permanent value to the economy. Although received with some caution at first, the Walloon craftsmen quickly justified their presence in the locality. They became, as they had promised, important employers of local men. When joined by the Norman 'rebels and heretics' who came to Southampton in 1572, they took an increasing part in the social and economic life of the borough. By the end of the century, there were well over two hundred aliens, mainly of northern French or Flemish extraction, listed as taxpayers in the town. Lieutenant Hammond, in 1635, estimated their congregation at the chapel of St Julian, God's House, at six or seven-score persons. Its register had opened in 1567, the date of the original Walloon settlement.[34]

Viewed overall, the startling down-swings and very much slower recoveries of Southampton's economy in the sixteenth century are likely to obscure what might be seen, in other particulars, as a retreat in reasonable order from an untenable trading position. If the town lost the riches of the Italian trade and failed to hold the loyalty of the Londoners, it gained valuable independence from the caprices of international commerce and from the whims of those who had used it too much to the advantage of themselves. If, furthermore, its leading burgesses successively left their ranks to find a new home amidst the gentry, it was luckier in attracting many of them back again, to assume command of the militia or to argue its case with the crown. In national counsels, Lord Chancellor Wriothesley's advocacy, through the second quarter of the century, was taken up by Sir Francis Walsingham in the fourth, whereas locally it was from the ranks of the landed families of the county that Southampton, increasingly, recruited its recorder, its parliamentary representatives, and even, on occasion, its mayor.[35] In anticipation of a revival of commerce overseas, the town kept its Customs House and port facilities in adequate repair, so that in 1565 it might confidently be reported that although suffering a 'decrease in traffic', Southampton 'is as well able to cope with trade as ever it was'.[36] But the prevailing preoccupation with departed glories abroad was not so strong as to prevent some sensible reforms at home. Southampton's role as a local market centre was threatened by the inadequacy of the traditional market on English Street, at St Lawrence church door. In 1570, over-ruling the opposition of interested parties in St Lawrence, the corporation undertook the construction of a new covered market at Holy Rood, under the Audit House. It was designed for the use of the 'very greate multitude' of countrymen repairing weekly to the market, as much as for that of the townsmen themselves. It replaced an open market area, 'whear no coverte nor any maner of defens is to save and kepe ther sayd victualls from the rayne and tempeste, which often tyms doth happen uppon those market dayes, wherby ther said victualls and neccessaris is greatly impayrid and as well the byers as the sellers therof therby muche the wors, as well in ther boddis as in the same victualls and necessaris ther so bought and sold in tyme of such tempestes'.[37]

Driven back on their own resources, the burgesses of Southampton exhibited a creditable resilience in the face of change. The uncalculating fanaticism of the Reformation had left their borough without facilities for education or accommodation for the aged and deserving poor. The generosity of two former mayors, John Capelin and Richard Butler, met at least a part of these needs. In 1554, by colour of letters patent of Edward VI granted the previous year, the new grammar school was founded and endowed. Butler's almshouses at St Mary's followed within the decade.[38] Later in the century, the Sendy charity at St Lawrence and at St Mary's almshouses further supported the poor.[39] Perhaps in a similar tradition of self-help, Southampton burgesses participated in Elizabethan voyages of discovery overseas. In 1582, the year that one of their number was setting down his thoughts on the current decay of the town, the burgesses gave a rousing send-off to the luckless Captain Edward Fenton, bound hopefully for China.[40] Later in the year, it was the Merchant Adventurers of Southampton who were the principal signatories of an agreement to finance Sir Humphrey Gilbert's almost equally inglorious journey of colonization and discovery to Newfoundland.[41]

Plainly, there was no lack in Elizabethan Southampton of the characteristic restlessness and ambition of the age, nor any of its patriotism and extravagance. There were certainly complaints in the contemporary court leet records of ruinous public buildings and decaying defences.[42] Yet on English Street, clustered in the fashionable parish of Holy Rood, the Audit House, Market Hall and Customs House were all newly-built or remodelled. On Westgate Street, above Ronceval, the Linen Hall and Tin Cellar, sharing a single building, had been equipped to meet a recent expansion in both the Channel Islands and the Cornwall trades. At the southern tip of Bull Street, the Beaulieu Wool House of the old town had become the Alum Cellar of the new.

Domestically, as the archaeology of the sixteenth-century town testifies, the burgesses of Southampton had not yet lost their taste for the luxuries which their fathers had imported from overseas. In the mid-century, the partial rebuilding of a tenement on Winkle Street was made the occasion for the laying of a fine floor of painted tiles, much superior in execution to the native product and a characteristic import from the Netherlands. From the Netherlands, too, came the first maiolicas and tin-glazes of the new fashion, and it was probably via Antwerp and the northern towns that the familiar stoneware bottles and beer-mugs of the Rhineland began to reach the port. There were lustres from Spain with the extravagantly ornamented chafing-dishes of Saintonge, whilst from Beauvais, in northern France, came those characteristically brightly-coloured sgraffiatos of the region, the forerunners of the English pictorial wares so generally popular in the next century.[43] As yet, there was no adequate local substitute for the fine glass of the Venetian lagoon. It was this that was chosen as an appropriate reward for those royal officials who, in one way or another, had advanced the cause of the borough in 1531, the occasion of the reduction of its farm.[44]

In the event, even the decay of the borough defences could be attributed to rational neglect. At Calshot Castle, well-gunned and strongly garrisoned in a crisis, the queen now had a fortress fit to seal the sea approaches to Southampton. It could be little to her purpose to put money into the obsolescent defences of the borough, or even to insist on their maintenance by others. Already, many years before the survey of 1585 pronounced it 'very ruynouse and in great decaye bothe within and without', Southampton Castle had been neglected, its lead gone, its timber down or rotten, and the shell of its walls alone surviving. The ditch, bordering the crumbling bailey wall on the landward side, had been parcelled up into garden plots, to be filled in steadily by the tenants until, by the time of another survey in 1636, only its line and approximate dimensions were remembered.[45] While slower to recognize the new position than the queen and her military advisers, the burgesses of Southampton, without pressure from the government, did little but minor repairs to their walls. But just as it was not simply poverty that explained this indifference, there was no lack of martial ardour to make up for it in other, more popular, ways. Seldom, indeed, had the pomp and professionalism of war held a higher place in general esteem. At Southampton, the musters were public occasions, opportunities for sport and display. The gunners, much envied, gathered to demonstrate their weapons, exactly as the young men of the town would one day meet to practise their markmanship at the close of Trinity Fair. In this thoroughly modern obsession, for all its roots in archery, we may discover much of the new quality of the age. Only recently, while removing a late-sixteenth-century level on the site at Cuckoo Lane, a diminutive bronze model of a wheel-lock pistol was recovered from under the shadow of the surviving town wall.[46] It was a warlike toy, and it had its own savage intimations for the future. The site from which it came had been 'liberated' for archaeology by the bombing of 1940. Where the sore is, proverbially, the finger will be.

Notes

1 Lucy Toulmin Smith (ed.), *The itinerary of John Leland in or about the years 1535–1543*, i:278. For the Marini tenancy at West Hall and for a good account of Guidotti's career, see Alwyn Ruddock, *Italian Merchants and Shipping*, pp. 243–5, and 'Antonio Guidotti', *Proc. Hampshire Field Club*, 15 (1941–3), pp. 34–42.

2 Alwyn Ruddock, *Italian Merchants and Shipping*, pp. 246–8; G. V. Scammell, 'Ship-owning in England, *c.* 1450–1550', *T.R.H.S.*, 5th series, 12 (1962), pp. 105–22. For the

office of town clerk and Mille's part in developing it, see A. L. Merson's introduction to the *Third Book of Remembrance*, i:xiii, xix–xx.

3 P.R.O. C1/1223/46.

4 P.R.O. E326/11798; S.C.R.O. SC3/1/1, p. 65; Alwyn Ruddock, op. cit., pp. 266–7. An instructive parallel existed at contemporary Exeter, where the majority of mayoral families had settled comparatively recently in the borough (Wallace T. MacCaffrey, *Exeter, 1540–1640*, pp. 256–7).

5 P.R.O. SP12/209/48.

6 *L. & P. Henry VIII*, xiv:2:155; Alwyn Ruddock, 'London capitalists and the decline of Southampton in the early Tudor period', *Ec.H.R.*, 2nd series, 2 (1949–50), pp. 150–1.

7 W. G. Hoskins, 'English provincial towns in the early sixteenth century', *T.R.H.S.*, 5th series, 6 (1956), pp. 9–10; Sylvia L. Thrupp, *The Merchant Class of Medieval London, 1300–1500*, pp. 191–206.

8 Michael E. Mallett, *The Florentine Galleys in the Fifteenth Century*, pp. 259–60.

9 P.R.O. SP12/156, and Alwyn Ruddock, *Italian Merchants and Shipping*, p. 260. For a full transcript of the 1582 documents, see J. L. Wiggs, 'The seaborne trade of Southampton in the second half of the sixteenth century', Southampton M.A., 1955, Appendix B.

10 *Third Book of Remembrance*, i:20–6, ii:148; *Sign Manuals and Letters Patent*, i:35–7.

11 T. Astle *et al.* (eds), *Taxatio ecclesiastica Angliae et Walliae, auctoritate Papae Nicholai IV, circa A.D. 1291*, pp. 210–11; J. Caley and J. Hunter (eds), *Valor Ecclesiasticus, temp. Henrici VIII, auctoritate regia institutus*, ii:19–20.

12 P.R.O. E179/173/175, E179/174/364; S.C.R.O. SC13/2/2. Similar distinctions between parishes have been observed by W. G. Hoskins, 'English provincial towns in the early sixteenth century', *T.R.H.S.*, 5th series, 6 (1956), p. 19, and 'An Elizabethan provincial town: Leicester', in *Studies in Social History, a Tribute to G. M. Trevelyan*, ed. J. H. Plumb, p. 43.

13 *Third Book of Remembrance*, i:52–3. For a useful discussion of early Tudor legislation against vagrancy, see W. K. Jordan, *Philanthropy in England, 1480–1660*, pp. 83–6.

14 *Third Book of Remembrance*, i:13. Wright was a town sergeant in 1485/6; he is thought to have died in about 1518.

15 P.R.O. SP12/156.

16 E. M. Carus-Wilson and Olive Coleman, *England's Export Trade, 1275–1547*, p. 149; Peter Ramsey, 'Overseas trade in the reign of Henry VII: the evidence of customs accounts', *Ec.H.R.*, 2nd series, 6 (1953–4), pp. 173–82. For a comparable economic miracle at Exeter, see E. M. Carus-Wilson, *The Expansion of Exeter at the Close of the Middle Ages*, passim.

17 Alwyn Ruddock, 'London capitalists and the decline of Southampton in the early Tudor period', *Ec.H.R.*, 2nd series, 2 (1949–50), pp. 137–51.

18 Alwyn Ruddock, 'Antonio Guidotti', *Proc. Hampshire Field Club*, 15 (1941–3), pp. 34–42.

19 P.R.O. C1/1037/50; *L. & P. Henry VIII*, xi:541, xii:2:367, xiii:1:442.

20 S.C.R.O. SC5/1/37, f. 22v; *Statutes of the Realm*, iii:351–2. The problem of the fee farm and the circumstances of its reduction are very fully discussed by A. L. Merson in the introduction to *The Third Book of Remembrance*, i:xxi–xxxi.

21 *Charters*, ii:22–9.

22 *Cal. State Papers Venetian, 1603–7*, p. 124.

23 Ibid., *1555–6*, pp. 535–6; *Charters*, ii:36–9; *Letters Patent*, ii:117–25; Alwyn Ruddock, 'London capitalists and the decline of Southampton in the early Tudor period', *Ec.H.R.*, 2nd series, 2 (1949–50), p. 149.

24 *Cal. State Papers Domestic, 1581–90*, p. 7.

25 P.R.O. SP12/156.

26 *Third Book of Remembrance*, i:27–8; *L. & P. Henry VIII*, xvii:400; B.M. Lansdowne 11/24, 12/64; *Black Book*, iii:166–7.

27 S.C.R.O. SC3/1/1, p. 69v; *Third Book of Remembrance*, i:60–1.

28 *Letters*, pp. 88–9.

29 F. J. Fisher, 'The development of London as a centre of conspicuous consumption in the sixteenth and seventeenth centuries', *T.R.H.S.*, 4th series, 30 (1948), passim.

30 L. G. Wickham Legg (ed.), 'A relation of a short survey of the western counties', in Camden Society, 3rd series, 52 (1936), pp. 55–6; reprinted by Robert Douch, *Visitors' Descriptions of Southampton, 1540–1956*, pp. 9–10. The circumstances of the sixteenth-century Channel Islands trade are discussed by J. L. Wiggs, op. cit., pp. 89–96, 126–8.

31 P.R.O. SP12/156.

32 *Letters*, pp. 134–7. For a discussion of ship-owning at Southampton through the last quarter of the sixteenth century, see R. C. Anderson's introduction and table in the *Book of Examinations*, pp. xxvii–xxxi, 63–74; also J. L. Wiggs, op. cit., chapter vi.

33 *Cal. State Papers Foreign*, xxiii:162; S.C.R.O. SC4/3/120; J. L. Wiggs, op. cit., chapter v.

34 H. M. Godfrey (ed.), *Registre de l'Église Wallonne de Southampton*, Publications of the Huguenot Society, 4 (1890), p. 3; *Cal. State Papers Domestic, Addenda, 1566–79*, pp. 31–2; Ibid., *Spanish, 1568–79*, p. 432; S.C.R.O. SC14/2/9; Davies, pp. 405–6.

35 A. L. Merson, 'Elizabethan Southampton', in *Collected Essays on Southampton*, eds J. B. Morgan and Philip Peberdy, p. 63. A

common practice in this century was the grant of free burgess-ships to prominent men, whether of the county or the court. Sir John Worsley had earned his, conferred on 20 August 1537, 'for divers considerations by him done touching the liberties of the town'. Other free burgesses had already included the abbots of Beaulieu, Netley, Waverley and Quarr. In later years, burgess-ships would be granted to the earls of Southampton, Sir Thomas Leighton, Sir Humphrey Gilbert, Sir Henry Carey, Sir Walter Raleigh and many others (S.C.R.O. SC3/1/1, pp. 57v, 62, 67v–69, 85, 90, 95, 97, 100, 102, etc.).

36 B.M. Add. MS. 25460, f. 141.

37 *Third Book of Remembrance*, ii:110–12.

38 B.M. Add. MS. 14265; S.C.R.O. SC4/2/409; *Black Book*, iii:124–5, 154–65.

39 Win.Coll.Mun. 17888.

40 *Cal. State Papers Colonial, East Indies, China and Japan*, ii:79.

41 Ibid., *America and West Indies*, ix:14–17.

42 *Court Leet Records*, passim.

43 *Southampton Excavations*, forthcoming.

44 S.C.R.O. SC5/1/37, f. 22v.

45 P.R.O. E178/2031 and 5634. Sections recently cut through the ditch fill have confirmed both the date of the filling and the dimensions given in the surveys (*Southampton Excavations*, forthcoming).

46 *Southampton Excavations*, forthcoming; for a general discussion of contemporary military fashions, see John Hale, 'War and public opinion in the fifteenth and sixteenth centuries', *Past & Present*, 22 (1962), pp. 18–33.

Appendices

Appendix 1

a. Biographical notes

Abingdon, Thomas of, *fl.* 1334–55. Married Margaret, formerly the wife of Robert atte Barre and his executor (P.R.O. E101/22/11). Elected bailiff in 1351 and 1354; parliamentary burgess in 1348 and 1355 (Davies, pp. 172, 201 (corrected); P.R.O. E372/196). Appointed controller of customs in 1334, to be confirmed in this office for a ten-year term on 6 May 1336 (*Cal.P.R. 1334–8*, pp. 52, 115, 260–1). Executor of Thomas Marlebrew in 1349 (P.R.O. E326/9359). Held properties in French Street and Above Bar (Bodleian, Queen's College MS. 339, 340; P.R.O. SC12/14/62; S.C.R.O. SC4/2/85).

Ace, Benedict, *fl.* 1230–50. Father of John Beneyt, later rector of Gussage All Saints (God's House Deeds 353); other sons included Thomas and possibly Odo, although the latter is more likely to have been the son of Azo Beneyt (Benedict) who appears on several occasions as a contemporary of Benedict Ace (Ibid., 577). Mayor with few, if any, intermissions from 1230 to 1249 (St Denys Cart. 167; P.R.O. E326/4492; *Cat.Anc. Deeds*, ii:D121; Davies, p. 170). Keeper of the king's wines at Southampton from 1232/3, or possibly earlier, an office in which he was later usually associated with Richard de la Prise (P.R.O. E372/77, 89; *Cal.C.R. 1237–42*, p. 71). Associated with Walter le Fleming in business and other affairs from 1230 (e.g. *Cal.C.R. 1227–31*, p. 285, *1234–7*, p. 94; P.R.O. E372/84, 86; *Cal. Liberate R. 1245–51*, p. 209). Lived in St Michael's, on Bull Street, probably on the corner of Vyse Lane (St Denys Cart. 249), but had other properties on English Street, just north of New Corner, and in Hill (Ibid., 190; *Cal.C.R. 1234–7*, pp. 275–6). His Shirley properties may have descended via Odo to William Ace 'of Freemantle', Odo's son, who owned much property in the 1330s and 1340s in Freemantle, Millbrook, Shirley and Hill (Win.Coll.Mun. 17855–8, 17861–7, 17872–9). Shops on, or near, Westgate Street, 'late of Benedict Ace', are mentioned in 1274 (J. M. Rigg (ed.), *Calendar of the Plea Rolls of the Exchequer of the Jews*, ii:119–20). But Benedict was dead, certainly, in 1267/8, and had probably died at least a decade before (P.R.O. E372/111, 112).

Ambrose, Christopher, *fl.* 1462–98. A Florentine by birth, becoming denizen in 1472 (Alwyn Ruddock, *Italian Merchants and Shipping*, pp. 183–4). His second son, Robert Ambrose, was admitted to a burgess-ship on 9 October 1508 (S.C.R.O. SC3/1/1, p. 54v). Bailiff in 1481–2, sheriff in 1483–4, mayor in 1486–7 and 1497–8 (S.C.R.O. SC4/3/10; Davies, p. 175). As a merchant and factor of Florence, listed among aliens resident in Southampton 1462–8 (P.R.O. E179/173/131–4). Dealt, among other commodities, in wine, cloth, leather, alum and woad (e.g. P.R.O. C1/29/357, C1/31/80, C1/37/13, C1/64/960; S.C.R.O. SC5/1/18, f. 31; *Port Books, 1469–81*, ii:144 and passim). Held property principally in the south-east quarter of the town, including land and buildings outside God's House Gate, a garden plot and barn south of Winkle Street and next to the town wall, and important tenements north of Porters Lane, held from Winchester College (S.C.R.O. SC4/1/1, SC4/3/14–16, SC5/1/15, f. 6b, SC5/1/23, f. 2b; Win.Coll.Mun. 17840; God's House Deeds

465). (N.B. For further details of Christopher Ambrose's career and trading interests, see Dr Ruddock's forthcoming volumes in the Southampton Record Series.)

Andover, Thomas of, *fl.* 1262–75. Father of Thomas (St Denys Cart. 126; S.C.R.O. SC4/2/8). Bailiff in 1262–3 (Davies, p. 170). Dealt in wine and wool, exporting twenty sacks of the latter in 1273 (*Cal.P.R. 1272–81*, p. 22). Concerned in a dispute over wine imports with merchants of Gascony in 1268, and over the balance and weights at the Weigh House with men of the earl of Warwick in 1275 (Ibid., *1266–72*, p. 282, *1272–81*, p. 117). Owned an important tenement, probably his dwelling, on the west side of English Street, parish of Holy Rood, with some property in the suburb on East Street (St Denys Cart. 126, 289; S.C.R.O. SC4/2/2).

Armorer, Thomas, *fl.* 1400–28. Married Isabella and then Matilda, who survived him (*Black Book*, i:78–9; S.C.R.O. SC4/2/259). Steward in 1400–1 and 1402–3 (S.C.R.O. SC4/2/179–80, 187). Bailiff in 1404–5, 1406–8, 1409–15; parliamentary burgess in 1413 and 1414 (Davies, pp. 173, 202). Granted in 1414, in consideration of past services, exemption from all likely duties to king or town (*Black Book*, ii:2–5). As one of four aldermen, witnessed deeds dated 27 April 1417 and 17 January 1417/18 (S.C.R.O. SC4/2/229, 233). Owned tenements on both the east and the west sides of English Street, the latter in the parish of St Lawrence; also tenements in St Michael's on both sides of French Street, and plots in the suburb west of Above Bar Street, including the field known as 'Little Hampton' (*Black Book*, i:78–79, 80–3, 144, ii:23, 26, 38; S.C.R.O. SC4/2/292–3). Matilda is named as his widow in a deed dated 30 November 1430 (S.C.R.O. SC4/2/259).

Aylward, Robert, *fl.* 1430–54. Steward in 1430–1 (S.C.R.O. SC4/2/259, 262–3); elected bailiff in 1433, mayor in 1436, 1441, 1449 and 1453 (Davies, pp. 173–4 (corrected)). Traded principally to Salisbury and the west in wine, soap and dyestuffs, with interests also in cloth and iron (*Brokage Book, 1443–4*, passim; P.R.O. E101/128/31, 34). Host to foreign merchants in 1444 (P.R.O. E179/173/110). Associated with Walter Fetplace in trading ventures and in dealings concerning William Nicholl's lands (P.R.O. E101/128/31; S.C.R.O. SC4/2/271). As alderman, witnessed deeds dated 8 May and 27 December 1445 (S.C.R.O. SC4/2/276, 277a).

Bacon, William, *fl.* 1365–92. There were two William Bacons simultaneously burgesses of Southampton, each holding important offices in the town. It was William Bacon 'the elder' who was appointed surveyor of works at the castle in 1383 (*Cal.P.R. 1381–5*, p. 334), being presumably the William Bacon 'of Bristol' who was associated with John Polymond and John Thorp throughout these works (e.g. P.R.O. E364/13/G and E364/20/B). As William Bacon 'senior', he was parliamentary burgess in 1382 (Davies, p. 201), collector of customs in 1386 (P.R.O. E364/20/G), and mayor in 1388–9 (God's House Deeds 380). Presumably, it was this William Bacon who was living in 1378 in English Street (*Cal.C.R. 1377–81*, p. 213), to be distinguished in this way from the William Bacon 'of St Michael's', parliamentary burgess with John Polymond in 1380 (Davies, p. 201). The latter, then, may have been the William Bacon 'junior' who became steward in 1372–3 and mayor in 1373–4 (S.C.R.O. SC4/2/108, 111; Davies, p. 172). It is tempting to identify him with the William Bacon Wytegod who died a bastard without issue in 1392–3, briefly survived by his widow, Isabel. The bulk of his property, recorded in inquests and court proceedings in 1397 and 1402, lay in St Michael's, and it may be that it derived at least in part from John Wytegod, former mayor and a considerable property-owner in the parish (P.R.O. C47/60/8/297, *Cal.C.R. 1399–1402*, pp. 425–7; *Cal.Inq.Misc. 1399–1422*. pp. 104–5). Certainly, John Wytegod and William Bacon appear together on at least three witness lists in 1366–8 (S.C.R.O. SC4/2/101–3). Should this identification be correct, it would suggest that the John Bacon, citizen and grocer of London, who claimed in 1409 and 1413 to be the son and heir of the late William Bacon, was in fact the son of William Bacon 'senior' (God's House Deeds 365; *Black Book*, i:146–9).

Bagge, Richard, *fl.* 1312–24. Survived by Richard, his son and heir (Win.Coll.Mun. 17847). Bailiff in 1319–20 (Davies, p. 171). In 1312 associated with Thomas Nostschilling in the receipt of stolen wines (*Cal.C.R. 1307–13*, pp. 487–8). Acted in 1316–17 as the intermediary in a transaction concerning former

Halveknight property on Simnel Street (S.C.R.O. SC4/2/15–19). Lost his ship *La Seint Denis*, and a valuable cargo of salt, to Breton pirates in 1319 (*Cal.C.R. 1318–23*, p. 209). Witnessed deeds in 1321 and 1324 (S.C.R.O. SC4/2/30, 34). Died before 1332, when Richard, his son, granted to Nicholas de Moundenard the two shops and chamber bequeathed to him by Richard Bagge 'senior'. They were situated on the east side of English Street, parish of St Lawrence (Win.Coll.Mun. 17847).

Banastre, Nicholas, *fl.* 1416–36. An associate of William Soper in the building of the *Gracedieu*, begun in the autumn of 1416 (P.R.O. E364/57/I). Appointed, on 5 March 1423, to the controllership of the king's ships at Southampton, two days after he had been named, with William Soper and John Foxholes, as a commissioner for the sale of certain surplus ships of the king's navy (*Cal.P.R. 1422–9*, pp. 57, 64, 70; *Cal.C.R. 1422–9*, p. 58). In 1416/17 held a tenement on Broad Lane immediately west of the great corner tenement then of Sir Richard de Montague (P.R.O. E326/11785). Acquired 'Suttonesplace' in Shirley in 1420; three years before, the estate had come to William and Alice Nicholl, with a tenement on English street (*Cal.C.R. 1419–22*, p. 62; *Black Book*, ii:15–16; S.C.R.O. SC4/2/244). It was probably this estate which had come to be known by 1493 as the manor called 'Banaster Court', to be listed in that year among the possessions of the late Thomas Banastre (*Cal.Inq.P.M.*, xiii:368–9). Nicholas himself was still active in 1436 (S.C.R.O. SC4/2/267–8).

Barber, John le, *fl.* 1316–30. Husband of Christina la Ryder; father of Nicholas and one other son (S.C.R.O. SC4/2/60; Bodleian, Queen's College MS. 257). Elected bailiff in 1321, 1323, 1324 and 1329; parliamentary burgess in 1327 (Davies, pp. 171, 200). With William Sampson and William le Horder, clerk for the recognizance of debts at Southampton from 1316 to 1327 (S.C.R.O. SC2/6/1, SC4/2/42; P.R.O. CP40/272, m. 81). Was closely associated for many years with the hospital at God's House. In 1321, when 'town clerk', received a gift of wheat from the hospital for his good offices; in 1326 was pardoned his rent; and in 1329 did business at God's House, dining at high table at least twice (*R.C.H.M.*, 6th report, pp. 565, 567; Bodleian, Queen's College MS. 257). In 1327, in the subsidy accounts of that year, was assessed at 40*s*. (P.R.O. E179/173/4, m.17v). In that same year, was judged to be insufficiently qualified to serve as coroner (*Cal.C.R. 1327–30*, p. 11). Held three shops on the south side of East Street just inside the gate, which his son, Nicholas, later exchanged with St Denys; also a tenement and garden on the east side of English Street, parish of St Lawrence (St Denys Cart. 133, 135–7, 170; P.R.O. E326/8036, 9314, 9332). Other properties included an important tenement with cellar and shop on the west side of English Street, parish of Holy Rood, and two messuages, also described as shops, at the Strand, parish of All Saints Without (S.C.R.O. SC4/2/46, 60–1, 63).

Barber, Robert le, *fl.* 1290–1303. Son of Roger and brother of Simon le Barber (God's House Deeds 658). Husband of Isabella; father of Richard and Matilda, later wife of Gaillard de Moundenard (Win.Coll.Mun. 17761). Alderman or bailiff in 1290–1; alderman again in 1291–2, in 1298–9 and in a year, possibly 1296–7, between (Davies, p. 170; St Denys Cart. 260; S.C.R.O. SC4/2/11). Associated with Peter de Lyon and John of Holebury in financial arrangements concerning the galley built at Southampton in 1295 (P.R.O. E101/5/2). Partner of Robert le Mercer and John of Holebury in a large shipment of wool (P.R.O. E372/158). Held four shops on East Street, a tenement on the east side of English Street, parish of Holy Rood, and the great tenement known as 'La Chayne' on Porters Lane (*Cat.Anc. Deeds*, i:B1413; St Denys Cart. 151; S.C.R.O. SC4/2/4; Win.Coll.Mun. 17761). Does not appear as principal or witness after *c.* 1303.

Barbflete, John, *fl.* 1372–1412. Grandson of Richard de Barbflete; son of John Barbflete and Joan la Smale, daughter of William le Smale (S.C.R.O. SC4/2/56, 108). He may never have married, for he is known to have dined regularly at high table at God's House and would seem to have died without issue (Bodleian, Queen's College MS. 296, 301, 312, 316A & B; God's House Deeds 1091). Elected bailiff in 1402 (Davies, p. 173). At various times held a tenement on the east side of French Street, tenements and shops on the west side of English Street, and another tenement on Simnel Street (*Cal.C.R. 1399–1402*,

p. 426, *1409–13*, p. 132; Win.Coll.Mun. 17833; S.C.R.O. SC4/2/108, 112, 119, 133, 155, 196). His will, dated 4 April 1412, was proved on 24 July. The hospital at God's House was principal legatee (God's House Deeds 1091).

Barbflete, Nicholas de, *fl.* 1267–95. Husband of Agatha and Alice (J. Speed, *History of Southampton*, p. 135). Survived by his son and next heir, Nicholas, who reappears in 1300 as the purchaser of the pesage of wool in the port (*Cal.Inq.P.M.*, iii:154; *Cal. Fine R.*, i:359; *Cal.P.R. 1292–1301*, p. 492; P.R.O. E372/157). Spanish merchants were lodging with him in 1267 (*Cal.P.R. 1266–72*, p. 169). Appointed in 1269 to the keepership of the king's wines at Southampton (Ibid., p. 392). In 1275 concerned with Thomas of Andover and others in a dispute over weights at the Weigh House (Ibid., *1272–81*, p. 117). Bailiff at least once in the 1280s (St Denys Cart. 21). In 1290 granted his spring at Hill to the friars, to make a conduit to their house in the town (*Cal.P.R. 1281–92*, p. 12). Held the manor of Shirley and Hill, which descended to Richard de Barbflete, son of Robert, and thence by way of Matilda of Holebury, his widow, to Roger Norman (*Cal.C.R. 1346–9*, p. 258). Died in 1295 (*Cal.Inq.P.M.*, iii:154; *Cal. Fine R.*, i:359).

Barbflete, Richard de, *fl.* 1303–28. Son of Robert de Barbflete and Lucya Fortin; brother of Nicholas, Robert, Rosya and Isabella, who married Thomas le Barber 'of Bristol'. Married Matilda, daughter and heir of John of Holebury, having by her a son, John, and a daughter, Alice, who married William Jardyn (S.C.R.O. SC4/2/41, 43–4; God's House Deeds 402, 413, 419). Bailiff in 1315–6 (Win.Coll.Mun. 17897). Alderman in 1317–18 (Davies, p. 171). Held an important tenement on French Street, south of Broad Lane, which he bequeathed to his son (S.C.R.O. SC2/6/2, SC4/2/45; Bodleian, Queen's College MS. 340); also a house on the east side of English Street, parish of Holy Rood (S.C.R.O. SC4/2/45). Assessed at 40*s.* in 1327 (P.R.O. E179/173/4, m.17v). Made his last appearance as a witness in that year, and must have died in or before 1329, having at that time an interest in the manor of Shirley and Hill, formerly of Nicholas de Barbflete, who may have been his uncle (S.C.R.O. SC4/2/45; *Cal.C.R. 1346–9*, p. 258). Was possibly the Richard 'de Biflet' who was dismissed from the office of tronage of wool in Southampton in November 1328, because he 'does not behave himself well in the said office' (*Cal.C.R. 1327–30*, p. 341).

Barre, John atte, *fl.* 1372–95. Probably the son of John atte Barre (d. before 1349) and grandson of John de Puteo; husband of Joan and father of Agnes (S.C.R.O. SC4/2/87; Win.Coll.Mun. 17833). Steward in 1374–5 (S.C.R.O. SC4/2/112; Win.Coll.Mun. 17814, 17892, 17905). At one time had an interest in the great corner tenement on English Street and Broad Lane, formerly of Henry de Lym, but sold this to Sir John de Montague in 1378 (P.R.O. E326/11787, 11805). May have been in financial difficulties in 1380, for he was bound in that year to Roger Mascall in a debt of £80 (S.C.R.O. SC4/2/127–9, 137). Properties included a tenement on the east side of English Street, parish of Holy Rood, in which he may have lived; also a tenement on the west side of the street, in the parish of St Lawrence, with a vacant plot on Broad Lane behind his former corner tenement there, and rents on the property immediately south of that tenement (S.C.R.O. SC4/2/119, 133, 144; P.R.O. E326/11805; Win.Coll.Mun. 17833). Died before 1397, survived by his wife, Joan (S.C.R.O. SC4/2/169).

Barre, Robert atte, *fl.* 1313–39. Son of John de Puteo, also known as John atte Barre, and of Hawise his wife; brother of John and Nicholas atte Barre; husband of Margaret, subsequently the wife of Thomas of Abingdon (*Cat.Anc. Deeds*, ii:B3385; St Denys Cart. 211; Bodleian, Queen's College MS. 339; P.R.O. E101/22/11). Elected bailiff in 1326, 1328, 1330, 1332, 1333, 1334 and 1336; parliamentary burgess in February 1323/4 and February 1337/8 (Davies, pp. 171, 200). Collector of customs at Southampton, with Henry le Fleming (*Cal.C.R. 1339–41*, p. 419). Receiver of the king's money and victuals in the town, probably from 1337 or earlier (Ibid., *1333–7*, p. 641, *1337–9*, pp. 304–5, *1339–41*, p. 175). Assessed at 100*s.* in the subsidy accounts of 1327 and 1332 (P.R.O. E179/173/4, m. 17v, E179/242/15a, m. 8v). Was living, in 1326/7, in a tenement on the west side of English Street, opposite St Lawrence Church (St Denys Cart. 192). Held other properties in the eastern suburbs, on both sides of English Street in the parish of Holy Rood, and on the sea shore at West Hithe by the gate of Simnel

Street (Ibid., 62; S.C.R.O. SC4/2/45, 56, 57; P.R.O. E326/8897, 9351). Died in June or July 1339 (*Cal.C.R. 1339–41*, p. 175).

Bassingrom, William (senior), *fl.* 1291–1316. Husband of Petronilla la Halveknight; father of Joan, Matilda (m. John Driberd), Agnes and Felicia (m. John of Chilworth). It was probably his son, Thomas, who was killed by Walter le Halveknight in 1312/13 (St Denys Cart. 177–80; P.R.O. E210/9312, E326/9340; *Cal.C.R. 1307–13*, p. 506). Elected bailiff in 1300, and for at least one other session, when John of Shirley was alderman (S.C.R.O. SC4/2/4; Win.Coll.Mun. 17896; Davies, p. 170). Between 1298/9 and 1303, acquired the former Isembard tenement, once of Ralph and then of James Isembard, on the east side of English Street, parish of St Lawrence (St Denys Cart. 173–6). Inherited, by right of his wife, Petronilla, an important share in West Hall, partitioned by the executors of Thomas le Halveknight in 1303/4 (P.R.O. E327/163; St Denys Cart. 242; God's House Deeds 476; S.C.R.O. SC4/2/396). In 1314, compelled by financial difficulties to lease his West Hall property for a seven-year term (B.M. Add.Ch. 685). Died in 1316, making provision in his will for the sale of half of the former Isembard messuage in St Lawrence, to meet his outstanding debts (St Denys Cart. 177).

Bassingrom, William (junior), *fl.* 1307–18. His relationship to William Bassingrom 'senior' is unclear, although he could possibly have been his son. Husband of Isabella and father of Luke, Richard and Matilda; grandfather, by Matilda, of Isabella (Bodleian, Queen's College MS. 1072; S.C.R.O. D/LY/23/1, SC2/6/1). Elected bailiff in 1311 and 1317; parliamentary burgess in 1313 (Davies, pp. 171, 200). Concerned in the confiscation, in 1313, of goods of Frisian merchants (*Cal.C.R. 1307–13*, p. 535). Probably lived in Simnel Street, where he had his capital tenement and shop called 'la putselde'. But also had a corner tenement by the fish market in St Michael's Square. By the terms of his will, proved at St Michael's Church in May 1318, these properties were to go, after the death of their mother, to Luke and Richard respectively (Bodleian, Queen's College MS. 1072; *R.C.H.M.*, 6th report, p. 552). Another legatee, Nicholas Bassingrom, is described as his clerk. Nicholas was appointed joint-executor of William's will, was assessed at 40*s*. in 1327 and 30*s*. in 1332, and reappeared in 1336 as the holder of a tenement on the west side of English Street, parish of St Lawrence (P.R.O. E179/173/4, m. 17v, E179/242/15a, m. 8v; S.C.R.O. SC4/2/58). Isabella, relict of William Bassingrom, was still alive in 1330/1. She had allowed great arrears of rent to accumulate on her tenement on the east side of Bull Street, in St Michael's. The property was resumed by God's House and re-granted to Henry de Lym (God's House Deeds 590). Mysteriously, William Bassingrom was still witnessing deeds in June 1318 and in 1319/20 (S.C.R.O. SC4/2/24, 28).

Benet, John, *fl.* 1393–1420. Elected bailiff in 1403, mayor in 1409, 1413 and 1418 (Davies, p. 173). Served as steward in 1404–5 (S.C.R.O. SC4/2/193, 196). In 1407 and 1410, was among those alleged to have withheld rents from God's House and St Denys (*Cal.C.R. 1405–9*, pp. 178–82, *1409–13*, pp. 132–3). Accounted, during his mayoralty, for works on the castle and at God's House Gate, a four-year programme beginning in July 1417 (P.R.O. E364/55/F). Lived, from 1393 or before, in a tenement, with a 'great gate', north of the fish market, but also held other property in St Michael's, on the west side of French Street and at New Corner (S.C.R.O. D/CJ/30; *Black Book*, i:139–43; *Cal.C.R. 1422–9*, p. 47). On his death, probably in the summer of 1420, left money to the town to take up and re-lay the pipes of the friary water conduit, and to build a new conduit house at Holy Rood. John Fleming was one of his executors (S.C.R.O. SC4/2/238).

Bettes, James, *fl.* 1518–39. Father of Thomas Bettes; grandfather of James, and probably of William Bettes (S.C.R.O. SC3/1/1, pp. 67v, 90; P.R.O. Req. 2/279/51; *Third Book of Remembrance*, ii:20n, iii:9n). Appointed, on 7 December 1518, to a collectorship of customs at Southampton, in succession to Sir John Dawtrey (*L. & P. Henry VIII*, ii:2:1415–6). Friend and patron of Henry Huttoft, asking in 1522 for a collectorship of customs for him, in place of Richard Palshid (Ibid., iii:1041–2). A correspondent of Thomas Cromwell's on the subject of the patronage of St Mary's Chantry, 1529–35 (Ibid., iv:2:2649, vii:143, ix:26). In 1536 seeking the help of Cromwell to meet, or hold off, debts 'incurred by reason of certain strangers that I trusted' and still not paid by the end of the following year (Ibid., xi:541, xii:2:367). With Nicholas Dey, then mayor, took charge of the contents of the friary on its surrender in October 1538 (Ibid., xiii:2:212). Died, probably, in 1539–40 (*Third Book of Remembrance*, i:56n). After his death, his son and grandsons farmed the former St Denys lands at Northam, holding them from Sir Francis Dawtrey, with Kingsland and the St Denys interest on Hoglands (Ibid., ii:20–1, 119n; P.R.O. Req. 2/279/51, E310/24/131/6, 25).

Blund, Thomas le, *fl.* 1270–95. Elected bailiff in 1270 and 1272, with at least two other periods of office while Robert le Mercer was alderman; himself alderman in 1294–5 (Davies, p. 170; St Denys Cart. 99, 200; *Cat. Anc. Deeds*, ii:B3311). The second of that name in the town, for an earlier 'Thomas Blundus' had been bailiff in 1248–9, appearing also in witness lists of 1230 and 1250 (Davies, p. 170; St Denys Cart. 92, 167). It was probably this earlier Thomas le Blund who was viewer of the king's works, with Thomas de Puteo, in 1257 (*Cal. Liberate R. 1251–60*, p. 413).

Bonhait, Robert, *fl.* 1269–86. A descendant, very probably, of the brothers William and Warin Bonhait (God's House Deeds 522; St Denys Cart. 167, 258). Married Alice, daughter of Walter le Fleming, who died some years before him (God's House Deeds 356, 517). Father of John and probably grandfather of Richard Bonhait. John, described as a 'smith', later occupied a tenement on the west side of English Street, backing on the castle ditch; Richard, in the accounts of the lay subsidy of 1332, was assessed at 20*s*. (P.R.O. E179/242/15a, m. 8v, E210/6997; St Denys Cart. 99; S.C.R.O. SC4/2/5, 6, 9, 10, 11, 26, 29, 41, 44, 46). Robert himself was both bailiff and alderman at least twice in the 1270s and 1280s (St Denys Cart. 21, 63, 98, 200; Win.Coll.Mun. 17895). In 1273, he founded a chaplaincy at St Michael's church in memory of his wife, Alice. The endowment included a house on the west side of French Street, parish of St Michael's, formerly the tenement of Simon le Franceys, grandfather of Alice, in which Alice and Robert themselves had lived. It was sited opposite the great stone houses once of Richard of Leicester (God's House Deeds 356, 369, 517). Robert also owned a tenement on the east side of English Street, in which he may later have lived. It was sited in the parish of Holy Rood, 'towards the sea' (S.C.R.O. SC4/2/7; God's House Deeds 369, 517).

Bourgoyne, John de, *fl.* 1291–1302. Husband of Cecilia, daughter of Henry le Long (S.C.R.O. SC4/2/10). Bailiff in 1295–6 and on at least one other occasion during the 1290s (Davies, p. 170; S.C.R.O. SC4/2/7, 8). Bought, in 1296 or thereabouts, an important stone-built tenement, with a 'great gate', from his father-in-law. It cost him £40 in silver, and was sited on the west side of French Street, north of West Hall, parish of St Hohn. Seems to have lived there until his death in, or before, 1303; but the tenement had reverted to the Long family by 1326, when it was divided between John and Hugh le Long, the surviving sons of Henry (S.C.R.O. SC4/2/10, 36–7, 396).

Brackley, Walter of, *fl.* 1316–45. Elected alderman in 1326; it was either this Walter or a namesake who served as bailiff from 1336 to 1340, through the crisis of the French raid and its aftermath (Davies, p. 171 (corrected); P.R.O. E210/9312). From 1316, regularly witnessed charters and other documents in the company of other leading burgesses (S.C.R.O. SC4/2/14, 20–1, 25–7, 33, 35–7, 39–40, 45, 48, 56–7, 63, 65–6, 79–80, 404). In the lay subsidy accounts of 1327 and 1332, assessed at £10 and £25 respectively, featuring as one of the wealthier men in the town (P.R.O. E179/173/4, m. 17v, E179/242/15a, m. 8v). By 1342, had come to hold an important share in the partitioned West Hall, which he had probably acquired before 1335. This descended, by way of his heirs, to Adam and Margery Brabason (Bodleian, Queen's College MS. 4G10; S.C.R.O. SC4/2/57). Made his last appearance as a witness in August 1345 (S.C.R.O. SC4/2/80).

Bradway, Richard, *fl.* 1387–1415. Husband of Alice; father of Richard 'junior'; grandfather of Richard, who married Christina and had a son, William (Davies, pp. 376–7; *Cal.C.R. 1447–54*, p. 237; *Black Book*, ii:6). Elected steward in 1387 and 1391; bailiff in 1397 and 1398; mayor in 1405, appearing thereafter as an alderman; parliamentary burgess in 1399 (S.C.R.O. SC4/2/151, 175–6, 178, 198, 201, 209–10, 212, 218, 222, 407–8; Davies, pp. 172–3, 201). Shown, in 1407 and

1410, to have been withholding substantial rents from both God's House and St Denys (*Cal.C.R. 1405–9*, pp. 178–82, *1409–13*, pp. 132–3). In 1396 acquired from the executors of John Polymond a stone house and cellar on the north side of Porters Lane (S.C.R.O. SC4/2/164–5; P.R.O. C146/9697). Concerned earlier, with Polymond and Alexander Dey, in the alleged fraudulent mishandling of William Bacon Wytegod's estate (*Cal.C.R. 1399–1402*, pp. 425–7). Main properties centred on St Lawrence, on both sides of English Street. But also owned a croft of arable land in the St Mary suburb, behind East Street. Died in December 1415 (Davies, pp. 376–7; P.R.O. E326/6691, 9068; *Black Book*, i:24–5, 48–51).

Bulehuse, John de la, *fl.* 1220–43. Son of Hugh of Hampton and nephew, or close relative, of Thomas de la Bulehuse (God's House Deeds 342, 751). Husband of Alice, daughter of William of St Laurence; father of Simon, John, Bartholomew, Joseph and one other son, and of Cecilia, probably the Cecilia who married Richard le English (St Denys Cart. 63–4; P.R.O. E372/98; J. M. Rigg (ed.), *Calendar of the Plea Rolls of the Exchequer of the Jews*, i:57). In 1221 presented the Southampton farm at the Exchequer, co-operating later in various royal works with Richard of Leicester, Robert le Moigne, and Benedict Ace, with whom he was associated in a sale of the king's wines in 1242/3 (P.R.O. E372/65, 68, 69, 87). Steward in 1240–1 and bailiff on at least one occasion in the 1230s (St Denys Cart. 207; *Cat.Anc. Deeds*, iii:D121; Davies, p. 170). Lived in a corner house in St Michael's, possibly at New Corner. Owned six acres in Hoglands, which came eventually to St Denys, and had other properties and interests in French Street, in the northern suburbs and in Newtown (St Denys Cart. 36, 63–4, 67, 73, 254, 258). Held a large stone house on the east side of English Street, in 1269 'once called the vault of John de la Bulehuse' and possibly the property in Holy Rood he had acquired originally from Beaulieu Abbey (God's House Deeds 366; B.M. Loans 29/330, f. 123). Died before 1244, survived by his wife and six children (J. M. Rigg (ed.), op. cit., i:57; P.R.O. E372/98). Simon reappears as bailiff before 1258 and as alderman in 1270–1; he was in prison in 1254, paying a fine for his release (P.R.O. E372/98; *Cal.C.R. 1253–4*, p. 72; *Cat.Anc. Deeds*, ii:B3280; Davies, p. 170). Bartholomew, deeply in debt to Jews of Winchester in 1268, four years later confirmed the reversion of his father's property in Hoglands to St Denys. He made other transfers of land to St Denys in Above Bar and in St Mary's, the latter to endow obits at the priory for his parents, his wife, Isabel, and himself (*Cal.C.R. 1264–8*, p. 462; J. M. Rigg (ed.), op. cit., i:167; St Denys Cart. 63–4; P.R.O. E326/4257; *Cat.Anc. Deeds*, ii:B3284). Roger and Juliana de la Bulehuse, both of whom feature in thirteenth-century deeds, were the children of Thomas de la Bulehuse, a notable figure in the town at the beginning of the century (God's House Deeds 603; *Pipe Roll 13 John*, p. 186). Roger had partnered Richard of Totnes in 1238–9 in the supervision of repairs at the castle and its quay (P.R.O. E372/83). He was still alive in 1270, when he quitclaimed to James Isembard his father's great tenement on Bull Street, known as the Bulehuse, later Bull Hall (God's House Deeds 600, 604).

Burche, William atte, *fl.* 1338–43. Married Isabella, formerly wife of William atte Hurne, a sea captain like himself (P.R.O. E210/9312; *Cal.C.R. 1323–7*, p. 611). In 1343, master of *La Jonette*, arrested by command of the king for leaving the port of Brest without permission, having gone there on his service (Ibid., *1343–6*, p. 129). Lived, very probably, on the east side of English Street, parish of St Lawrence (P.R.O. E210/9312, E326/9325, 9332, 9341). His property on the other side of the street was badly damaged in the raid of 1338. In 1341, he granted it away for life on a rebuilding lease, possibly influenced by the experience of his kinsman Adam, a lessee of property of God's House. Adam atte Burche and Alice, his wife, had held a tenement, burnt in the raid, on French Street, opposite the east end of St Michael's church. They re-negotiated their lease on 25 February 1340, securing the reduction by half of their rent as the precondition for rebuilding (S.C.R.O. SC4/2/67–8; God's House Deeds 565). The family relationships of the Burches are obscure. Adam and Richard atte Burche feature in the lay subsidy accounts of 1332; they were assessed at 30*s*. and 100*s*. respectively (P.R.O. E179/242/15a, m. 8v). Besides these, there was a Robert atte Burche, later of Eling, married to Elena and then to Alice. He was captain of a ship called *La Margarete* in the late 1330s, of which another kinsman, Walter atte Burche, was joint-patron with Henry Imberd. His lands in Eling were inherited from his father, Edward atte Burche (St Denys Cart. 235; S.C.R.O. SC4/2/91, 100–1; P.R.O. E372/194). Juliana atte Burche, described as a widow in 1368, had property in St Michael's, part of which she granted to John Polymond in that year. The remainder was still held by her grandson, John Bray, in 1400, as son and heir of Alice Bray, her daughter (Win.Coll. Mun. 17885–6). Gillot atte Burche was a sister at God's House in 1375–6 (Richard Harris, 'God's House, Southampton, in the reign of Edward III', Southampton M.A. dissertation, 1970, p. 16).

Byndon, Thomas de, *fl.* 1307–41. Probably the son of John and Juliana de Byndon, like himself property-owners in Holy Rood (P.R.O. E327/695; St Denys Cart. 233). Husband of Joanna (P.R.O. E372/192). Alderman, with Nicholas de Lyon and Hugh Sampson as bailiffs, before 1315, with other terms of office in 1316–17, 1324–5, 1331–2 and 1336–7; he may also have been alderman in 1329–30; parliamentary burgess in 1332 (S.C.R.O. SC4/2/19, 21, 22, 25, 31, 36, 46, 48; Davies, pp. 171, 200). Assessed, in the lay subsidy accounts of 1327 and 1332, at £20 and £30 respectively (P.R.O. E179/173/4, m. 17v, E179/242/15a, m. 8v). At various times, collector of the town farm for Queen Isabella, collector of customs and receiver of wool for the king (*Cal.C.R. 1327–30*, p. 243, *1337–9*, p. 361, *1339–41*, pp. 550–1). As a prominent ship-owner in the port, was frequently called upon to supply ships for the royal service and to help the king in matters of prize and fleet muster (e.g. P.R.O. E372/170, 171, 184, 210; *Cal.P.R. 1324–7*, p. 317; *Cal.C.R. 1327–30*, p. 434, *1337–9*, p. 27, *1339–41*, p. 343). Seems to have dealt principally in victuals and in wine, owning a wine tavern of his own (P.R.O. SC8/237/11828, SC8/324/E.625; *Cal.C.R. 1330–3*, pp. 147–8; *Cat.Anc. Deeds*, ii:B3406). In 1321, completed negotiations, begun some years before, for the purchase and transfer to St Denys Priory of a new site for Holy Rood church, immediately east of the old (*Cat.Anc. Deeds*, ii:B3443; *Cal.P.R. 1317–21*, p. 535; P.R.O. C143/140/19, E326/4491). His property concentrated at the south end of English and French streets, including the site of the later Customs House. He seems to have lived there both before and after the raid of 1338, in which his tenements sustained some damage (Bodleian, Queen's College MS. 339, 340; *Cat.Anc. Deeds*, ii:B3406). To judge from the agistment of men-at-arms of *c.* 1341, he had become by that date the wealthiest man in the town, with the probable exception of Roger Norman who does not feature in the list (P.R.O. C47/2/39/42). Died in, or before, 1342 (St Denys Cart. 237; *Cat.Anc. Deeds*, ii:B3408).

Chamberleyn, John, *fl.* 1410–54. Husband of Joan (S.C.R.O. SC4/2/285). Father of the Thomas Chamberleyn who was parliamentary burgess in 1453 and executor of William Soper's will (Davies, p. 202; *Black Book*, ii:112–13, 122–5; *History of Parliament* (*Biographies*), *1439–1509*, pp. 171–2). Was in receipt of a royal pension of 6*d.* per day, granted originally by Henry IV and confirmed by Henry V on his accession to the throne (P.R.O. E372/272). In the last years of Henry V, clerk of the king's works at Portsmouth (P.R.O. E364/57/I). In 1432/3, described as a goldsmith (P.R.O. E372/278). Lived in a large tenement 'with three roofs and two vaults' on the west side of English Street, towards the northern boundary of Holy Rood (S.C.R.O. SC13/1). He had it on a 24-year lease from Walter Fetplace 'senior', at a rent of £4 (S.C.R.O. SC4/2/269, 285). The John Chamberleyn who was lodging at God's House in 1396–7 was of Cornish origin, presumably the brother, or other close relative, of Thomas Chamberleyn, father of William, Ralph and Robert. He died in, or before, 1421, leaving a widow, Joan, and a son, William (Bodleian, Queen's College MS. 296, 316b; God's House Deeds 431–2).

Chamberleyn, William, *fl.* 1419–45. Son of Thomas Chamberleyn, of Grampound in Cornwall, the purchaser in 1400 of the Botiller lands in St Michael's, Holy Rood and the East Street suburb, and probably the same Thomas Chamberleyn who featured in the God's House accounts of the 1390s (*Cal.C.R. 1441–7*, pp. 205–6; *Black Book*, i:56–61; Bodleian, Queen's College MS. 315a, 316a). Husband of Margery; father of William and Joan; brother of Ralph and Robert Chamberleyn (*Black Book*, ii:34–5; *Cal.C.R. 1422–9*, pp. 462–3; God's House Deeds 436, 438). Parliamentary burgess, usually with William Soper, in 1419, 1420, 1427, 1429, 1431, 1432, 1433, 1435 and 1442 (Davies, p. 202; *History of Parliament* (*Biographies*), *1439–1509*, p. 172). In 1428/9, acted for the town in securing the enrolment of its charter and in obtaining letters patent (*Stewards' Books*, i:34–9). In 1423 and 1427, negotiated with Rome, on behalf of himself and his wife, the right to obtain a plenary indulgence at the hour of death and to maintain a private oratory (*Cal.Pap.Reg.*, *Papal Letters*, vii:303, 337). Connected, by way of his brother, Ralph Chamberleyn, with the wealthy Inkepenne family of Winchester. Ralph married Alice, daughter of Richard Inkepenne, bringing back to his own Southampton family the considerable properties in Freemantle, Millbrook and Shirley originally granted to Robert de Inkepenne by the Aces, William and John (Win. Coll.Mun. 17868–9). In 1433, William acquired certain Winchester properties from Margery, widow of Robert Inkepenne, and in 1438 was himself holding Richard Inkepenne's former Winchester tenements (Ibid., 17871; *Cal.C.R. 1429–35*, p. 288). At various times, held lands and rents on both sides of English Street, parish of Holy Rood; on the west side of French Street, parish of St Michael; on Simnel Street; on the north side of St Michael's Square, to the south of St Michael's church; and in the suburbs of Above Bar, East Street and Newtown (God's House Deeds, 433, 434, 437, 438; S.C.R.O. SC4/2/245, 251, 252, 265, 349; *Cal.C.R. 1422–9*, pp. 47, 462–3; *Black Book*, ii:32–5). Died on 6 April 1445 (*History of Parliament* (*Biographies*), *1439–1509*, p. 172).

Claramunda, *fl.* 1250–60. Survived two husbands, Brunus (probably Brunus 'de Byllote') and Stephen Jociaume (St Denys Cart. 87; P.R.O. E327/633). Her relationship to the Gloucesters is obscure, but Claramunda may have been the sister of Walter of Gloucester, for his sons (William, Richard and Nicholas) claimed, after her death, to be holding her property by hereditary right, and one of his three daughters, Claremund, could well have been named after her (P.R.O. E210/5324; God's House Deeds 510–11; St Denys Cart. 81). In 1253, granted exemption from all royal tallages (*Cal.P.R. 1247–58*, p. 209). In 1258, sold wine to the king and was probably trading in her own right (*Cal.Liberate R. 1251–60*, p. 438). Held for life, at a rent of 40*s*., the great tenement on the western shore known as 'Ronceval'. She seems to have lived there, assembling other properties and interests in the area, including a tenement immediately south of Bull Hall and a plot of land between Ronceval itself and the Fleming property at Martin's Hall (*Cat.Anc. Deeds*, ii:B3436–7; P.R.O. E210/5324; *Cal.C.R. 1279–88*, p. 87). Also had extensive suburban interests in the northern suburb and at the Strand (St Denys Cart. 36, 57, 67, 72–3, 78–81, 84–7). A benefactress of Quarr Abbey, to which she granted her tenement south of Bull Hall, but perhaps more particularly of St Denys Priory, to which she transferred suburban and other rents to endow a fund for the purchase of communion wine (*Cat.Anc. Deeds*, ii:B3437; God's House Deeds 603–4; St Denys Cart. 87). Died, apparently without surviving children, in 1260, or just before. Her personal possessions at the time were said to have included a chest of jewellery and plate (*Cal.P.R. 1258–66*, pp. 92–3, 104–5).

Clerk, John le, *fl.* 1343–81(?). First appears in 1343 as a 'mariner', married to Alice and holding a tenement on the west side of English Street, parish of Holy Rood (S.C.R.O. SC4/2/73). Before 1361 was married again, this time to Joan, widow of Thomas atte Marche and daughter and heiress of Hugh Sampson (Bodleian, Queen's College MS. 4G10; S.C.R.O. SC4/2/92). Joan had a daughter, another Joan, probably by her previous marriage. Her daughter's son, John Hargreve, was quitclaiming property to the Chamberleyns early in the next century (*Cal.C.R. 1422–9*, p. 47). Elected bailiff in 1344; mayor in 1354, 1362 and 1363; parliamentary burgess in 1351, 1355, 1358, 1361, 1363, 1365, 1372 and 1373 (Davies, pp. 172, 201). While mayor in 1355, supervised the repair of a ship in the service of Edward, the Black Prince. The connection seems to have been cultivated, for on 1 August 1363 the prince granted John le Clerk a pension of £10 'for good service in past and future' (*Register of Edward the Black Prince, 1351–65*, pp. 143, 504). In 1360, reported to have lost his temper and to have threatened to break the heads of those who came to clear his garden, or orchard, in Newtown to improve the defences of the town. John Fysmark acted as mediator on his behalf (*Cal.Inq.Misc. 1348–77*, pp. 154–5). Other properties included Hugh Sampson's portion of West Hall, descended to him by way of his wife and her former husband, Thomas atte Marche; also, briefly, La Chayne (with John Wytegod); a tenement called 'la Wayehus', or 'le Wolhous', on the east side of Bull Street; and properties on the east side of English Street, parishes of

Holy Rood and St Lawrence (Bodleian, Queen's College MS. 4G10; *Cal.Inq.P.M.*, xv:25–6; Win.Coll.Mun. 17779; S.C.R.O. SC2/6/3, SC4/2/92, 102, 105, 106, 407). One of the collectors of the poll tax in Southampton, both in 1377 and 1381 (P.R.O. E179/173/31, 46, E359/8b, m. 18, 8c, m. 4). But this may have been another John le Clerk, for the original John is described as John le Clerk 'senior' in 1388, in a charter relating to property adjoining his former tenement on Bull Street (S.C.R.O. SC4/2/407).

Dawtrey, Sir John, *fl.* 1490–1518. Son of Andrew Dawtrey, of Sussex; married Jane and then Isabel, who survived him to marry Richard Lyster; father of Francis, later farmer of the St Denys demesnes, and Anne, who married Sir John Ernley (*History of Parliament* (*Biographies*), *1439–1509*, p. 263; *L. & P. Henry VIII*, vi:403, xiii:2:99). Admitted to a free burgess-ship in 1490, by which time he already held a customership in the port, soon afterwards beginning the building of his fine house on the corner of St Michael's Square and Blue Anchor Lane, now the Tudor House Museum (S.C.R.O. SC5/3/1, fos 7, 15; *Oak Book*, i:159). Parliamentary burgess in 1491–2 and 1495 (*History of Parliament* (*Biographies*), *1439–1509*, p. 263). Controller of customs by 1500, serving as victualler for the king and becoming particularly active in the preparations for the war of 1512–14, during which, among other things, he supervised the then heavy expenditure on the repair of the town defences (Op. et loc. cit.; *Third Book of Remembrance*, i:10–12; *Assize of Bread Book*, p. 60; *L. & P. Henry VIII*, i:2: 1504–5, ii:2:1461–2, iii:2:1041–2, *Addenda*, i:2:4; P.R.O. E101/517/19; S.C.R.O. SC5/1/30). In addition to his important tenement on St Michael's Square, held, from 1501, the lease of West Quay, or a portion of it, having had an interest there since 1495/6, or earlier (*Book of Remembrance*, i:9; S.C.R.O. SC4/1/1). His other properties included a tenement and three cottages on the east side of Bull Street, parish of St Michael, and a wool-house in St John's (*L. & P. Henry VIII*, xiii:2:99; *Black Book*, iii:10; S.C.R.O. SC4/3/27). Knighted in 1515, and died on 24 November 1518 (*History of Parliament* (*Biographies*), *1439–1509*, p. 263; *L. & P. Henry VIII*, ii:2:1415–6).

Emory, John, *fl.* 1428–44. Possibly the John Emory 'junior' whose marriage to Christine, daughter and joint-heir of John Fysmark 'the elder', brought him, in 1398, the tenement known as 'la Chayne' on Porters Lane, with another tenement on Simnel Street (Win.Coll.Mun. 17763). Bailiff in 1428–9, 1430–1 and 1431–2; mayor in 1433–4 and 1440–1 (Davies, p. 173 (corrected); *Local Port Book, 1439–40*, pp. 100–1; P.R.O. E101/128, 31). In 1443, partnered Robert Aylward in a large purchase of bitumen and soap, but his interest was primarily in the wine trade, with the occasional lesser transaction in victuals, dyestuffs and iron (P.R.O. E101/128/34; also *Brokage Books* and *Local Port Books*, passim).

English, Richard le, *fl.* 1260(?)–1309. Possibly the Richard 'called Anglicus' who was joint-executor of Claramunda and husband of Cecilia de la Bulehuse, daughter of John (St Denys Cart. 63–4, 72, 80). Father of Richard and John le English, the latter probably the Sir John le English who witnessed, on 7 July 1347, a charter concerning Freemantle, Millbrook and Shirley lands (P.R.O. E329/193; Win.Coll.Mun. 17855). Brother, or other close relative, of Bartholomew le English, who was husband of Rosya, daughter and co-heir of Thomas Stout, and father of William le English. Bartholomew was parliamentary burgess in January 1306/7 (S.C.R.O. SC2/6/2; P.R.O. E329/193; Davies, p. 200). Held, and probably lived in, a tenement on the north side of St Michael's Square, with several plots in Hoglands (God's House Deeds 581–4; P.R.O. E329/193). Was coroner before his death in 1309 (*Cal.C.R. 1307–13*, p. 188).

Fetplace, Walter, 'senior', *fl.* 1412–49. Husband of Alice, daughter of John and Christina Cosyn; kinsman of Walter Fetplace 'junior' (*Black Book*, ii:28–33; *History of Parliament* (*Biographies*), *1439–1509*, p. 321). Elected steward in 1412, bailiff in 1414, and mayor in 1419, 1426, 1432, 1439 and 1444 (*Stewards' Books*, i:vii–viii; Davies, pp. 173–4 (corrected); P.R.O. E101/128/35). Traded principally in dyes and mordants, but also handled other commodities, including wool, cloth and wine (P.R.O. E101/128/31, E122/141/24, E122/184/3, SC8/111/5504; *Brokage Books* and *Local Port Books*, passim; Alwyn Ruddock, *Italian Merchants and Shipping*, pp. 191–2; W. J. Carpenter Turner, 'The brokage books of Southampton. A Hampshire merchant and some aspects of medieval transport', *Proc. Hampshire Field Club*, 16 (1944–7), pp. 173–7).

Lived on English Street, parish of Holy Rood, immediately south of Peter James's Broad Lane corner tenement (P.R.O. E326/11799, 11804). Also owned the great tenement, further up the street to the north, leased by him to John Chamberleyn on 14 December 1436 (S.C.R.O. SC4/2/269, 285). Died in 1449 (*History of Parliament* (*Biographies*), *1439–1509*, p. 321n).

Fetplace, Walter, 'junior', *fl.* 1449–87. Son of John Fetplace, of Denchworth (Berkshire), and kinsman of Walter Fetplace 'senior' (*History of Parliament* (*Biographies*), *1439–1509*, p. 321). Husband of Joan; father of Walter, of Alice, later the wife of Walter Tancok, and of at least one other daughter (God's House Deeds 532; *Black Book*, iii:48–9). As sheriff in 1456–7, compiled the return of aliens then resident in the town (P.R.O. E179/173/139). Mayor from 20 May 1463, replacing the deposed John Payne; re-elected mayor for 1463–4 and 1464–5 (Davies, p. 174). Parliamentary burgess for 1472–5 (*History of Parliament* (*Register*), *1439–1509*, p. 417). As one of the displaced candidates for the mayoralty, was concerned in the mayoral riots of 1460 (Alwyn Ruddock, *Italian Merchants and Shipping*, p. 176). Later accused of malpractice himself while mayor, favouring the defendant in an action and unlawfully retaining the goods of an outlaw (P.R.O. C1/29/435; *Letters Patent*, ii:34–49). Was living, in 1454, in the parish of Holy Rood, in a tenement late of William Nicholl (S.C.R.O. SC13/1). Died in, or about, 1487, his will being dated 28 April that year (*Black Book*, iii:48). Survived by his son, Walter, who in 1495/6 was holding property in St Michael's inherited from his father, and who lived himself in that parish (God's House Deeds 532; S.C.R.O. SC4/1/1).

Fleming, Henry le, *fl.* 1327–57. Son of John le Fleming; husband of Margaret; father of Benedict, Robert and Henry, who married Joan and died without issue in 1373 (*Cat.Anc. Deeds*, ii:B3405; Bodleian, Queen's College MS. 1087). Elected bailiff in 1331, mayor in 1344; parliamentary burgess in 1329, 1334, 1336 and 1338 (Davies, pp. 171–2, 200). Collector of customs, with Robert atte Barre, before Robert's death in 1339, probably continuing as such for another eighteen months, at least, with Peter de Pakenham, Robert's successor (*Cal.C.R. 1339–41*, p. 419, *1341–3*, pp. 680–1). In 1345 paid heavy fines at the Exchequer for past customs frauds (P.R.O E372/190). Was acting as local attorney for a group of alien merchants in 1347, and in 1348 himself shipped cloth to Gascony (*Cal.C.R. 1346–9*, pp. 302–3, 560). Assessed at £25 in 1332, and featured again in the agistment of men-at-arms for *c.* 1341 as one of the wealthier merchants in the town (P.R.O. C47/2/39/42, E179/242/15a, m. 8v). Held a tenement in Holy Rood, once of John le Fleming, with other property in St Michael's, by the fish market (Bodleian, Queen's College MS. 340; *Cat.Anc. Deeds*, ii:B3405). With Nicholas de Moundenard, John Fysmark 'senior', and Nicholas Sampson 'junior', was one of the four *echevins* of the town in 1350–1 (*Oak Book*, ii:130–1). Died, a great benefactor to the friary, in 1357 (J. Speed, *History of Southampton*, p. 135).

Fleming, John le, *fl.* 1295–1336. Great-grandson of Walter le Fleming; grandson of John le Fleming and Petronilla, sister of James Isembard; son of either Walter or Giles le Fleming; father of Walter and Henry le Fleming (P.R.O. E326/8900; Bodleian, Queen's College MS. 340, 1076). It was either this John le Fleming or his uncle, John the clerk, who found a crew for, and equipped, the royal galley in 1295 (P.R.O. E101/5/12; for the uncle, see S.C.R.O. D/CJ/28, St Denys Cart. 134, 172, 242). Mayor in 1319–20; parliamentary burgess in 1298, 1306, 1313, 1315, 1327, 1329 and 1330 (Davies, pp. 171, 199–200). In 1326, was trading with his son, Henry, and William de Inkepenne, a burgess of Southampton but of the prominent Winchester family, to Ireland and the Channel Islands (*Cal.P.R. 1324–7*, p. 318). From 1299, closely associated with God's House Hospital, for which he frequently did business (*R.C.H.M.*, 6th report, pp. 557, 560, 562–6). Seems also to have acted as the agent for Beaulieu Abbey in the town (B.M. Loans 29/330, f. 55). Owned tenements in Holy Rood, including the great corner tenement at the Broad Lane and High Street junction, once of Walter le Fleming; also a windmill in All Saints Without, and other suburban properties. Lived in the corner tenement, and left it in his will, dated 1336, to Walter, his son, who must soon have disposed of it to Henry de Lym (Bodleian, Queen's College MS. 339, 340, 1076). Walter featured in the subsidy accounts of 1327, but was assessed there at only 20*s*. He does not appear in the 1332 accounts, and may by then have left the town (P.R.O. E179/173/4, m. 17v, E179/242/15a, m. 8v).

Fleming, John, *fl.* 1407–54. Grandson of Henry and Margaret Fleming; son of Benedict, being the heir of Benedict's childless brother, Henry; father of Gabriel, who married Agnes, and of a daughter, later the wife of Andrew James; grandfather of John Fleming, a considerable man in the early-sixteenth-century town (*Black Book*, iii:50–3; *Book of Remembrance*, iii:2–3; P.R.O. C1/16/277; Bodleian, Queen's College MS. 1087; S.C.R.O. SC4/2/201). Clerk of recognizances in 1439, already holding a record of service to the town (Win. Coll.Mun. 17767; *Stewards' Books*, ii:28–9, 62–3). Mayor for two successive terms, from 1445 to 1447 (Davies, p. 174, and God's House Cartulary). Recorder from 1448, being parliamentary burgess in 1449–50 (*History of Parliament* (*Biographies*), *1439–1509*, pp. 337–8). While mayor, deprived Thomas White, John Payne's son-in-law, of his burgess-ship, this being one of the earlier moves in the squabble between Payne and his opponents (P.R.O. C1/16/352). The charges of corrupting the law, subsequently brought against him by White, were probably exaggerated, but Fleming's reputation was not a savoury one, and he had already been implicated, among other things, in the alleged annoyance of William Overy's tenants, complained of by Agnes, Overy's widow (S.C.R.O. D/CJ/28). His own properties included rents in French Street; also probably the plots in the eastern suburbs and the cellars in St Michael's later held by Gabriel, his son (*Black Book*, iii:50–3; P.R.O. SC11/597). Lived in All Saints, on the west side of English Street, north of Castle Lane and either opposite, or just to the south of, All Saints church. His grandson, John Fleming, was living there in 1515, when he negotiated private access to the town water conduit at All Saints; he was still the principal property-owner in All Saints in 1524, being assessed at £66. 13*s*. 4*d*. for the purpose of the subsidy of that year (S.C.R.O. SC4/2/333–4, SC13/1; P.R.O. E179/173/175).

Fleming, Walter le, *fl.* 1210–58. Brother of James le Fleming and uncle of Peter, James's son (God's House Deeds 313; St Denys Cart. 87). Husband of Joan, probably the daughter of Simon le Franceys, and of Margery, who survived him; father of Henry, John, Roger and Alice, who married Robert Bonhait (Bodleian, Queen's College MS. 1071; God's House Deeds 356; *Cal.C.R. 1247–51*, p. 456). First appears, already listed with the more important men in the town, in 1211/12 (*Pipe Roll 13 John*, p. 186). Starting in 1229 or earlier, was bailiff many times while Benedict Ace was mayor, probably replacing him as chief officer in 1249 (St Denys Cart. 92, 115, 167; *Cat.Anc. Deeds*, ii:B3368, 3377, 3383, 3441; P.R.O. E372/94; *Cal.Ch.R. 1226–57*, p. 345; *Cal.C.R. 1247–51*, p. 257). Owned several ships, including *La Heitee*, *La Jonette* and *La Pauline*, trading in wine and wool (*Cal.C.R. 1227–31*, p. 199, *1234–7*, p. 53, *1251–3*, p. 91, *1254–6*, p. 106; P.R.O. E372/84, 85). Also dealt, to a lesser extent, in salt and cloth (*Cal. Liberate R. 1245–51*, p. 321; *Cal.P.R. 1216–25*, p. 452). Undertook frequent commissions for the king, co-operating in these and in trading ventures with Benedict Ace (*Cal.C.R. 1227–31*, p. 285, *1242–7*, p. 102, *1247–51*, p. 54, *1251–3*, pp. 355, 466–7; *Cal. Liberate R. 1240–5*, p. 178; P.R.O. E372/86). Lived in the great corner tenement on the junction of English Street and Broad Lane, south of the lane; also had tenements on French Street and on the western shore, with houses in Chichester, Portsmouth and Winchester (P.R.O. E327/328; Bodleian, Queen's College MS. 1071). A benefactor of the friary, which was sited opposite his capital messuage (*Cat.Anc. Deeds*, iii:D121). Generous gifts to the friars were a feature of his will, dated 5 January 1257/8 (Bodleian, Queen's College MS. 1071).

Flete, John, *fl.* 1376–1403. Possibly the father, or husband, of Margery Flete who occurs in 1423 as the owner of his former English Street property (P.R.O. E326/9081). Frequently the associate in office of John Polymond, being elected bailiff while Polymond was mayor in 1381, 1384, 1385, 1391 and 1392; also parliamentary burgess with Polymond in 1382 and 1384. Bailiff again in 1390–1 and 1394–5; mayor in 1395–6 and 1397–8 (Davies, pp. 172, 201). In 1395, a collector of the wine subsidy (P.R.O. E122/138/13). In 1376 and 1377, associated with John Polymond, William Bacon and others in the illegal forestalling of victuals and other merchandise at Southampton, 'making singular profit thereby' (*Cal.P.R. 1377–81*, p. 81). As mayor in 1397–8, conducted the first public enquiry into the lands of the late William Bacon Wytegod (P.R.O. C47/60/8/297). Held a tenement, in which he may have lived, on the west side of English Street, parish of St Lawrence (P.R.O. E326/9334, Win.Coll.Mun. 17818). Was dead by 1405/6, leaving a widow (P.R.O. E326/8517).

Forst, John, *fl.* 1308–32. Brother of Walter and Henry Forst; related, very probably, to the Richard Forst who was bailiff in 1318–19 and mayor in 1321–2 (Davies, p. 171; *Cal.P.R. 1327–30*, p. 216). Parliamentary burgess in 1322 and 1327 (Davies, p. 200). Was exporting wool in 1307/8, with Walter Forst, Robert le Mercer and others (P.R.O. E122/136/6). With his two brothers, Walter and Henry, led an attack, in 1327, on the persons and property of Thomas de Byndon and of the Flemings, Henry and John, alleging misappropriation of the town farm (*Cal.C.R. 1327–30*, p. 243; *Cal.P.R. 1327–30*, pp. 212, 216). Henry Forst, assessed at 100*s*., appears in the accounts of the lay subsidy of 1327 (P.R.O. E179/173/4, m. 17v). In 1332 there was a Roger Forst in the town, assessed at 40*s*., and two John Forsts, assessed at 66*s*. 8*d*. and 15*s*. respectively (P.R.O. E179/242/15a, m. 8v). It is probable that one of these last was the John Forst who was elected mayor in 1339, 1341 and 1348, holding that office again in 1353 (Davies, pp. 171–2; *Cat.Anc. Deeds*, ii:B3420). In 1341–2, a John Forst accounted with Nicholas Sampson for local customs in the port (P.R.O. E122/137/11).

Fortin, William, *fl.* 1237–52. Father of John and grandfather of Lucya Fortin, who married Robert de Barbflete (*Cal.Inq.Misc. 1219–1307*, p. 162; S.C.R.O. SC4/2/41; St Denys Cart. 77). Possibly the son of either Walter or Denys Fortin, both important men in the town through the first decades of the thirteenth century (*Pipe Roll 4 John*, p. 78, *13 John*, p. 186; B.M. Loans 29/330, fos 122–4; God's House Deeds 695). Fortinus, one of three burgesses accounting for the borough farm in 1164–6, was perhaps the ancestor of them all (*Pipe Roll 10 Henry II*, p. 27, *11 Henry II*, p. 44, *12 Henry II*, p. 109). Bailiff in 1247–8 and for at least one other term (Davies, p. 170; *Cat.Anc. Deeds*, ii:B3383; St Denys Cart. 68). With others of his family, owned extensive properties in Newtown and St Mary's, being a benefactor there of the friary (P.R.O. E327/470; St Denys Cart. 56; God's House Deeds 760). Keeper of the king's houses at Southampton when he died on 30 November 1252. Roger de Lokinton was appointed keeper in his place on 18 December 1252, but the actual charge of works and buildings seems to have fallen to John Fortin, William's son. John neglected his charge, permitting the houses to be looted for building materials, as reported to the king in 1260 (*Cal.P.R. 1247–58*, p. 168, *1258–66*, p. 104; *Cal.Inq.Misc. 1219–1307*, p. 162). It was John Fortin who was a supporter of the Montforts and the baronial faction against the king (*Cal.Inq. Misc. 1219–1307*, p. 216).

Fysmark, John, *fl.* 1329–60. Father of John, William and Isabella, who married William Malmeshull 'senior' (S.C.R.O. SC4/2/113–4). John, his son, was probably the John Fysmark 'the elder' who died in or before 1398, his property being partitioned on 17 March that year between his children, Christine, wife of John Emory 'junior', and John Fysmark 'of Totton' (Win.Coll.Mun. 17763). Christine's portion at 'La Chayne' descended to John Fysmark 'senior', probably the great-grandson of the original John and father himself of John Fysmark 'junior' and Katerine. The tenement was sold to Gabriel Corbet in December 1439 (Win.Coll.Mun. 17764, 17766–8, 17770; *Black Book*, ii:72–5. The original John Fysmark first appears in the subsidy accounts of 1327, assessed at 20*s*., the same rate as Henry Fysmark. Henry no longer features in the 1332 accounts, in which John was assessed at 10*s*. only (P.R.O. E179/173/4, m. 17v, E179/242/15a, m. 8v). John was mayor in 1346–7; parliamentary burgess in 1348 and 1351 (Davies, pp. 172, 201 (corrected); Win.Coll. Mun. 17865; *Stewards' Books*, i:vii). In 1350–1, he was one of the four *echevins* of the town (*Oak Book*, ii:130–1). When improvements to the eastern defences threatened John le Clerk's garden in 1360, John Fysmark interceded on his behalf with Sir Henry Peverel, the keeper (*Cal.Inq.Misc. 1348–77*, pp. 154–5). Died probably some years before 1375 (S.C.R.O. SC4/2/113–14).

Gervase 'le Riche', *fl.* 1182–96. Son of Turbert of Hampton; brother of Roger, usually known as 'Master Roger'; husband of Isabella, and uncle of Walter (God's House Deeds 802; Bodleian, Queen's College MS. 4G10; *Pipe Roll 2 John*, p. 206). Rendered account for the borough farm for the decade beginning 1182, appearing from 1185 as 'provost' of Southampton (*Pipe Rolls 28–34 Henry II*, *2–3 Richard I*, passim). In 1190–1, was partnered by Walter of Gloucester both in the accounting for, and in the supervision of, works at the castle; the next year shared the account with William Brewer, who took it over from him entirely in 1192–3 (*Pipe Rolls 2–4 Richard I*, passim). Founder and principal benefactor of God's House Hospital, to which he gave rents in the town and estates outside it, one of them the neighbouring grange at Padwell (God's House Deeds 310, 313, 802). Built and lived at the great tenement known as 'West Hall' (Ibid., 310, 313). On his death in 1196/7, the tenement descended to Isabella, his widow, and then to Walter, his nephew. Master Roger, known to have had a house on French Street, must also have lived either in, or very close to, West Hall (*Pipe Roll 8 Richard I*, p. 196; Bodleian, Queen's College MS. 4G10; God's House Deeds 751).

Gloucester, Walter of, *fl.* before *c.* 1250. Probably the son, or grandson, of the Walter of Gloucester who supervised works at the castle and accounted for part of the borough farm in 1190–1 (*Pipe Roll 2 Richard I*, pp. 131–2; God's House Deeds 337). Brother of John of Gloucester and possibly of Claramunda, wife of Stephen Jociaume (P.R.O. E326/9145). Father of Richard, William, Nicholas, Joan, Claremund and Margery (God's House Deeds 510–11; St Denys Cart. 81). His sons' claim to be the heirs of Claramunda involved them in a succession of disputes and settlements concerning her former property (P.R.O. E210/5324, E327/633; St Denys Cart 81; J. M. Rigg (ed.), *Calendar of the Plea Rolls of the Exchequer of the Jews*, ii:95–6, 119–20).

Guidotti, Antonio, *fl.* 1517–55. Married Dorothy, daughter of Henry Huttoft; father of John (Alwyn Ruddock, 'Antonio Guidotti', *Proc. Hampshire Field Club*, 15 (1941–3), pp. 35, 41). In 1524 already prospering, his assessable goods being valued at £33. 6*s*. 8*d*. (P.R.O. E179/173/175). Admitted to a free burgess-ship on 14 January 1534. Deprived of his burgess-ship in 1541–2, some years after the initial collapse of his fortunes, but restored to it on 18 December 1543 'for that [he] hath alweis ben a loving man to the towne yn all there affares' (S.C.R.O. SC3/1/1, p. 66; *Third Book of Remembrance*, ii:2). Lived on English Street, parish of Holy Rood, and hired warehouse space from the town (P.R.O. C1/1223/46). A Florentine by birth, he traded for some years very successfully to the Mediterranean, in association with his brother Giovanni Baptista. Got into difficulties in 1535 and fled the country, leaving a considerable burden of debt on his father-in-law, who had himself profited greatly by Antonio's earlier successes (*L. & P. Henry VIII*, viii: 346, xi:239, xiii:1:206, 253). The recovery of his fortunes seems to have begun with his release from the Fleet in March 1542 (Ibid., xvii:67). Thereafter, he continued his trading career, making another career also in diplomacy. He died in Florence on 28 November 1555, survived by Dorothy (Alwyn Ruddock, op. cit., pp. 39–41).

Gunter, William, *fl.* 1475–96. Brother of Henry Gunter, and uncle of William and John, the sons of Henry and Joan; husband of Agnes and then of Alice, formerly wife of John James, who survived him (*Black Book*, ii:152–5; *Port Books, 1469–81*, i:62). Elected sheriff in 1475, mayor in 1477, 1485 and 1493 (*Book of Remembrance*, i:72, 74). On 1 April 1476, granted an annual rent of twenty shillings by the prior and convent of St Denys, in consideration of his 'good counsel given to the Priory' (S.C.R.O. SC4/2/305). Held lands in Eling, a tenement in Salisbury, and two substantial tenements on the east side of English Street, one of them the 'Dolphin' (*Black Book*, ii:134–5, 154–7). Lived in a tenement 'with two vaults' on the west side of English Street, parish of Holy Rood, formerly of John James (S.C.R.O. SC4/3/17, *Black Book*, ii:172–3). Made his will on 1 August 1492, 'seeing that the peril of death comes upon me'. But lived to be elected mayor the following year, and to see that his last wishes were enrolled in the town's 'Black Book'. Declaring a wish to be buried next to John James, 'lately buried' at St Mary's, he left the bulk of his property to the town of Southampton to endow a chantry at Holy Rood, specifying John James again among those for whom the benefits of the chantry were intended. William Justice was to be one of his executors (*Black Book*, ii:152–61). Still alive in 1496, but dead by 1500 (Ibid., ii:172–3; S.C.R.O. SC4/3/17).

Halveknight, Thomas le, *fl.* 1270–99. Husband of Christina and possibly the brother of Robert le Demichevalier, a contemporary; father of John, Thomas, Roger and Walter, and of Petronilla, wife of William Bassingrom 'senior' (St Denys Cart. 17, 242). Paid a small fine in 1275 'for a trespass' against the king, probably a by-product of the anti-Jewish incident of the previous year (J. M. Rigg (ed.), *Calendar of the Plea Rolls of the Exchequer of the Jews*, ii:219). In the 1280s, or thereabouts, bought 'la Bulehuse' and another Bull, Street property from James Isembard (God's House Deeds 601, 605). Died in 1299, or just before, the owner of a tenement on English Street (*Cat.Anc. Deeds*, ii:B3287). But his capital messuage was Gervase's former mansion at West Hall, elaborately partitioned among his heirs in 1303/4 (P.R.O. E327/163; God's House Deeds 476; St Denys Cart. 242; S.C.R.O. SC4/2/396).

Holebury, John of, *fl.* 1294–9. Father of Matilda, who married Richard de Barbflete (God's House Deeds 402). In November 1294, appointed joint supervisor with Robert le Mercer of the building of the galley, travelling with Robert le Barber to London in the spring of 1295 to collect wages for the crew (P.R.O. E101/5/2). Associated with both Robert le Mercer and Robert le Barber in a large shipment of wool (P.R.O. E372/158). Bailiff when Robert le Barber was alderman in 1298–9, and on at least one other occasion (Davies, p. 170). Dead in 1308/9, having held a tenement on the east side of English Street, which descended to Matilda and Richard, her husband (God's House Deeds 402).

Holmhegge, Nicholas, *fl.* 1435–61. Married, before 1445, Joan, formerly the wife of William Ledys and William Marche; stepfather of John Marche; father of Gregory, who married Agnes (S.C.R.O. SC4/2/277; *Cal.C.R. 1476–85*, p. 206). Bailiff in 1441–2; mayor in 1443–4 and 1454–5; parliamentary burgess in 1450 (Davies, pp. 174, 202 (corrected); P.R.O. E101/128/35; *History of Parliament* (*Biographies*), *1439–1509*, p. 464). Traded principally in victuals, although he had some dealings also in sweet wine, iron and cloth (*Local Port Book, 1435–6*, p. 26; *Brokage Book, 1443–4*, passim; *Port Books, 1469–81*, ii:202; P.R.O. E101/128/31, m. 36). Lived at the north end of the parish of St Michael's, having acquired, by way of his wife, a considerable block of properties at New Corner (S.C.R.O. SC13/1, SC4/2/277). Died in 1461, survived by Joan. Together, Nicholas and Joan had made provision before his death for the foundation of a chantry at St Mary's, with an obit at Holy Rood. The endowment of the chantry consisted of a total of thirteen messuages in the town, four of them on the west side of English Street, parish of Holy Rood, the other nine in French Street (S.C.R.O. SC4/2/292–3). A full account of the 'mind' of Nicholas and Joan Holmhegge, kept on 18 June 1496, survives in the town terrier of that date (S.C.R.O. SC4/1/1). Shortly before its suppression, the rents attaching to the chantry totalled £6. 13*s.* 4*d.*; the incumbent, who had no other living, was John Baker. The obit at Holy Rood was worth ten shillings (P.R.O. E301/52). A dispute over the inheritance in 1465/6 led to a case in the town court and the arrest of Gregory Holmhegge (P.R.O. C1/28/96, C1/31/22). Gregory reappears in 1479, making provision for his wife, Agnes, to whom he assigned a messuage, with vault and adjacent garden, in English Street, parish of St Lawrence, to take effect on his death. He did this in fulfilment of a promise of his father, Nicholas, and in compensation for the moneys paid to him by the friends of Agnes on their betrothal (*Cal.C.R. 1476–85*, p. 206).

Horder, Adam le, *fl.* 1277–1308. Husband of Joan, daughter of Henry Brian (S.C.R.O. SC4/2/3). Father of Robert and Katerina, and may also have been the father of William (St Denys Cart. 65; S.C.R.O. SC4/2/20). A close relation, very probably, of Thomas and Walter le Horder, both of whom slightly pre-date him in the records (*Cat.Anc. Deeds*, ii:B3452, *Cal.P.R. 1272–81*, p. 23; St Denys Cart. 21, 63, 64; P.R.O. E326/4478). Bailiff in 1288–9 and 1291–2; alderman in 1303–4 (Davies, p. 170; St Denys Cart. 151; P.R.O. E329/21). Collector of the new customs, with Robert le Mercer, in 1303–5; his son, Robert, was also a collector of customs in 1303/4 (P.R.O. E122/197/5, E327/163). Traded in wool, in 1277 obtaining permission to export fifty sacks (*Cal. Chancery R., Various, 1277–1326*, p. 2). Before 1291, held the shop at the east end of Holy Rood church, which was later to be the site of the rebuilt church (*Cat.Anc. Deeds*, ii:B3437). Also had extensive interests in the northern suburbs, with two shops on English Street, parish of St Lawrence, rents from houses in St Michael's, by the fish market, and an important tenement on the southern shore (*R.C.H.M.*, 6th report, p. 552; St Denys Cart. 21–3, 59, 61; *Cat.Anc. Deeds*, ii:B3458; S.C.R.O. SC4/2/1, 3, 6, 20; Bodleian, Queen's

College MS. 339, 340). In 1305, built a windmill at 'Foulflod', later to become the property of William le Horder (*R.C.H.M.*, 6th report, pp. 553, 560).

Horder, William le, *fl.* 1312–46. Possibly the son of Adam le Horder; husband of Agnes; father of John, Nicholas, Richard, Lawrence and Margaret (St Denys Cart. 306; S.C.R.O. SC4/2/84). With William Sampson and John le Barber, clerk for the recognizance of debts at Southampton, 1316–27 (S.C.R.O. SC2/6/1, SC4/2/42; P.R.O. CP40/272, m. 81). In 1327, both he and John le Barber were considered insufficiently qualified to hold office as coroners (*Cal.C.R. 1327–30*, pp. 7, 11). In the subsidy accounts of 1327 and 1332, assessed at 20*s.* and £10 respectively (P.R.O. E179/173/4, m. 17v, E179/242/15a, m. 8v). In 1312, held the windmill at Full Flood originally built by Adam le Horder, being still in possession of the mill in 1342 (*R.C.H.M.*, 6th report, p. 553 (date corrected); Bodleian, Queen's College MS. 340). Was among those who followed Petronilla la Fleming as the occupant of the corner tenement on English Street and Broad Lane, formerly of Walter le Fleming and later of John le Fleming and Henry de Lym (Bodleian, Queen's College MS. 1076). But in later years is more likely to have lived in the north-west quarter of the parish of St Michael's, by Pilgrims Pit, where Agnes, his widow, certainly lived after her husband's death (St Denys Cart. 306). Their son, Nicholas, still held a tenement there in 1364, which then became property of Beaulieu Abbey (*Cal.Inq.Misc. 1348–77*, p. 241). John, Nicholas's brother, is recorded as holding, in 1351, an empty plot on the west side of English Street, parish of Holy Rood; the previous year, he had been elected one of the *jurats* of the town (P.R.O. E326/10928; *Oak Book*, ii:130–1).

Horn, John, *fl.* 1247–79. Husband of Joan and of Rose Gildenye, who survived him; step-father of Joan, daughter of Rose by a previous marriage (St Denys Cart. 195, 205, 219; S.C.R.O. SC4/2/6). In 1260–1, joint supervisor with William Baldwin of an expensive programme of works on the chapel and on other buildings of the castle (P.R.O. E372/105). By his marriage with Joan, acquired a tenement on the west side of English Street adjoining the meat market, just north of New Corner; further consolidated and enlarged this property by the acquisition of neighbouring tenements of Benedict Ace and Nicholas le Weyte (St Denys Cart. 189–90, 198–206; P.R.O. E315/42/130, E326/6669, 9151, 9166, E327/157). Had extensive interests in the northern suburbs (St Denys Cart. 17, 23–32, 54, 58–9, 86); also two acres in Kingsland, to the east (Ibid., 361). His will, dated 10 September 1279, was proved on 20 September in the same year. He left his capital messuage in St Lawrence, with other properties, to Rose, his wife, for the term of her life. On her death, the bulk of the estate was to go to St Denys Priory to maintain a canon, celebrating mass three times a week for the souls of the testator, his wife and all the faithful departed. A rent of three shillings was assigned to St Lawrence for the upkeep of a lamp and the endowment of an obit (Ibid., 208).

Hurne, Roger atte, *fl.* 1327–38. Presumably related to William and Richard atte Hurne, contemporaries and both seafaring men like himself (*Cal.C.R. 1323–7*, p. 611; P.R.O. E210/9312, E372/203; S.C.R.O. SC4/2/134). Parliamentary burgess in 1335 and 1336 (Davies, p. 200). In 1327, associated with Thomas de Byndon and Hugh Sampson in the transport of the king's treasure to Aquitaine, finding a ship similarly in 1338 to carry equipment and horses to the Duchy (*Cal.C.R. 1327–30*, pp. 14, 434; P.R.O. E372/210). An exporter of wool, and both patron and master of his ship *La Trinite* (P.R.O. E372/194). Possibly because he was at sea at the time, or living overseas, was not listed in either of the subsidy accounts of 1327 and 1332, although William atte Hurne featured in both, assessed at 40*s.* and 30*s.* respectively (P.R.O. E179/173/4, m. 17v, E179/242/15a, m. 8v).

Huttoft, Henry. *fl.* 1506–40. Brother of Thomas Huttoft; father of John and of Dorothy, the wife of Antonio Guidotti (S.C.R.O. SC3/1/1, p. 66v; Alwyn Ruddock, 'Antonio Guidotti', *Proc. Hampshire Field Club*, 15 (1941–3), p. 35). Admitted to a free burgess-ship on 7 October 1506 in consideration of services already rendered to the town (S.C.R.O. SC3/1/1, p. 54). Elected court bailiff in 1520, sheriff in 1521, mayor in 1525 and 1534 (*Third Book of Remembrance*, i:64–5). In 1522, recommended by James Bettes for a collectorship of customs, on the grounds that he had been brought up to the job in his youth by Sir John Dawtrey, Bettes's own predecessor as collector in the port (*L. & P. Henry VIII*,

iii:2:1041–2). Finally appointed collector of customs on 11 March 1534 (Ibid., vii:175). In 1524 already a very wealthy man, being assessed in the subsidy accounts of that year at the high figure of £133. 6*s*. 8*d*., after Richard Lyster the highest in the town; four of his servants were also listed in the assessment, one of them at £10 (P.R.O. E179/173/175). Active in the sweet wine trade, frequently in association with his son-in-law (Alwyn Ruddock, op. cit., p. 35, and *Italian Merchants and Shipping*, in particular pp. 246–8). Was energetic in the service of Thomas Cromwell, whom he claimed, in 1535, to have known already for twenty-five years; also helped Thomas Wriothesley, in both cases chiefly on matters concerning the lands of dissolved religious houses (*L. & P. Henry VIII*, vi:455, viii:346, ix:127, xi:490, xii:1:287, xii:2:274, xiii:1:6–7, 210, 282–3, xvi:2:263). Acquired for himself an interest in the friary site, of which for a time he was custodian (P.R.O. E315/442, SC6/7407). Lived in the parish of St Michael, probably at Bull Hall which he had rebuilt to be the 'chefest' of the 'many very fair marchauntes houses' noted by John Leland in the town (Lucy Toulmin Smith (ed.), *The Itinerary of John Leland*, i:278). It was the only thing on which he would admit extravagance (*L. & P. Henry VIII*, viii:346). Brought into severe financial difficulties by the debts of his son-in-law, Antonio Guidotti (Op. et loc. cit.; also xii:1:113, 239, xiii:1:253, xiv:379–80, xv:150, xvii:153). Replaced as overseer of customs in 1540 (Ibid., xvi:174). His son, John, elected to a burgess-ship on 12 October 1535, also took a part in the events of the Dissolution, being associated with Richard Mille, the son of John Mille, as receiver of the Beaulieu estates (S.C.R.O. SC3/1/1, p. 66v; P.R.O. E315/363, 442). John Huttoft was granted the office of clerk of the signet in October 1539, shortly afterwards to be nominated secretary to Anne of Cleves (*L. & P. Henry VIII*, xiv:2:155, xv:9).

Huttoft, Thomas, *fl.* 1515–54. Brother of Henry Huttoft; father of Thomas, Barnabe, Nicholas, William, Elizabeth and Mary (H.R.O. will of Thomas Huttoft, 1554). Admitted to a burgess-ship on 3 July 1515, paying a reduced fine as the former apprentice of Nicholas Cowart, twice mayor (S.C.R.O. SC3/1/1, p. 57v). Water bailiff in 1522–3, court bailiff in 1523–4, sheriff in 1527–8 (*Third Book of Remembrance*, i:64–5). Assessed at £20 in the subsidy accounts of 1524 (P.R.O. E179/173/175). For a decade or more from *c*. 1534, weigher of wools in the town, also holding the Tin House during those years (Ibid., i:63n). In 1522, owner of a ship called the *Mary James* (*L. & P. Henry VIII*, iii:2:1102). Lived in a valuable corporation tenement on the west side of Bull Street, parish of St Michael, leased immediately after his death to James Brand, the newly-appointed recorder of the town (S.C.R.O. SC4/3/32). Huttoft's careful apportionment of goods between his surviving children shows his house to have been luxuriously furnished with imported tapestries, carpets, cushions and chests (H.R.O. will of Thomas Huttoft, 1554).

Imberd, Richard, *fl.* 1332–59. Possibly the grandson of James Isembard and may have been the brother of Henry Imberd, joint-patron with Walter atte Burche of *La Margarete* (P.R.O. E372/194). Husband of Christina and father of Nicholas (S.C.R.O. D/CJ/23; Win.Coll.Mun. 17880). Did not feature in the subsidy accounts of 1327, in which Henry Imberd was assessed at 60*s*. However, both Henry and Richard Imberd were listed in 1332, assessed at 100*s*. and 40*s*. respectively (P.R.O. E179/173/4, m. 17v, E179/242/15a, m. 8v). Bailiff in 1337–8; mayor in 1342–3; parliamentary burgess in 1341 and 1348 (Davies, pp. 172, 200–1; P.R.O. E326/9341). Kept account of the local customs for the months immediately following his mayoralty (P.R.O. E122/137/12). Held land in Freemantle from John and William Ace in 1344, and would seem to have held a mortgage on the Ace lands in Freemantle, Millbrook, Shirley and Hill between 1346 and 1348, when they were acquired by the Inkepennes of Winchester (Win. Coll.Mun. 17854, 17859, 17863, 17865–7, 17877, 17880). Held tenements on the east side of English Street, including the two properties immediately north of St Lawrence church. Very probably lived in that parish, for he appointed its priest one of the executors of his will, dated 5 March 1359, and endowed an obit at the church (S.C.R.O. D/CJ/23; P.R.O. E210/9312, E326/8036, 9341). His son, Nicholas, died before 1372, still in possession of at least one St Lawrence tenement (Win.Coll.Mun. 17771).

Inweys, Adam, *fl.* 1332–59. First features in the subsidy accounts of 1332, assessed already at the high figure of £20 (P.R.O. E179/242/15a, m. 8v). Elected bailiff in 1340 and 1347, mayor in 1357, 1358 and 1359; parliamentary burgess in 1340 and 1343 (Davies, pp. 171–2, 200). Collector of customs in the port from 1341, or earlier, remaining such until at least 1349 (P.R.O. E122/193/10; Win.Coll.Mun. 17917). As bailiff in 1347/8, took charge for the king of the lands of the bankrupt Nicholas de Moundenard (P.R.O. SC6/981/26). In 1360, while mayor, interceded with Sir Henry Peverel for John le Clerk, whose garden in Newtown was threatened by modifications to the defences (*Cal.Inq.Misc. 1348–77*, pp. 154–5). Exported wool on a large scale in 1338–9, trading to Bordeaux (*Cal.C.R. 1337–9*, p. 456, *1339–41*, p. 132).

Isembard, James, *fl.* 1270–89. Son of Ralph Isembard and Joan of St Laurence; brother of Petronilla, wife of John le Fleming; possibly the grandfather of Richard and Henry Imberd, both active in the town in the second quarter of the fourteenth century (St Denys Cart. 134, 172; P.R.O. E326/9331). Bailiff in 1286–7 (Davies, p. 170). By *c.* 1270, held 'la Bulehuse' in Bull Street, parish of St Michael, possibly by right of his aunt, Alice, who had married John de la Bulehuse. Acquired the adjoining property, once of Claramunda, from the abbot and convent of Quarr Abbey, but sold both tenements to Thomas le Halveknight (God's House Deeds 600–1, 603–5; *Cat.Anc. Deeds*, ii:B3447). Pleaded his case before the king on Monday 1 August 1289, his lands having been taken into the king's hands for his default against John de Hardington (*Cal.C.R. 1288–96*, p. 50). A tenement of his, on the west side of Bull Street, is mentioned in a deed dating to Thomas de Byndon's first term of office as alderman. It could be that he was still alive at this date, but this James Isembard could possibly have been his son (S.C.R.O. SC2/6/2).

Isembard, Ralph, *fl.* before *c.* 1250. Probably the son, or other close relative, of the 'Hysenbard' who appears as a witness to one of the earliest God's House charters (God's House Deeds 802). Husband of Joan, sister of Simon and daughter of William of St Laurence; father of James and of Petronilla, who married John le Fleming, Walter le Fleming's son (Ibid., 695; P.R.O. E326/9331; St Denys Cart. 134, 172). Bailiff in 1222–3; described as 'reeve of Hamton and steward of God's House' in an early-thirteenth-century deed, Walter Fortin being mayor (Davies, p. 170; God's House Deeds 348). Acquired through his wife the former St Laurence capital tenement in the parish of St Lawrence (God's House Deeds 695). Dead before 1268, by which time his own capital tenement had descended to Petronilla, his daughter, who was using it to house foreign merchants visiting the town (*Cal.P.R. 1266–72*, p. 242).

James, Andrew, *fl.* 1443–78. Probably the son of Peter James; son-in-law of John Fleming and of John Payne in succession (P.R.O. C1/16/352; Alwyn Ruddock, *Italian Merchants and Shipping*, p. 170; also 'John Payne's persecution of foreigners', *Proc. Hampshire Field Club*, 16 (1944–7), p. 32). Elected bailiff in 1446; mayor in 1452; parliamentary burgess in 1453 and 1461 (*Book of Remembrance*, i:66, 68; Davies, pp. 174, 202 (corrected); *History of Parliament (Biographies), 1439–1509*, pp. 496–7). On 7 July 1473, appointed deputy at Southampton, with William Saunders, of the king's chief butler (*Cal.P.R. 1467–77*, p. 393). Is known to have made considerable purchases of wine in 1443, trading the next year principally to Oxford, Abingdon and Salisbury (P.R.O. E101/128/31, m. 36; *Brokage Book, 1443–4*, passim). Still trading in 1469–70 as an exporter of cloth (*Port Books, 1469–81*, i:14, 55). Actively engaged in the factional squabbles in the town through the fifties and sixties (P.R.O. C1/16/352, C1/29/405; Alwyn Ruddock, op. cit., pp. 170, 176–8). Lived on the east side of English Street, parish of Holy Rood, north of Holy Rood church (S.C.R.O. SC13/1).

James, Peter, *fl.* 1413–50. Husband of Joan; father of William and Catherine, probably also of Andrew and John (S.C.R.O. SC4/2/246; *Black Book*, ii:56–9, 92–5). Elected steward in 1413; bailiff in 1416 and 1417; mayor in 1428, 1434, 1435, 1442 and 1447; parliamentary burgess in 1427 (*Stewards' Books*, i:vii–viii; Davies, pp. 173–4, 202 (corrected); P.R.O. E101/128/31, m. 32, E179/173/107). While mayor in 1428–9, joined William Chamberleyn and John Fleming in the purchase for the town of West Hall (*Stewards' Books*, i:10–11, 30–3). Associated in trading ventures with Walter Fetplace, dealing principally in wines (*Brokage Books* and *Local Port Books*, passim; P.R.O. E101/128/31, m. 28, E122/184/3, SC8/111/5504). Held property on both sides of English Street, parish of Holy Rood, including the great tenement on the southern corner of Broad Lane and English Street, formerly of the Flemings, Henry de Lym and Sir John de Montague, in which he probably lived (P.R.O. E326/11799, 11800, 11804; S.C.R.O. SC4/2/246, 289). Quarrelled with his daughter, Catherine, over property left to her by her first husband, Andrew Payne; the case was brought before the courts by Catherine and her second husband, John Serle (P.R.O. C1/15/184, C1/73, 144–5). Was dead before 1457, by which year his widow, Joan, had re-married, her second husband being Walter Bacyn (S.C.R.O. SC4/2/289). John James, who died in 1471 without surviving issue, left his wife, Alice, the tenement in which they lived on the west side of English Street, parish of Holy Rood (*Black Book*, iii:24–9; S.C.R.O. SC4/2/296, 301–2). But the principal James property on the Broad Lane corner site descended to William James, whose son, Henry, sold the family tenement to William Justice early in the sixteenth century, while still retaining an interest in the three adjoining tenements along Broad Lane to the west (P.R.O. E326/11784, 11789, 11792; *Black Book*, ii:92–5, iii:36–45; *Third Book of Remembrance*, i:18–19). By 1524, Henry James had become resident in the ward of St Michael with St John, being assessed there at £5 in the subsidy accounts of that year. His son, William, was assessed at £20 in the account, being then resident in Holy Rood (P.R.O. E179/173/175). William James and his own son, Lawrence, were both burgesses of Southampton in their turn, being admitted to burgess-ships in 1518 and 1547 respectively; the former became also a citizen and draper of London (S.C.R.O. SC3/1/1, pp. 59, 74; *Third Book of Remembrance*, i:18n).

Justice, William, *fl.* 1469–1510. Husband of Alice; father of William (P.R.O. E326/11792; S.C.R.O. SC3/1/1, p. 55). Elected junior bailiff in 1489; senior bailiff in 1492; sheriff in 1495; mayor in 1501 (*Book of Remembrance*, i:75–6). Appears first in October 1469, handling a small consignment of congers, with John James standing pledge for him; re-appears in 1481 importing wine, still not a burgess in his own right (*Port Books, 1469–81*, i:4, ii:150). Bought the James corner tenement on Broad Lane for £63, but challenged in its ownership by Thomas Thomas, who subsequently secured possession for himself (P.R.O. E326/11784, 11789, 11792, E329/429; *Black Book*, iii:36–45). Still alive in September 1510, when William, his eldest son and next heir, was admitted to a burgess-ship (S.C.R.O. SC3/1/1, p. 55).

Lange, Walter, *fl.* 1374–1408. Nephew of Thomas Lange 'of Weymouth'; husband of Joan, possibly the daughter of Thomas le Cust (S.C.R.O. SC4/2/112, 117, 119, 120). Steward in 1382–3; mayor in 1393–4 and 1407–8; parliamentary burgess in 1397, 1398 and 1406 (Davies, pp. 172–3, 201–2; *Stewards' Books*, i:vii; S.C.R.O. SC4/2/138). Owner of very considerable properties on the east side of English Street, parish of Holy Rood, including the tenement immediately north of the friary site, once of the Barbfletes and Nicholas de Moundenard, and the tenements adjoining it to the north again; also held a rent in St Michael's and a house and plots in the northern suburbs (S.C.R.O. SC4/2/112, 119, 120, 135, 143, 144, 169, 171–3, 175, 189, 190).

Leicester, Richard of, *fl.* before *c.* 1235. Father of William and Richard; possibly related to the earls of Leicester, and certainly well-connected locally with members of both the St Laurence and the Bulehuse families (S.C.R.O. D/CJ/1; God's House Deeds 343; St Denys Cart. 66). Held responsible, with Simon of St Laurence and Joceus de Bray, then bailiffs, for a deficiency on the town farm, incurred in 1213–14 and a burden to all of them for many years thereafter (P.R.O. E372/62–70). Shortly afterwards, in 1216/17, again in association with Simon of St Laurence, with Thomas de la Bulehuse and others, was concerned in the arrest and detention of horses and servants of Sir Richard Scarcaville, a local incident in the civil war, subsequently brought to the attention of the king's justices (W. W. Shirley (ed.), *Royal and other historical letters illustrative of the reign of Henry III*, i:8–10). In 1223–4, joint supervisor with John de la Bulehuse of works on the king's quay and the prison (P.R.O. E372/68). Steward during an early mayoralty of Walter Fortin (God's House Deeds 695; P.R.O. E326/6723). Towards the end of his life, drawn into a quarrel with William, his son, over possession of a tenement in the town. The dispute led to the imprisonment of William and ended, more happily, with his release early in 1235 (*Cal.C.R. 1234–7*, p. 39). Probably the builder of the 'great stone houses' known to have been his on the east side of French Street, parish of St Michael's. Almost certainly, he would have lived there, but had had to dispose of them before December 1221, possibly to meet his debts (St Denys Cart. 92, 251–3). Also held for a time, from John de la Bulehuse, land and buildings on the east side of Above Bar Street, in the northern suburb, later sold to Stephen Jociaume and Claramunda, his wife (Ibid., 67).

London, John of, *fl.* 1299–1315. Husband of Blanche and Joan Loveraty, later the wife of Roger Norman; father of Andrew, John, Henry, Menesina and Alice (*Cal.P.R. 1301–7*, p. 102, *1307–13*, p. 507, *1324–7*, p. 110). For services in Gascony and elsewhere, the king granted John of London 'of Bordeaux', then described as his 'serjeant', a free burgess-ship of Southampton, with exemption from all taxes in the town. The grant was dated 17 March 1299, being extended on 10 January 1303 to cover his wife, sons and daughters as well. On 24 May 1306, the extension of the grant to include free burgess-ships of Winchester gave 'Margery' as the name of his wife: either a second wife or a mistake for the first. Certainly, he had re-married by November 1312, when his privileges were further extended to cover Joan (Ibid., *1292–1301*, pp. 398–9, *1301–7*, pp. 102, 434, *1307–13*, p. 507). In 1309, serving as Southampton deputy to the king's chief butler (Ibid., *1307–13*, p. 190). Was holding the cocket seal in November 1311, when required to return it to Henry de Lym, then collector of customs on wool, woolfells and hides (*Cal.C.R. 1307–13*, p. 386). As a ship-owner, one of his ships being *La Naudeu*, continued to maintain a connection at Bordeaux, storing at least some of his imported wines at the great cellar he was renting from God's House Hospital in 1304–6 (Yves Renouard (ed.), *Gascon Rolls, 1307–17*, pp. 65, 444–5; *R.C.H.M.*, 6th report, p. 560). Also traded in wax, selling an important consignment to the king in July 1305 (P.R.O. E122/197/5). In 1315, probably the year of his death, received a gift of two cheeses from God's House, 'for divers courtesies shown to the House'. His widow, Dame Joan, continued the connection, helping out the hospital with loans on at least two occasions (*R.C.H.M.*, 6th report, pp. 564, 566, 567). As Joan Loveraty, widow of William of Cardiff, she was lending large sums of money to Hugh Sampson and Eborard Franceys, of Bristol, in 1319 and 1320 (S.C.R.O. SC2/6/1). Presumably John of London was her second husband. She had married her third, Roger Norman, by 1322 (God's House Deeds 672; *Black Book*, i:116).

Long, Henry le, *fl.* 1272–97. Contemporary and possibly the brother of Richard le Long; father of John and Hugh le Long, and possibly also of Roger, husband of Christina la Long and father of Bartholomew. Of his daughters, Alice had a daughter of her own, Felicia; 'Anneys' became Anneys Fyskel; and Cecilia married John de Bourgoyne (St Denys Cart. 64, 101, 123; S.C.R.O. SC4/2/10, 36–7). First recorded as a witness in 1272 (St Denys Cart. 63). With Walter le Horder, exporting twenty sacks of wool in 1273 (*Cal.P.R. 1272–81*, p. 23). Lived in the parish of St John in a stone tenement with cellars and shops on the west side of French Street, north of West Hall. Like West Hall itself, Henry le Long's tenement stretched from French Street, on the east, to Bull Street, on the west. He sold it, shortly before the turn of the century, to his son-in-law, John de Bourgoyne, but it had reverted to his heirs by 1326, when the capital messuage in French Street and Henry le Long's extensive properties on Simnel Street, parish of St Michael, were partitioned among them (S.C.R.O. SC4/2/10, 36–7).

Ludlow, John, *fl.* 1478–1500. Probably the son of the John Ludlow who, in the 1450s, was holding a tenement on the east side of English Street, parish of Holy Rood, next to a tenement of William Soper; possibly related to the Richard Ludlows, father and son, who were his contemporaries in the town (Davies, p. 377; Win.Coll.Mun. 17788; *Black Book*, ii:102–3). Mayor in 1478–9 (Davies, p. 175). By the end of the century, had held for over a decade the six messuages and two gardens in Holy Rood formerly of the Fetplace family, to which he was related. Before selling them outright in 1499/1500 to Thomas Thomas, had leased them to Thomas, who himself chose to live in the great tenement immediately south of the James capital messuage, in which Walter Fetplace 'senior' used to live (P.R.O. E326/11792, 11794–6).

Lym, Henry de, *fl.* 1307–44. Husband of Petronilla; father of James and another Petronilla (Win.Coll.Mun. 17827–8; God's House Deeds 1098). With John of Shirley, collector of customs at Southampton from *c.* 1307 (P.R.O. E122/136/6, 8, 17; *Cal.C.R.*

1307–13, pp. 275–6, 386). Bailiff before 1311; alderman in 1320–1 and 1329–30, with an earlier spell probably before 1315; parliamentary burgess in 1311, 1313, 1315, 1324 and 1328 (Davies, pp. 171, 200 (corrected)). One of the wealthier burgesses of his day, being assessed at £30 and £20 in the subsidy accounts of 1327 and 1332 (P.R.O. E179/173/4, m. 17v, E179/242/15a, m. 8v). Associated with Thomas de Byndon, John le Fleming, Nicholas de Moundenard, Robert atte Barre and other leading burgesses in the enforced purchase of bad wine at Portchester in 1324/5 (P.R.O. C47/60/6/184; *Cal.C.R. 1327–30*, p. 147). In 1330, founded a chantry at Barton Oratory on the Isle of Wight, endowing it with a substantial gift of lands in Southampton and elsewhere (P.R.O. C143/210/28; Win.Coll. Mun. 17827). Obtained letters patent in 1334 pardoning an earlier outlawry, exemplified in 1341 after the original document had been burnt in the raid of 1338 (*Cal.P.R. 1340–3*, p. 79). In the last years of his life, lived in the corner tenement on Broad Lane and English Street, formerly property of the Fleming family (Bodleian, Queen's College MS. 339–40). Witnessed a deed of January 1344, and probably died that year (Win.Coll.Mun. 17828, 17867).

Lyon, Peter de, *fl.* 1278–1301. Three times bailiff in the 1290s: in 1290–1, 1294–5 and one other term. Alderman in 1300–1, and possibly also in 1295–6, with John de Puteo (atte Barre) and John le Monir as bailiffs; parliamentary burgess, with John atte Barre, in November 1295 (Davies, pp. 170, 199 (corrected); P.R.O. E326/9349; St Denys Cart. 159; Win.Coll.Mun. 17896). While bailiff in 1294–5, took a part in supervising the building of the galley, going to London with Robert le Barber, early in 1295, to discuss progress at the Exchequer (P.R.O. E101/5/2). Held property in Holy Rood, on the east side of English Street (God's House Deeds 358; S.C.R.O. SC4/2/7). Probably related to Nicholas de Lyon, who was bailiff during Thomas de Byndon's first mayoralty, and who may have been Peter's son. Nicholas is known to have had a messuage on the west side of Above Bar Street, backing on the field called Hampton, which he sold to Richard and Elena Forst (God's House Deeds 723; S.C.R.O. SC2/6/2). He reappears as witness to a quitclaim of 1319/20, although, puzzlingly, a 'widow' of Nicholas de Lyon is recorded in an early rental of God's House, now re-dated to 1307–8 (St Denys Cart. 101; *R.C.H.M.*, 6th report, p. 552 (corrected)). A Thomas de Lyon and a Juliana de Lyon both feature in the subsidy accounts of 1332, assessed at 15*s.* and 20*s.* respectively (P.R.O. E179/242/15a, m. 8v).

Lyster, Thomas, *fl.* 1505–45. A relative, possibly the brother, of Sir Richard Lyster, chief baron of the exchequer and later chief justice. Husband of Alice; father of Elizabeth (B.M. Add. Ch. 7219). Admitted to a burgess-ship on 25 May 1505 (S.C.R.O. SC3/1/1, p. 52v). Elected steward in 1509; water bailiff in 1511; court bailiff in 1512; sheriff in 1514; mayor in 1517, 1527, 1536 and 1544 (*Third Book of Remembrance*, i:64–5). As a resident of Holy Rood, assessed at £100 in 1524 (P.R.O. E179/173/175). Described as an 'alderman of the said town and merchant adventurer' when his late apprentice, John Overy, was admitted to a burgess-ship in 1538/9 (S.C.R.O. SC3/1/1, p. 70). Held property from the town on both sides of English Street, parish of Holy Rood; also the 'George' and other properties on the west side of Above Bar Street, in All Saints Without; probably lived himself on the east side of English Street, parish of Holy Rood (S.C.R.O. SC4/2/348, 351, SC4/3/21, 25, 49; *Third Book of Remembrance*, i:57–8; B.M. Add. Ch. 7219). His relative, Sir Richard Lyster, married Isabel, widow of Sir John Dawtrey, thus acquiring Sir John's great house on the corner of St Michael's Square and Blue Anchor Lane, now the Tudor House Museum (*L. & P. Henry VIII*, vi:403). By 1524, Richard Lyster was already, by a substantial margin, the richest man in the town, having assessable goods there worth £250. Eight of his servants also feature in the subsidy accounts of that year (P.R.O. E179/173/175). It was probably Richard's son, Michael, who was admitted to a burgess-ship on 12 September 1536 (S.C.R.O. SC3/1/1, p. 68).

Marche, Thomas atte, *fl.* before *c.* 1342. Husband of Joan, daughter and heiress of Hugh Sampson, who survived him and married John le Clerk; father of Richard atte Marche (Bodleian, Queen's College MS. 4G10; *Cal.C.R. 1402–5*, p. 174; S.C.R.O. SC4/2/188). Mayor in 1340–1; parliamentary burgess in 1339 (Davies, pp. 171, 200). Collector of customs, with Adam Inweys, in 1341–2 (P.R.O. E122/193/10). In 1340–2, holding the portion of West Hall formerly of Hugh Sampson

(Bodleian, Queen's College MS. 339, 340). The West Hall property descended to John le Clerk, Joan's second husband, but subsequently reverted to Richard atte Marche, who entered the Church and became a chaplain, and who very probably inherited also from Thomas the tenements on the east side of English Street, parish of Holy Rood, in the disposing of which he was particularly active in the early 1380s (Bodleian, Queen's College MS. 4G10; *Cal.C.R. 1422–9*, pp. 462–3). The hospital at God's House benefited in 1381 from this distribution to the extent of £10 in rents from a tenement and shops newly built, adjoining Richard's tenement on its north (God's House Deeds 428). Richard atte Marche featured regularly thereafter in the internal accounts of the hospital, on many occasions dining there with his servant (Bodleian, Queen's College MS. 262, 305, 306, 307). A Thomas atte Merssh, married to Agnes, is recorded as transferring a tenement in St Michael's to John Barbflete in 1405 (*Black Book*, i:86). He had appeared earlier, with John le Clerk and others, as a collector of the poll tax of 1381 (P.R.O. E179/173/46).

Marsh, Adam, *fl.* 1419–39. Husband of Joan, who survived him for over two decades; probably related to the William Marche who was parliamentary burgess in 1437 and mayor in 1437–8, who had a son, John, and whose widow, Joan, married Nicholas Holmhegge (S.C.R.O. SC4/2/275, 277, 294). Steward in 1419–20; bailiff in 1425–6 and 1435–6 (*Stewards' Books*, i:vii; Davies, p. 173). Was importing a tun of wine in December 1435 (*Local Port Book, 1435–6*, pp. 24–5). Lived in the parish of St Lawrence, possibly in the tenement he had himself rebuilt on the west side of English Street; also held tenements in All Saints and properties as far dispersed as Dorset and Sussex (S.C.R.O. SC4/2/255a, 275, 294). Died in, or before, 1439; the accounts for his obit at St Lawrence, as kept on 14 August 1496, survive in the corporation terrier of 1495–6 (S.C.R.O. SC4/1/1, SC4/2/270).

Mascall, John, *fl.* 1397–1422. Probably the son of Roger and Felicia Mascall; married Joan and then Margery (*Black Book*, i:117; Davies, p. 377). Elected bailiff in 1405, 1409 and 1411; mayor in 1414, 1420 and 1421; parliamentary burgess in 1421 and 1422 (Davies, pp. 173, 202). Before 1397, had lived in the former Moundenard tenement immediately north of the friary (*Black Book*, i:52–3). In 1402, bought a reversion on two tenements on the west side of English Street; also held property in the northern and north-eastern suburbs, part of which he disposed of in 1411 (Ibid., i:68–71, 117). With Walter Fetplace, bought certain St Lawrence properties from the executors of Richard Bradway 'senior' in 1418/19 (Davies, pp. 376–7). Was dead, probably, before March 1428 (P.R.O. E326/11799; Davies, p. 377). The accounts of his obit, kept on 10 November 1495, are preserved in the corporation terrier of 1495–6. The obit was still being kept on the suppression of the chantries in the next century (S.C.R.O. SC4/1/1; P.R.O. E301/52).

Mascall, Roger, *fl.* 1368–88. Husband of Felicia, daughter or step-daughter of Nicholas de Moundenard; probably father of John Mascall, later in occupation of Roger's lands (S.C.R.O. D/CJ/24, D/LY/23/3, SC4/2/103, 162–3; *Black Book*, i:52–3). Bailiff in 1368–9; parliamentary burgess in 1386 (Davies, pp. 172, 201). In 1368, bought the Moundenard suburban properties from the executors of Christina, his mother-in-law (S.C.R.O. D/CJ/ 25, 26, 27, SC4/2/103). Through his wife, Felicia, also acquired an interest in the Moundenard tenement on the east side of English Street, immediately north of the friary site, a part of which had come to her on Nicholas de Moundenard's death (S.C.R.O. D/CJ/24). In 1377, acquired a mortgage on the full property from Nicholas Sherwynd, its rebuilder. Two years later, arranged a mortgage himself on the same property with John Clerk, of Lymington, who was still holding the tenement in the last years of the century, although it was John Mascall who lived there (S.C.R.O. SC4/2/116a, 122–5, 162–3, 171–2). In 1380, holding a mortgage on John atte Barre's lands. The details of the transaction are obscure, but it was probably from John atte Barre that Roger Mascall acquired his permanent interest in the properties south of Broad Lane (S.C.R.O. SC4/2/126–33, 136–7, 140, 143; P.R.O. E326/11799). In 1381, further acquired a vacant plot on the west side of English Street, parish of St Lawrence, immediately south of a tenement of John atte Barre, stretching from the street on the east to the castle moat on the west (S.C.R.O. SC4/2/134). Acting in 1388 as an executor of William Waldern, in a matter concerning entry rights at West Hall, in which he himself had an interest (S.C.R.O. SC4/2/406; Bodleian, Queen's College MS. 4G10). Died before 1393 (S.C.R.O. SC4/2/156).

Mercer, Robert le, *fl.* 1270–1314. Possibly a descendant of Thomas le Mercer and relative of John, William and Adam le Mercer, the first of these a direct contemporary similarly engaged in the export of wool (St Denys Cart. 49; P.R.O. E122/136/1, 6; God's House Deeds 616, 726; Win.Coll.Mun. 17842–3, 17846). Bailiff in 1270–1 and again, unusually, in 1290–1; alderman in 1284–5, 1288–9, 1295–6 and for at least three other sessions in the 1290s and early 1300s (Davies, pp. 170–1 (corrected); *Cat.Anc. Deeds*, ii:B3311). In 1274–5 implicated in the anti-Jewish riot at Southampton (J. M. Rigg (ed.), *Calendar of the Plea Rolls of the Exchequer of the Jews*, ii:302). An exporter, on a large scale, of wool, sometimes in association with other leading Southampton merchants, including John of Holebury and Robert le Barber (*Cal. Chancery R., Various, 1277–1326*, p. 2; P.R.O. E122/136/1, 6, E372/158). Collector of new customs, with Adam le Horder, in 1303–5 (P.R.O. E122/197/5). Joint supervisor, with John of Holebury, of the construction of the galley in 1294–5 (P.R.O E101/5/2). Had acquired lands, in 1291, in the parish of South Stoneham, a few miles to the north-east of the town (*Cal.C.R. 1288–96*, p. 245). Died in 1314, remembered as a benefactor of the friary, to which he had given the site of its new stone church (J. Speed, *History of Southampton*, p. 135).

Middleton, Thomas, *fl.* 1382–1422. Husband of Joan and then, late in life, of Margaret (Win.Coll.Mun. 17792; *Black Book*, i:152–3). Elected mayor in 1401, 1402 and 1403; parliamentary burgess in 1399 and 1402 (Davies, pp. 173, 201–2). As clerk to the town court, witnessed deeds of the early 1380s; accounted for tunnage and poundage in the port in 1413 (S.C.R.O. SC4/2/135, 140, 144; P.R.O. E122/140/2–3). Obviously a man of considerable wealth, he was probably the builder of the great warehouse known as the 'Wool House' and now the Maritime Museum; certainly, he financed the building of an important new quay, fitted with a crane of its own, at the Watergate (*Cal.Inq.Misc. 1399–1422*, pp. 186–7, 228; S.C.R.O. SC4/2/210; *Local Port Book, 1439–40*, pp. xxxvi-xxxvii). An executor of both John Polymond and John Barbflete (Win.Coll.Mun. 17790; God's House Deeds 479). Early in the fifteenth century, associated with many other leading burgesses in the withholding of rents from God's House and St Denys (S.C.R.O. D/LY/7/18; *Cal.C.R. 1405–9*, pp. 178–82, *1409–13*, pp. 132–3). Held and probably lived at Bull Hall for many years, and had other properties and interests in the parishes of St Michael, St John, Holy Rood, St Lawrence and All Saints Without (God's House Deeds 607; S.C.R.O. SC4/2/151, 210; *Black Book*, i:48–51, 84, 106–13, 152–7). Had married his second wife, Margaret, by 1414, and it was with her that he was granted, in 1420, the right to maintain a private oratory at their home (*Black Book*, i:152–3; *Cal. Pap. Reg., Papal Letters*, vii:342). In 1422 was appointed an executor of John Renaud, a former mayor, whose legacies included the gift of a scarlet fur-trimmed gown and red silk belt to Thomas Middleton's son, unnamed (P.R.O. E327/775).

Mille, John, *fl.* 1509–51. Father of Richard, John, George and Thomas (*L. & P. Henry VIII*, xix:1:281; S.C.R.O. SC3/1/1, pp. 66v; *Third Book of Remembrance*, i:xix). Became town clerk, probably, in 1509, holding that office jointly with the recordership until his death in 1551; parliamentary burgess in 1523 and 1529 (Davies, p. 203; *Third Book of Remembrance*, i:66–7, ii:158–9). In December 1540, appointed overseer of customs in place of Henry Huttoft (*L. & P. Henry VIII*, xvi:174). In 1545, acting as clerk for the recognizance of debts at Southampton, having already served in 1542 as commissioner for the debts of Henry Huttoft (Ibid., xvii:153; *Black Book*, iii:80–1). Described as a 'merchant adventurer' in 1538/9; also active in transactions concerning the lands of the dissolved religious houses, in particular those of St Denys Priory and the abbeys of Beaulieu and Quarr (S.C.R.O. SC3/1/1, p. 55v; P.R.O. E315/363, 442, LR2/269, SC6/Henry VIII/3340, 7413; *L. & P. Henry VIII*, ix:127, 313, xiii:1:6–7, 281, 580, xiii:2:124, xix:1:78, xxi:1:352). Badly in debt in 1538, alleging that he had been tricked by the Venetians (Ibid., xiii:1:442; P.R.O. C1/1037/50). But handling large sums for the king in 1540, during works on local fortifications (*L. & P. Henry VIII*, xv:306). Held considerable properties in St John's, including 'le Vernecle' from the corporation, probably living in that parish. His house was among those singled out by John Leland for special praise (S.C.R.O. SC4/2/351–2; Lucy Toulmin Smith (ed.), *The Itinerary of John Leland*, i:278). Died in 1551, being succeeded both as town clerk and as recorder by his son, Thomas (*Third Book of Remembrance*, ii:158–9). Thomas Mille's son and heir, Richard, was admitted to a burgess-ship in 1582, by which time Thomas was dead (S.C.R.O. SC3/1/1, p. 96).

Moigne, Bernard le, *fl.* 1273–83. Probably related to Robert le Moigne, a former bailiff and benefactor of St Denys; father of Cecilia, who married a merchant of Lucca (St Denys Cart. 92; Davies, p. 170; P.R.O. E210/5745). In 1273, exporting twenty sacks of wool (*Cal.P.R. 1272–81*, p. 24). As bailiff in 1275, implicated in the non-payment of fines by Southampton burgesses, arising from the anti-Jewish riot of the previous year (J. M. Rigg (ed.), *Calendar of the Plea Rolls of the Exchequer of the Jews*, ii:249). In 1283, involved personally in a dispute with a merchant of Cork, in which both sides retaliated by arresting the goods of other merchants of their respective towns (P.R.O. C47/10/14/9; *Cal.P.R. 1281–92*, pp. 98–9). Probably lived on the east side of Bull Street, opposite Bull Hall, at the north-west corner of the parish of St John (God's House Deeds 601). This tenement descended to his daughter, Cecilia, to become the property, in succession, of at least three Luccan merchants (P.R.O. E210/5745). Peter le Moigne and another Bernard le Moigne both held property in the early-fourteenth-century town (Win.Coll.Mun. 17884; P.R.O. SC8/61/3039, SC8/128/6351).

Moundenard, Nicholas de, *fl.* 1325–57. Married Margery and then Christina; father, or step-father, of Felicia, daughter of Christina, who married Roger Mascall; very probably related to Gaillard de Moundenard, who married Matilda, daughter of Robert le Barber (*Cal.C.R. 1323–7*, p. 648; S.C.R.O. D/LY/23/3; Win.Coll.Mun. 17761). Elected bailiff in 1325, 1329, 1330 and 1331; mayor in 1332; one of the four *echevins* in 1350 (Davies, p. 171 (corrected); P.R.O. E326/9340; *Oak Book*, ii:130–1). In 1324/5, associated with Thomas de Byndon and other leading burgesses in the enforced purchase of bad wine at Portchester (P.R.O. C47/60/6/184; *Cal.C.R. 1327–30*, p. 147). Already one of the wealthier burgesses, assessed at £30 in the subsidy accounts of 1327 and 1332 (P.R.O. E179/173/4, m. 17v, E179/242/15a, m. 8v). From February 1337 to January 1339, collector of customs and subsidies, with Laurence de Mees (P.R.O. E372/184). Briefly imprisoned in the Tower of London in 1339, accused of customs frauds and the misappropriation of moneys raised on murage, quayage and barbicanage grants (*Cal.C.R. 1339–41*, p. 241; *Cal.P.R. 1340–3*, pp. 312, 326, 441). By 1347, when his lands were taken into the king's hands for debt, was carrying the whole burden of the £502. 10*s*. 6¼*d*. still owing at the end of his joint customership (P.R.O. E122/137/14, E372/184, SC6/1282/1). He never managed to pay it off, for the debt continued to feature in the pipe rolls for several decades, standing at £497. 10*s*. 6¼*d*. in 1363, six years after his death (P.R.O. E372/208). Owner of the great tenement immediately north of the friary site; also held an important tenement south of Broad Lane, between tenements of Henry de Lym and Roger Norman, with shops in St Lawrence and other properties on Simnel Street and in All Saints Without, including probably 'Moundenardescourt' (S.C.R.O. SC4/2/41, 43–4; Bodleian, Queen's College MS. 339, 340; Win.Coll.Mun. 17847; P.R.O. SC6/981/26–7; *Cal.Inq.Misc. 1392–9*, pp. 63–4; *Cal.Inq.P.M., Henry VII*, i:368–9). Died in 1357, leaving the bulk of his remaining property to Christina, who survived him another ten years at most (S.C.R.O. D/LY/23/3, D/CJ/24, SC4/2/103; *Cal.Inq.Misc. 1348–77*, p. 93).

Nicholl, William (senior), *fl.* 1388–1440(?). The family relationships of the Nicholls are obscure, and have been much debated (*Black Book*, i:52n; *Letters Patent*, ii:16n; *Southampton Letters*, p. 10n). It was William Nicholl 'senior' who was husband of Elena and Catherine, and possibly of Juliana; he was probably father of William 'junior' and Oliver, and stepfather of Catherine, presumably the daughter of Juliana (God's House Deeds 430; S.C.R.O. SC4/2/164–5, 306, 309; *Black Book*, ii:58–9; *Letters Patent*, ii:16–17; *Southampton Letters*, pp. 6–10). Elected bailiff in 1401 and 1407; it was probably this William again who became mayor in 1411, 1417, 1422 and 1427, although the William Nicholl who was mayor in 1438–9 is more likely to have been his son (Davies, p. 173 (corrected); *Stewards' Books*, i:vii). Partnered William Soper in 1412 as an importer of La Rochelle wine (S.C.R.O. SC4/2/223). Probably it was both the William Nicholls who were actively engaged in the twenties and thirties in the importing and distribution of wine, iron, dyestuffs and miscellaneous victuals (*Port Books, 1427–30, Local Port Book, 1439–40, Brokage Book, 1439–40,* passim). Family properties included tenements in St John's and Holy Rood, among them an important tenement on the north side of Porters Lane and the messuage immediately north of the friary site, acquired from Walter Lange by William Nicholl 'senior' (P.R.O. E326/11799, 11800; Win.Coll.Mun. 17835, 17840; S.C.R.O. SC4/2/164–5, 193, 210–12, 229–32; *Black Book,* 1:50–3). Outside the town, the family held lands at South Stoneham, and rents and other interests as far dispersed as Surrey and Cornwall (S.C.R.O. SC4/2/253–4, 260–1, 271–3, 306–9). A William Nicholl, married to Alice, probably William Nicholl 'junior', appears as early as 1422 (S.C.R.O. SC4/2/243). It was this William who founded a chantry at St Mary's, endowing also an obit at Holy Rood; the obit was kept in the names of William Nicholl and of his wives, Agnes and Alice, but also mentioned Richard Thomas, who had married Juliana, widow of William Nicholl 'senior' (P.R.O. E301/52; S.C.R.O. SC4/1/1; Davies, pp. 422–4, placing the chantry at Holy Rood). If Juliana was indeed the wife of William Nicholl 'senior', he must have died before the year 1442, by which date she was already married to Richard Thomas (S.C.R.O. SC/4/2/273).

Norman, Roger, *fl.* 1322–47. Married Joan, formerly the wife of John of London; father of Giles (God's House Deeds 672; *Cal.Inq.P.M.,* xi:194, 208). Mayor in 1328–9 and 1330–1; parliamentary burgess in 1328, 1332 and 1339 (Davies, pp. 171, 200). In 1325, by virtue of his marriage to Joan, successfully claimed for himself a free burgess-ship of Southampton, to which she was already entitled (P.R.O. SC8/234/11672–3; *Cal.P.R. 1324–7,* p. 110). Probably the richest burgess of his day, he was assessed at £40 in the subsidy accounts of 1327 and 1332 (P.R.O. E179/173/4, m. 17v, E179/242/15a, m. 8v). Traded on a large scale in wool, owning ships of his own, which he frequently used on commissions for the king (P.R.O. E372/209, 210, SC6/1282/1). His service to the crown in this and other ways was recognized by the grant, in 1337, of free warren on his demesne lands, and by exemption, in 1338, from any additional military obligations (*Cal.Ch.R. 1327–41,* p. 389; *Cal.P.R. 1338–40,* pp. 56, 252). Properties in Southampton included an important messuage on the west side of English Street, south of Broad Lane, between tenements of Thomas de Byndon on the south and Nicholas de Moundenard on the north (Bodleian, Queen's College MS. 339, 340). Featuring as a substantial contributor to the cost of rebuilding Holy Rood church, he was probably a resident of that parish (Davies, p. 353). Had other tenements and rents in Holy Rood and East Street, with lands in Millbrook, Shirley and Chilworth, and estates in Wiltshire, Gloucestershire, Essex and Suffolk (Win.Coll.Mun. 17872–4, 17911–14; *Cal.C.R. 1346–9,* p. 258, *Cal.Ch.R. 1327–41,* p. 389; P.R.O. E326/9330). Granted a temporary respite from knighthood in June 1341, to last until the end of the year (*Cal.P.R. 1340–3,* p. 229). It was as 'Sir Roger Norman, knight' that he witnessed a charter of July 1347, concerning lands of William Ace in Freemantle, Millbrook, Shirley and Hill (Win.Coll.Mun. 17855).

Nostschilling, Thomas, *fl.* 1312–34. Married Florence, formerly the wife of Thomas Stout; father of John, who married Agnes (S.C.R.O. SC2/6/2; P.R.O. E326/9381). Elected bailiff in 1326, 1332 and 1333 (Davies, p. 171). In 1312, associated with Richard Bagge as joint-receivers of stolen wines worth £30 (*Cal.C.R. 1307–13,* pp. 487–8). Still trading in wine in 1324/5, when compelled with other leading Southampton burgesses to buy bad wine at Portchester (P.R.O. C47/60/6/184; *Cal.C.R. 1327–30,* p. 147). A man of considerable wealth, he was assessed at £40 and £25 in the subsidy accounts of 1327 and 1332 (P.R.O. E179/173/4, m. 17v, E179/242/15a, m. 8v). His marriage to Florence Stout brought him a tenement at the southern tip of French Street, on the sea front (S.C.R.O. SC2/6/2). It was probably his Stout and English family connections which led to the purchase, in 1325/6, of 1½ acres in Hoglands, inherited by Richard le English from his father, Richard 'senior', and next to land which Thomas Nostschilling had already acquired from John le English, brother of Richard 'junior' (P.R.O. E329/193). When his son, John Nostschilling, died in 1361, he was living at Eling, a few miles to the north-west of the town. John Nostschilling left his properties in Winchester and Southampton to his wife, Agnes, for the term of her life, with reversions to named religious institutions in the area (P.R.O. E326/9381). But he had neglected to secure royal licences, against the terms of the mortmain legislation, and his lands escheated to the crown on Agnes's death. In Southampton, they consisted of six acres in Hoglands and the Magdalene fields, and five tenements, three on English Street, one on East Street in the suburbs, and the fifth on French Street, parish of St John (P.R.O. C143/376/19; Win.Coll. Mun. 17779; *Cal.Inq.P.M.*, xiii:272).

Overy, William (senior), *fl.* 1388–1428. Married Agnes; father of Juliana, William and, probably, John (S.C.R.O. D/CJ/28; *Oak Book*, i:85). Steward in 1393–4; mayor in 1398–9 and 1406–7; parliamentary burgess in 1426 (Win.Coll.Mun. 17790–1; *Stewards' Books*, i:vii; Davies, pp. 173, 202). With John Polymond in 1388, required to release a Breton barge arrested by them for non-payment on supplies for Brest Castle (*Cal.C.R. 1385–9*, pp. 541–2). In 1407, said to have been withholding from God's House a rent due on property on the south side of St Michael's Square, next to the church (Ibid., *1405–9*, pp. 178, 180). Owned a house on the west side of English Street, parish of Holy Rood (S.C.R.O. SC4/2/202, 273). Still alive in April 1428, when he appeared as witness to a quitclaim by Sir Henry Plesington (*Cal.C.R. 1422–9*, p. 454). After his death, his widow, Agnes, was to complain of John Fleming 'annoying' her tenants; in the same letter, she commended William Soper for his help, and for the friendship he had always shown to herself and to her children (S.C.R.O. D/CJ/28).

Overy, William (junior), *fl.* 1472–85. Son of William Overy 'senior'; husband of Joan, father of Isabel and Joan, and possibly also of Thomas Overy, who was elected junior bailiff in 1485, sheriff in 1487, and mayor in 1488, 1489 and 1490 (*Oak Book*, i:85; *Black Book*, iii:52–3; *Book of Remembrance*, i:74–5). Was clerk to the town, probably for several years; became sheriff in 1472 and mayor in 1474 (*Oak Book*, i:85; Davies, p. 174). While sheriff in 1473, translated the ancient gild ordinances, presenting his translation to the town in 1478 (*Oak Book*, i:85–100). Already a knight before 1483/4, when attainted for treason, with other men of Southampton, probably in connection with the duke of Buckingham's rebellion and Henry Tudor's unsuccessful attempt to land at Poole. Pardoned shortly after Henry's accession in 1485 (*Rot.Parlm.*, vi:246, 273). William Overy's widow is mentioned in 1499, but William himself seems likely to have died some years before (*Black Book*, iii:52–3). It was Thomas Overy, who, while mayor, attempted to reform the town administration, introducing a new set of ordinances (*Oak Book*, i:xli–xlii, 151–60). A few years later, as captain and governor of Jersey, he may have been instrumental in fostering the Channel Islands trade of the town (J. L. Wiggs, 'The seaborne trade of Southampton in the second half of the sixteenth century', Southampton M.A., 1955, p. 91; *History of Parliament* (*Biographies*), *1439–1509*, p. 653).

Palshid, Richard, *fl.* 1496–1524. Town clerk from 1502, combining that office with the recordership from about 1506; probably gave up both offices when appointed collector of customs on 22 June 1509 (*Third Book of Remembrance*, i:66–7; *L. & P. Henry VIII*, i:1:53). In November 1500, acting as attorney for Thomas Thomas in a transaction concerning the latter's Southampton tenements (P.R.O. E326/11790). In London on the town's business in 1508/9 (S.C.R.O. SC5/1/27a, f. 7). In 1519/20, supervised the building of the new Customs House at Southampton (S.C.R.O. SC5/3/1, f. 45). Since 1496, had held the Watergate and adjoining house from the town, on a repairing lease, making it his home (S.C.R.O. SC4/1/1, SC4/3/14, 19, SC5/1/30, f. 37v; *Black Book*, ii:170–1). In 1522, reported to be dying (*L. & P. Henry VIII*, iii:2:1041–2). But was still alive in April 1524, when assessed at £100 for the purpose of the subsidy of that year (P.R.O. E179/173/175).

Payne, John, *fl.* 1428–67. Brother of Thomas Payne and Edith; married twice, the second time to Joan Childe, widow of a Londoner; father of John 'junior', of Catherine, Jane, Margery and one other daughter; father-in-law of Thomas White and Andrew James (Alwyn Ruddock, *Italian Merchants and Shipping*, pp. 170–1, and 'John Payne's persecution of foreigners', *Proc. Hampshire Field Club*, 16 (1944–7), passim). Elected sheriff in 1449; mayor in 1450, 1451 and 1462, being deposed from the mayoralty in May 1463; parliamentary burgess in 1435, 1447 and 1450 (Davies, pp. 174, 202 (corrected); *History of Parliament* (*Biographies*), *1439–1509*, pp.

669–70; *Cal.C.R. 1447–54*, p. 237). Traded in wine, iron, canvas, cloth and dyestuffs, oil and victuals (*Port Books*, *Local Port Books*, and *Brokage Books*, passim). Leader of the anti-foreign faction in the town through the middle years of the century (Alwyn Ruddock, *Italian Merchants and Shipping*, pp. 170–3, 176–80; P.R.O. C1/16/352, C1/26/385, C1/29/150, 403, etc.; *Cal.P.R. 1452–61*, p. 639). Retreated to London in 1463 and died there, a very wealthy man, in 1467 (Ruddock, op. cit., pp. 173, 180). In 1454, both the John Paynes lived in the parish of St John, whereas Thomas Payne lived in Holy Rood, in the great tenement north of the friary (S.C.R.O. SC13/1). Almost certainly, it was another Thomas Payne, the grandson of John Payne 'senior', who was mayor in 1472–3 (Davies, p. 174; *History of Parliament* (*Biographies*), *1439–1509*, p. 670n). In 1469–71, this Thomas Payne was trading in wine and some cloth, later founding an important chantry at Holy Rood (S.C.R.O. SC5/1/27b, f. 8; Davies, p. 422).

Polymond, John, *fl.* 1364–93. Husband of Alice (Win.Coll.Mun. 17885). Mayor in 1365–6, 1369–70, 1380–3, 1384–6 and 1391–3; parliamentary burgess in 1365, 1373, 1380–2 and 1384 (Davies, pp. 172, 201). Collector of customs and subsidies in the port from 1371, or earlier, frequently in association with William Bacon or John Thorp (P.R.O. E101/31/24, E122/136/30, E122/137/9a, E364/20/B; *Cal.C.R. 1389–92*, pp. 135, 239, *1409–13*, p. 186). With the two William Bacons and John Thorp again, active for many years in the king's service, supervising musters, surveying or arresting goods, and organizing works, in particular the construction of the new keep at Southampton Castle (P.R.O. E358/5, m. 16d, E364/12/E, E364/13/G, E364/14/C, E364/15/B, E372/222, 224, 236; *Cal.C.R. 1377–81*, p. 296, *1381–5*, pp. 63, 259, 261, 472–3, *1392–6*, pp. 69–70; *Cal.P.R. 1370–4*, pp. 72, 393, 485, *1377–81*, pp. 174, 241, 281, 313, 446, *1381–5*, pp. 279, 564, *1385–9*, pp. 236–7, 258). Between 1379 and 1384, rebuilt the Weigh House on its traditional site on French Street, opposite West Hall (*Cal.Inq.Misc. 1377–88*, p. 42; *Cal.P.R. 1381–5*, p. 476; *Cal.C.R. 1409–13*, pp. 45–6). On 28 October 1383, in recognition of past services, granted exemption from all municipal and royal offices, should he wish it; there is no evidence that he did, although he had clearly sought and must have welcomed the privilege (*Cal.P.R. 1381–5*, p. 320). In the last years of Edward III's reign and early in the reign of Richard II, associated with William Bacon, John Flete and others in illegal activities in the town, including prohibited sales to the king's enemies, forestalling, fraudulent customs and the taking of excessive profits on the collection of subsidies; escaped with pardons (Ibid., *1377–81*, pp. 79, 81, *1381–5*, p. 281). Himself a ship-owner and large-scale exporter of cloth (Ibid., *1388–92*, p. 27; P.R.O. E122/138/8, SC8/136/6767). Lived in the great tenement called 'Ongerisplace', between French Street and English Street, north of Brewhouse Lane; in 1454 it was known as 'Polymond's Hall', and later went under the name of 'Hampton Court' (God's House Deeds 417, 572; S.C.R.O. SC13/1). Other properties included an important group of tenements north of Porters Lane, with other tenements and rents on both sides of English Street, parish of Holy Rood, on the west side of the same street, parish of St Lawrence, on French Street and in the eastern suburbs; he also briefly held a valuable mortgage on the former Moundenard tenement immediately north of the friary (S.C.R.O. SC2/6/3, SC4/2/115–16, 156, 158, 164–5; God's House Deeds 680, 784; Win.Coll.Mun. 17763, 17779, 17780, 17790, 17885, 17893; P.R.O. C47/60/8/303, E326/9068; *Cal.Inq.Misc. 1348–77*, p. 241). Died between February 1393 and April 1394 (*Cal.C.R. 1392–6*, pp. 46, 69–70, 184–5; S.C.R.O. SC2/6/3, SC4/2/158; Win.Coll.Mun. 17790).

Puteo, John de (also known as John atte Barre), *fl.* 1288–before 1312. Son of Nicholas de Puteo, and presumably a descendant of Sampson de Puteo, a former bailiff, and Thomas de Puteo, joint viewer with Thomas le Blund of works at the king's castle and quay (St Denys Cart. 23, 207; P.R.O. E326/4492, *Cat.Anc. Deeds*, iii:D121; *Cal. Liberate R. 1251–60*, p. 413). Married Hawise, who survived him; father of John, Nicholas and Robert atte Barre (*Cat.Anc. Deeds*, ii:B3385; St Denys Cart. 211). Bailiff in 1288–9, 1291–2 and for at least one other term in the 1290s, when Peter de Lyon was alderman; parliamentary burgess, with Peter de Lyon, in 1295 (Davies, pp. 170, 199; P.R.O. E326/9349). Held a tenement and three shops on English Street, parish of St Lawrence; also a shop on the east side of the same street, parish of Holy Rood, and land in the northern suburbs, part of which he inherited from his father, Nicholas

(*Cat.Anc. Deeds*, ii:B3385; S.C.R.O. SC4/2/7; St Denys Cart. 22–3, 59–60, 77, 211). The family interest in All Saints Without seems to have been a strong one, for Sampson de Puteo and his wife, Isabel, actually lived in a messuage on the east side of Above Bar Street, north of the Bargate (St Denys Cart. 143). John de Puteo must have died before 1312, for there is mention of his widow in that year (*R.C.H.M.*, 6th report, p. 553).

Ravenston, William, *fl.* 1395–1410. Husband of Alice (S.C.R.O. SC4/2/187). Mayor in 1399–1400, in which role he began, at the instance of the king, a fresh programme of works on the defences (P.R.O. E364/37/B; Davies, p. 173). In 1403, took a repairing lease on the Watergate towers, later to be rebuilt by William Soper (S.C.R.O. SC4/3/2). Also held property on the east side of English Street, and came into a tenement on the west side of the same street, parish of Holy Rood, formerly of John Polymond. In March 1406, acquired the former Stout lands at the southern tip of the parish of St John, getting them from John Spicer and Thomas Coventre, to whom they had descended via Thomas, brother of the original purchaser, John le Spicer of Salisbury (S.C.R.O. SC4/2/182–4, 187, 197–9, 202, 207, 209). Was dead before June 1418, when mention is made of his widow, although another William Ravenston, 'clerk', was active in the town a decade later (S.C.R.O. SC4/2/237, 253–4).

St Laurence, Simon of, *fl.* 1196–1229. Probably the son of Robert of St Laurence, for many years tax farmer of the town, whose widow, Cecilia, succeeded him in that office in 1180 (*Pipe Roll 26 Henry II*, p. 148). Simon's other family relationships are difficult to disentangle, for he is described variously as the brother and the son of William of St Laurence, bailiff in 1205–6 (*R.C.H.M.*, 4th report, pp. 452–3; God's House Deeds 695; Davies, p. 170). But the most likely explanation seems to be that he was the uncle of the Simon who claimed to be William's son and heir rather later in the century. And if that is so, he was also the uncle of Agatha, sister of Simon 'junior', of Joan, who married Ralph Isembard, and of Alice, who became the wife of John de la Bulehuse (B.M. Loans 29/330, fos 123v, 124v; God's House Deeds 695; St Denys Cart. 63). Simon 'senior' was probably the father of Bovo of St Laurence, for it was Bovo who, from 1230, was being held responsible for the deficit on the farm incurred originally when Simon was bailiff in 1213–14. Bovo continued to carry the charge, although steadily reducing it, until his own death in 1256/7 (P.R.O. E372/62–101). Simon was already witnessing charters at the turn of the century, and was clearly an important man in the town by 1211–12 (God's House Deeds 802; *R.C.H.M.*, 4th report, pp. 452–4; *Pipe Roll 13 John*, p. 186). He was associated with Richard of Leicester both in the deficit on the farm of 1213–14 and in the Sir Richard Scarcaville incident three years later (W. W. Shirley (ed.), *Royal and other historical letters illustrative of the reign of Henry III*, i:8–10). He was not the only member of his family to cross the king. Already in 1208/9, Ralph of St Laurence, possibly another brother, had been fined sixty marks for 'having the benevolence' of John (*Pipe Roll 10 John*, p. 68).

Sampson, Hugh, *fl.* 1314–36. Possibly the son of the Hugh Sampson whose widow, Lucy, was holding tenements in the town in 1295/6 and 1307/8 (S.C.R.O. SC4/2/7; *R.C.H.M.*, 6th report, p. 552). Husband of Constance; father of Joan and presumably either brother or father of Thomas and Nicholas 'senior' (Bodleian, Queen's College MS. 4G10, 340; *Cal.P.R. 1334–8*, pp. 297–8). Bailiff, with Thomas de Byndon as alderman, before 1315; alderman himself in 1318–19, 1323–4, 1325–6 and 1333–4; parliamentary burgess in 1335 (Davies, pp. 171, 200 (corrected); P.R.O. E326/9340; *Cal. Memoranda R. 1326–7*, p. 294; *Cal.P.R. 1324–7*, p. 317). Collector of customs at Southampton from 1323, or earlier, until his death (P.R.O. E122/136/28–9; *Cal. C.R. 1327–30*, pp. 69–70, 434, *1333–7*, p. 58; *Cal.P.R. 1334–8*, pp. 297–8). In the twenties, a ship-owner on a considerable scale, suffering severe losses from piracy on at least one occasion (*Cal.P.R. 1324–7*, p. 276; *Cal.C.R. 1327–30*, pp. 298, 466–7). It was these, perhaps, that were influential in reducing his assessment for subsidy from £40 in 1327 to only 10*s*. in 1332 (P.R.O. E179/173/4, m. 17v, E179/242/15a, m. 8v). Early in 1331, summoned, with Thomas Sampson, to give advice to the king on nautical matters (Ibid., *1330–3*, p. 283). Lived, in 1335, on the east side of English Street, parish of Holy Rood (S.C.R.O. SC4/2/57). But had amassed by then a considerable property on Bull Street and French Street, parish of St John, including Henry le

Long's former capital messuage north of West Hall, Walter le Halveknight's share of West Hall, and a vacant plot in the area (S.C.R.O. SC4/2/33, 35–6, 39, 404). Nicholas Sampson was living in the vicinity, probably in one of these tenements, in August 1335. The West Hall property descended to Hugh Sampson's daughter, Joan, and to her husbands, Thomas atte Marche and John le Clerk; it included, by then, the shares earlier acquired by John of Shirley and bought by Hugh Sampson from his widow, Felicia (S.C.R.O. SC2/6/2, SC4/2/57; Bodleian, Queen's College MS. 4G10). As a wealthy burgess, active in trade, Hugh Sampson had handled considerable sums of money during his life, both as a borrower and as a lender (e.g. *Cal.C.R. 1327–30*, pp. 90, 92; S.C.R.O. SC2/6/1). On his death, before July 1336, his goods were arrested to cover his debts, at the suit of Thomas de Byndon, an old-time associate and fellow collector of customs. In defiance of the town bailiffs, who had taken them under lock and key, Constance Sampson and her friends rescued her late husband's effects, valued at over £200 (*Cal.P.R. 1334–8*, pp. 297–8).

Sampson, Nicholas (senior), *fl.* 1319–45. Brother of Thomas Sampson; close relative, probably either brother or son, of Hugh Sampson; husband of Isabel; father, or uncle, of Nicholas Sampson 'junior', bailiff in 1341–2, steward in 1342–3 and 1348–9, collector of customs in 1346, and probably the Nicholas who was an *echevin* of the town in 1350–1 (S.C.R.O. SC2/6/2, SC4/2/57, 77, 83–5; Win. Coll.Mun. 17804; *Oak Book*, ii:130–1). Nicholas 'senior' was himself bailiff in 1320–1 and 1334–5, being alderman for two years in succession from 1337–9, through the crisis of the French raid (Davies, p. 171 (corrected); St Denys Cart. 179, 181; P.R.O. E210/9312, E326/9152, E372/210; *Cal. Fine R.*, v:124; *Cat.Anc. Deeds*, ii:A3244). In 1338, shortly before the raid, was exporting wool in *La Bertelmew*, of which he was patron (P.R.O. E372/194). It was probably his knowledge of shipping as much as his experience of the raid which subsequently recommended him to the king as an adviser on the defence of the realm and on its shipping (*Cal.C.R. 1339–41*, p. 449). In the subsidy accounts of 1327 and 1332, Nicholas Sampson was assessed at £6. 13*s*. 4*d*. and £10 respectively; his brother, Thomas, in the same accounts was assessed at £5 and 33*s*. 4*d*. (P.R.O. E179/173/4, m. 17v, E179/242/15a, m. 8v). Nicholas lived on the west side of French Street, parish of St John; he also acquired a tenement on West Hithe, just south of the castle, which became the property of Hugh Sampson shortly before his death, subsequently descending to Thomas atte Marche (S.C.R.O. SC4/2/57; Bodleian, Queen's College MS. 339–40). In 1325/6, while Hugh Sampson was alderman, Nicholas acquired a tenement on the north side of Simnel Street, parish of St Michael. It was possibly there that his brother, Thomas Sampson, was living in August 1335 (S.C.R.O. SC4/2/32, 57). Still active, in what appears to have been a property exchange, in June–August 1345 (S.C.R.O. SC4/2/77, 80). A St Denys rental of June 1349 records Nicholas Sampson as the holder of two plots of land by Houndwell, although it is not clear which Nicholas, 'senior' or 'junior', was intended (P.R.O. SC12/14/62).

Shirley, John of, *fl.* 1294–1327. Probably the son of Roger and Isabel of Shirley, and brother of Nicholas, Roger 'junior' and Simon; possibly a descendant of the Nicholas of Shirley who made over his rights on Southampton Common to the burgesses in 1228; husband of Felicia (St Denys Cart. 161–6; *Black Book*, iii:134–9; S.C.R.O. SC4/2/403). Bailiff in 1298–9 and for at least one other term in the 1290s, when Robert le Mercer was alderman and Thomas le Blund was the other bailiff; alderman himself at least twice at the beginning of the new century, and again in 1311–12; parliamentary burgess in 1302 and 1311 (Davies, pp. 170–1, 199–200 (corrected); St Denys Cart. 142; P.R.O. E326/5745; *Cat.Anc. Deeds*, ii:B3311). With Henry de Lym, collector of customs at Southampton from *c.* 1307 (P.R.O. E122/136/6, 8, 17; *Cal. C.R. 1307–13*, pp. 275–6). Following the partition of West Hall in 1303/4, acquired the shares of John, Thomas and Roger le Halveknight, already having a substantial interest there by 1307/8 (S.C.R.O. SC4/2/398–401, 403; *R.C.H.M.*, 6th report, p. 552). His widow, Felicia, sold these shares to Hugh Sampson, probably before 1335 (Bodleian, Queen's College MS. 4G10).

Soper, William, *fl.* 1410–59. Son of Robert and Clemency Soper, of Winchester; married Isabel and then Joan (S.C.R.O. D/LY/7/25; *Black Book*, ii:58–9, 102–3). Steward in 1410–11; mayor in 1416–17 and 1424–5;

parliamentary burgess in 1413, 1414, 1419, 1420, 1421, 1423, 1427, 1429, 1431, 1432, 1433, 1442 and 1449 (*Stewards' Books*, i:vii; Davies, pp. 173, 202 (corrected); *History of Parliament* (*Biographies*), *1439–1509*, p. 782). Active in the king's service from the start of Henry V's reign, beginning a long association with the navy in 1414. Supervised ship-building, repairs and supply, being appointed clerk of the king's ships while the building of the *Gracedieu* was in progress, and holding the office of keeper and governor of the king's ships from 1423 until 1442 (*Cal.P.R. 1422–9*, p. 64, *1441–6*, p. 58; also Mrs Carpenter Turner's articles in *The Mariner's Mirror*, 40 (1954), pp. 44–72, 270–81, and M. Oppenheim, *A history of the administration of the Royal navy*, pp. 16–17). For services to the crown, in receipt of a pension from the king from 1417 (P.R.O. E122/140/13). Collector of tunnage and poundage in the port from November 1413; with John Foxholes, collector of customs on wool, woolfells and hides from July 1421 (P.R.O. E122/140/6, E364/55/F; *Cal.P.R. 1416–22*, p. 392). Himself active in trade, in association with Walter Fetplace, William Nicholl and others, dealing principally in wine and wool, with some iron, oil and miscellaneous merchandise (S.C.R.O. SC4/2/223; B.M. Cotton Vesp. XIII:51; P.R.O. E122/184/3; *Cal.P.R. 1416–22*, p. 295; *Port Books, 1427–30*, passim, although it is noticeable that in the later *Local Port Books* and *Brokage Books* he scarcely features, except in the despatch of occasional cartloads of wine and luxury goods to London, possibly for his own use, or as gifts to influential friends). Took his turn as host to foreign merchants, as he was doing in March 1443 and February 1444 (P.R.O. E101/128/35, E179/173/107). But spent much of his time in London, frequently representing the town in parliament and attending to the details of the payment of its farm (*Port Books, 1427–30*, pp. 86, 116; *Local Port Book, 1435–6*, pp. 124–7). In 1420, granted the right to maintain a private oratory in his house (*Cal.Pap.Reg.*, *Papal Letters*, vii:337). He certainly had such an oratory, or chapel, in 1430 at the estate and hunting-lodge he maintained on the edge of the New Forest, of which he was a verderer (M. E. Mallett, *The Florentine galleys in the fifteenth century*, pp. 259–60). His interests in Southampton itself included a long lease on the tenement at the south-west tip of English Street, next to the Watergate and later to be the site of the Customs House. He held the property immediately to the north, with other plots south of Broad Lane; and by 1433 had rebuilt the Watergate itself, holding it thereafter at a nominal rent from the town and subletting it to John Ingoldesby from October 1439 (Win.Coll.Mun. 17835; P.R.O. E326/11785, 11792, 11804; S.C.R.O. SC4/3/4, 6–7, SC13/1). A benefactor of the friary, of which he was a near-neighbour. He was beginning to make arrangements there for his own burial and memorial masses as early as 1452, when he assigned his country estates to the endowment of an obit at the friary church. Made other like arrangements in 1458 when drawing up his last will and testament. Died in 1459, and was buried in the marble tomb he had already had constructed for himself on the south side of the friary nave. Left a widow, Joan, who was to hold, for her life, William's extensive properties on the east side of English Street, including two tenements and a cellar newly built in the friary cemetery, with the rent still due from John Ingoldesby on the Watergate (S.C.R.O. D/LY/7/25; *Black Book*, ii:98–115, 122–5).

Southwick, Richard of, *fl.* 1268–90. Husband of Juliana, who survived him; father of Rose and Juliana (S.C.R.O. SC4/2/8; St Denys Cart. 260). Held a tenement and other properties on the east side of Bull Street, on the southern edge of the parish of St Michael; also a messuage, with curtilage and the land adjoining, in the north-western suburb, on the Strand (God's House Deeds 594–7, and Cartulary f. 17v; St Denys Cart. 55, 83, 260, 269–70). Died in 1290, or shortly before (St Denys Cart. 260). A seal matrix bearing his name was recently recovered from a cesspit attached to a great stone house on the western shore, south of Westgate Street; it was associated with pottery and other objects of late-thirteenth-century date (*Southampton Excavations*, forthcoming). It may be that he was living there during the last years of his life, for it is certainly true that he had given up at least one of his Bull Street properties by 1283/4 (God's House Deeds 597). An earlier seal, attached to a deed some twenty years pre-dating his death, is of a rather different form (Ibid., 594). The name 'Southwick', variously rendered 'Suwik', 'Suwyk', 'Suwyke', 'Sutwyk', 'Sutwike', 'Suthewik' and 'Suthewike', is as likely to derive from the lands of 'Suth Wyk' in Portswood, as from the more obvious Southwick, near Fareham (St Denys Cart. 297).

Stout, Thomas, *fl.* 1283–1317. Possibly the brother of Luke Stout, a contemporary with property adjoining his own on the east side of Bull Street; husband of Florence, later the wife of Thomas Nostschilling; father of Rosya, who married Bartholomew le English, and Isabel, who married John de Ronde (S.C.R.O. SC2/6/2). Bailiff before 1303, when John of Shirley was alderman; alderman himself before 1314 and in 1315–16 (Davies, p. 171 (corrected); S.C.R.O. SC4/2/401; St Denys Cart. 142; Win.Coll.Mun. 17897–8, 17908). Traded in wine, owning the ship called *La Nicholas* which was still working the wine routes for his widow, Florence (*Cal.C.R. 1313–18*, p. 460; P.R.O. SC6/1282/1). Held from 1283, or earlier, very considerable properties at the southern end of the town, on both sides of Bull Street, but principally between Bull Street and French Street and on the quay linking the two. These descended to his heirs, Florence, Rosya and Isabel, becoming the property, in the 1340s, of John le Spicer, of Salisbury. From John they came to his brother, Thomas le Spicer, who had disposed of part of the property to Thomas Coventre, of Oxford, before passing the remainder on to his own son, John. In March 1406 the former Stout tenements came back into local ownership when William Ravenston acquired them from Thomas Coventre and John Spicer, nephew of their original purchaser (God's House Deeds 596–7; S.C.R.O. SC2/6/2, SC4/2/197–9).

Thomas, Sampson, *fl.* 1517–47. Son of Thomas and Elizabeth Thomas; brother of Frances and Joan; husband of Maud (P.R.O. C1/1372/3, E326/12251). Admitted to a burgess-ship in 1517; sheriff in 1519–20; mayor in 1523–4 and 1535–6 (S.C.R.O. SC3/1/1, p. 58; *Third Book of Remembrance*, i:64–5). Controller of customs at Southampton in the 1540s (*L. & P. Henry VIII*, xxi:2:84). In 1524 assessed, in the subsidy accounts of that year, at the high figure of £66. 13*s*. 4*d*. (P.R.O. E179/173/175). Was a close friend and trading associate of the Anglo-Genoese merchant, Niccolo de Egra, then holding West Hall from the town (Alwyn Ruddock, *Italian Merchants and Shipping*, pp. 247, 251). Lived himself on the east side of English Street, parish of Holy Rood, securing for his own use, in 1535, a private supply of water, to be drawn from the friary conduit (P.R.O. E326/6957). It was probably to improve the supply that he leased, shortly afterwards, the friary washing yard, continuing to hold it, on very favourable terms, following the Dissolution (P.R.O. SC6/Henry VIII/7407; B.M. Harl. Roll I.14; *L. & P. Henry VIII*, xvii:698). Involved in a prolonged dispute with the Huttofts, like himself 'great occupiers' in the town (*Third Book of Remembrance*, i:39–40; *L. & P. Henry VIII*, xiii:1:430). Died, without issue, certainly before 1555, but probably nearer 1547/8 (P.R.O. C1/1372/3).

Thomas, Thomas, *fl.* 1486–1509. Of Welsh birth, the son of John Thomas who settled in London; married Elizabeth, who survived him; father of Sampson, Frances and Joan, who married John White, having by him a daughter, Elizabeth, later the wife of George Oglander (P.R.O. C1/1372/3, E326/11798, 12251). Parliamentary burgess, with John Dawtrey, in 1495 (Davies, p. 203; *History of Parliament* (*Biographies*), *1439–1509*, pp. 846–7). From 1486, controller of customs in the port, an office in which Dawtrey succeeded him (S.C.R.O. SC5/3/1, f. 15; *Black Book*, ii:162). Lived during those years in Holy Rood, south of Broad Lane, in the tenement once of Walter Fetplace 'senior', let and then sold to him, with other Fetplace properties in the parish, by John Ludlow (P.R.O. E326/11792, 11794–6). In 1493, bought from the town a cellar at La Chayne, holding other properties from the corporation and God's House in St John's and in the Newtown suburb (S.C.R.O. SC4/1/1, SC5/3/1, f. 15; God's House Deeds 791; *Black Book*, ii:162). After a legal wrangle, bought in 1507 the former James corner tenement on Broad Lane and English Street, briefly held by William Justice (P.R.O. E326/11789, 11792, E329/429; *Black Book*, iii:36–45). Had clearly settled at Southampton before his death, desiring to be buried at the friary next to his mother. But held considerable London properties and spent much of his time there. His will, dated 26 September 1508, named Richard Palshid, already his attorney in 1500, among his executors. His wife, Elizabeth, was to hold his tenements until her death, meanwhile using her own judgment as to how much to pass on to their children (P.R.O. E326/11790, 11798). Died in December 1509, but was in deep trouble at the time of his death, probably on account of his association with

Sir Richard Empson and Edmund Dudley, the late king's unpopular officers (*History of Parliament* (*Biographies*), *1439–1509*, pp. 846–7).

Welles, Thomas (junior), *fl.* 1534–50. Probably a relative of Thomas Welles 'the elder', who was admitted burgess five years later than himself; husband of Margaret; stepfather of William Knight, who married Elizabeth (S.C.R.O. SC3/1/1, p. 70v; *Black Book*, iii:90). Admitted to a burgess-ship on 1 July 1535; court bailiff in 1539–40; sheriff in 1547–8 (S.C.R.O. SC3/1/1, p. 66; *Third Book of Remembrance*, i:65, ii:154). In succession to James Bettes, held a customership at Southampton from 1539/40 (*L. & P. Henry VIII*, xi:130; S.C.R.O. SC13/2/1). Associated with Thomas Wriothesley, later earl of Southampton, as a pensioner of Hyde Abbey shortly before the Dissolution, and was at Titchfield, Wriothesley's newly-acquired estate, in January 1538, helping John Mille and Henry Huttoft restore it to some order (*L. & P. Henry VIII*, xiii:1:6–7, xiv:2:75). On 1 September 1534, anticipating the Dissolution, had himself acquired from Netley Abbey the lease of a substantial tenement on the west side of English Street, parish of Holy Rood (P.R.O. E318/603, SC6/Henry VIII/3326). Subsequently bought this property from John Mille, to transfer it, with another tenement and a vacant plot and garden in St Michael's, to William and Elizabeth Knight (*Black Book*, iii:90–2; *L. & P. Henry VIII*, xxi:1:352). Held the friary site in 1540–1, violently resisting an attempt the following year to dispossess him. In subsequent proceedings, it was alleged that Welles had stripped the friary buildings of lead and timber, and had set up bowling-alleys on the site (B.M. Harl. Roll I.14; P.R.O. E315/165, f. 5). Was probably alive still in August 1550, when his wife was said to have been holding seditious conversations with her nephew, the keeper of Crockham Park, Berkshire (*Letters*, pp. 78–9). Dead before May 1551 (B.M. Harl. 606, f. 35v).

Wytegod, John, *fl.* 1348–69. Husband of Joan (*Cal.Inq.P.M.*, xv:26). Probably related to the Walter Wytegod who featured in the subsidy accounts of 1327 and 1332, assessed at £5 and £3. 6*s*. 8*d*. respectively (P.R.O. E179/173/4, m. 17v, E179/242/15a, m. 8v). Bailiff in 1348–9; mayor in 1361–2 and 1367–8; parliamentary burgess in 1358, 1362, 1363 and 1368 (Davies, pp. 172, 201). In 1365, one of the collectors of customs at Southampton (R. R. Sharpe (ed.), *Calendar of Letters from the Mayor and Corporation of the City of London*, pp. 132–3). In that year, alleged to have been bribing a royal clerk to make payments and assignments in his favour (*Cal.C.R. 1364–8*, p. 122). A vintner, he traded to Gascony for wines and was planning a venture there in December 1369 (Ibid., *1369–74*, p. 51). Was probably a resident of the parish of St Michael, holding property by St Michael's Square and the tenement on the western shore now known as 'King John's Palace', immediately south of Wytegod's Lane, now Blue Anchor Lane. In 1360, among the improvements recommended for the town defences was the blocking of his seaward postern 'with a wall as thick as the wall of the cellar' (*Cal.Inq.Misc. 1348–77*, p. 154; *Black Book*, i:85, ii:51). Also held a tenement on the west side of English Street, parish of Holy Rood, a vacant plot on the same side of the street, parish of St Lawrence, and the site of La Chayne, north of Porters Lane, the last initially with John le Clerk (S.C.R.O. SC2/6/3, SC4/2/93; *Cal.Inq.P.M.*, xv:26; Win. Coll.Mun. 17805–6).

b. Family alliances

The tables in Figure 10 have been compiled to illustrate dynastic intermarriage within the Southampton burgess class. They are not to be seen as complete family trees, even at the present state of knowledge. In particular, the Fleming family did not die out with the children of John le Fleming and Petronilla Isembard. There are Flemings in Hampshire to this day. In Southampton, the direct male line of the Fleming family is traceable through the remainder of the Middle Ages.

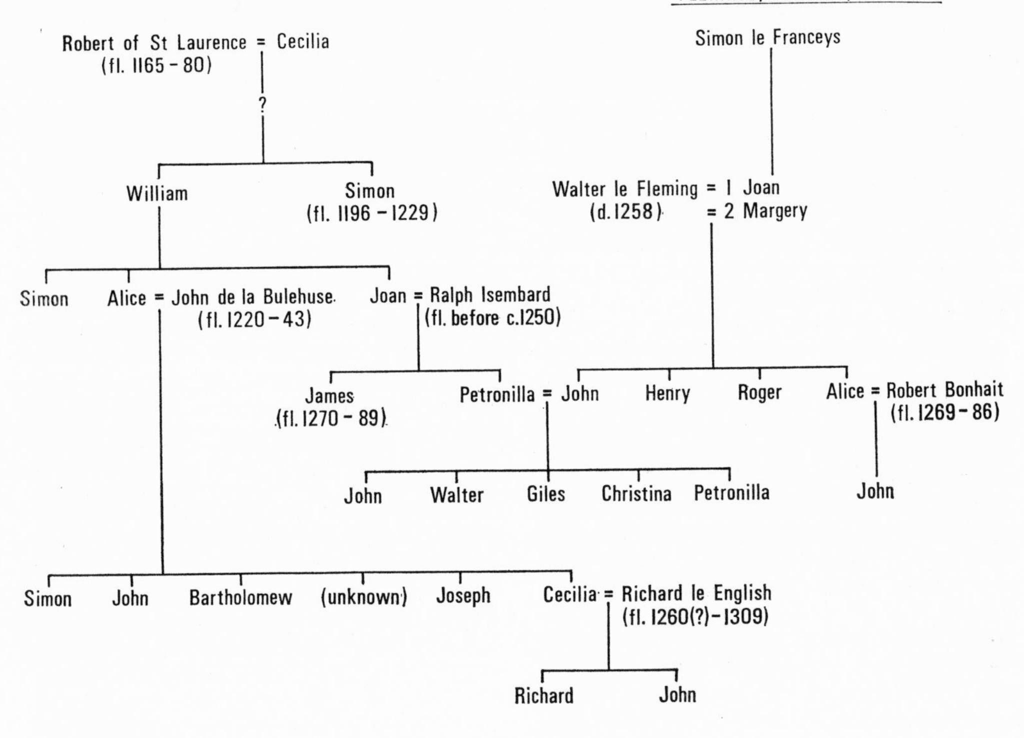

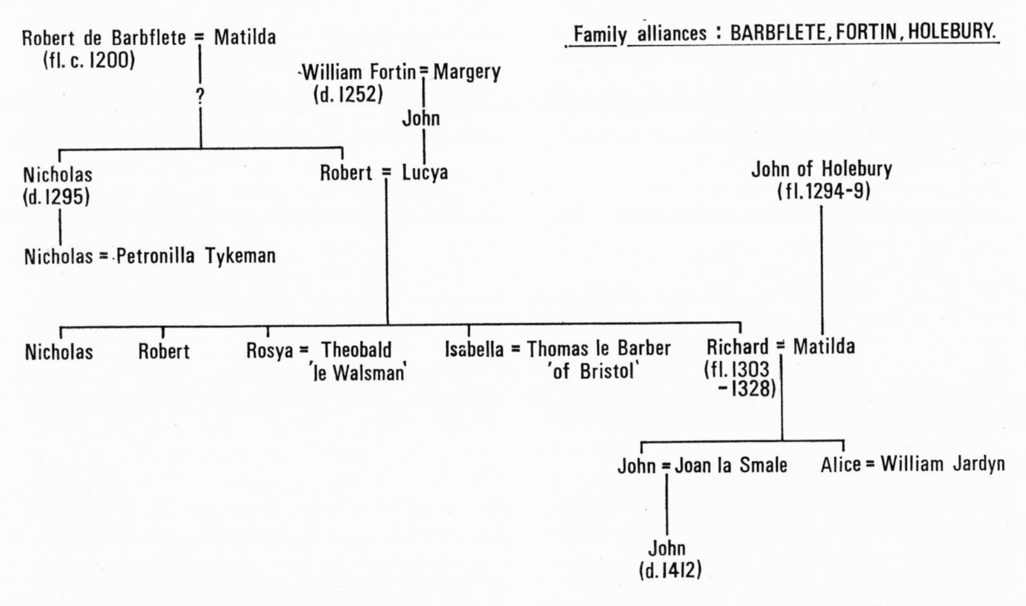

Figure 10 Genealogical tables: family alliances in the thirteenth- and fourteenth-century borough

c. Population and social stratification in medieval Southampton

Population

Population estimates are notoriously subjective, and medieval historians are rightly suspicious of them. But when applied to a single location over a long period of time, such estimates may begin to show some pattern. It is to this pattern rather than to any absolute magnitudes that a value may be attached. At Southampton, within our period, there are four points in time at which data become available for population studies. Of these, the earliest is also the least satisfactory.

1. Domesday Book, 1086 (650–850). Although of some use in comparisons with other towns, the Domesday record for Southampton is less than adequate as evidence of the size of the community in 1086. In the absence of any thorough modern analysis of the Domesday borough evidence, Professor J. C. Russell's figure of 773 persons at Southampton is likely to remain the only acceptable working estimate.[1] Yet, as J. H. Round pointed out many years ago, the Southampton Domesday entry is defective even in the little it attempts to record. It lists, for example, no fewer than 79 royal tenants in the borough, to set against an opening total of only 76. And the value it possesses lies rather in the record it preserves of French (65) and English (31) settlement in the years immediately following the Conquest.[2]

2. Poll tax, 1377 (1,600). Clergy and children under the age of fourteen were omitted from the lay poll tax returns of 1377. But with these exceptions, and in marked contrast to the less successful tax of 1381, evasion in 1377 is generally reckoned to have stood at scarcely more than 5 per cent. At Southampton it may have been less, for the named collectors, John Polymond and his associates, were already well-tried administrators on appointment. By their reckoning, there were 1,152 persons, male and female, taxable in the borough in 1377; their successors, in 1381, counted 1,051.[3] These were years of depression and depopulation in the borough. Consequently, Professor Russell's allowance for omissions in the 1377 returns, at 50 per cent of the total, may very well be over-generous.[4] A population figure at about 1,600 in 1377 is probably nearer the mark.

Once arrived at, a population estimate for 1377 may be used to suggest a pre-plague total for the town, although only at the risk of compounding such error as is already incorporated in the later figure. It is Professor Russell's view, re-expressed as recently as 1969, that the population of the plague-affected areas receded by as much as 40 per cent over the three decades following the Black Death. Of this, the Black Death itself may have accounted for about half the loss.[5] But to reach the pre-plague figure by a simple addition of Russell's 40 per cent would be to ignore the specially adverse conditions in the town by 1377, the product of the war with France and of desertion by the burgesses themselves in the face of the heavy burden of defence. If the 1377 figure was indeed an unnaturally low one, something would have to be added to the pre-plague estimate by way of compensation. It is suggested, therefore, that the pre-plague population of Southampton would have been nearer 2,500, and may have been two or three hundred more. It had probably remained that way for at least fifty years, in keeping with the general stabilization of population in England, which seems to have occurred at the turn of the thirteenth and fourteenth centuries.

3. Terrier, 1454 (1,800–2,000). An inventory, compiled in 1454 for the purpose of apportioning responsibility for repair of the defences, listed 'all the capital tenements, messuages, cottages, cellars, warehouses and vacant plots situated and lying within the walls of the town of Southampton and extending to the streets and lanes in the said town'.[6] The wording of the terrier is sometimes unhelpful, but it is possible to say that there were between 420 and 430 occupied properties within the walls, ranging from the great houses of the wealthy burgesses to the cottages of their servants and journeymen. If a household multiplier of 3½ is applied, the figure for residents in the walled town would be about 1,500. But it has frequently been felt that Professor Russell's multiplier is too low, particularly for these later periods, and it may be safer to apply a multiplier of 4, bringing the total to nearer 1,700. The balance of properties in the terrier, with its comparatively low figure for cottages, suggests that a fair proportion of the poorer townspeople lived in the suburban areas outside the walls. If an entirely arbitrary figure of 20 per cent is added for these, the total population of the borough and its immediate environs in 1454 may have reached a figure of between 1,800 and 2,000, showing a measure of recovery in keeping with the return of modest prosperity to the town.

4. Lay subsidy, 1524 (1,750–1,950). The 1454 total is convincingly supported by the returns for the lay subsidy of 1524. In what was perhaps the most effective general tax devised since 1377, the local assessors of 1524 were required to make returns covering all persons in the town having land, goods or wages to the value of £1 a year, or more. On the usual reckoning, between a third and a half of the total population escaped the tax, for the most part by reason of poverty. At Southampton, in addition, provision must be made for those names (rather less than a quarter of the total for the ward) missing from the damaged account of St Michael with St John; some allowance is necessary for the presence in the accounts of servants (not always householders) and widows (perhaps living on their own); and the taxpayers of Portswood should be excluded from the total. Using multipliers again of 3½ and 4, and making generous provision for non-taxpayers, the returns of 1524 suggest a population for the borough and its suburbs of between 1,750 and 1,950.[7] With another trade recession in the offing and a war in progress, this was not a prosperous time for the port. Many townsmen made a living from casual employment on the quayside, and it would seem not unreasonable to suppose an incidence of poverty at Southampton rather higher than the average for boroughs of comparable size. Although population figures generally had begun to pick up, and would rise dramatically through the latter part of the sixteenth century, it is doubtful whether this movement was fully reflected at Southampton. If it were so, one might expect a recovery to pre-plague figures by 1600. But reverses in international trade had deprived the borough of much of its economic resilience, and if population built up again, as it must have done in time, an increasing part in this growth would have been taken by low-income earners and by the destitute poor.

Many estimates of medieval population depend on the calculation of life expectations, and it may be of interest to comment here on the implications of the *floruits* assembled in the first part of this appendix. The coverage is restricted to the ruling class, and in many cases the evidence is defective. Nevertheless, it can be said that the usable *floruits* indicate a working span, for somewhat over 45 per cent of the total, of between twenty and thirty years. In the next largest group, at about 25 per cent, working lives extended to between thirty and forty years. Some 13 per cent worked for forty years or more, and only 15 per cent for less than twenty. Nobody can say at what point in their careers the majority of the burgesses first made an appearance in the records. But they did so, usually, as householders, as the principals in trading transactions, or as witnesses, lending the weight of their names to the deeds and other legal documents of co-burgesses. In the circumstances, a starting-age at twenty may not be unrealistic, suggesting a life-span for this comfortably-off class in the region of fifty years. On any reckoning, a strikingly high percentage of the burgesses lived to be over sixty.

Social stratification

Although usually imperfect as the source material for population estimates, the same records may sometimes yield information of value relating to social patterns in the town. At Southampton, the subsidy returns of 1524 have been used already in the calculation of a population figure for that year. But both this and the earlier lay subsidies were assessed on personal wealth, or, perhaps more to the point, on a contemporary collector's estimate of that wealth, agreed at a conventional figure usually in consultation with the assessed. Whereas the limitations of such returns as a record of absolute riches have long been recognized, it is yet possible to see them as a contemporary portrayal of social stratification in the community, a valuable extension of knowledge in an area otherwise little recorded.

The lay subsidy returns of 1327 and 1332, touching less than a quarter of the community, are of little value in the calculation of population figures. But they have uses other than that. Tabulated below, the figures from the returns suggest a rough classification by wealth within the tax-paying class, already used by Dr Pelham to point a revealing contrast with the neighbouring community at Winchester.[8] In addition, the names listed in the returns both confirm our impression of the dominant voices in the town and allow a rare glimpse of the better-off artisan and tradesman class, included at the bottom of the scale. In 1327, the wealthiest men in the town were Roger Norman, Hugh Sampson and Thomas Nostschilling, each assessed at £40, with Henry de Lym and Nicholas de Moundenard closely following, at £30. By 1332, Hugh Sampson, probably as a result of his recent severe losses at sea, had dropped far behind. Henry de Lym's assessment had been reduced to £20, and Thomas Nostschilling's to £25. Thomas de Byndon, assessed at only £20 in 1327, was now rated at £30. The assessments of Roger Norman and Nicholas de Moundenard remained the same, at £40 and £30 respectively. The lowest assessments, £1 in 1327 and usually below £1 in 1332, attached to men very frequently identified by an occupational surname of some kind. By far the largest group of such surnames was to be found in this class, and almost all of its members were included below the £5 limit. Of course, many of these occupational surnames had become family names, continuing in use regardless of the trade of the holder. But at least it remains possible to record that there were masons, turners and smiths working in the local building trades; that shearers, tanners, cordwainers, glovers and tailors were employed in the clothing industry; that there were spicers, poulterers, vintners, tappers and taverners among the victuallers; and potters, barbers, gardeners and mulewards representing the miscellaneous trades.[9]

Deficient coverage is a serious weakness of these earlier lay subsidies. But if this is less the case in 1524, it needs to be said that the improved coverage of the later returns should warn us against comparisons between the two. In 1524, in contrast to the earlier returns, the

Table 1 *Subsidies of 1327 and 1332*

Assessable goods	*1327 (1/20th)*	*1332 (1/10th)*
Under £1	—	30 (27·3%)
£1 to £2	65 (50%)	31 (28·2%)
£2 to £5	39 (29·3%)	19 (17·3%)
£5 to £10	15 (11·1%)	15 (13·6%)
£10 to £20	5 (3·6%)	5 (4·5%)
£20 to £40	8 (6%)	10 (9·1%)
Total taxpayers	132	110

majority of regular wage labourers are thought to have been included in the accounts. The Southampton collectors listed wage-earners in the lower categories. Wage labourers and servants, with a large group of householders and other self-employed, assessed on wages or goods to the value of £1, constituted about 50 per cent of the taxpayers in the town. Another 35 per cent of the total was made up of those assessed at between £2 and £10, including some wage-earners among them. There were no wage-earners in the next group, just under 12 per cent of the total, assessed at between £10 and £40. Only 3 per cent were judged to be worth £40 or more. If paupers and the lowest levels of wage-earners are assumed to have constituted a minimum of 30 per cent of the community, escaping assessment altogether, it becomes possible to rewrite these figures as percentages of the town population as a whole. In their new form, they will be seen to compare closely with the figures published by Dr Hoskins for contemporary Leicester. Neither at Leicester nor at Southampton can much be said of the really poor. But in those assessed at £1 we may reasonably identify an employed working class, making an adequate living so long as employment persisted in the port. At Southampton, it constituted some 36 per cent of the total population of the borough; at Leicester, about 30 per cent. A 'lower middle class', individually assessed at between £2 and £10, made up another 25 per cent of the population at Southampton, 30 per cent at Leicester. In those assessed at between £10 and £40, Dr Hoskins sees the 'solid core' of the middle classes: some 8 per cent at Southampton, 7 per cent at Leicester. The wealthy, only 2 per cent at Southampton and 3 per cent at Leicester, usually paid tax on an assessment very much higher than £40.[10] In the sixteenth-century borough, sharp divisions, already apparent two centuries before, persisted between the very wealthy and the men of middling condition. A small group of burgesses still concentrated power at the top, constituting an aristocracy of wealth. Of its members, Peter Stoner, Richard Caplyn and Walter Baker each paid tax on an assessment of £40, Sampson Thomas, John Perchard and John Fleming on £66. 13*s*. 4*d*., Thomas Husee on £80, Richard Palshid and Thomas Lyster on £100, Henry Huttoft on £133. 6*s*. 8*d*., and Richard Lyster on the large assessment of £250. With the exception of Richard Lyster, who was building his career in the law, each of these men either had held already, or would hold in the future, high public office in the borough. As the servants of the king and of the borough, they expected (and usually received) good rewards.

Table 2 *Subsidy of 1524*

Assessable goods	*Holy Rood*	*St Lawrence*	*All Saints*	*St Michael with St John*	*Tithing of Portswood*	*Totals*
£1	41	16	61	41	18	177 (50%)
£2 to £10	37	16	35	33	3	124 (35·2%)
£10 to £40	14	8	10	10	—	42 (11·8%)
£40 and over	5	2	1	3	—	11 (3%)
Total taxpayers	97	42	107	87/105	21	354/372
(tax paid)	(£33. 0*s*. 12*d*.)	(£13. 10*s*. 0*d*.)	(£12. 18*s*. 4*d*.)	(£41. 4*s*. 10*d*.)	(13*s*. 6*d*.)	(£101. 7*s*. 8*d*.)

Note Part of the return for St Michael with St John has rotted away, removing what can be calculated as a little less than a quarter of the list of taxpayers. It is suggested that the total number of taxpayers in the ward was probably about 105, calculated on the basis of the total tax paid in the ward, the figure for which has survived (as above).

Social exclusiveness in the borough may be demonstrated in another way. The subsidy of 1524 was collected by ward, the four wards corresponding with the parishes of Holy Rood, St Lawrence, All Saints and St Michael with St John. To these was added, for the purpose of the return, an account for the tithing of Portswood. Noticeably, those paying the higher taxes concentrated in the southern parishes: Walter Baker, Henry Huttoft and Richard Lyster in St Michael with St John; Peter Stoner, Sampson Thomas, John Perchard, Thomas Lyster and Richard Palshid in Holy Rood; Thomas Husee and Richard Caplyn in St Lawrence. Only John Fleming chose to live in All Saints, where his father and grandfather had held the family tenement before him. At Portswood, a distant suburb, the wealthiest taxpayer was Robert Baker, assessed at only £7. At the other end of the scale, it was in All Saints and at Portswood that the highest percentages were recorded of taxpayers assessed at only £1. St Lawrence, a small parish with house frontages exclusively on English Street, showed the lowest percentage of working-class taxpayers, as well as the highest percentage, relatively, of solid-core middle class. It was to the middle class, clearly, that the St Lawrence properties had most appeal, perhaps because of their suitability for retailing. Wealthier men, the leading figures of the town, usually handling overseas trade, chose to live nearer the shore, in the parishes of Holy Rood, St Michael and St John.

Some further confirmation of these preferences may be obtained from the record of town properties compiled in the previous century for the corporation. The terrier of 1454 records a total of twenty-six capital tenements within the walled town: twelve in Holy Rood, six in St Michael's, five in St John's, two in St Lawrence's and only one (the Fleming tenement again) in All Saints. Two other classes of occupied property, tenements and cottages, were recorded in the terrier. Of these, there were substantially more tenements than cottages in the parishes of Holy Rood, St Michael, St John and St Lawrence. Only in All Saints Within were the numbers of cottages and tenements approximately equal. Through the walled town as a whole, about 6 per cent of the occupied properties were ranked as capital tenements, some 60 per cent as tenements (including 'small' tenements), and just over 30 per cent as cottages. Clearly, the figures support the assumption that the majority of the really poor lived outside the walls, in the suburbs of All Saints Without and St Mary's. But it may be worth observing that cottage properties were by no means excluded from the wealthier parishes in the south of the town, where they probably housed the servants and journeymen of the burgesses. In the parish of St Michael, in particular, the incidence of cottage property was high, although still falling short, in proportion, of the figure recorded in the poorer northern parish of All Saints Within.[11]

Over a much longer period, some sort of rough check on burgess preferences may be made by assembling the information relating to places of residence included in the biographies published in Appendix 1a above. Interestingly, whereas the wealthy burgess of the thirteenth-century town usually made his home, on this evidence, in the parishes of St Michael or St John, a pronounced shift of fashion in favour of Holy Rood had occurred by the following century, to become more obvious still in the fifteenth century as the western shore fell derelict and Thomas Middleton's new quay at the Watergate came into service. In the sixteenth century, although the waterfront was never re-settled on its former scale, the parish of St Michael had experienced a recovery, wealthy property-holders settling by St Michael's Square or along Bull Street, to the south. Despite the Fleming preference for All Saints, witnessed in the fifteenth and sixteenth centuries, that parish never became generally popular among members of the wealthier burgess class. In the suburbs, if we discount the large properties purchased as country retreats by prominent late-medieval burgess families, there is only one recorded instance of an important burgess operating from a suburban tenement. Sampson de Puteo, bailiff at least twice in the first decades of the thirteenth century, lived with his wife, Isabel, in a tenement north of the Bargate, on the east side of Above Bar Street. A contemporary of Benedict Ace, John de la Bulehuse and Walter le Fleming, he belonged to a generation which could have had no difficulty in recalling the unbroken spread of settlement through All Saints parish, before its partition by the ramparts of the northern defences. To Sampson de Puteo, the ramparts were an innovation, not necessarily to be regarded in the choice of a permanent residence. To Sampson's successors, they were to become the accepted northern limit of secure settlement.

Table 3 *Parish of residence, from information in the biographies* (*Appendix 1a*)

	C13	*C14*	*C15*	*C16*	*Totals*
Holy Rood	1	8	10	5	24
St Michael	9	6	3	4	22
St John	5	2	2	1	10
St Lawrence	2	4	1	–	7
All Saints	–	–	2	1	3

Notes

1 J. C. Russell, *British Medieval Population*, p. 50.
2 *V.C.H., Hampshire*, i:433, 516.
3 P.R.O. E359/8b, m. 18; E179/173/46.
4 J. C. Russell, op. cit., p. 142.
5 J. C. Russell, 'Population in Europe, 500–1500', *The Fontana Economic History of Europe*, i:1:42, to be read with the same author's 'The preplague population of England', *The Journal of British Studies*, v:2 (1966), pp. 1–21.
6 S.C.R.O. SC13/1. Recently published as the latest volume of the Southampton Records Series.
7 P.R.O. E179/173/175. Excluding the tithing of Portswood and making allowance for the missing names in the St Michael with St John ward, there were approximately 351 townspeople paying tax in 1524.
8 R. A. Pelham, 'Medieval Southampton', in *A Survey of Southampton and its Region*, ed. F. J. Monkhouse, pp. 211–12.
9 P.R.O. E179/173/4, m. 17v, E179/242/15a, m. 8v.
10 P.R.O. E179/173/175; W. G. Hoskins, 'An Elizabethan provincial town: Leicester', in *Studies in Social History*, ed. J. H. Plumb, pp. 44–5.
11 S.C.R.O. SC13/1.

Appendix 2

Select tenement histories

1 Bull Hall: junction of Bull (Bugle) Street and Westgate Street

Originally the capital tenement of Thomas de la Bulehuse, father of Roger and Juliana, and an important figure in the town in the early years of the thirteenth century. Partitioned on Thomas's death, the tenement itself descended to Roger de la Bulehuse, while the south part of the site, with a tenement and shop of its own, came to Juliana, Roger's sister. Juliana sold, or otherwise disposed of, her share to Claramunda, who gave it to Quarr Abbey (Isle of Wight). But by *c.* 1270 both portions had come into the possession of James Isembard, a nephew of Alice, wife of John de la Bulehuse (*Cat.Anc. Deeds*, ii:B3447; God's House Deeds 600, 603–4). Probably in the 1280s, James Isembard sold Bull Hall to Thomas le Halveknight, later, and perhaps already, the owner of West Hall, the great tenement on the other side of Bull Street, further down the street towards the sea (God's House Deeds 601, 605). Thomas le Halveknight died in, or shortly before, 1299. In 1303/4, his West Hall property was partitioned among his heirs of the body, but Bull Hall, whether by purchase or inheritance, came to Luke Stout, a leading member of a family with important property interests at the south-western tip of the town. Luke developed his property in 1326 by the lease of the former Quarr Abbey plot to the south of Bull Hall, now vacant and the property of God's House Hospital (Ibid., 606). But by 1338 the Hall had come into the hands of William le Wariner and Amice, his wife, who similarly leased the adjoining God's House plot that year, promising to build on it. William still held both these properties in 1342, although his proposals for redevelopment had perhaps been upset by the raid four years before (Bodleian, Queen's College MS. 340; God's House Deeds 608). Certainly, although Thomas Middleton was probably living at Bull Hall itself in 1389, the plot to the south, on which he took a long lease that year from God's House, was still vacant; it bordered another vacant plot, to the south again, formerly of John le Clerk 'senior', and was bounded on the west by a garden (God's House Deeds 607). Thomas Middleton sold Bull Hall, on 15 April 1414, to John and Clemency Renaud (*Black Book*, i:152–7). The Renauds lived in a tenement on the west side of English Street, parish of Holy Rood, but held Bull Hall with Polymond Hall and other important properties in the town, presumably as investments. When John Renaud died in 1422, he left his considerable possessions to Clemency, his widow, with the reversion to his young kinsman and heir, Nicholas Renaud, should he survive to the age of twenty-one; Thomas Middleton was one of the executors. Middleton, in 1414, had retained the garden to the south of Bull Hall, which he leased from God's House in 1389. Very likely, he still held it in 1422, for John Renaud's will mentions no more than a share in the gardens to the south of the Hall, held from God's House (P.R.O. E327/775). By 1454 Bull Hall, like West Hall to the south, had been let to the Italians. One of their more important resident agents in the town, the Genoese Galeazzo di Negro, held it from John Serle, second husband of Catherine and son-in-law of Peter James (S.C.R.O. SC13/1). He was paying a rent of forty shillings, granted to the town for ten years in 1457 by Catherine Serle, in part payment of the arrears accumulated by John, her late husband, while Bargate broker (*Book of Remembrance*, i:33, 35). The Hall was still rented to Genoese merchants in 1471, being then the residence of Giovanni Andrea Vivaldi (Alwyn Ruddock, *Italian Merchants and Shipping*, p. 131; S.C.R.O. SC5/1/13). By 1526, Bull Hall had become the property of Henry Huttoft, who was probably its rebuilder, making of it the 'chefest' of the 'many very fair marchauntes houses' remarked by John Leland in the town a decade or so later. It continued to be bounded by gardens on the south, as it would be in later generations when held by the earls of Southampton (Bodleian, Queen's College MS. 2570; S.C.R.O. SC5/1/37, f. 5, SC5/1/41, f. 4v; *Third Book of Remembrance*, ii:9n; H.R.O. Wriothesley Deeds, 5M53/451–4).

2 La Chayne: on the north side of Porters Lane, west of the Customs House

The tenement known as 'La Chayne' makes its first appearance in the records in the will of Isabella, widow of Robert le Barber, dated 2 January 1312/13 and proved on 9 May 1315. For a twelve-year term, Isabella granted the northern moiety of La Chayne to John de Moundenard, a long-established landholder in the area with a tenement immediately to the north. It was then to revert to Matilda and Gaillard de Moundenard, daughter and son-in-law of Isabella, to be held by them with the southern moiety, already their own by an earlier charter of the same donor (Win.Coll. Mun. 17761; *R.C.H.M.*, 6th report, p. 557). Matilda herself was dead by September 1341. The tenement descended, still partitioned, to her children, but was probably consolidated by Isabel, her daughter, to whom the others granted their moiety, perhaps to join with her own (Win.Coll.Mun. 17762). In 1348/9, the plot called 'La Chayne' was held by Richard Elmsley, together with a tenement on English Street and another void plot. Richard died in the Black Death, leaving his properties to Isabel, his wife, possibly Isabel de Moundenard, daughter of Gaillard and Matilda, who held them for a further fifteen years until her own death, after which they lay vacant for more than four years. By way of Walter Couk, a native of Worcestershire (Richard Elmsley's own home county), who then claimed to be Richard's next heir, the plot called 'La Chayne' came after a year to John le Clerk and John Wytegod. Three years later, John le Clerk released his rights in the plot to John Wytegod and his heirs. It was held by Wytegod until his death in *c.* 1370, when it passed to William Bacon. But Richard Elmsley, a bastard, had died without surviving heirs of his body. Consequently, his lands should have escheated to the king. An inquisition, held in the town before the king's escheator on 14 June 1379, established the circumstances of his Southampton properties. They were granted by the king to John Slegh on 9 November 1381 (*Cal.Inq.P.M.*, xv:25–6; *Sign Manuals and Letters Patent*, i:56–9). La Chayne, in 1381, had been described as a 'vacant plot'. Soon afterwards, it came into the possession of the Fysmark family, and it was probably the Fysmarks who rebuilt it. Certainly, when John Fysmark 'senior' sold it in 1439 to Gabriel Corbet, a naturalized Venetian, there was a tenement on the site, entered from Porters Lane by way of a gate and passage running under the upper room, or 'solar', of Walter Fetplace's bakehouse. Fetplace's messuage was on the east of the site. On the west, La Chayne was bounded by a messuage of William Nicholl (Win.Coll.Mun. 17763–4, 17766–8, 17770; *Black Book*, ii:72–5; Alwyn Ruddock, *Italian Merchants and Shipping*, pp. 160–1). When Gabriel Corbet died in 1463, La Chayne and his other Southampton properties descended to his daughter-in-law, Isabel, with the reversion to Winchester College. Isabel, originally the wife of Thomas Corbet, married again, and it was not until January 1491 that she and her second husband transferred these tenements to the college. On 10 June 1496, another naturalized Italian, Christopher Ambrose, leased La Chayne, already holding from the college a corner tenement to the east, used as a Customs House (Win.Coll.Mun. 17799, 17800, 17840; S.C.R.O. SC4/3/14; God's House Deeds 465). The general description 'La Chayne' had come, by this time, to cover at least two properties in the area. In addition to the college property, which was still in the same ownership in the seventeenth century, there was a cellar and adjoining plot belonging to the corporation, also commonly known as 'La Chayne'. It was sold to Thomas Thomas in 1493, came to God's House in 1515 by way of his widow and Edward Rigge, and reverted to the town shortly afterwards (S.C.R.O. stewards, books, passim, also SC4/1/2, SC4/3/71 and SC5/3/1, f. 15; Bodleian, Queen's College MS. 501–3; B.M. Add. Ch. 17449).

3 Ronceval: on the western shore, north of Westgate Street

The tenement took its name from Roncevaux (Roncesvalles) Priory, to which this and other Southampton tenements were granted in, or before, 1231 by William Marshal, earl of Pembroke (*Cal.Ch.R. 1226–54*, pp. 167–8). Demised for life, at a rent of forty shillings, to Claramunda who held it, and probably lived there, until her death in *c.* 1260. Descended to William and Richard of Gloucester, and was mortgaged by them some years later to Benedict, a Jew of Winchester. In 1273, or just before, Richard of Gloucester and a party of friends and relations ejected Benedict from the tenement and carried away his goods. Benedict successfully petitioned for reinstatement, but it was probably this and other similar grievances that led to the anti-Jewish riots at Southampton in 1274 (*Cal.C.R. 1279–88*, p. 87; *Cal.Inq.Misc. 1219–1307*, p. 155; J. M. Rigg (ed.), *Calendar of the Plea Rolls of the Exchequer of the Jews*, ii:95–6, 119–20, 130–1). On Benedict's death, Ronceval came into the hands of the king, to be restored on 28 May 1281 to the priory (*Cal.C.R. 1279–88*, p. 87). Nothing more is known of the property until 1362, when, following the death of Sir Henry Peverel earlier that year, it was granted by his executors to Stephen Michel, a Southampton burgess (S.C.R.O. D/LY/7/4). Michel re-granted it, with a cellar and tenement on the south side of Broad Lane, to John Brown and Nicholas Sherwynd, the re-developer of the former Moundenard tenement north of the friary. The grant was dated 25 September 1367, and was followed by further transactions in 1388, by which time the Bechefonts, John and Robert, had acquired an interest in the tenement (S.C.R.O. SC4/2/102, 146–7). It need not have been much after this that William Ravenston came into the property, to be succeeded by William Nicholl. In addition to his other former Nicholl tenements, Thomas Payne was holding Ronceval, still described as a 'capital tenement', in 1454 (S.C.R.O. SC13/1). Its access to Westgate Street probably preserved Ronceval from the worst effects of the wall-building in that quarter, which had led to the decay of other similarly-sited tenements before the end of the previous century. But by the time it came into corporation ownership, which it had done before 1482/3, Ronceval had come to be used most commonly as a store, being hired as such to visiting galley patrons and others (e.g. S.C.R.O. SC5/1/17, 19, 21, 22, 25). Although its value, over the next two centuries, continued to be relatively high, the several buildings on the site at Ronceval were usually leased by different tenants and given over to ship-repairing and carpentry. In the corporation terrier of 1617, the dimensions of the site were given as 84 by 44 feet; its buildings were described as a cellar with a loft over it, a 'skeeling', or lean-to warehouse, along the length of the town wall, and a shop 'with two roofs' on Westgate Street (S.C.R.O. SC4/1/2, SC4/3/77, 116, 120; B.M. Add.Ch. 17449).

4 West Hall: between Bull (Bugle) Street and French Street, north of Rochelle Lane

Built for his own use by Gervase 'le Riche', for many years collector of the town farm and 'provost' of Southampton (God's House Deeds 310, 313). Descended, on Gervase's death in 1196/7, to Isabella, his widow, and then to Walter, his nephew and heir (Bodleian, Queen's College MS. 4G10; *Pipe Roll 2 John*, p. 206, *6 John*, p. 129). Before 1299, came into the possession of Thomas le Halveknight, to be partitioned between his heirs in 1303/4. At that time, its buildings were disposed about a courtyard, entered through a main gate on French Street, opposite St John's church; they included a hall and several chambers, with cellars and stables, a kitchen and bakehouse, a garden and a well (P.R.O. E327/163; God's House Deeds 476; St Denys Cart. 242; S.C.R.O. SC4/2/396). Within the next three decades, John of Shirley, Hugh Sampson and Walter of Brackley each acquired shares in West Hall, the Shirley portion coming subsequently to Hugh Sampson by purchase from Felicia, John of Shirley's widow. On Sampson's death in 1336, his West Hall interest was divided unequally between Constance, his widow, and Joan, his daughter. In 1342, Constance still retained one part of the Hall, Joan and her husband, Thomas atte Marche, held two, and Walter of Brackley had a fourth (S.C.R.O. SC4/2/398–401, 403/4; Bodleian, Queen's College MS. 340, 4G10). Walter of Brackley's share was to be acquired from his heirs by Adam Brabason, whose widow, Margery, then continued to hold it after his death. It came subsequently to Robert Boteshout, who held it first with Roger Mascall and then, before 1393, with John Polymond. Joan Sampson's share went with her to her second husband, John le Clerk, but then descended, probably in 1365, to Richard atte Marche, the child of her first marriage. Richard was certainly holding the property in the 1380s, and may well have continued to do so until his death in *c.* 1403 (Bodleian, Queen's College MS. 4G10; S.C.R.O. SC4/2/406, 408; *Cal.C.R. 1402–5*, p. 174). Some part, at least, of these holdings then came to Thomas Appleby (S.C.R.O. SC13/1; P.R.O. SC11/597). But West Hall, by 1429, had become the property of Robert Lange, very probably a relative of the Walter Lange who had been such a considerable landholder in Southampton at the turn of the century. In 1429, Robert sold the Hall for £120 to the mayor and burgesses of Southampton, to be held as an investment by the town. It was leased immediately to Paolo Morelli, a Florentine agent long resident in the port (*Stewards' Books, 1428–34*, pp. 8–9, 10–11, 30–3). Subsequently, West Hall became the headquarters of a number of Italian enterprises, remaining the residence of the Genoese Marini family for almost a century (Alwyn Ruddock, *Italian Merchants and Shipping*, in particular pp. 98–105, 130–1, 233–54). It was mortgaged briefly in 1538 to cover a deficit on the farm, but had been redeemed by 1544 and was still town property in 1553/4, when pledged to cover the endowment of the new free grammar school founded in 1553, of which the mayor and his officers were governors (*Third Book of Remembrance*, i:56–7; S.C.R.O. SC4/2/409, SC5/1/40, f. 30v; B.M. Add. MS. 14265). The school itself, originally established on a site near God's House, removed to the West Hall buildings, by arrangement with the corporation, in the 1690s (Davies, p. 314).

5 The Barbflete, Moundenard and Nicholl tenement: immediately north of the friary site, on the east side of English (High) Street, parish of Holy Rood

The Barbflete family, important in the town from the beginning of the thirteenth century, acquired its interests north of the friary probably well before 1300. Robert de Barbflete, who married Lucya Fortin, held and almost certainly occupied the great tenement immediately north of the friary, perhaps the nucleus of the family properties in the parish of Holy Rood. It descended, on his death, to Lucya, his widow, to his sons, Nicholas and Robert, and to his daughters, Rosya and Isabella. Richard, another son, inherited the valuable family property to the north, which was to descend to John Barbflete, his grandson. It was from Rosya, and more particularly from Nicholas, that Nicholas de Moundenard in 1329 purchased Robert's former capital tenement, paying the considerable sum of £40 for Nicholas de Barbflete's share of it (S.C.R.O. SC4/2/41, 43–4). It is evident, even so, that Nicholas de Barbflete did not sell the whole of his inheritance in 1329. The Barbflete capital tenement remained partitioned until consolidated by Walter Lange at the end of the century. Its northern portion was left by Petronilla, Nicholas de Barbflete's widow, to Matthew Gentilcorps, who granted it in 1333 to William le Smale and Isabella, his wife (S.C.R.O. SC4/2/50, 52–4). Evidently, it was by way of William le Smale, father of Joan who married John Barbflete 'the elder', that the property returned to the Barbflete family, to be disposed of later in the century by John Barbflete 'the younger' (S.C.R.O. SC4/2/108, 112, 119, 133, 140). In the meantime, Nicholas de Moundenard's ownership of the southern portion had coincided with the devastations of the French raid of 1338. A decade after the raid, between 1348 and 1351, the tenement was described as ruinous and worth no more than 40*d.* a year (P.R.O. SC6/981/26). On Nicholas de Moundenard's death, in 1357, there was a tenement on the south part of the site and a vacant plot on the north (S.C.R.O. D/LY/23/3). But it would have been beyond Nicholas's means to re-develop the whole site adequately, and the expensive task of rebuilding was left to Nicholas Sherwynd, almost two decades later. Probably, Nicholas Sherwynd had obtained the property from Roger and Felicia Mascall, the heirs of Christina, widow of Nicholas de Moundenard. Certainly, it was Roger Mascall who arranged, on 1 October 1377, a mortgage of £63. 6*s*. 8*d*. on the new tenement, to replace an identical short-term mortgage held by John Polymond and expiring the day before (S.C.R.O. SC4/2/115–6a). For some years at least before 1397, John Mascall was living in Sherwynd's rebuilt tenement, and William and Elena Nicholl had been further developing the site in 1388 (*Black Book*, i:52–3, God's House Deeds 430). But ownership had passed, again by way of a mortgage, to John le Clerk, of Lymington, in 1379–80, and it was from John le Clerk that Walter Lange obtained the property in 1396 as perhaps the final stage of a long process of property consolidation in the immediate area (S.C.R.O. SC4/2/112, 117–25, 135, 143–4, 162–3, 171–3, 175). He did not hold it for long, transferring it almost immediately, on 28 December 1397, to William and Elena Nicholl, who likewise were to accumulate important property interests in the vicinity (*Black Book*, i:50–3; S.C.R.O. SC4/2/229–32, 243–4, 264). By 1454, the Nicholl interests north of the friary, with other Nicholl properties including Ronceval, had come into the hands of Thomas Payne, brother of John Payne and a considerable man in the town. Thomas lived in the capital tenement central to these properties, renting out the lesser tenements on either side (S.C.R.O. SC13/1). The northern tenement, by the end of the century, had become the property of Winchester College, whereas the two southern tenements had come to the town, very probably as a part of the endowment of Thomas Payne's important chantry foundation at Holy Rood church. All three were held on lease in 1549 by Thomas Rigges, a former mayor (S.C.R.O. SC4/3/30).

6 The Fleming, Lym and James tenement: south corner of Broad Lane and English (High) Street

Probably built by Walter le Fleming, whose capital messuage it became, and possibly the house for which Walter negotiated a building agreement with Beaulieu Abbey concerning use of the party wall to support his timbers and the springing of his cellar vault (P.R.O. E327/328; Bodleian, Queen's College MS. 1071; B.M. Loans 29/330, fos 125–125v). By way of Margery, Walter's widow, the tenement descended to John le Fleming 'junior', son of Petronilla and John 'senior', and grandson of Walter. Petronilla la Fleming, who survived her husband by two decades, was the daughter of Ralph Isembard. It is known that she was using both the Isembard and Fleming former capital messuages in the 1260s as lodgings for foreign merchants (*Cal.P.R. 1258–66*, p. 258, *1266–72*, pp. 242, 325). For a time, early in the fourteenth century, the corner tenement on Broad Lane was held by William le Horder, but it reverted to the Flemings with John le Fleming, great-grandson of Walter, who held it until his death in 1336 (Bodleian, Queen's College MS. 1076). John's son and heir, another Walter, must have sold the tenement to Henry de Lym within a short space of his father's death. Henry was certainly living there by 1340, and had probably held it since before the raid of 1338 (Bodleian, Queen's College MS. 339). It is most unlikely that the property could have escaped damage in the raid. There is abundant archaeological evidence of contemporary destruction immediately north of Broad Lane, and both Henry de Lym and Thomas de Byndon, his near-neighbour to the south, are said to have sustained losses in the raid (*Southampton Excavations*, forthcoming; *Cal.P.R. 1340–3*, p. 79; *Cat.Anc. Deeds*, ii: B3406). Although the immediate succession after Henry de Lym is unclear, John atte Barre had acquired an important interest in the property before 1378, when he sold it to Sir John de Montague, then military commander in the town (P.R.O. E326/11787, 11805). Sir John's widow, Margaret, was holding the tenement in 1389, to be replaced before the end of the century by Sir Richard de Montague, a relative of Sir John, possibly his son (P.R.O. C47/60/3/65; *Cal.C.R. 1389–92*, p. 193, *1396–9*, p. 274; *Cal.Inq.Misc. 1392–9*, pp. 194, 196–7; *Black Book*, i:69n). Sir Richard continued to hold, and add to, his Southampton properties until April 1416, when he sold the Broad Lane corner tenement to Walter Fetplace 'senior' and Peter James (P.R.O. E326/11785, 11800, 11802, E329/430). By 1428, Peter James had come into sole possession of the tenement, with Walter Fetplace as his next-door neighbour, immediately to the south. It was described, at the time, as a great corner tenement overlying two vaults, with curtilage and garden adjacent, and seems to have stretched some distance back along Broad Lane to the west, with its kitchen set at the rear. Certainly, recent excavations on the line of Broad Lane have confirmed the exceptional length of the tenement (P.R.O. E326/11799, 11804; *Southampton Excavations*, forthcoming). On the death of Peter James, the corner tenement, with other Broad Lane properties, descended to his son, William, who sold off the three tenements along the lane to the rear (*Black Book*, ii:92–5). It was William's son, Henry, who finally disposed of the main part of the family property originally acquired by his grandfather nearly a century before. He still held property on Broad Lane in 1524/5, but he had long before sold the corner tenement for £63 to William Justice, in a transaction which was questioned in the courts and which ended in the transfer of the property in 1507 to Thomas Thomas, for some years already Henry James's neighbour to the south (P.R.O. E326/11784, 11789, 11792, E329/429; S.C.R.O. SC5/1/33, f. 6v; *Black Book*, iii:36–45). It is probable that Sampson Thomas succeeded to the tenement on his father's death shortly afterwards. But he lived on the other side of English Street, and it is not clear how he disposed of his Broad Lane interests.

It is worth noting that the continued use of the Broad Lane tenement as high-class burgess housing throughout the later Middle Ages was matched at the other great tenements to the south. An extensive re-development of the area, on the archaeological evidence, certainly occurred at the turn of the twelfth and thirteenth centuries, and it cannot have been much later that Walter le Fleming first built his great stone tenement on the Broad Lane site (*Southampton Excavations*, forthcoming). By the second quarter of the fourteenth century, as probably for many years before, the most influential burgesses of the day clustered south of Broad Lane. Henry de Lym held the Fleming tenement; his immediate neighbour to the south was Nicholas de Moundenard; to the south again, Roger Norman held a tenement, bounded by the property of Thomas de Byndon on the English Street and Porters Lane junction (Bodleian, Queen's College MS. 339–40). A century later, Walter Fetplace 'senior' lived in the former Moundenard tenement as a neighbour of Peter James; it would become, in due course, the property of John Ludlow and Thomas Thomas. The great corner tenement of Thomas de Byndon, as probably the tenement once of Roger Norman as well, had been taken over by William Soper (P.R.O. E326/11792, 11794–6, 11799, 11804; Win.Coll.Mun. 17835). Property in the area continued to command a high price in the mid-sixteenth century. A house on the west side of English Street, parish of Holy Rood, fetched £62 in 1552 (*Black Book*, iii:94–5).

Bibliography and Index

Bibliography

a. Manuscript sources

1 Bodleian Library, Oxford

Queen's College Manuscripts: God's House cartulary; deeds, rent-rolls and domestic accounts of the hospital at God's House; Southampton wills

2 British Museum, London

Additional Charters and Rolls: 685, 7219, 17449
Additional Manuscripts: 14265, 25460
Cotton Manuscripts: Vesp. XIII
Harleian Manuscripts: I.14; 606
Lansdowne Manuscripts: 11/24, 12/64
Loans: 29/330

3 Hampshire Record Office, Winchester

Wills of Thomas Bayly (1515), Rawlinus Grete (1512), Thomas Goddard (1555), Charles Harrison (1558), Thomas Huttoft (1554), Richard Mershe (1558), Jane Rygges (1558), Richard Vaughan (1546), Richard Winson (1517)
Wriothesley Deeds

4 Public Record Office, London

a. *Records of the Chancery*

C1 Early Chancery Proceedings
C3 Chancery Proceedings, Series II
C47 Miscellanea of the Chancery
C143 Inquisitions ad quod damnum
C146 Deeds

b. *Records of the Exchequer*

E36 The Treasury of the Receipt of the Exchequer, Books
E101 The King's Remembrancer, Various Accounts
E117 The King's Remembrancer, Church Goods
E122 The King's Remembrancer, Customs Accounts
E178 The King's Remembrancer, Special Commissions of Inquiry
E179 The King's Remembrancer, Subsidy Rolls
E210 The King's Remembrancer, Deeds, Series D
E301 The Augmentation Office, Certificates of Colleges and Chantries
E310 The Augmentation Office, Particulars for Leases
E315 The Augmentation Office, Miscellaneous Books
E318 The Augmentation Office, Particulars for Grants of Crown Lands
E321 The Augmentation Office, Proceedings of the Court of Augmentations
E326 The Augmentation Office, Ancient Deeds, Series B
E327 The Augmentation Office, Ancient Deeds, Series BX
E329 The Augmentation Office, Ancient Deeds, Series BS
E359 Lord Treasurer's, Remembrancer's and Pipe Offices, Accounts of Subsidies, Aids, etc.
E364 Lord Treasurer's, Remembrancer's and Pipe Offices, Rolls of Foreign Accounts (Pipe Office)

E372 Lord Treasurer's, Remembrancer's and Pipe Offices, Pipe Rolls (Pipe Office)
LR2 Office of the Auditors of Land Revenue, Miscellaneous Books

c. *Records of the Court of Common Pleas*

CP40 Plea Rolls

d. *Records of the Court of Requests*

Req. 2 Proceedings

e. *Special Collections*

SC1 Ancient Correspondence
SC6 Ministers' and Receivers' Accounts
SC8 Ancient Petitions
SC11 Rentals and Surveys, rolls
SC12 Rentals and Surveys, portfolios

f. *State Paper Office*

SP12 State Papers Domestic, Elizabeth I

5 Southampton Civic Record Office

D/CJ Photostats of documents deposited in the Hampshire Record Office
D/LY Documents deposited by the Public Library
SC2/6 Registrations with the Corporation
SC3/1/1 Admissions of Burgesses
SC4/1/1 Terrier of 1495/6
SC4/1/2 Terrier of 1617
SC4/2 Various Deeds, Bonds and Agreements
SC4/3 Corporation Leases
SC5/1 Stewards' Books
SC5/3 Mayors' Account Books
SC13/1 Terrier of 1454
SC13/2 Muster Books
SC14/2 Parliamentary Tax Assessments

6 Calendars, typescript and manuscript

God's House Deeds
St Denys Cartulary
Winchester College Muniments

b. Printed sources

1 Publications of the Southampton Record Society and of the Southampton Record Series

ANDERSON, R. C. (ed.), *Letters of the Fifteenth and Sixteenth Centuries from the Archives of Southampton*, 1 vol. in 2, Southampton Record Society, 1921.
ANDERSON, R. C. (ed.), *The Assize of Bread Book, 1477–1517*, Southampton Record Society, 1923.
ANDERSON, R. C. (ed.), *The Book of Examinations, 1601–1603, with a list of ships belonging to Southampton in the years 1570–1603*, Southampton Record Society, 1926.
AUBREY, ELINOR R. (ed.), *The History and Antiquity of Southampton, with some conjectures concerning the Roman Clausentum, by John Speed, written about the year 1770*, Southampton Record Society, 1909.
BUNYARD, BARBARA D. M. (ed.), *The Brokage Book of Southampton, from 1439–40*, Southampton Record Society, 1941.
CHAPMAN, A. B. WALLIS (ed.), *The Black Book of Southampton*, 3 vols, Southampton Record Society, 1912–15.
COBB, HENRY S. (ed.), *The Local Port Book of Southampton for 1439–40*, Southampton Record Series, 1961.
COLEMAN, OLIVE (ed.), *The Brokage Book of Southampton, 1443–4*, 2 vols, Southampton Record Series, 1960–1.
FOSTER, BRIAN (ed.), *The Local Port Book of Southampton for 1435–36*, Southampton Record Series, 1963.
GIDDEN, H. W. (ed.), *The Charters of the Borough of Southampton*, 2 vols, Southampton Record Society, 1909–10.
GIDDEN, H. W. (ed.), *The Sign Manuals and Letters Patent of Southampton*, 2 vols, Southampton Record Society, 1916–19.
GIDDEN, H. W. (ed.), *The Book of Remembrance of Southampton*, 3 vols, Southampton Record Society, 1927–30.
GIDDEN, H. W. (ed.), *The Stewards' Books of Southampton, from 1428*, 2 vols, Southampton Record Society, 1935–9.
HAMILTON, GERTRUDE H., and AUBREY, ELINOR R. (eds), *Books of Examinations and Depositions, 1570–1594*, Southampton Record Society, 1914.

HEARNSHAW, F. J. C., and HEARNSHAW, D. M. (eds), *Southampton Court Leet Records*, 1 vol. in 4, Southampton Record Society, 1905–8.
MERSON, A. L. (ed.), *The Third Book of Remembrance of Southampton, 1514–1602*, 3 vols, Southampton Record Series, 1952–65.
QUINN, D. B., and RUDDOCK, ALWYN A. (eds), *The Port Books or Local Customs Accounts of Southampton for the Reign of Edward IV*, 2 vols, Southampton Record Society, 1937–8.
RUDDOCK, ALWYN A., *Italian Merchants and Shipping in Southampton, 1270–1600*, Southampton Record Series, 1951.
STUDER, PAUL (ed.), *The Oak Book of Southampton of c. A.D. 1300*, 3 vols, Southampton Record Society, 1910–11.
STUDER, PAUL (ed.), *The Port Books of Southampton, or Anglo-French accounts of Robert Florys, water-bailiff and receiver of petty customs, A.D. 1427–1430*, Southampton Record Society, 1913.

2 Other primary sources

A descriptive catalogue of ancient deeds in the Public Record Office, 6 vols, London, 1890–1915.
ARNOLD, THOMAS (ed.), *Henrici archidiaconi Huntendunensis historia Anglorum. The history of the English, by Henry, archdeacon of Huntingdon, from A.D. 55 to A.D. 1154, in eight books*, Rolls Series, London, 1879.
ARNOLD, THOMAS (ed.), *Symeonis monachi opera omnia*, 2 vols, Rolls Series, London, 1882–5.
ASTLE, T., AYSCOUGH, S., and CALEY, J. (eds), *Taxatio ecclesiastica Angliae et Walliae, auctoritate P. Nicholai IV, circa A.D. 1291*, Record Commissioners, London, 1802.
BAIGENT, FRANCIS JOSEPH (ed.), *The registers of John de Sandale and Rigaud de Asserio, bishops of Winchester (A.D. 1316–1323)*, Hampshire Record Society, 8 (1897).
BALLARD, ADOLPHUS, and TAIT, JAMES (eds), *British Borough Charters, 1216–1307*, Cambridge, 1923.
BATESON, MARY (ed.), *Records of the Borough of Leicester*, 3 vols, London and Cambridge, 1899–1905.
BATESON, MARY (ed.), *Borough Customs*, 2 vols, Selden Society, 18 (for 1904) and 21 (for 1906).
BIRD, W. H. B. (ed.), *The Black Book of Winchester (British Museum, Additional MS. 6036)*, Winchester, 1925.
BOND, E. A. (ed.), *Chronica monasterii de Melsa, a fundatione usque ad annum 1396, auctore Thoma de Burton, abbate*, 3 vols, Rolls Series, London, 1866–8.
BUCHON, J. A. C. (ed.), *Les chroniques de sire Jean Froissart*, 3 vols, Paris, 1835.
Calendar of various chancery rolls (supplementary close rolls, Welsh rolls, scutage rolls) preserved in the Public Record Office, A.D. 1277–1326, London, 1912.
Calendar of the charter rolls preserved in the Public Record Office, 6 vols, London, 1903–27.
Calendar of the close rolls preserved in the Public Record Office, London, 1892– (in progress).
Calendar of the fine rolls preserved in the Public Record Office, London, 1911– (in progress).
Calendar of inquisitions miscellaneous (chancery) preserved in the Public Record Office, London, 1916– (in progress).
Calendar of inquisitions post mortem and other analogous documents preserved in the Public Record Office, London, 1904– (in progress).
Calendar of inquisitions post mortem and other analogous documents preserved in the Public Record Office, Henry VII, 3 vols, London, 1898–1955.
Calendar of the liberate rolls preserved in the Public Record Office, Henry III, London, 1916– (in progress).
Calendar of memoranda rolls (exchequer) preserved in the Public Record Office, Michaelmas 1326–Michaelmas 1327, London, 1968.
Calendar of entries in the papal registers relating to Great Britain and Ireland, papal letters, London, 1893– (in progress).
Calendar of the patent rolls preserved in the Public Record Office, London, 1891– (in progress).
Calendar of state papers, colonial series, preserved in the State Paper Department of Her Majesty's Public Record Office, London, 1860– (in progress).
Calendar of state papers, domestic series, of the reigns of Edward VI, Mary, Elizabeth, preserved in the State Paper Department of Her Majesty's Public Record Office, 12 vols, London, 1856–72.
Calendar of state papers, foreign series, of the reign of Elizabeth, preserved in the State Paper Department of Her Majesty's Public Record Office, London, 1863– (in progress).
Calendar of letters and state papers relating to English affairs, preserved principally in the archives of Simancas, 4 vols, London, 1892–9.

Calendar of state papers and manuscripts relating to English affairs, existing in the archives and collections of Venice, and in other libraries of northern Italy, London, 1864– (in progress).
CALEY, J., and HUNTER, JOSEPH (eds), *Valor ecclesiasticus, temp. Henr. VIII, auctoritate regia institutus*, 6 vols, Record Commissioners, London, 1810–34.
CHANEY, E. F. (ed.), *La danse macabre des charniers des Saints Innocents à Paris*, Manchester, 1945.
Close Rolls of the reign of Henry III preserved in the Public Record Office, 14 vols, London, 1902–38.
COOPLAND, G. W. (ed.), *Le songe du vieil pelerin (Philippe de Mézières)*, 2 vols, Cambridge, 1969.
DAVID, C. W. (ed.), *De Expugnatione Lyxbonensi. The conquest of Lisbon*, Oxford, 1936.
DAVIS, H. W. C., JOHNSON, CHARLES, CRONNE, H. A., and DAVIS, R. H. C. (eds), *Regesta regum anglo-normannorum, 1066–1154*, 3 vols, Oxford, 1913–68.
DEANESLEY, MARGARET (ed.), *The incendium amoris of Richard Rolle of Hampole*, Manchester, 1915.
DEEDES, CECIL (ed.), *Registrum Johannis de Pontissara, episcopi Wyntoniensis, A.D. MCCLXXXII–MCCCIV*, 2 vols, Canterbury and York Society, 19 (1915) and 30 (1924).
DELISLE, M. LEOPOLD (ed.), *Recueil des actes de Henri II*, 4 vols, Chartes et diplômes relatifs à l'histoire de France, Paris, 1909–27.
D'EVELYN, CHARLOTTE (ed.), *Peter Idley's instructions to his son*, London, 1935.
DILKS, THOMAS BRUCE (ed.), *Bridgwater Borough Archives*, 4 vols, Somerset Record Society, 48 (1933), 53 (1938), 58 (1945) and 60 (1948).
DOUGLAS, DAVID C., and GREENAWAY, C. W. (eds), *English Historical Documents, 1042–1189*, London, 1953.
EDWARDS, E. (ed.), *Liber monasterii de Hyda; comprising a chronicle of the affairs of England, from the settlement of the Saxons to the reign of King Cnut, and a chartulary of the abbey of Hyde, in Hampshire, A.D. 455–1023*, Rolls Series, London, 1866.
FURNIVALL, F. J. (ed.), *The Babees Book, the Bokes of Nurture of Hugh Rhodes and John Russell, etc.*, Early English Text Society, 32 (1868).
FURNIVALL, F. J. (ed.), *Harrison's Description of England in Shakspere's Youth, being the second and third books of his 'Description of Britain and England'*, 3 vols, New Shakspere Society, London, 1877–1908.
GAIRDNER, JAMES (ed.), *Letters and papers illustrative of the reigns of Richard III and Henry VII*, 2 vols, Rolls Series, London, 1861–3.
GAIRDNER, JAMES (ed.), *The historical collections of a citizen of London in the fifteenth century*, Camden Society, new series, 17 (1876).
GALBRAITH, V. H. (ed.), *The Anonimalle chronicle, 1333 to 1381, from a MS. written at St Mary's abbey, York*, Manchester, 1927.
GODFREY, HUMPHREY MARETT (ed.), *Registre de l'Église Wallonne de Southampton*, Publications of the Huguenot Society of London, 4 (1890).
GOODMAN, A. W. (ed.), *Chartulary of Winchester Cathedral*, Winchester, 1927.
HARDY, SIR THOMAS DUFFUS, and MARTIN, CHARLES TRICE (eds), *Lestorie des engles solum la translacion Maistre Geffrei Gaimar*, 2 vols, Rolls Series, London, 1888–9.
HARDY, WILLIAM, and HARDY, EDWARD L. C. P. (eds), *A collection of the chronicles and ancient histories of Great Britain, now called England, by John de Wavrin, lord of the manor of Forestel*, 3 vols, Rolls Series, London, 1864–91.
HINGESTON, F. C. (ed.), *Royal and historical letters during the reign of Henry the Fourth, king of England and of France, and lord of Ireland. A.D. 1399–1404*, Rolls Series, London, 1860.
HOSTE, ANSELM, and LIMA, ROSE DE (ed. and trans.), *For Crist Luve. Prayers of Saint Aelred, Abbot of Rievaulx*, The Hague, 1965.
HOWES, EDMUND, *Annales, or, A Generall Chronicle of England, begun by John Stow: continued and augmented with matters Foraigne and Domestique, Ancient and Moderne, unto the end of this present yeere, 1631*, London, 1631.
HOWLETT, RICHARD (ed.), *Monumenta Franciscana. Vol. ii. Being a further collection of original documents respecting the Franciscan order in England*, Rolls Series, London, 1882.
HUGHES, PAUL L., and LARKIN, JAMES F. (eds), *Tudor Royal Proclamations*, 3 vols, New Haven (Conn.), 1964–9.
JONES, PHILIP E. (ed.), *Calendar of Plea and Memoranda Rolls preserved among the Archives of the City of London at the Guildhall, A.D. 1323–1482*, 6 vols, Cambridge, 1926–61.

KÖLBING, EUGEN (ed.), *The Romance of Sir Beves of Hamtoun*, Early English Text Society, extra series, 3 vols in 1, 1885–94.

LEACH, ARTHUR F. (ed.), *Beverley Town Documents*, Selden Society, 14 (1900).

LEGG, L. G. WICKHAM (ed.), 'A relation of a short survey of the western counties made by a lieutenant of the military company in Norwich in 1635', *Camden Miscellany xvi*, Camden Society, 3rd series, 52 (1936).

Letters and papers, foreign and domestic, of the reign of Henry VIII, preserved in the Public Record Office, the British Museum, and elsewhere in England, 23 vols in 38, London, 1862–1932.

LITTLE, A. G. (ed.), *Fratris Thomae, vulgo dicti de Eccleston, tractatus De adventu fratrum minorum in Angliam*, Manchester, 1951.

LUARD, H. R. (ed.), *Annales monastici*, 5 vols, Rolls Series, London, 1864–9.

LUARD, H. R. (ed.), *Matthaei Parisiensis, monachi sancti Albani, chronica majora*, 7 vols, Rolls Series, London, 1872–83.

LUARD, H. R. (ed.), *Flores historiarum*, 3 vols, Rolls Series, London, 1890.

LUMBY, JOSEPH RAWSON (ed.), *Chronicon Henrici Knighton, vel Cnitthon, monachi Leycestrensis*, 2 vols, Rolls Series, London, 1889–95.

MCGRATH, PATRICK (ed.), *The Marchants Avizo, by I(ohn) B(rowne), Marchant, 1589*, Cambridge (Mass.), 1957.

MAGNÚSSON, ERÍKR (ed.), *Thómas saga erkibyskups. A life of Archbishop Thomas Becket in Icelandic, with English translation, notes and glossary*, 2 vols, Rolls Series, London, 1875–83.

MARSDEN, R. G. (ed.), *Documents relating to law and custom of the sea, A.D. 1205–1648*, 2 vols, Navy Records Society, 49 (1915) and 50 (1916).

MARTIN, CHARLES TRICE (ed.), *Registrum epistolarum fratris Johannis Peckham, archiepiscopi Cantuariensis*, 3 vols, Rolls Series, London, 1882–5.

MASTERS, BETTY R., and RALPH, ELIZABETH (eds), *The church book of St Ewen's, Bristol, 1454–1584*, Publications of the Bristol and Gloucestershire Archaeological Society, Records Section, 6 (1967).

MAYOR, JOHN E. B. (ed.), *Ricardi de Cirencestria speculum historiale de gestis regum Angliae*, 2 vols, Rolls Series, London, 1863–9.

MICHELL, R., FORBES, N., BEAZLEY, C. R., and SHAKHMATOV, A. A. (eds), *The Chronicle of Novgorod, 1016–1471*, Camden Society, 3rd series, 25 (1914).

NICHOLS, J. G. (ed.), *Literary Remains of King Edward the Sixth*, 2 vols, Roxburghe Club, 1857.

OPPENHEIM, M. (ed.), *Naval accounts and inventories of the reign of Henry VII, 1485–8 and 1495–7*, Navy Records Society, 8 (1896).

Pipe Roll Society Publications, London, 1884– (in progress).

POTTER, K. R. (ed.), *Gesta Stephani: the deeds of Stephen*, London, 1955.

POTTER, K. R. (ed.), *The Historia Novella by William of Malmesbury*, London, 1955.

RAINE, ANGELO (ed.), *York Civic Records, 1475–1588*, 8 vols, Yorkshire Archaeological Society, Record Series, 1939–53.

Register of Edward the Black Prince preserved in the Public Record Office, 4 vols, London, 1930–3.

RENOUARD, YVES (ed.), *Gascon Rolls preserved in the Public Record Office, 1307–1317*, London, 1962.

RIGG, J. M., and JENKINSON, HILARY (eds), *Calendar of the Plea Rolls of the Exchequer of the Jews*, 3 vols, The Jewish Historical Society of England, 1905–29.

RILEY, HENRY THOMAS (ed.), *Munimenta Gildhallae Londoniensis: Liber Albus, Liller Custumarum et Lilber Horn*, 3 vols, Rolls Series, London, 1859–62.

RILEY, HENRY THOMAS (ed.), *Ypodigma Neustriae, a Thoma Walsingham, quondam monacho monasterii S. Albani, conscriptum*, Rolls Series, London, 1876.

Rotuli parliamentorum; ut et petitiones, et placita in parliamento, 6 vols including index volume, London, 1783 and 1832.

Royal Commission on Historical Manuscripts, 4th and 6th reports, London, 1874 and 1877.

RYE, WILLIAM BRENCHLEY (ed.), *England as seen by foreigners in the days of Elizabeth and James the First. Comprising translations of the journals of the two dukes of Wirtemberg in 1592 and 1610*, London, 1865.

RYMER, THOMAS (ed.), *Foedera, conventiones, litterae, et cujuscunque generis acta publica, inter reges Angliae et alios imperatores, reges, pontifices, principes, vel communitates, ab ineunte saeculo duodecimo, viz. ab anno 1101, ad nostra usque tempora, habita aut tractata*, 20 vols, London, 1727–35.

SHARPE, REGINALD R. (ed.), *Calendar of Letters from the Mayor and Corporation of the City of London, circa A.D. 1350–1370, enrolled and preserved among the archives of*

the Corporation at the Guildhall, London, 1885.
SHIRLEY, WALTER WADDINGTON (ed.), *Royal and other historical letters illustrative of the reign of Henry III, from the originals in the Public Record Office*, 2 vols, Rolls Series, London, 1862–8.
SMITH, LUCY TOULMIN (ed.), *The itinerary of John Leland in or about the years 1535–1543*, 5 vols, London, 1906–10.
SNEYD, CHARLOTTE AUGUSTA (ed.), *A relation, or rather a true account, of the island of England; with sundry particulars of the customs of these people, and of the royal revenues under King Henry the Seventh, about the year 1500*, Camden Society, 37 (1847).
SPONT, ALFRED (ed.), *Letters and papers relating to the war with France, 1512–1513*, Navy Records Society, 10 (1897).
The statutes of the realm, from original records and authentic manuscripts, 11 vols in 12, Record Commissioners, London, 1810–28.
STEVENSON, JOSEPH (ed.), *Letters and papers illustrative of the wars of the English in France during the reign of Henry the Sixth, king of England*, 2 vols in 3, Rolls Series, London, 1861–4.
STUBBS, WILLIAM (ed.), *Gesta regis Henrici secundi Benedicti abbatis. The chronicle of the reigns of Henry II and Richard I, A.D. 1169–1192, known commonly under the name of Benedict of Peterborough*, 2 vols, Rolls Series, London, 1867.
STUBBS, WILLIAM (ed.), *Chronica Rogeri de Houedene*, 4 vols, Rolls Series, London, 1868–71.
STUBBS, WILLIAM (ed.), *Memoriale fratris Walteri de Coventria. The historical collections of Walter of Coventry*, 2 vols, Rolls Series, London, 1872–3.
STUBBS, WILLIAM (ed.), *Radulfi de Diceto decani Londoniensis opera historica. The historical works of Master Ralph de Diceto, dean of London*, 2 vols, Rolls Series, London, 1876.
STUBBS, WILLIAM (ed.), *The historical works of Gervase of Canterbury*, 2 vols, Rolls Series, London, 1879–80.
Stubbs, William (ed.), *Chronicles of the reigns of Edward I and Edward II*, 2 vols, Rolls Series, London, 1882–3.
STUBBS, WILLIAM (ed.), *Willelmi Malmesbiriensis monachi de gestis regum anglorum libri quinque; historiae novellae libri tres*, 2 vols, Rolls Series, London, 1887–9.
TALBOT, C. H. (ed.), *The life of Christina of Markyate, a twelfth-century recluse*, Oxford, 1959.
THOMPSON, EDWARD MAUNDE (ed.), *Chronicon Angliae, ab anno domini 1328 usque ad annum 1338, auctore monacho quodam santi Albani*, Rolls Series, London, 1874.
THOMPSON, EDWARD MAUNDE (ed.) *Adae Murimuth: continuatio chronicarum. Robertis de Avesbury: de gestis mirabilibus regis Edwardi tertii*, Rolls Series, London, 1889.
WEINBAUM, MARTIN (ed.), *British borough charters, 1307–1660*, Cambridge, 1943.
WHEATLEY, HENRY B., and ASHBEE, EDMUND W. (eds), *The Particular Description of England, 1588 (William Smith)*, London, 1879.
WRIGHT, THOMAS (ed.), *Political poems and songs relating to English history, composed during the period from the accession of Edw. III to that of Ric. III*, 2 vols, Rolls Series, London, 1859–61.

c. Secondary sources

1 Works of reference

BRITTON, C. E., *A Meteorological Chronology to A.D. 1450*, London, 1937.
CARUS-WILSON, E. M., and COLEMAN, OLIVE, *England's Export Trade, 1275–1547*, Oxford, 1963.
COLVIN, H. M. (ed.), *The History of the King's Works*, 2 vols and case of plans, London, 1963.
HARVEY, JOHN, *English Medieval Architects. A Biographical Dictionary down to 1550*, London, 1954.
KNOWLES, DAVID, and HADCOCK, R. NEVILL, *Medieval Religious Houses, England and Wales*, London, 1953.
The Victoria History of the Counties of England, London, 1900– (in progress).
WEDGWOOD, JOSIAH C., *History of Parliament (Biographies and Register), 1439–1509*, 2 vols, London, 1936–8.
WHITING, BARTLETT JERE, *Proverbs, Sentences and Proverbial Phrases from English writings mainly before 1500*, Cambridge (Mass.), 1968.

2 Other secondary sources

ADDYMAN, P. V., and HILL, D. H., 'Saxon Southampton: a review of the evidence', *Proceedings of the Hampshire Field Club and Archaeological Society*, 25 (1968), pp. 61–93.

ALLIN, PATRICIA F. D., 'Medieval Southampton and its Jews', *Transactions of the Jewish Historical Society of England*, 23 (1970–1), pp. 87–95.

ALLMAND, C. T., 'A note on denization in fifteenth-century England', *Medievalia et Humanistica*, 17 (1966), pp. 127–8.

ANDERSON, R. C., 'English galleys in 1295', *The Mariner's Mirror*, 14 (1928), pp. 220–41.

ANDERSON, R. C., *Oared Fighting Ships*, London, 1962.

BEARDWOOD, ALICE, 'Mercantile antecedents of the English naturalization laws', *Medievalia et Humanistica*, 16 (1964), pp. 64–76.

BIDDLE, MARTIN, 'Excavations at Winchester 1967. Sixth interim report', *The Antiquaries Journal*, 48 (1968), pp. 250–84.

BLENCH, J. W., *Preaching in England in the late Fifteenth and Sixteenth Centuries. A study of English sermons 1450–c. 1600*, Oxford, 1964.

BONNEY, HELEN, '"Balle's Place", Salisbury: a 14th-century merchant's house', *The Wiltshire Archaeological and Natural History Magazine*, 59 (1964), pp. 155–67.

BRAITHWAITE, P. R. P., *The Church Plate of Hampshire*, London and Winchester, 1909.

BRIDBURY, A. R., *England and the Salt Trade in the Later Middle Ages*, Oxford, 1955.

BRIDBURY, A. R., *Economic Growth: England in the Later Middle Ages*, London, 1962.

BROOKE, ROSALIND B., *Early Franciscan Government, Elias to Bonaventure*, Cambridge, 1959.

BROOKS, F. W., *The English Naval Forces, 1199–1272*, London, 1933 (reprinted 1962).

BROWN, E. H. PHELPS, and HOPKINS, SHEILA V., 'Seven centuries of building wages', *Economica*, new series, 22 (1955), pp. 195–206.

BROWN, E. H. PHELPS, and HOPKINS, SHEILA V., 'Seven centuries of the prices of consumables, compared with builders' wage-rates', *Economica*, new series, 23 (1956), pp. 296–314.

BURCH, C. E. C., *Minstrels and Players in Southampton, 1428–1635*, Southampton, 1969.

BURGESS, L. A., *The Origins of Southampton*, Leicester, 1964.

BURWASH, DOROTHY, *English Merchant Shipping, 1460–1540*, Toronto, 1947.

CARPENTIER, ÉLISABETH, 'Autour de la peste noire: famines et épidémies dans l'histoire du XIVe siècle', *Annales*, 17 (1962), pp. 1062–92.

CARUS-WILSON, E. M., 'The effects of the acquisition and of the loss of Gascony on the English wine trade', *Bulletin of the Institute of Historical Research*, 21 (1946–8), pp. 145–54.

CARUS-WILSON, E. M., *The Expansion of Exeter at the Close of the Middle Ages*, Exeter, 1961.

CARUS-WILSON, E. M., 'The medieval trade of the ports of the Wash', *Medieval Archaeology*, 6–7 (1962–3), pp. 182–201.

CHENEY, C. R., 'Church-building in the Middle Ages', *Bulletin of the John Rylands Library*, 34 (1951–2), pp. 20–36.

COLEMAN, OLIVE, 'Trade and prosperity in the fifteenth century; some aspects of the trade of Southampton', *Economic History Review*, 2nd series, 16 (1963–4), pp. 9–22.

COLVIN, H. M. (ed.), 'Domestic architecture and town-planning', in *Medieval England*, ed. A. L. Poole, Oxford, 1958.

COORNAERT, EMILE, 'Les ghildes médiévales (V^e^–XIVe siècles)', *Revue Historique*, 199 (1948), pp. 22–55, 208–43.

COPE, J. HAUTENVILLE, 'Church goods in Hampshire, A.D. 1552', *Papers and Proceedings of the Hampshire Field Club*, 7 (1914–16), pp. 67–98, and 8 (1917–19), pp. 1–39.

CRAEYBECKX, JAN, *Un grand commerce d'importation: les vins de France aux anciens Pays-Bas (XIIIe–XVIe siècles)*, Paris, 1958.

CRAWFORD, O. G. S., 'Trinity chapel and fair', *Papers and Proceedings of the Hampshire Field Club and Archaeological Society*, 17 (1949–52), pp. 45–53.

DAVIES, J. SILVESTER, *A History of Southampton*, Southampton and London, 1883.

DICKINSON, R. E., 'The town plans of East Anglia', *Geography*, 19 (1934), pp. 37–50.

DOUCH, ROBERT, *Visitors' Descriptions of Southampton, 1540–1956*, Southampton, 1961.

EDEN, CECIL H., *Black Tournai Fonts in England. The Group of Seven Late Norman Fonts from Belgium*, London, 1909.

ENGLEFIELD, HENRY C., *A Walk through Southampton*, Southampton, 1805 (2nd edition).

FARRER, WILLIAM, 'An outline itinerary of King Henry the First', *English Historical Review*, 34 (1919), pp. 303–82, 505–79.

FAULKNER, P. A., 'Medieval undercrofts and town houses', *The Archaeological Journal*, 123 (1966), pp. 120–35.

FISHER, F. J., 'The development of London as a centre of conspicuous consumption in the sixteenth and seventeenth centuries', *Transactions of the Royal Historical Society*, 4th series, 30 (1948), pp. 37–50.

FOX, AILEEN, 'The underground conduits in Exeter, exposed during reconstruction in 1950', *Report and Transactions of the Devonshire Association*, 83 (1951), pp. 172–8.

FREEMAN, A. Z., 'A moat defensive: the coast defense scheme of 1295', *Speculum*, 42 (1967), pp. 442–62.

FURLEY, J. S., *City Government of Winchester from the Records of the XIV and XV Centuries*, Oxford, 1923.

GANSHOF, F. L., *Étude sur le développement des villes entre Loire et Rhin au Moyen Age*, Paris and Brussels, 1943.

GILCHRIST, J., *The Church and Economic Activity in the Middle Ages*, London, 1969.

GRAS, N. S. B., *The Early English Customs System*, Cambridge (Mass.), 1918.

HALE, JOHN, 'War and public opinion in the fifteenth and sixteenth centuries', *Past & Present*, 22 (1962), pp. 18–33.

HIGOUNET, CHARLES, *Bordeaux pendant le haut moyen âge*, Bordeaux, 1963.

HILL, J. W. F., *Medieval Lincoln*, Cambridge, 1948.

HOSKINS, W. G., 'An Elizabethan provincial town: Leicester', in *Studies in Social History, a Tribute to G. M. Trevelyan*, ed. J. H. Plumb, London, 1955.

HOSKINS, W. G., 'English provincial towns in the early sixteenth century', *Transactions of the Royal Historical Society*, 5th series, 6 (1956), pp. 1–19.

JAMES, MARGERY K., 'The fluctuations of the Anglo-Gascon wine trade during the fourteenth century', *Economic History Review*, 2nd series, 4 (1951), pp. 170–96.

JAMES, MARGERY K., *Studies in the Medieval Wine Trade*, ed. Elspeth M. Veale, Oxford, 1971.

JONES, DOUGLAS, *The Church in Chester, 1300–1540*, Chetham Society, 3rd series, 7 (1957).

JORDAN, W. K., *Philanthropy in England, 1480–1660. A study of the changing pattern of English social aspirations*, London, 1959.

KERLING, N. J. M., *Commercial relations of Holland and Zeeland with England from the late 13th century to the close of the Middle Ages*, Leiden, 1954.

LANE, F. C., 'Tonnages, medieval and modern', *Economic History Review*, 2nd series, 17 (1964–5), pp. 213–33.

LAUGHTON, L. G. CARR, 'The cog', *The Mariner's Mirror*, 46 (1960), pp. 69–70.

LECLERCQ, JEAN, VANDENBROUCKE, FRANÇOIS, and BOUYER, LOUIS, *La Spiritualité du Moyen Age*, Paris, 1961.

LIPMAN, V. D., *The Jews of Medieval Norwich*, The Jewish Historical Society of England, London, 1967.

LITTLE, A. G., 'Introduction of the Observant Friars into England', *Proceedings of the British Academy*, 10 (1921–3), pp. 455–71.

LITTLE, A. G., 'Introduction of the Observant Friars into England: a bull of Alexander VI', *Proceedings of the British Academy*, 27 (1941), pp. 155–66.

LOBEL, M. D. (ed.), *Historic Towns. Maps and plans of towns and cities in the British Isles, with historical commentaries, from earliest times to 1800*, volume 1, London and Oxford, 1969.

MACCAFFREY, WALLACE T., *Exeter, 1540–1640. The Growth of an English County Town*, Cambridge (Mass.), 1958.

MCNEILL, JOHN T., and GAMER, HELENA M., *Medieval Handbooks of Penance*, New York, 1938 (reprinted 1965).

MALLETT, MICHAEL E., *The Florentine Galleys in the Fifteenth Century*, Oxford, 1967.

MARTIN, A. R., *Franciscan Architecture in England*, British Society of Franciscan Studies, 18 (for 1933–4).

MARTIN, G. H., 'The English borough in the thirteenth century', *Transactions of the Royal Historical Society*, 5th series, 13 (1963), pp. 123–44.

MEAD, WILLIAM EDWARD, *The English Medieval Feast*, London, 1931.

MERSON, A. L., 'Elizabethan Southampton', in *Collected Essays on Southampton*, eds J. B. Morgan and Philip Peberdy, Southampton, 1958.

MONKHOUSE, F. J. (ed.), *A Survey of Southampton and its Region*, Southampton, 1964.

MOODY, HENRY, *Hampshire in 1086. An Extension of the Latin Text, and an English Translation of the Domesday Book, as far as it relates to Hampshire*, Winchester, 1862.

MOREY, ADRIAN, *Bartholomew of Exeter, Bishop and Canonist. A Study in the Twelfth Century*, Cambridge, 1937.

O'NEILL, B. H. ST J., 'Southampton town

wall', in *Aspects of Archaeology in Britain and Beyond*, ed. W. F. Grimes, London, 1951.
O'NEILL, B. H. ST J., *Castles and Cannon, a Study of Early Artillery Fortifications in England*, Oxford, 1960.
OPPENHEIM, MICHAEL, *A history of the administration of the Royal navy and of merchant shipping in relation to the navy from 1509 to 1660, with an introduction treating of the preceding period*, London, 1896.
OWST, G. R., *Literature and Pulpit in Medieval England*, Cambridge, 1933.
PANTIN, W. A., 'The development of domestic architecture in Oxford', *The Antiquaries Journal*, 27 (1947), pp. 120–50.
PANTIN, W. A., 'Medieval English town-house plans', *Medieval Archaeology*, 6–7 (1962–3), pp. 202–39.
PANTIN, W. A., 'Some medieval English town houses', in *Culture and Environment, Essays in Honour of Sir Cyril Fox*, eds I. Ll. Foster and L. Alcock, London, 1963.
POWER, EILEEN, 'The wool trade in the fifteenth century', in *Studies in English Trade in the Fifteenth Century*, eds Eileen Power and M. M. Postan, London, 1933 (reissued 1966).
PRITCHARD, V., *English Medieval Graffiti*, Cambridge, 1967.
RAINE, ANGELO, *Medieval York: a topographical survey based on original sources*, London, 1955.
RAMSEY, PETER, 'Overseas trade in the reign of Henry VII: the evidence of customs accounts', *Economic History Review*, 2nd series, 6 (1953–4), pp. 173–82.
RENN, D. F., 'The Southampton arcade', *Medieval Archaeology*, 8 (1964), pp. 226–8.
RENOUARD, YVES, 'Le grand commerce des vins de Gascogne au moyen âge', *Revue Historique*, 221 (1959), pp. 261–304.
RENOUARD, YVES, *Bordeaux sous les rois d'Angleterre*, Bordeaux, 1965.
ROBSON-SCOTT, W. D., *German Travellers in England, 1400–1800*, Oxford, 1953.
RUDDOCK, ALWYN, 'Antonio Guidotti', *Papers and Proceedings of the Hampshire Field Club and Archaeological Society*, 15 (1941–3), pp. 34–42.
RUDDOCK, ALWYN, 'The Greyfriars in Southampton', *Papers and Proceedings of the Hampshire Field Club and Archaeological Society*, 16 (1944–7), pp. 137–47.
RUDDOCK, ALWYN, 'John Payne's persecution of foreigners in the town court of Southampton in the fifteenth century. A study in municipal misrule', *Papers and Proceedings of the Hampshire Field Club and Archaeological Society*, 16 (1944–7), pp. 23–37.
RUDDOCK, ALWYN, 'Alien hosting in Southampton in the fifteenth century', *Economic History Review*, 16 (1946), pp. 30–7.
RUDDOCK, ALWYN, 'London capitalists and the decline of Southampton in the early Tudor period', *Economic History Review*, 2nd series, 2 (1949–50), pp. 137–51.
RUSSELL, J. C., *British Medieval Population*, Albuquerque, 1948.
RUSSELL, J. C., 'The preplague population of England', *The Journal of British Studies*, v:2 (1966), pp. 1–21.
RUSSELL, J. C., 'Population in Europe, 500–1500', in *The Fontana Economic History of Europe*, London, 1969– (in progress).
SABINE, ERNEST L., 'Butchering in medieval London', *Speculum*, 8 (1933), pp. 335–53.
SABINE, ERNEST L., 'Latrines and cesspools of medieval London', *Speculum*, 9 (1934), pp. 303–21.
SABINE, ERNEST L., 'City cleaning in medieval London', *Speculum*, 12 (1937), pp. 19–43.
SALTER, H. E., *Medieval Oxford*, Oxford, 1936.
SALZMAN, L. F., *Building in England down to 1540. A documentary history*, Oxford, 1952 (reprinted with additions in 1967).
SAUNDERS, A. D., 'Hampshire coastal defence since the introduction of artillery, with a description of Fort Wallington', *The Archaeological Journal*, 123 (1966), pp. 136–7
SAWYER, P. H., 'The wealth of England in the eleventh century', *Transactions of the Royal Historical Society*, 5th series, 15 (1965), pp. 145–64.
SCAMMELL, G. V., 'Shipowning in England, c. 1450–1550', *Transactions of the Royal Historical Society*, 5th series, 12 (1962), pp. 105–22.
SHERBORNE, J. W., 'Indentured retinues and English expeditions to France, 1369–1380', *English Historical Review*, 79 (1964), pp. 718–46.
SHILLABER, CAROLINE, 'Edward I, builder of towns', *Speculum*, 22 (1947), pp. 297–309.
STENTON, SIR FRANK, 'Norman London', in *Social Life in Early England*, ed. Geoffrey Barraclough, London, 1960.
TAIT, JAMES, *The Medieval English Borough. Studies on its origins and constitutional history*, Manchester, 1936.
THRUPP, SYLVIA, *The Merchant Class of Medieval London, 1300–1500*, Chicago, 1948 (reprinted Ann Arbor, 1962).

THRUPP, SYLVIA, 'A survey of the alien population of England in 1440', *Speculum*, 32 (1957), pp. 262–73.
TIERNEY, BRIAN, *Medieval Poor Law. A sketch of canonical theory and its application in England*, Berkeley and Los Angeles, 1959.
TITOW, J., 'Evidence of weather in the account rolls of the bishopric of Winchester, 1209–1350', *Economic History Review*, 2nd series, 12 (1959–60), pp. 360–407.
TOUCHARD, HENRI, *Le commerce maritime Breton à la fin du moyen âge*, Paris, 1967.
TURNER, W. J. CARPENTER, 'The brokage books of Southampton. A Hampshire merchant and some aspects of medieval transport', *Papers and Proceedings of the Hampshire Field Club and Archaeological Society*, 16 (1944–7), pp. 173–7.
TU RNER, W. J. CARPENTER, 'The *Little Jesus of the Tower*, a Bursledon ship of the early fifteenth century', *Papers and Proceedings of the Hampshire Field Club and Archaeological Society*, 18 (1953–4), pp. 173–8.
TURNER, W. J. CARPENTER, 'The building of the *Gracedieu*, *Valentine* and *Falconer* at Southampton, 1416–1420', *The Mariner's Mirror*, 40 (1954), pp. 55–72.
TURNER, W. J. CARPENTER, 'The building of the *Holy Ghost of the Tower*, 1414–1416, and her subsequent history', *The Mariner's Mirror*, 40 (1954), pp. 270–81.
UNWIN, GEORGE, *The Gilds and Companies of London*, London, 1925 (2nd edition).
URRY, WILLIAM, *Canterbury under the Angevin Kings*, London, 1967.
WEINBAUM, MARTIN, *The Incorporation of Boroughs*, Manchester, 1937.
WELCH, EDWIN, *Southampton City Charters*, Southampton, 1966.
WILLIAMS, GWYN A., *Medieval London. From commune to capital*, London, 1963.
WOLFF, PHILIPPE, 'English cloth in Toulouse (1380–1450)', *Economic History Review*, 2nd series, 2 (1949–50), pp. 290–4.
WOOD, MARGARET, *The English Medieval House*, London, 1965.
WOOD-LEGH, K. L., *Perpetual Chantries in Britain*, Cambridge, 1965.

3 Unpublished theses and dissertations, etc.

BODEN, CAROLINE E., 'The borough organization of Southampton in the sixteenth century', London M.A., 1920.
BURGESS, L. A., 'A topographical index of Southampton' (typescript deposited at Southampton City Reference Library), undated.
CARR, ANTHONY M., 'A documentary survey of property in medieval Southampton' (typescript deposited at Southampton University Library, 1969).
HARRIS, RICHARD, 'God's House, Southampton, in the reign of Edward III', Southampton M.A. dissertation, 1970.
JAMES, MARGERY K., 'The Gascon wine trade of Southampton during the reigns of Henry VI and Edward IV', Oxford B.Lit., 1948.
JAMES, MARGERY K., 'The non-sweet wine trade of England during the fourteenth and fifteenth centuries', Oxford D.Phil., 1952.
WIGGS, J. L. (afterwards Mrs Thomas), 'The seaborne trade of Southampton in the second half of the sixteenth century', Southampton M.A., 1955.

Index